Praise

GREAT WHIT

"It takes a skilled writer and repor[...]
fresh, and in his book, *Great White* [...]
ing the age and the personalities that led to the creation of a
modern-day Colossus ... Taliaferro's lens in this book is broad and
his eye is inquisitive, roaming widely to give the complete story ...
At the last page, the readers is left with a sense of having learned
much about an obscure and complicated chapter of American
history. There is also the wistful hope that there might have been
just a little more. And in the writing game, this truly is the sign of a
tale well told."

—SAN ANTONIO EXPRESS-NEWS

"Crisp ... this book is a strange mix of the glorious and the disturb-
ing ... a major book about the American character—and the early
20th-century monument that was an expression of that brash, confident collective personality."

—KANSAS CITY STAR

"Taliaferro's description of how [Mount Rushmore] came to be
makes for a ... colorful and entertaining history lesson here and
now."

—BOSTON GLOBE

"Taliaferro's narrative sparkles ... The most fascinating aspect of
[his] book is a recurring theme that's just as relevant now as it was
in Borglum's day: Monuments are controversial."

—FORBES FYI

"Taliaferro's reporting is impossible not to enjoy ... deliciously
reduces one of our nation's largest and most bizarre artistic under-
takings to its most valuable and entertaining details ... This book is
an insightful period piece, appreciably enriching—and no minivan
required."

—AUSTIN AMERICAN-STATESMAN

"John Taliaferro's engrossing *Great White Fathers* gives us fascinating facts aplenty ... *Great White Fathers*, never tedious, meshes art, history, politics and abnormal psychology into an absorbing account of how a familiar symbol of national hubris was made."

—*Savannah News*

"Taliaferro makes nonfiction read like a historical saga ... Not since Alfred Hitchcock's *North by Northwest* ... has there been as much excitement about Mt. Rushmore as the release of this book, and it's for good reason."

—*Sioux Falls Argus Leader*

"Taliaferro details in superlative prose, with fascinating depth and splendid sensitivity."

—*Cleveland Plain Dealer*

"All who visit Mt. Rushmore must ask themselves what possessed anyone to commit such an act of patriotic hubris. John Taliaferro tells us, and a great deal more, in a fascinating account that combines history, politics, art, and the Sturgis motorcycle rally."

—H. W. Brands, author of *The Age of Gold*

"*Great White Fathers* is partly about art history, partly about the artistic psyche, and all about patriotism. This book is an important addition to the literature that explores what it means to be an American."

—Dan O'Brien, author of *Buffalo for the Broken Heart*

Great White Fathers

GREAT WHITE
FATHERS

The Story of the Obsessive Quest

to Create Mount Rushmore

JOHN TALIAFERRO

PUBLICAFFAIRS   NEW YORK

Book design by Mark McGarry, Texas Type & Book Works.
Set in Dante.

Library of Congress Cataloging-in-Publication data
Taliaferro, John, 1952–
Great white fathers: the story of the obsessive quest to create Mount Rushmore /
John Taliaferro.—1st ed.
p. cm.
Includes index.
ISBN 1-58648-205-x (pbk)
1. Mount Rushmore National Memorial (S.D.)—History.
2. Burglum, Gutzon, 1867–1941. I. Title.
F657.R8 T35 2002
978.3'93—dc21
2002069681

10 9 8 7 6 5 4 3 2 1

For Malou

It was a happy lot for children to grow up to manhood or womanhood with the Great Stone Face before their eyes, for all the features were noble, and the expression was at once grand and sweet, as if it were the glow of a vast, warm heart, that embraced all mankind in its affections, and had room for more. It was an education only to look at it. According to the belief of many people, the valley owed much of its fertility to this benign aspect that was continually beaming over it, illuminating the clouds, and infusing its tenderness into the sunshine.

NATHANIEL HAWTHORNE · "The Great Stone Face"

The true artist has the planet for his pedestal; the adventurer, after years of strife, has nothing broader than his own shoes.

RALPH WALDO EMERSON · "Uses of Great Men"

CONTENTS

PREFACE

HIDING IN PLAIN SIGHT

G UTZON BORGLUM hoped that ten thousand years from now, when archaeologists came upon the four presidential heads he sculpted on a mountainside in the Black Hills of South Dakota, they would gain an immediate and graphic understanding of American civilization. "This colossus is our mark," Borglum wrote in 1936 while still at work on the mountain. "Cut in the backbone of this western world, high in the heavens, fearless we have carved it, defying the elements ... confident that [it] shall endure eons after civilizations upon civilizations have come, read, pondered, wondered and passed away. I am assured that these carvings will endure as long as the Rocky Mountains endure; their message will outlast Egypt's entombed mortality, Greece's gift of grace and loveliness."

Rather than wait thousands of years, I have allowed only six decades to pass before examining the artifact that is Mount Rushmore. Yet I have sought to answer the questions that any archaeologist would ask. Who are the four men carved upon this remote mountain in the center of the continent? Why were they chosen? How were they carved? By whom? If this is a shrine (as Borglum declared it to be), who are its priests and pilgrims? And what is the nature of the temples and settlements that surround the central altar?

Rushmore, needless to say, means different things to different people. Native Americans regard it as a desecration of the sacred *Paha Sapa*, the "hills of black." Environmentalists regard Rushmore as a mutilation of Mother Earth. "Why should we add to . . . the work of nature with the puny work of man?" Black Hills resident Maude Hoover intoned in 1924, when she first got word of Borglum's intent. Cher—actress, singer, and icon in her own right—honestly believed that the sculpture was a natural formation.

But to millions of others, Rushmore symbolizes all that is fine and noble in America, joining the Liberty Bell and the Statue of Liberty as the nation's most luminescent beacons of democracy. Indeed, Rushmore has a way of vanquishing its skeptics. Many of those who at first see only folly or ego in the ambition to blow a half million tons of rock from a perfectly good mountain in order to honor four dead presidents soften when they behold the finished product up close. "I never would have believed that so seemingly useless a creation was so necessary to humanity," confessed Herman Oliphant, one of Gutzon Borglum's many converts.

It is hard to imagine anyone attempting anything so bold as Mount Rushmore again. Separate from environmental concerns is the matter of hero worship, or the lack thereof. As a rule, we seem to have lost our desire to cast our leaders as Great Men. The mole that Borglum carved on Lincoln's cheek is a foot in diameter. The warts that journalists and historians have highlighted on presidents in recent years—from Thomas Jefferson's miscegenation to William Jefferson Clinton's libido and lying—are uncountable and surely have rendered their subjects uncarvable. The era of hiding in plain sight is over.

But Rushmore is about more than presidents. Arguably, the central figure of the memorial is not Washington, Jefferson, Roosevelt, or Lincoln, but rather it is Borglum himself. Only he could have carved and completed Mount Rushmore, and for better or worse, he is every bit as emblematic of America as the four presidents he memorialized—in his passion, his persistence, his patriotism, and last but not least his prejudices.

"I lead a one-man war pretty near all the time and my battlefield is the world and my enemies are mainly fools," Borglum wrote to Helen Keller in 1939. This pronouncement fairly well sums up Borglum's estimation of himself. That he made it to Helen Keller, whom he met while both happened to be in Europe, is not unusual, either, for Borglum seemed to have at least passing acquaintance with an extraordinary number of the most prominent figures of his day—from Rodin to robber barons, Roosevelt (Teddy) to Roosevelt (Franklin), the Wright brothers to Frank Lloyd Wright. Borglum wasn't everyman, as his remark to Keller makes plain, but there was a time when he seemed to be everywhere at once. And just as his Mount Rushmore was meant to leave a permanent imprint of America, so too did Borglum make an indelible impression on all he met. Some regarded him as the next Michelangelo. Others viewed him as the heir to Ahab, obsessed in his pursuit of his own white leviathan. The National Park Service administrators who had to deal with him month in and month out called him "temperamental." Less politic observers chose words such as "truculent," "pugnacious," "unforgiving." Some went as far as "raving," "paranoid," "megalomaniacal."

As for my own opinion, I feel the same about Borglum as I do about Mount Rushmore. Both man and mountain are inspiring; both are unsettling. Inspiring because they strive to embody the highest ideals possible; unsettling because they are so adamant in their conviction that one man's, or one nation's, designs can be so unequivocal, so inviolable, so bald-faced. Patriotism, as Samuel Johnson reminded, is often a refuge for scoundrels. Not that Borglum was a scoundrel—not entirely,

anyway. But as a man of extraordinary will and vision, he also gener-
ated enormous controversy, along with immense art. Although he was
the son of immigrants, he railed against the dangers of further immigration, a stridency that eventually led to his involvement with extrem-
ists such as the Ku Klux Klan. He harbored a remarkably progressive
attitude toward American Indians, yet he saw nothing inappropriate
about carving four glowering white guardians in the heart of their
homeland. And to read his speeches and correspondence is to conclude
that the most formidable impediment to carving the Shrine of Democracy was democracy itself. The granite was easy; moving the public
and especially the politicians drove him up the wall, and perhaps even
to an early grave.

Above all, what Mount Rushmore teaches us is that the best American stories are not simple; they are complex and contradictory, brilliant
and murky, at times uplifting, at other times ironic, even tragic. Two of
the most memorable events to occur at Mount Rushmore in the last
half century are the chase scene at the end of Alfred Hitchcock's *North
by Northwest* and the takeover of the mountain (twice) by the militant
American Indian Movement. (AIM was also suspected in the 1975
bombing of the Rushmore visitor center, but no arrests were ever
made.) At the time, each was considered a threat to the sanctity as well
as the physical integrity of the memorial. Yet I would suggest that all
have enriched our appreciation of Mount Rushmore as a mirror of our
culture. Borglum was right: Rushmore is "the mark of American civilization," part Rosetta, part Rorschach. Exactly how that mark will be
read by the future, ten thousand or even ten years hence, remains to be
seen.

AMERICAN HORSE

O F ALL THE DIRECTIONS from which one can approach Mount Rushmore, the least traveled is from the north. However so, this was the choice I made for a day's journey that commenced at dawn on August 6, 2000, at the battleground of Slim Buttes in the upper left-hand corner of South Dakota and concluded at twilight one hundred miles south in the Black Hills, where I arrived in time for the playing of the National Anthem beneath the Great White Fathers of Rushmore. By design, my pilgrimage was to be a whimsical course in the culture of the Great Plains, the Black Hills, and Mount Rushmore itself. Beyond that, I hoped to come to terms with, if not America entirely, then at least my own Americanness.

The Slim Buttes appear to have changed little since September 9, 1876, the day an encampment of Lakota—as the westernmost Sioux prefer to be called (other Sioux are *Dakota* or *Nakota*)—was overrun by General George Crook's cavalry. Like the Black Hills, the buttes are islands in a vast plain, a narrow, twenty-mile-long atoll of limestone ridges and woody reefs bracketed by the Grand and Moreau Rivers and jutting five hundred feet above the rolling upholstery of grass. Natives came here for shelter, food, and fuel ten thousand years before the first white men happened along, like crusaders, and named the most prominent of the Slim Buttes the Castles.

I understand the urge to claim Slim Buttes for one's own, for I have done so myself. I have met very few people, including South Dakotans, who have been there. Even those who have heard of the buttes are vague about their whereabouts. Indians, to be sure, know about them, as do local ranchers, hunters, and of course the U.S. Forest Service, the buttes' legal guardian. To me, though, Slim Buttes seems like no-man's-land, halfway between the bare-bones towns of Buffalo and Bison. I had happened on them on a zigzag tour of the prairie the summer before and spent my first night in their folds quite alone. On this, my second visit, as I awoke in the back of my Suburban just below the Castles, I discovered that the rumbling in the night had not been thunder but the arrival of two bikers who had paused on their trek to the annual Sturgis motorcycle rally in the Black Hills. They had slept on the ground beside their Harleys. I half-expected to see pony reins clutched in their hands, nightriders too weary to picket their horses. Instead they had marked their bed ground with Bud bottles and Fritos bags. At daybreak, we toasted each other—I with my Minute Maid, they with more Budweiser. Soon they were in the saddle, belching down the trail toward Highway 20, then southward to the big powwow in Sturgis. I would pass through Sturgis myself, but I still had business in these buttes.

A couple of miles east of the Castles, fifty yards or so off the pavement, protected by a braided wire fence, stand a stone obelisk, three grave markers, and a naked flagpole. A plaque on the obelisk provides a dispassionate, if ethnocentric, summary of the events of September 9, 1876: "On this spot stood the village of 37 lodges, captured at daybreak by Capt. Anson Mills with 150 men, and held until the arrival of Gen.

Crook's army. . . . Twenty Sioux took refuge in the wash coulee faced by this tablet, and five were killed. In the afternoon there was an attack by 2000 Indians." The three marble headstones memorialize "Edw. D. Kennedy, Co. C, 5 U.S. Cavalry . . . Jonathan White, U.S. Scout . . . and John Wenzel, Co. A, 3 U.S. Cav." The fallen Native Americans are not identified.

How quickly Sioux fortunes had reversed. At the battle of the Little Bighorn, just ten weeks earlier, the Sioux had scored their greatest triumph. By the starkest contrast, Slim Buttes—smaller, more obscure, scarcely a battle at all—marked the beginning of the final days of Sioux freedom. True, the Plains Indians, including the Sioux, had been losing ground for at least a generation and were already relegated to reservations. Yet not until Slim Buttes did it become clear just how dear the price of Little Bighorn would be. White America was no longer fixed on containment and pacification of the first Americans. It was now bent on revenge.

General Crook had been scuffed badly at the battle of the Rosebud just nine days before Custer's comeuppance at the Little Bighorn. Shaken and chagrined, he had hoped to even the score with his nemesis Crazy Horse, the elusive and already legendary leader of the Lakota. But Custer jumped the gun and perished with 262 of his troopers before Crook and the rest of the cavalry could get to the fray. Now tagged "Rosebud George," Crook was left with the task of tracking the Lakota and their allies, the Cheyenne, as they dispersed to summer hunting grounds, to Canada (in the case of Sitting Bull), and back toward the Sioux reservation from which they had strayed earlier that spring. Forming the Big Horn and Yellowstone Expedition, composed of 1,500 cavalry, 450 infantry, assorted scouts, and a pool of newspapermen, Crook set out from the Tongue River of eastern Montana Territory on August 5, 1876, headed for Fort Abraham Lincoln on the Missouri, anticipating a monthlong, three-hundred-mile march. Hopeful of overtaking Indians along the way, the expedition traveled light, carrying minimal rations of hardtack, bacon, and flour. Each soldier was allowed one blanket and the clothes on his back. Like Custer, forty-seven-year-old Crook was a Civil War veteran, and also like Custer, he preferred civilian clothes to military dress while in the field. In place of a spirited charger, he often rode a mule.

We do not know whether Crook was obliged to eat his own mount during the journey, but before the campaign ended, horse and mule meat were staples of the military menu. For starters, Crazy Horse's Lakota, in leaving Little Bighorn, had burned the prairie behind them, making forage scarce. Next came bad weather. Summer ended abruptly, off cue, and rain, hail, and frigid wind were unceasing throughout the trip. With no tents and only meager provisions, soldiers grew hungry, then ill, many barely able to march or even ride. Horses and mules, already gaunt from lack of feed, balked in the mud, and dozens of them were shot and butchered where they fell. The camp mascot, a lumbering Newfoundland, attempted futilely to stalk prairie dogs.

Prudence suggested that the force press on toward Fort Lincoln for shelter and resupply, but the iron-willed Crook had other ideas. The freshest Indian trails led south, in the direction of Black Hills mining camps. With two days' rations remaining, the column plodded south with the noble aim of protecting white settlers from the marauding Crazy Horse, whose sign was everywhere, according to army scouts. Catching Indians also meant capturing their food and livestock, an exigency perhaps less strategic but now paramount. Meantime, a detachment of a hundred and fifty men, under Captain Anson Mills, was ordered ahead to the Black Hills in an urgent quest for provisions.

Late in the day on September 8, as Mills's men approached Slim Buttes, one of his scouts spotted a herd of grazing Indian ponies. Soon they located a village of three dozen tepees clustered in a coulee along present-day Gap Creek, a tributary of the Moreau. The troopers spent a miserable night hunkered beneath cottonwood trees in ankle-deep puddles. The fact that they were now within the boundaries of the

Great Sioux Reservation—ground on which, by government treaty, the Sioux actually belonged—was a topic the shivering soldiers likely never discussed.

When Mills's cavalry charged at dawn, the Lakota—Minneconjou, Oglala, and Brulé, perhaps two hundred and fifty in all—were tucked snugly in their lodges, entrance flaps tied shut against the dreary weather. Awakened by the sound of plunging horses, yelling soldiers, and bullets ripping through soggy tepee walls, the Indians slashed openings wherever they could and escaped into the warren of brush and coulees on the eastern shoulder of Slim Buttes. Even more surprising than the cavalry assault was the intensity of Lakota resistance. As soldiers ransacked the camp, Indians sniped from surrounding ridges, heartened by the knowledge that a much larger force of Lakota, including Crazy Horse, was somewhere to the south, perhaps only an hour or two away.

Meanwhile, messengers from Mills's unit had reached Crook, camped twenty miles to the north. Without delay, Crook forced his column, some on foot, some astride half-dead horses, down the trail, arriving at the Indian camp shortly before noon. By then, the Indians were scattered, and Mills's men were picking through the lodges. The booty was impressive. The summer's hunt had filled Lakota parfleches with five thousand pounds of dried meat and berries—groceries to last the winter and, as events would soon reveal, the last great harvest of buffalo in the tribe's history. In addition to the lode of food, the soldiers found evidence of another bloody summer activity. Amongst the robes, blankets, cooking utensils, and horse gear, they noticed a swallow-tailed guidon clearly taken from the Seventh Cavalry at the Little Bighorn. Grimmer still was the discovery of a leather gauntlet belonging to Captain Myles Keogh, who had perished with Custer.

Incensed by these and other macabre artifacts, Crook's troopers turned their attention to a small coulee several hundred yards above the camp. Here twenty or so Indians, mostly women and children, had sought refuge in the dense, virtually impenetrable brush. The South Dakota State Historical Society has officially named the events of the ensuing two hours "the Siege of the Ravine."

On the morning of my visit, the weather at Slim Buttes could not have been more different than that of September 9, 1876. At 7:30, as I parked my car at the highway obelisk, my dashboard thermometer read seventy degrees in the full sunshine. Grasshoppers had begun to rasp in the knee-high grass. I hiked a roundabout route—trespassing, I'm sure—first to where I guessed the Indian camp had been, but then along the creek bed to the ravine. Initially I thought I was mistaken, for the site was so tiny, no more than an acre in area. The ravine is perhaps fifteen feet deep and in places only that wide. The thought of twenty people burrowed into its thicket of box elders and buck brush made me shiver.

By early afternoon, soldiers had ringed the ravine, firing potshots into its overgrown recesses. In their zeal, three of the attackers, the three names on the plaque, fell here: Private Wenzel; Private Kennedy, who died the following day after amputation of a shattered leg; and the scout, White, better known as Buffalo Chips. Remarkably, the Siege of the Ravine did not turn into wholesale annihilation. The Indians, including their leader, American Horse, had dug themselves even deeper into the ravine with knives and fingernails, hoping that relief might still come from Crazy Horse's Lakota to the south. But as the day wore on and more of the Army's bullets found their mark, American Horse chose discretion over further valor and signaled surrender.

Among the first to emerge from the ravine was a young mother, wet, shivering, covered in mud, carrying her dead child in her arms. Soon came American Horse, a tall, lean warrior, assisted by a woman, perhaps his wife. He had been shot through the abdomen, and the woman had tied her shawl around his midriff to prevent his intestines from spilling onto the ground. With his waning strength, American Horse offered his rifle to General Crook. Amid howls of "No quarter" and "Put a knife in the son of a bitch" from the unquenchable soldiers, American Horse was led back to camp, where he was administered morphine by army contract surgeon Valentine McGillycuddy. American Horse, along with Private Kennedy, died in the night.

I sat by the ravine for several minutes, trying to imagine the horror that had transpired more than a century ago. This was no Wounded Knee, the massacre of 1890 in which three hundred Lakota corpses froze in the snow and public memory like so much graveyard sculpture. By comparison, official accounts claim that only five of the twenty or so Indians in the ravine died that day. Still, I wondered if even now there weren't uncounted skeletons secreted in the grotto below.

The battle of Slim Buttes was the last hurrah of the Sioux War. Crazy Horse and his Lakota held out through the winter of 1876–1877, but he was killed the following September, almost a year exactly after the battle of Slim Buttes. Sitting Bull and his band managed to hold out in Canada until July 1881, but they too surrendered without firing another shot and submitted to a future of rations and reservations. Since then, the Sioux have measured their losses in many ways. War, disease, and alcoholism have devastated lives, livelihood, and pride. Yet of all the indignities suffered by the Sioux, it is the loss of land—not only the Black Hills but also hunting grounds that reached east to the Great Lakes, west to the Rocky Mountains, south to the Platte River, and north into the Canadian prairie—that is hardest to countenance or to overcome.

By 10:00 A.M., I was speeding south toward the Black Hills and that landmark of landmarks, Mount Rushmore. Crook and his men had followed essentially the same route after the battle at Slim Buttes, and for most of the way, the general and his men were harassed by Indians, although both sides, despite formidable numbers, seemed satisfied with needling the other's flanks rather than squaring off in full-fledged combat. Most accounts suggest that Crazy Horse was indeed in the area.

His warriors had been worrying Black Hills miners for some weeks, but as with many chapters in Crazy Horse's life, one cannot be positive of his presence. Regardless, it was a badge of honor for his enemies to boast that they had fought the great warrior.

Crook's men took five days to cover the eighty miles to Deadwood, the nearest settlement. Rain, mud, and hostiles plagued them the entire way, and for some inexplicable reason, the troops continued to live on horsemeat, despite the bounty of buffalo meat they had discovered in the Lakota camp. Upon arrival in Deadwood, soldiers commemorated their "Starvation March" by hamming shamelessly for a traveling photographer. They pointed their rifles at the heads of stricken horses or staged mock fisticuffs for ownership of the carcasses. Stereoscopic slides of these shabby scenes were then sold to the public—initiating a bonanza of Black Hills souvenirs that today seems boundless.

As I approached the town of Sturgis on the northern fringe of the Black Hills, I was surrounded by a cavalry of a different stripe. The Sturgis Rally and Races were founded in 1938 by a group of motorcycle enthusiasts, the Jackpine Gypsies, as a sort of two-wheeled alternative to the annual Days of '76 rodeo in nearby Deadwood. Motorcycles proved to be reliable during World War II and were adopted as the chariot of choice by postwar rebels. Marlon Brando romanticized the biker life in *The Wild One* (1953), and Peter Fonda and Dennis Hopper were twice as winsome in *Easy Rider* (1969). The rise of the Hell's Angels and other motorcycle gangs alarmed police but made Harley-Davidson a household name.

In the early years, the Sturgis rally was as much about riding as it was about the biker image, and the journey to and from the Black Hills was at least half the fun. But by the 1970s, Sturgis had exploded into a hajj for hedonists, a cross between Mardi Gras and the running of the bulls. For ten days every August, a town of five thousand mild-mannered souls is overrun by more than half a million bikers and "bitches" (the term of endearment for a motorcycle passenger, female or male), everyone determined to strut his or her birthright of untamed individuality.

The good citizens of Sturgis long ago came to appreciate that if they couldn't lick 'em, they'd join 'em, and today the rally *is* the Sturgis economy. Bikers fill every motel room within a hundred-mile radius, and the overflow pitch camp in fields dedicated for their use by local landowners. The sprawling maze of merchandise, ranging from $50,000 customized bikes to $5 earplugs, rakes in millions of dollars—of which the town takes a healthy cut. Where once the presence of Hell's Angels and other highwaymen was the biggest menace to the town's well-being, now it's the pirating of the municipally owned "Sturgis" trademark by vendors of T-shirts and the like.

As I neared the outskirts of town, the traffic thickened. Biker camps lined both sides of Highway 79. Some people had pitched pup tents. Others enjoyed the comfort of motor homes, bike trailers attached. Reveille had apparently sounded late in the morning; whichever way I looked, I observed shirtless men and halter-topped women firing up hibachis or spitting toothpaste over barbwire fences. Many were mounting up. The drill apparently was to oversleep the night's hangover, then roll into Sturgis, Rapid City, Mount Rushmore, or any of the other Black Hills towns and hang out. According to a recent survey by Black Hills State University, two out of three Sturgis attendees come with no ambition of attending any specific events, of which there are scores.

On Main Street, bikes were backed into the curb for show and tell while their riders strolled the bars, tattoo parlors, and T-shirt stalls. Women paraded by in leather chaps and thongs. Men had only their guts and goatees to flaunt. Perhaps because of my recent experience at Slim Buttes, I couldn't help noting the similarities between today's bikers and Native Americans. Harley riders wear fringed leggings, Indian-style, and decorate their jackets and skin with feathered insignia. On my way into town, I was passed by a biker who had deer antlers on his handlebars and coyote tails flying from the back of his leather vest—American Horse redux.

Yet wildness is a relative concept. The chamber-of-commerce types in Sturgis—as well as the sheriff—would have you believe that the crowd gets more mature, upscale, and ... well, civilized every year. They point out that two thirds of rally-goers are family men and a full third earn more than $50,000 a year. Indeed it is true that cardiologists with hair plugs and software tycoons with cash to burn have taken to trucking their Harleys, often with their own pit crews, to the Nebraska or Wyoming border and then riding into Sturgis like middle-aged Tartars. Tattoos, once declarations of reckless abandon, are now regarded as calling cards of conformity. Some Sturgis stalwarts acquire new ones on each visit, the way our grandparents once collected decals on their steamer trunks.

Still, Sturgis has a long way to go before it becomes a Harley Chautauqua. The Christian Riders Ministry has a fair following, but it is no match for the daily Ladies World Champion Pickle Lickin' Contest or the nightly procession of "headlighters"—women riders flashing their breasts—a time-honored tradition of campground life. On the radio, I heard the Sturgis police chief downplaying this year's crop of invaders as a "Geritol crowd." He may have been right, but statistics suggest that Sturgis celebrants do not exactly take their Geritol straight. By week's end, more than three hundred bikers would be hauled in on drug charges, and twice as many would be busted for drunk driving—all this with the cops doing their damnedest to look the other way. The Hell's Angels may now have a website, but the fact remains that on any given day at Sturgis, you can still buy and consume all the pot and bathtub amphetamine your otherwise wholesome heart desires. Sturgis has outgrown Woodstock—and Altamont, for that matter—but then again, neither of those events sold "Rehab Is for Quitters" T-shirts by the gross.

★

After an hour or so, I escaped the labyrinth of leather and pushed farther into the Black Hills. I exited Interstate 90 at Rapid City and followed signs for Highway 16, the four-lane funnel that points to Keystone and Mount Rushmore.

The Black Hills are all about context. Like a birthmark on a smooth cheek, they rise five thousand feet above the surrounding prairie—the highest uplift of land (along with the Chisos Mountains of Texas's Big Bend) between Pikes Peak and the Pyrenees. Harney Peak, the tallest of the hills, is 7,242 feet above sea level. Although perhaps not as majestic as the Rockies, the Black Hills earn distinction as some of the oldest exposed rock on earth, a granite batholith (or pluton, depending on which geology text you prefer) formed more than two billion years ago. And as locals are proud to point out, the Black Hills happen to be located precisely at the center of the nation.

Their signature blackness, it turns out, is the result of trees, not rocks. To the traveler, the hills first appear as a low, dark nimbus on the horizon. Slowly the cloud solidifies, darkening as it grows closer. Finally, as the plains surrender to the first hogback of shale and sandstone ten miles out, one can discern that the black is actually the dark green of foliage on the steep rampart ahead. The trees are ponderosa pine mixed with aspen, juniper, and some lodgepole.

Rapid City, population sixty thousand, is the largest town in the Black Hills and the primary business center of western South Dakota—"West River" in local parlance, the river being the Missouri, which bisects the state two hundred miles east of the hills. The first tourists to the hills disembarked from the Chicago and North Western Railway at Rapid City and transferred to one of the small-gauge lines that wound into the hills, or else they drove by horse-drawn conveyance and eventually gas-powered automobile. Now, with millions visiting the hills each year, one can barrel straight to the front gate of Mount Rushmore on busy Highway 16, which has evolved into one of the most orgiastic tourist corridors in the world. The buffet of roadside attractions includes but is by no means limited to Reptile Gardens, Black Hills Maze, 1880 Train, Sitting Bull Crystal Caverns, Fort Hays Dances with Wolves Film Set, Cosmos Mystery Area, Old MacDonald's Farm, and Bear Country USA. The Rushmore name has such proven drawing power that dozens of Black Hills businesses have appropriated it: Rushmore Travel, Rushmore Tramway, Rushmore Trading Post, Rushmore Inn, Rushmore Cave, Rushmore Clinic, Rushmore Mall, Rushmore Waterslide, Rushmore Helicopters, Rushmore Taffy, Rushmore Gold, Rushmore Ammo, Rushmore Brewing Company, and a personal favorite, Rushmart, a pit stop for beleaguered pilgrims. For sheer density and intensity, Highway 16 rivals not so much the Strip in Las Vegas as the Via Dolorosa in Jerusalem, where the Stations of the Cross today are scrunched between shops offering everything from sheep heads to knock-off crowns of thorn.

I had already visited Mount Rushmore several times, though none of those trips had been as a child. My parents had never taken me on one of those mewly station-wagon vacations to the West. In fact, it was I who took them to Mount Rushmore for the first time in the mid-1990s. We had stayed overnight at the Alex Johnson, Rapid City's grand old hotel, and driven up Highway 16 first thing in the morning through dense fog. Just our luck, as we rounded a bend above Keystone, a mile below the mountain, the clouds opened and presented Mount Rushmore like a cameo.

If the issue with the Black Hills is context, then with Mount Rushmore it's scale. Gutzon Borglum touted his creation as the largest monument since the Pyramids. Each face is sixty feet tall, and the four together measure 180 feet across. (The greatest of the Pyramids is 481 feet high and 756 feet wide at the base. The Statue of Liberty is 305 feet tall, including its base; the Washington Monument, 556; the Eiffel Tower, 984; and the Gateway Arch in St. Louis, 630 feet tall, but all of these monuments function as *buildings*.) In the numerous polls and surveys and focus groups that have been conducted on behalf of Mount

Rushmore, no one has ever bothered to ask the most basic question: At first sight, does Rushmore seem larger than expected, or smaller? My guess—my experience, anyway—is *smaller*. Since construction was halted on Mount Rushmore in October 1941, the world has shrunk, even while it has been overrun by giants. We fly in jumbo jets, crane our necks at skyscrapers, lose ourselves on superhighways, watch blockbuster productions on big-screen televisions from our king-size beds. Even art is big: Think of Christo's *Valley Curtain*, Robert Smithson's *Spiral Jetty*, or the 120-foot-tall Louisville Slugger in the city of that name.

Yet if Mount Rushmore now seems modest compared to more recent creations, it manages to grow on you in a way that cannot be measured in feet or tons. When I approached Rushmore for the first time, I anticipated something supernatural, like the lofty mountain spires in an Albert Bierstadt painting. But much to my surprise and satisfaction, I found myself gazing upon something very human—human in form, naturally, but also human in execution. And this, I would later come to appreciate, is the glory of Mount Rushmore: It is a true piece of sculpture, not a building, not in the least architectural. Its forms are handmade suits of stone, tailored to fit the distinguished men who wear them.

To behold Mount Rushmore in 1927, the year that work on it commenced, and throughout the 1930s, while it was under construction, must have been a wondrous experience. Imagine motoring across the Midwest from, say, Chicago in a Model A over hot, dusty roads poorly marked and often barely passable. Finally, the Black Hills heave into sight, like a mirage at sea. Ascending the hills on a rugged track, absent any roadside attractions besides wildlife and the odd miner's shanty, it's almost impossible not to anthropomorphize the jumble of rocks. Hey, that looks like the Old Man of the Mountain. Over there, couldn't that be the head of an Indian? Finally—what's that? Is that a face? No—yes, it is.

The trip is so much more tacky today. The billboards have been coming at you for hundreds of miles—ballyhooing Rushmore itself, but also all the schlock that encircles it. (Billboards have become so integral to the South Dakota landscape and economy that in the 1960s, when Lady Bird Johnson's famous highway beautification legislation restricted their size and placement alongside federally funded roads, owners of several of the most prominent tourist attractions—Wall Drug, Reptile Gardens, Rushmore Cave, Al's Oasis—persuaded the state to resist compliance, a display of self-interest that nearly cost South Dakota hundreds of thousands in federal highway dollars. Even then, some businesses got around the law by painting their messages on the sides of truck trailers and parking them by the sides of major roadways.) By the time you've quit the interstate and run the gauntlet of Highway 16, the buildup virtually guarantees some degree of anticlimax. Nothing could live up to the hype, and at first glance, Mount Rushmore doesn't quite fill the windshield the way, for instance, Half Dome and El Capitan do as you enter Yosemite.

Just the same, gratification awaits. By now, most everyone recognizes Mount Rushmore. It's one of those universal icons, like Mickey Mouse or the Nike Swoosh—although an extraordinary percentage of those who can identify Rushmore collectively cannot name the four faces individually. (Answer, left to right: George Washington, Thomas Jefferson, Theodore Roosevelt, and Abraham Lincoln.) Admittedly, to see the actual Rushmore, *in toto, in situ,* is no longer an experience of virgin discovery. Rather, it's one of confirmation. A circuit is completed, and any early mental snapshots that we have harbored zoom to the fore—to be validated, revised, refined. We nod with recognition of a familiar flavor, though we are really only tasting it for the first time.

Before Keystone, five miles from Mount Rushmore, I took a slight detour, circling to the rear of the crenellated peaks, and approached Rushmore via Hill City on Highway 244. The road is two-lane and twisty, pines and boulders pressing close to the shoulders. I steered around a final curve, and suddenly Mount Rushmore was right on top of me, the profile of George Washington looming above, like a father standing over the bed of his child. In no time, I was around the final bend, through the entrance gate, and engulfed by the parking garage—a monster of stone and concrete completed in 1998 amid stubborn protest, for until the addition of the new garage and the adjoining visitor center and concession complex, Mount Rushmore—the carving, that is—was virtually unto itself. For seventy years, Rushmore was the dominant presence on the mountain. Now, with the recent additions, hundreds of thousands of square feet, it's not even the biggest man-made object. In the eyes of critics, the jewel of Rushmore is now diminished by its semiprecious setting.

The justification for the $60 million expansion at Mount Rushmore is straightforward: The memorial has become one of the most popular destinations in the United States, certainly among the national parks. Each year, three million people visit Yellowstone Park, more than two million acres of mountains, geysers, and wilderness. By comparison, Mount Rushmore National Memorial—1,278 acres, only twenty of which are readily accessible to the public—must accommodate two and a half million visitors. Rushmore is no longer a remote mountaintop; it's a city at the end of an expressway. Twenty-five thousand visitors on a summer day is normal.

Not that I had chosen a normal day to drop by. Dusk quickened as I walked through the entrance colonnade. Bikers were as conspicuous as clerics at the Vatican, their vestments just as black. They looked almost penitent as they shared the line for ice cream with a troop of sunburned Boy Scouts, the other uniform of the day. Other bikers filed into the Buffalo Dining Room to sup on the spaghetti-and-meatball dinner and a dessert of red Jell-O with whipped cream and an American flag on top.

The concession shops and the Grand View Terrace are linked by the Avenue of Flags, a polished stone pathway flanked by a succession of granite columns on which are mounted the flags of every state and territory. Sitting on the wall between New Hampshire and the Commonwealth of Northern Mariana Islands was a guy nursing an enormous cone of chocolate ice cream. His black T-shirt inveighed, "Fuck Off—I Have All the Friends I Need." A half moon rose off to the east of Abraham Lincoln.

Mount Rushmore grew as I neared the balustrade of the terrace, a broad granite deck overlooking an amphitheater and three hundred yards from the talus pediment of the four presidential heads. Once you put all the buildings behind you, Rushmore regains its grandeur and comes to you on its own terms; like a practiced politician, it draws you from the crowd and greets you personally. Each time I come, I try to notice something new, and this evening, in the fading light, I was struck by how withdrawn Roosevelt seemed, as if expressing his disdain for the present muster of rough riders. Like all great figurative sculpture, from Michelangelo's *David* to James Fraser's Indian relief for the old nickel—and unlike more mediocre sculpture, such as the Statue of Liberty or the nearby Crazy Horse Memorial—the faces of Rushmore have expressions: Washington is stern, Jefferson is bemused, Roosevelt is avuncular, and Lincoln is resolute.

As the time for the evening's lighting ceremony approached, I chose a place at the rail next to two guys in full leather. They were trying to sort out the faces. They knew Jefferson—the president most people have trouble identifying—but could not put a name to Roosevelt.

On my other side was a woman, also in leather, a ring on every finger. She was fiftyish, from Chattanooga, I overheard her say. This was her third year for Sturgis, and she'd made a point of visiting Mount Rushmore each time. "I tell you," she said to the woman on her other side, "when them lights go on and they play the National Anthem, it puts chills through you." The other woman, apparently an acquaintance of the moment only, asked how she felt about Lincoln, who, after all, did not exactly smile on the South during the Civil War. "Doesn't bother me at all," replied the lady in leather. "I wasn't in it—'less I've been reincarnated." Then, digressing: "My mother always wanted to be reincarnated and come back as a bird and shit on everyone who shit on her. . . . She passed seven years ago today." As the ceremony commenced, the woman began to whistle along to "It's a Grand Old Flag."

A park ranger stepped onto the stage of the amphitheater below us. "Welcome, bikers," she began and then had to wait a good thirty seconds till the hoots and whistles subsided. "We love having you people in the Black Hills." Next she segued into her set speech for the night, and the Harley faithful absorbed her condensed history of Rushmore and the Great White Fathers with an enthusiasm previously reserved for their ice cream. The gist goes something like this: America loves the difficult task. The presidents on Mount Rushmore were extraordinary men who did extraordinary things. Gutzon Borglum and the workers who expended blood, sweat, and tears to create Mount Rushmore were extraordinary men who did extraordinary things. Finally, we as ordinary people have within us the potential to do extraordinary things. We too can achieve the American Dream. More hoots and whistles from the audience.

It was time for the grand finale. The public address system fired up "The Star Spangled Banner." The twilight's last gleaming was gradually replaced by enormous spotlights that brightened the faces of Mount Rushmore. The woman from Chattanooga had taken the leather kerchief from her head and was singing along. She was flanked by the man in the "I've Got All the Friends I Need" T-shirt, who turned out to be her mate. He joined in too, though he mumbled the words. A woman just below me in the top row of the amphitheater, in a leather vest championing "Ladies of Harley—Sioux Falls Chapter," sang loudly in a gorgeous church soprano. I gazed about me: The whole crowd, bikers the majority, was singing along, many with hands over hearts. I spied at least one woman dabbing tears.

As I turned toward the exit, eager to beat the traffic, I was provided a final view of the memorial—this one emblazoned on the front of a nearby soft-drink machine. As I rolled into my motel bed in Keystone a half hour later, my thoughts drifted back to American Horse as he lay dying. I imagined his eyes fixed on firelight. I hoped that his death song had its own verse about the land of the free and the home of the brave. And in the matter of extraordinary men and their deeds, I knew I must dig deeper than Gutzon Borglum or a fallen Lakota.

chapter 2

THE THIEVES ROAD

GOLD TURNED THE Black Hills white, and no individual deserves more credit or blame for this transition of culture and color than Lieutenant Colonel George Armstrong Custer. On July 2, 1874, Custer left Fort Lincoln under orders from General Phil Sheridan, commander of the Department of the Missouri, and approved by President Ulysses S. Grant, to "examine" the Black Hills and surrounding territory. His command included ten companies of the Seventh Cavalry and two companies of infantry. Baggage and provisions were freighted in one hundred wagons, each pulled by six mules. All told, the cavalcade comprised one thousand men and two thousand animals.

Notable guests included Grant's son Frederick, who came along nominally as Custer's aide but mostly for the lark of it all. Also riding with Custer were his brothers Tom and Boston and brother-in-law James Calhoun, all three of whom would perish with him at the Little Bighorn two years later. The roster also included a biologist, a geologist, and the esteemed Yale zoologist George Bird Grinnell, plus several newspaper reporters, a photographer, and last but not least two experienced miners. The procession pulled out of Fort Lincoln to the jaunty strains of "Garry Owen," played by Custer's sixteen-piece band, mounted as always on white horses. Bounding in front were Custer's beloved greyhounds.

If the Black Hills were still largely terra incognita to whites in 1874, there was no question to whom they belonged. In 1868, Congress had ratified the Fort Laramie Treaty establishing the Great Sioux Reservation, 26 million acres of land in Dakota Territory west of the Missouri, including the Black Hills, plus hunting rights to another thirty million "unceded" acres stretching south to the North Platte River in Nebraska and west to the Big Horn Mountains in Wyoming. The treaty forbade whites to settle or even pass through the reservation, which was "set apart for the absolute and undisturbed use and occupation of the Indians herein named." Loophole language allowed admittance by "officers, agents, and employés of the Government as may be authorized . . . in discharge of duties," but even this provision did not begin to justify Custer's agenda. He insisted that his mission was "pacific," but he was prepared to unlimber his Springfield carbines and Gatling guns at the first sign of hostility from the Lakota. And while surveyors and scientists were arguably a benign presence, the inclusion of miners in the caravan would prove an enormous threat to Indian life and liberty.

What few people knew at the time of the Black Hills expedition is that Custer was acting as an unofficial publicist and scout for the Northern Pacific Railroad. Any intelligence he could provide on the resources of the Black Hills, especially any signs of gold, would stimulate settlement—still very much illegal—and thus aid the expansion of the troubled railroad, then stalled on its westward path at Bismarck on the Missouri. "There is no doubt," wrote one member of Custer's entourage, "that the conviction . . . that the hills would prove a region of fabulous wealth has induced the Government to undertake the present expedition."

To the Sioux, the Custer survey was nothing short of an invasion. Over time, Indians would come to refer to the cavalry's route through the Black Hills as "the Thieves Road." In a remarkably candid dispatch written in Bismarck before the trip began, *New York World* correspondent William E. Curtis acknowledged, "If it were only a summer jaunt to enable a few officers to pick up a few steps, a few scientists to pick up fossils, and to give the President's son and the mule train a change of air, and if the Indians were at peace and the frontier protected, there would be nothing especially to censure." But the reality was, "We are goading the Indians to madness by invading their hallowed grounds, and throwing open to them the avenues leading to a terrible revenge whose costs would far outweigh any scientific or political benefit to be extracted from such an expedition under the most favorable circumstances."

Two years hence, Curtis's dark prophecy would become Custer's epitaph.

The Fort Laramie Treaty had been very clear about Sioux rights to the Black Hills. Even so, the tribe's ancestral, pre-treaty claim was not exactly airtight. White archaeologists and historians assert that the Sioux originated east of the Appalachian Mountains, where they first made contact with Europeans in the 1600s. Steady settlement by whites crumpled the map of traditional Indian homelands, tipping many tribes, including the Sioux, westward. The Sioux are believed to have arrived in Minnesota, near the headwaters of the Mississippi, sometime in the early 1700s. The first Sioux may not have reached the Great Plains and the Black Hills until the end of the century, about the time of the American Revolution. Oral histories of other tribes suggest that the Sioux did not drive their enemies, the Crow, or displace their eventual allies, the Cheyenne, from the Black Hills till as late as the 1820s—a mere two generations before the Fort Laramie Treaty and the intrusion of Custer.

Most Sioux, especially the Lakota, who live nearest the Black Hills, scoff at this chronology, dismissing it as so much white—*wasicu*—revisionism. The more artifactual, linguistic, and anecdotal evidence that whites dig up, the more stubbornly the Lakota stand by their own genesis narrative, a debate that vaguely resembles the argument between those who take the Bible as fact and those who regard it as myth. Lakota belief holds that their ancestors once lived blissfully beneath the Black Hills in a world not so different from the Garden of Eden. Eventually, they emerged through an opening in the rock in the vicinity of present-day Wind Cave National Park, twenty-five miles south of Mount Rushmore. Indians even assign an approximate date to this genesis. Their oral history records a specific alignment of the Dried Willow constellation. Archaeoastronomers—pioneers of a fascinating and increasingly credible interdisciplinary field of science—deduce that this particular orientation of the stars above the Black Hills occurred sometime between 100 B.C. and 1600 B.C. In other words, the Lakota contend that their people have been present in the hills for at least two thousand years, possibly three thousand or even more. That's their gospel—"stellar theology," the Lakota call it—and they're sticking to it.

But regardless of how long the Lakota have been tenants of the hills, their spiritual link to them has been, and continues to be, extremely profound. Whites who wish to dismiss or minimize the Indian claim to the Black Hills suggest that the Lakota never actually spent long stretches of time there. No one, not even the Lakota, argues with this observation, but it is beside the point. The Lakota were a mobile tribe, married to the whims of the vast buffalo herds that wandered the plains. Home was a hunting ground the size of France, and while the Lakota may not have "dwelled"—not by any Euro-American definition of the word—in a single spot for months or years, there is no question that they frequented the Black Hills constantly, for specific purposes and according to a highly ritualized schedule.

Like their predecessors over the previous ten thousand years, the Lakota came to harvest young pines for tepee poles and to hunt deer, elk, bighorn sheep, and beaver. Beyond that, they came to practice their most sacred religious rites, from vision quests to sun dances. Church analogies again seem obvious—the spires of the Black Hills as Gothic steeples, peaks such as Devil's Tower and Bear Butte the Sioux equivalents of Mount Sinai or the Temple Mount—but these comparisons hardly do justice to the absolutely primal bond between the Lakota and the Black Hills. To them, the hills are both the center of the universe and a microcosm of it.

In Lakota belief, life is a circle, from birth to death to birth again. Accordingly, the Black Hills are a circle, too—an impression reinforced by the conspicuous loop of red soil and rock that neatly circumscribes the region, between the outer hogback of hills and the interior mountains. Symmetry, balance, seamlessness—these are the essential components of Lakota metaphysics, on earth as it is in heaven. "There I was standing on the highest mountain of them all, and round about me was the hoop of the world," Lakota holy man Black Elk said, describing a vision that carried him to the top of Harney Peak. "And while I stood there I saw more than I can tell and I understood more than I saw; for I was seeing in a sacred manner the shapes of all things in the spirit, and the shape of all shapes as they must live together like one being. And I saw that the sacred hoop of my people was one of many hoops that made one circle, wide as daylight and as starlight. . . . And I saw that it was holy." To Black Elk and his people, the Lakota *are* the Black Hills. To separate one from the other would break the circle, cut the heart from the body.

To outsiders, though, the notion of the Black Hills as fundamentally sacred was received as so much savage superstition, and the strange tales that emanated from the region in the years before whites ever set foot there stretched credibility, though their ominousness gave most travelers pause. While camped at the mouth of the Cheyenne River, Lewis and Clark encountered a French trapper, who told them of a great noise coming from the "Black Mountains." Edwin Denig, a white who lived among the tribes of the upper Missouri for thirty years in the early 1800s, likewise told of "[u]nnatural noises" emanating from the Black Hills, "which . . . are thought to be the moans of the Great White Giant, when pressed upon by rocks as a punishment for being the first aggressor in their territory. They say that he issues forth on occasions and his tracks . . . are twenty feet in length. He is condemned to perpetual incarceration under the mountain as an example to all whites to leave the Indians in quiet possession of their hunting grounds."

Such warnings meant no more to Custer than the Indians' legal claim to their sacred land.

Custer's route through the Black Hills is well documented, thanks to his own dispatches and the presence of reporters and a photographer. The expedition swung southwest through the present-day intersection of North Dakota, South Dakota (at the time North and South were one territory), Montana, and Wyoming. It passed by Slim Buttes, detouring briefly so one of the scouts could point out a cave covered with petroglyphs, which the *World*'s Curtis described as "the Sioux Erebus"—the Indian passage to the underworld. Custer finally entered the Black Hills on July 21, working southeastward. On the 23rd, having penetrated the outer ridges and crossed the "racetrack," the expedition entered a valley (today's Cold Spring Creek) of "the most wonderful as well as beautiful aspect," in Custer's words. "Every step of our march that day was amidst flowers of the most exquisite colors and perfume. . . . It was a strange sight to glance back at the advancing columns of cavalry, and behold the men with beautiful bouquets in their hands, while the head gear of their horses was decorated with wreaths of flowers fit to crown a queen of May."

The trip grew only more bountiful. A week later, Custer and a small party climbed Harney Peak, the altitude of which Custer's surveyor overestimated by two thousand feet. Because the mountain, the highest crag in the Black Hills, had already been named two decades earlier—for General William S. "White Whiskers" Harney—Custer claimed one of the peaks visible to the north for himself and named another for Major General Alfred Terry, commander of the Department of the Dakota and, incidentally, one of the signers of the Fort Laramie Treaty of 1868. On August 1, the expedition entered the valley of French Creek and pitched camp three miles east of the spot where, the following year, a "city" would be named for the intrepid Custer—and deservedly so, for his discoveries nearby, generously described and widely disseminated, made white settlement both imminent and irresistible.

The companies of cavalry spread their tents across the green valley and indulged their various appetites. Troopers played baseball. Each night the band and glee club performed. Fred Grant, the president's son, never strayed far from the sutler's supply of liquor and was said to have been drunk "nearly all the time." George Bird Grinnell catalogued more than 150 species of mammals and birds and collected numerous fossils, including the leg bone of a mammoth. Custer found the hunting splendid, and he was able to write to his wife, Libby, that "I have reached the hunter's highest round of fame . . . I have killed my Grizzley." (Today there are no bears of any species left in the Black Hills, except at Bear Country USA, the drive-through animal park on the road to Mount Rushmore.)

As Custer studied the land about him, the booster in him came to the fore. "In no portion of our country, not excepting the famous bluegrass region of Kentucky, have I ever seen grazing superior to that found growing wild in this hitherto unknown region," he wrote. "Not only is the land . . . conveniently located with streams of pure water flowing through its length and breadth, but nature oft-times seems to have gone further and placed beautiful shrubbery and evergreens in the most desirable locations. . . . The soil is that of a rich garden. . . . We have found the country in many places covered with wild raspberries. . . . Cattle could winter in these valleys without other food or shelter than that to be obtained from running at large."

As glowing as this endorsement was, it was eclipsed by news of a much more dazzling treasure. In a dispatch of August 2, Custer noted—this time with surprising restraint—that "gold has been found in several places and it is the belief of those who are giving their attention to this subject that it will be found in paying quantities. I have upon my table 40 or 50 small particles of pure gold, in size averaging that of a small pin head, and most of it obtained today from one panful of earth."

Rumors of gold had seeped from the Black Hills for years. "Came to these hills in 1833 seven of us," begins an inscription scratched on a stone and discovered half a century later. "All died but me Ezra Kind. Killed by Ind. . . . Got all the gold we could carry our ponys all got by the Indians I have lost my gun and nothing to eat and Indians hunting me." This was the last anyone heard of Ezra Kind, but Indians continued to show up at trading posts and forts with tantalizing bits of "the yellow metal that makes the *wasicu* crazy." Military forays to the fringes of the hills in the 1850s and 1860s turned up promising traces as well, but the soldiers did not linger long enough to strike it rich. Independent prospectors who dared to penetrate the heart of the Sioux Nation during that period were fortunate to get out with their lives.

Many people suspect that gold was the underlying motivation of the Custer expedition all along. Perhaps so, but when more traces of gold continued to surface along French Creek, Custer remained remarkably guarded in his descriptions. "Until further examination is made regarding the richness of the gold," he advised in his dispatch of August 2, "no opinion should be formed."

His fellow travelers were much more sanguine. A rider galloped from French Creek on the third, carrying news of the strike to Fort Laramie, Wyoming Territory, the nearest telegraph. Well before Custer had left the hills and returned to Fort Lincoln on August 30, the world had been alerted that gold had been taken "right from the grass roots." Headlines in the Chicago *Inter-Ocean* blared "GOLD! The Glittering

Treasure Found at Last ... A Belt of Gold Territory Thirty Miles Wide." The accompanying story exclaimed that "the expedition has solved the mystery of the Black Hills, and will carry back the news that there is gold here, in quantities as rich as were ever dreamed of." The truth was somewhat different, however. Custer's miners never did find more than encouraging color—"ten dollar diggin's"—but optimism ran unbridled nevertheless. Before leaving French Creek, twenty-one members of the expedition formed a mining company and staked claims up and down the banks. They could not have acted too soon. Five days before the expedition arrived home, a group of two hundred and fifty men "interested in the mineral sources of the Black Hills" had joined together in Sioux City, Iowa, and made plans to leave for the hills in mid-September. Meanwhile in Chicago, several thousand Irishmen were volunteering to dig enough Black Hills gold to fund the liberation of Ireland from the British.

Gold fever notwithstanding, the Black Hills were still very much off limits to whites, according to the treaty of 1868. Keeping prospectors from the hills, though, was an entirely separate proposition, and even those who favored protection of native interests saw trespass as inevitable. William Curtis, the *World* correspondent who had warned that Indian retribution would outweigh any benefits gleaned by white incursion, had changed his tune by the time he arrived back at Fort Lincoln. "I feel confident that fortunes will be made in extracting the mineral wealth of the Black Hills," he declared, although he added that "my advice to all would be to make haste slowly."

Yet even if gold were never unearthed in abundant quantities, the climate, fertility, and natural beauty of the hills were worth the trip, Curtis exhorted. "I write this, recognizing the fact that at present the existence of a treaty between the General Government and the Sioux prevents the settlements of this most desirable region. . . . But the remedy to this can easily be applied. The Government should promptly take steps to extinguish the claim of the Indians to the Black Hills."

Extinguishing of the Indians' legal claim would prove problematic, but the settlement of the hills by whites was a virtual stampede. The first group of gold miners, six wagons carrying twenty-eight men and women, arrived on French Creek around Christmas 1874 and built a stockade as defense against Indians (who never did attack). By the following summer, at least six hundred more argonauts had made the trip. Despite the constant fear of Indian depredations, the real threat to the early miners was the United States Army. Until another treaty could be negotiated, or the Black Hills purchased from the Sioux outright, the Army chose to honor the Fort Laramie pact and deployed troops to intercept incoming settlers and to expel those who had already set up camp. Yet for every interloper apprehended, dozens more slipped through. When a second government expedition, this one sponsored by the Bureau of Indian Affairs, arrived on French Creek in June 1875, its geologists found traces of gold almost everywhere they looked, although they also noted that "the placers at present . . . are not remarkably rich." Lieutenant Colonel Richard Irving Dodge, commander of the military escort, observed that the settlement of Stonewall, soon to be renamed Custer City, was well established, "with at least ten idlers for every working man."

By summer's end, the Army had thrown up its hands. At a meeting attended by Secretary of War William Belknap and Generals Crook and Sheridan, President Grant announced that forthwith the Army, while continuing to honor the spirit of the Fort Laramie Treaty, would no longer expend itself intercepting travelers to the Black Hills or removing those already settled there. By the end of the year, an estimated fifteen thousand whites had entered the hills, with thousands more on the way. "All the powers of the Administration cannot keep this country in the possession of the Indians," Dodge wrote to Crook from French Creek. "None but a ring ridden [meek] nation would ever think for one moment of leaving such paradise in the hands of miserable savages even did they use it, which is not the case." The Chicago

Inter-Ocean banged the drum of manifest destiny even more shamelessly: "What, to the roaming Yankee, are the links that bind the red man to the home of his fathers? He is but an episode in the advance of the Caucasian. He must decrease that the new comers may grow in wealth."

The United States government, to its modest credit, did not have a wholly larcenous heart. Better informed on the resources of the Black Hills, and with the gold rush at full throttle, it made a legitimate attempt to purchase the hills from the Sioux. Washington's offer was $6 million. But Chief Red Cloud and several of his fellow Lakota chiefs had visited mines and observed not only the gold extracted but also the enthusiasm of the miners for their work. Accordingly, Red Cloud demanded $70 million for the hills. Neither side would budge, and no bargain was struck. (In later years, whites would admonish Sioux who insisted that the hills had never been for sale, asserting that the issue was not a willingness on the part of the Indians but simply a matter of price.)

With that, relations between the United States and the Sioux Nation went to hell. Indians continued to roam from the government agencies, the hubs of supply and administration established within the reservations: Red Cloud (named for Oglala Chief Red Cloud), Spotted Tail (for Brulé chief Spotted Tail), Rosebud, Cheyenne River, Standing Rock, and Crow Creek. Government rations were notoriously short and the housing shoddy, and of all the Great Plains tribes, the Lakota seemed to have the greatest difficulty adopting the white man's program of farming and education. By the terms of the 1868 treaty, still very much on the books, the Sioux were allowed to hunt westward into the Powder, Tongue, and Big Horn river basins—where they also continued to skirmish with whites and the Crow. Diehards such as Crazy Horse of the Oglala and Sitting Bull of the Hunkpapa were not going to give up the old ways without a fight, and they exhorted their "hang around the fort" brethren to shake off the entropy that was sapping their strength and self-esteem. Fearing a major blowup and citing Indian violence as a breach of treaty, the Secretary of the Interior announced that all Indians who were discovered off the reservation after January 1876—even those moving about in the larger unceded lands permitted under the 1868 treaty—would be regarded as "hostile." The line had been drawn in the prairie dirt, and the Great Sioux War of 1876–1877 awaited only the arrival of summer and the guidons of generals Crook, Terry, John Gibbon, and of course Custer.

We know what happened next. The Army tried to surround Crazy Horse and Sitting Bull, sending Gibbon from the west, Crook from the south, and Terry and Custer from the east. Gibbon bogged down in the spring snow. Crook tangled prematurely with Crazy Horse on the Rosebud. Custer broke off from Terry and rushed ahead. At the battle of the Little Bighorn, Crazy Horse, Sitting Bull, Gall, Rain in the Face, and a cast of thousands of Sioux, Cheyenne, and Arapaho repelled Custer's attack on June 25 and killed 263—the worst drubbing the Army would ever suffer at the hands of Indians.

The price the Indians paid for victory was huge, ruinous. The battle of Slim Buttes, two and a half months after Little Bighorn, was but one blow in the military's broader campaign to avenge Custer and to contain the "savage" Sioux on significantly reduced reservations. On August 15, while thousands of Sioux were still at large, Congress issued another ultimatum: no more rations until the Lakota agreed to give up all lands outside their immediate reservation, *plus all reservation land west of the 103rd meridian*—namely, the Black Hills. A presidential commission arrived at Red Cloud Agency on September 26, 1876, with the aim of gathering Lakota assent to the "sign or starve" agreement. Reluctantly the Lakota elders put their marks on the paper, although most said either that they did not understand its terms or that they had no intention of abiding by them. One chief covered his head with a blanket in shame as he "touched the pen." Soon chiefs at the other agencies followed suit. The commissioners had announced from the start that their underlying wish was to "save [the Indians] from death and lead them to civilization." In their missionary zeal, however, none seemed to have given any heed to Article XII of the treaty of 1868, which reads: "No treaty for the cession of any portion or part of the reservation ... shall be of any validity or force ... unless executed and signed by at least three fourths of all the adult male Indians." The number of X's on the latest agreement fell far short of the three quarters required to override the 1868 treaty. Even the most conservative estimate of warriors who had participated at Little Bighorn made clear just how faulty this math was.

The legality of the new Black Hills agreement will remain a topic of virulent debate for as long as the hills are part of white America and there are Indians alive to protest that fact. But as far as the boomers were concerned, the Black Hills were up for grabs, free and clear. By February 1877, the month the agreement was ratified, the population of Deadwood was already well over five thousand. The diggings in Custer City, along French Creek, had never amounted to much, as predicted by the early assays, but new settlements of Hill City, Crook City, Rapid City (also known as Hay Camp), and Spearfish were going great guns. Just upstream from Deadwood, the brothers Fred and Moses Manuel had struck a promising lead (pronounced "leed," an outcropping of ore) and took $5,000 in gold from it in the first year. Having earned their homestake—enough money to buy homes—they sold their holdings to San Francisco investor George Hearst (father of William Randolph Hearst) and two partners for $70,000. During the next 120 years, more than twelve hundred tons of gold bullion would be extracted from the Homestake mine in Lead, South Dakota. Even in the 1990s, as production at the mine came to an end, the value of the gold dust that washed out of miners' clothes in the laundry—Homestake owned their coveralls—exceeded $100,000 a year. For a time, Homestake's shafts, eight thousand feet straight down, were the deepest in North America, and its open pit, now listed on the National Registry of Historic Places, could swallow scores of Mount Rushmores.

But while miners were staking claims from one end of the Black Hills to the other, small bands of Lakota were still at large, refusing to come into the agencies. Newspapers sensationalized ongoing Indian "atrocities" against whites, but in fact such incidents, while regrettable, were vastly outnumbered by white attacks on Indians. The commissioners of newly formed Lawrence County put a bounty of $250 "for the body of each and every Indian, killed or captured, dead or alive." Setting its own bounty of $50, Deadwood rationalized that "killing Indians was conducive to the health of the community."

An even graver threat to the health of the community was white inhumanity toward whites. Robbery, claim-jumping, high-grading, and other outbursts of chicanery were chronic and often fatal. Walking along Deadwood's muddy main street on a Sunday afternoon in 1876, a correspondent for *Scribner's Monthly* opined, "I never in my life saw so many hardened and brutal-looking men together." One of those men shot "Wild Bill" Hickok in the back during a card game. Another Deadwood denizen, "Calamity Jane" Canary, is rumored to have been awarded her nickname not so much for her proto-feminist gumption but for the venereal curse she conveyed to her innumerable patrons. Sanitation in general was appalling in the mining camps, and dysentery, tuberculosis, and cholera were perhaps the most merciless killers of all.

Vice and violence lent a certain backhanded charm to the gold camps, thanks to the *Police Gazette* and dime novels, yet nothing quite so picturesque was befalling the Lakota. As Deadwood boomed, Sitting Bull and his proud followers were slowly starving in southern Saskatchewan. A more heartbreaking and—in light of the future affairs of the Black Hills—trenchant story is that of Crazy Horse's final days. Just as the massacre at Wounded Knee would eventually be compared to that at My Lai in Vietnam, so Crazy Horse would become an Indian Christ-figure.

Why Christ? For one thing, as with Jesus Christ, we know little about Crazy Horse. No photograph of him exists. Likenesses such as the five-hundred-foot-tall Crazy Horse Memorial now being carved in the Black Hills near Mount Rushmore and the 1982 Crazy Horse commemorative stamp are guesswork at best. His life story is equally sketchy. He was born around 1840 just north of the Black Hills. He was a quiet child and an aloof adult. Very much an ascetic, he did not go in for the paint and decorative accessories so characteristic of his fellow Lakota. He wore a single hawk feather in his hair and a pebble tied behind one ear. He was no pacifist, as evidenced by his bloody participation in the Fetterman Massacre of 1871 and the battles of the Rosebud and the Little Bighorn in 1876, plus numerous clashes with Indians. Nor was he chaste; he even had an affair with another man's wife. Above all, though, we have chosen to cast him as a mystic who, like Christ, was prone to wander off into the "wilderness" alone. And like Christ, he did not choose to lead; that role was chosen for him. Indeed, the outcome of his life seems to have been predestined.

Crazy Horse and several hundred followers had spent the winter of 1876–1877 in the Powder River Basin, avoiding the army and trying as best they could to feed themselves and their horses. Game was scarce, however; the buffalo herds had been decimated, and Crazy Horse's Lakota were weak and losing resolve. Finally in May, Crazy Horse embraced the inevitable and led his people into Red Cloud Agency. Although they gave up their arms and ponies, Crazy Horse's acquiescence was hardly a surrender, for the reservation Indians welcomed him as a returning hero. The only Lakota not happy to see him were those, like Red Cloud, who were ensconced in positions of reservation authority. Crazy Horse's unbowed dignity was a constant reminder of their own submissiveness.

At Red Cloud Agency, Crazy Horse began negotiating for his own reservation on the Powder River. Meanwhile, his Judases spread rumors that he was going to break out, that he would not be satisfied till he had killed every white man on earth. He told Dr. Valentine McGillycuddy, now the surgeon at Camp Robinson, the military post adjacent to Red Cloud Agency, "We did not ask you white men to come here. The Great Spirit gave us this country as home. You had yours. . . . We do not want your civilization." Finally, it was decided that Crazy Horse was too dangerous to be left to his own devices, and his arrest was ordered. The intention was to banish him to a prison in the Dry Tortugas of Florida.

Crazy Horse, escorted by a large contingent of soldiers and Indian police, rode willingly into Camp Robinson on September 5, 1877, believing that he could sort out, or at least articulate, some of his differences with the authorities there. Hundreds of Indians lined the parade ground to observe the arrival of the strong-hearted Oglala. He assumed that he was being led to the adjutant's office. Instead he was steered toward the guardhouse by his former friend, now Indian policeman, Little Big Man. Next came the crucifixion, unintentional perhaps but no less vivid. When Crazy Horse resisted, Little Big Man pinned both of his arms. A white soldier leapt forward and bayoneted the defenseless Crazy Horse in the side. He died later that night in the presence of his father and his friend Touch the Clouds. Dr. McGillycuddy was there, too, as he had been with American Horse a year earlier. Extreme unction was again a syringe of morphine.

Crazy Horse's parents took his body in a coffin to Spotted Tail Agency, then moved it again several days later. It is said to have been placed on a scaffold somewhere near Wounded Knee Creek on what is now the Pine Ridge Reservation, but no one knows for sure—or if they do, they're not saying. We have few heroes like Crazy Horse in American history. Unlike Chief Joseph, Crazy Horse never surrendered. Unlike Geronimo, he was never imprisoned. Unlike Red Cloud, he never signed a treaty. Unlike Sitting Bull, he never allowed his shadow to be captured by the camera. He never even slept in a white man's bed. And because his grave is a mystery, for thousands of Indians he is still very much at large. He still lives. Today, numerous places in the Black Hills are named for Custer: a town, a county, a mountain, a state park. But the spirit of Crazy Horse is everywhere. And those who sense his presence also nurture the belief that the Black Hills, like the promised land, may one day belong to the Lakota again.

Textbooks call the decade following the death of Crazy Horse "the Great Dakota Boom." Getting to the Black Hills was still not easy, but it was becoming less of an odyssey. Steamboats, stagecoaches, and freight wagons offered fairly reliable service, and in 1886, the first railroad reached the hills. With the rails came rigorous promotion exhorting settlement along their routes. Soon the territorial government of Dakota opened its own immigration bureau to bruit the region's charms in the crowded cities of the East and as far away as Europe. Gold remained the big draw, but miners were also having some luck with quartz, mica, and tin. Agriculture was another big enticement, as anticipated by Custer and so many others. Serendipitously, the 1870s were wet years on the northern plains, leading to the empirical gaffe that "rain follows the plow." On the prairie, Norwegian, Swedish, German, Bohemian, and Russian immigrants plowed up an aeon of grass and staked their futures on wheat and corn. As the more fertile ground east of the Missouri was snatched up, the grid of homesteads extended westward, attended by the railroads. Between 1876 and 1889, when Dakota Territory split into two states, the population of its southern portion tripled, to 330,000. A decade after the arrival of the first whites on French Creek in December 1874, the population of the Black Hills exceeded thirty thousand.

And even as the dime novels continued to mythologize the escapades of Wild Bill, Calamity Jane, and Deadwood Dick, the Black Hills endeavored to clean up their image. One of the many brochures aimed at prospective mining investors assured that the gunslingers, bushwhackers, and mountebanks had all been purged or tamed. "Time quiets all passions," promised the pamphleteers, and "the law is respected in a manner that would put many an older community to shame." The message, in so many words, was: Your money is safe here, and bring the family while you're at it—an avowal that nowadays is the subtext of every highway billboard within a six-hundred-mile radius of the Black Hills.

From the start, Black Hills promoters realized that there were other ways to attract newcomers besides mining, farming, or logging. "In no place on God's green earth is the flora more beautiful or a greater variety found," declared a booklet published by the Deadwood Board of Trade. The streams were "crystal," the springs "suggestive of angel whispers," the weather "as lovely as that of Italy." It followed that in a setting this Arcadian, the recreational and recuperative charms would be superb. In the decades after the Civil War, America had taken to cycling, the beach, and "physical culture." Spas, once the retreat of gentry, were now popular among the middle class. The lakes and springs of the Black Hills, along with the elevation (high and cool, but not too high or too cool), fit the bill perfectly, and at Hot Springs, a town in the southern hills, the minerals were in the water as well as the rock. Hot Springs baths were advertised as a remedy for everything from syphilis to sciatica. (Today the big attraction of Hot Springs is not the water's heat or health but the height of its waterslide.) Cave touring had also caught on across the country, and Wind Cave in the Black Hills, with its ninety miles of passageways, was already attracting the curious by the 1890s. In 1903, it became the nation's seventh national park.

White people's gain meant even greater hardship for the Lakota. In 1889, Congress subtracted another nine million acres from the Great Sioux Reservation, which was then parceled into six smaller reservations. An even more traumatic blow to the Lakota people was the government's backlash against the Ghost Dance. In the spring of 1890, a delegation of Lakota had returned to South Dakota from a trip to

Nevada, where they had gone to gather firsthand the message of Wovoka, a Paiute medicine man who had experienced a powerful messianic vision. During a solar eclipse a year earlier, Wovoka had glimpsed impending apocalypse. He predicted that in the spring of 1891 whites would be swept from the earth, or at least back to Europe, and all Indian "believers" would be joined by their ancestors in a paradise where the grass was green and the game plentiful as before.

Wovoka's vision offered optimism at a time when the Lakota had lost yet another hunk of their homeland. The range would not support their livestock, never mind buffalo. Perversely, the government announced it was slashing rations in half to encourage self-sufficiency. "There was no hope on earth and God seemed to have forgotten us," Chief Red Cloud reflected. "Some said they saw the Son of God [in Wovoka]; others did not see Him. . . . The people did not know; they did not care. They snatched at the hope." They did so by praying, singing, and dancing the Ghost Dance described in Wovoka's vision. Followers worked themselves into trances that allowed them rapturous glimpses of the promised land. Wovoka enjoined them to follow a set of commandments that were reminiscent of Moses' decalogue. Those who heeded the commandments, danced the Ghost Dance, and wore their ceremonial Ghost Shirts believed they were impervious to white harm, even bullets.

The Ghost Dance caught on like lightning striking pine needles. There were still plenty of fence sitters—"I was puzzled and did not know what to think," Black Elk recalled—but the zealotry of the true believers threw off a disproportionate heat. Sunday became the Ghost Dancers' Sabbath. When agency authorities outlawed the new religion, Indians chased off police who tried to break up their gatherings. Traditional leaders seized the occasion to reassert the old ways, urging the people to discard white clothes, white housing, white education, and white language.

The apocalypse did arrive, but not as Wovoka had pictured it. The

Black Hills and prairie surrounding the reservations were more densely settled than they had been ten years before, and whites who regarded the West as already "won" now flew into a panic, convinced that rampaging Sioux were about to scalp them in their beds. On November 15, the agent at Pine Ridge telegraphed Major General Nelson Miles, new commander of the Division of the Missouri: "Indians are dancing in the snow and are wild and crazy. . . . We need protection and we need it now." Miles obliged by calling out the cavalry to quell what was still essentially a religious revival. As it happened, the cavalry he sent was the Seventh, Custer's old unit, with a number of Little Bighorn survivors still in its ranks.

While the Army was moving onto Pine Ridge, tribal police were dispersed to round up known troublemakers. In the eyes of whites, Public Enemy No. 1 was still Sitting Bull, who had returned from Canada nine years earlier, had toured amiably with Buffalo Bill's Wild West show, and was now living on the Standing Rock Reservation. He had not been among the first to embrace the Ghost Dance, but he welcomed it nonetheless. When police surrounded Sitting Bull's house on December 15, a gunfight erupted, and the Hunkpapa leader was shot dead. At the sound of gunfire, his horse, a gift from Buffalo Bill, sat down and began performing tricks, as it had been taught to do on similar cue for audiences across America and Europe.

Another one of the alleged troublemakers was Chief Big Foot, Sitting Bull's half-brother. Also a disciple of the Ghost Dance, Big Foot feared reprisal after the death of Sitting Bull and decided to bring his band of 350 followers into Pine Ridge to demonstrate their peaceful intentions. On December 28, soldiers of the Seventh Cavalry surrounded Big Foot's band at a campsite on Wounded Knee Creek. Big Foot, weak from pneumonia, flew a white flag beside his tent. When cavalrymen attempted to disarm his people, a scuffle broke out. Regardless of who took the first shot—a subject still conjectured—there is no question who shot last. Firing at will with carbines, pistols, and

Hotchkiss guns, the soldiers killed nearly three hundred Indians, mostly women and children, unarmed, defenseless. A blizzard pounced upon the killing field that night, and frozen corpses still held their ghoulish poses when stacked in wagons six days later. Thus ended the Ghost Dance. More than thirty soldiers also died at Wounded Knee, mostly from their own crossfire. Eighteen were awarded the Congressional Medal of Honor for their putative bravery on December 28, 1890.

South Dakota author Leland Case once remarked that the history of the Black Hills lacked a medieval period. The transition from ancient times to modern was simply too rapid. Immigrants came fast on the heels of explorers. Tourists arrived even before the Indians had laid down their weapons. And then, just as suddenly, the twentieth century arrived.

After Wounded Knee, the next major turning point in the history of western South Dakota was the First World War, or rather its aftermath. The war years capped a period of remarkable growth and prosperity for America's breadbasket. Between 1890 and 1917, more than 100,000 newcomers settled in South Dakota's West River, taking advantage of the Enlarged Homestead Act, which expanded claims from 160 to 320 acres, and the Dawes Allotment Act, which enabled whites to take up unoccupied land on Indian reservations. Life on the high plains was made that much more inviting, thanks to the introduction of new drought-hearty strains of wheat, advances in the technology of farming and milling, and continued expansion of the railroads. Moreover, war had triggered a huge demand for grain and livestock. Between 1910 and 1918, the price of South Dakota wheat, corn, and beef more than doubled. In some West River counties, land values tripled or quadrupled.

But as quickly as prices soared, they then plummeted with the postwar decline in demand for commodities. By 1920, South Dakota had entered a slump that would last another two decades. Over the next five years, the value of the average West River farm shrank to half its wartime appraisal. During that same period, half the farms in these formerly booming counties failed. More South Dakota banks shut their doors in the 1920s than in the more infamous Depression of the 1930s. In the Black Hills, mining sputtered, too. Able-bodied veterans returned home and could not get their old jobs back. Existing mines laid off workers. New mines went undug, and miners left the hills. Too many of those who remained were living hand to mouth.

One of the first men to venture a solution to the region's flagging economy was Doane Robinson, the state historian. Before he was done, he had not only written the history of South Dakota; he had also made a good deal of it himself.

Throughout the cultural history of the West, one continually comes across the archetype of the farm-raised, world-curious youth who, in adulthood, applies his or her native intellect and determination to a life of the mind that appears, at first glance, an extraordinary overachievement but upon reflection seems spawned entirely by his or her roots. We think of O. E. Rölvaag, born of Norwegian homesteaders, whose novel *Giants in the Earth*—published in 1927, just as work commenced on Mount Rushmore—established him as the Tolstoy of the Dakota steppes; or Nebraska's Willa Cather, whose evocative portraits of prairie society are at once nostalgic and fatalistic. Nowhere near as famous or refined as these two, Doane Robinson nonetheless sprang from the same sod.

He was born in Wisconsin in 1856; then, as a young man, he filed for a homestead in Minnesota. Along with farming, he studied law and soon set up practice in newly minted South Dakota, a state too young to have a published history of any heft. Robinson solved that. In 1901, he founded the South Dakota State Historical Society, and as its first secretary, he authored a series of books, most notably a two-volume *History of South Dakota* and the groundbreaking *A History of the Dakota or Sioux Indians*, which begins: "The course of the Sioux as a tribe is now completed. He has fought his last war, he has discarded the blanket and donned the habiliments of civilization." Where others saw a primitive past and a coarse adolescence, Robinson discerned the germ of culture for whites as well as Indians. As a naturalized son of South Dakota, he was proud of the state's history and beauty and was among the first to regard them as marketable amenities. As early as 1898, he had written a tract entitled "Dakota for Health Seekers," in which he equated the state with eastern retreats such as the Catskills or Saratoga. By the 1920s, with South Dakota wheezing from the war letdown, he began evangelically touting the state's exciting heritage as one of the keys to its future. "There is in most of us an inherent combination of curiosity and reverence that makes us regard the scenes of historic achievement . . . with something of awe and satisfaction," he wrote.

One of his fellow believers was Peter Norbeck, the first native Dakotan to become governor. Another son of Norwegian immigrants, Norbeck had made a modest fortune digging wells and then had climbed the ladder from the South Dakota senate to lieutenant governor, then to governor and later to the U.S. Senate. Norbeck was a Roosevelt Republican, and like Theodore Roosevelt, he was a dedicated conservationist. Although he was born and raised in the eastern part of the state, he had grown to appreciate the Black Hills as South Dakota's crown jewel. In 1919, Governor Norbeck consecrated 73,000 acres of the eastern hills as a state park (the second largest state park in the United States, after Anzo Borrego in California's Mojave Desert), which he named for the region's most celebrated invader and stocked with one of the last remaining buffalo herds in the country. With Custer State Park as a drawing card, now more than ever the Black Hills could be billed as a destination for those in search of wholesome beauty and Old West diversion. Norbeck and Doane Robinson were optimistic that tourism could become the newest leg supporting the economic table of South Dakota.

Yet the same old problem still existed. The Black Hills weren't really near anywhere else, weren't even on the way to or from anywhere else. The question facing Robinson, Norbeck, and their fellow promoters was how to persuade travelers to bend their itineraries to include the Black Hills. The twentieth-century vacationer already had an abundance of choices for western adventure: the Grand Canyon and the Southwest; Pikes Peak and the Colorado Rockies; the Tetons, Yellowstone, and Glacier National Park in the northern Rockies; and Yosemite and the myriad charms of California. Given all these magnificent options, why would anyone detour to the outback of South Dakota? By way of answer, Doane Robinson suggested carving a series of enormous historical figures on the side of one of the Black Hills.

CHAPTER 3

GARDEN OF THE GODS

G IVING TRAVELERS a reason to visit the Black Hills was only half of Doane Robinson's battle. The other half was getting them there. South Dakota's leading historian and most enthusiastic advocate knew that if he built a compelling enough diversion, travelers would find a way to come. And once they started coming, better roads would follow. Or something like that.

The chronicle of the Black Hills in the twentieth century—including that of Mount Rushmore—parallels the course of automobile tourism in America. Travel for pleasure and adventure has always been part of the national character, but not until after the First World War did Americans of any number take to the roads in their own cars. Before then, they journeyed by train to the seashore, the mountains, and our national parks, many of which—Grand Canyon and Glacier, for instance—were developed by the railroads.

Touring by automobile was not for the fainthearted in the first two decades of the century. The nation had no comprehensive network of highways, and most rural roads were old wagon ruts, gumbo when wet, washboarded and dusty the rest of the time. Maps and road signs were sporadic and unreliable. In 1903, at a time when transcontinental rail travel took only four days, H. Nelson Jackson and Sewall K. Crocker took a record sixty-four days to muscle a one-cylinder, twenty-horsepower Winton from San Francisco to New York.

Henry Ford introduced the Model T in 1908, and suddenly the country had an affordable, reliable, gas-powered conveyance. The family car had arrived and with it the family vacation. Still, the roads were treacherous. Of the nation's three million miles of road in 1904, only 140 miles were "hard" surfaced and only 150,000 miles were "improved" in any way. Scarcely any of the "good" roads were in the West. In 1905, Peter Norbeck had made the first automobile trip from the South Dakota capital, Pierre, to the Black Hills, sticking as best he could to the existing wagon trail established by freighters. The first day, his party hit rain and was stranded in a farmhouse for three days. "After the roads dried up a little," he related, "we proceeded to Rapid City but had a team [of horses] help us along for twenty or thirty miles. We found the water too high in the Cheyenne River to cross on our own power but fortunately three cowboys came along and kindly hitched their ropes to the car and towed us across on a gallop. We reached Rapid City without [further] trouble. We were then caught in a heavy snow storm and had to leave the car and take the train for home via Sioux City [Iowa]."

Faced with similar vicissitudes, American motorists refused to keep still. Magazines and Sunday rotogravures carried accounts of "auto touring" adventures, nearly all harrowing, but most with happy endings. Published memoirs bore titles such as *Log of an Auto Prairie Schooner* and *It Might Have Been Worse: A Motor Trip from Coast to Coast*. In 1915, etiquette maven Emily Post made a car trip from New York to the Golden Gate, a wicker hamper carrying her silver tea set strapped to the fender. Her account of the journey was laced with advice on what to wear and how much to spend—a sure sign that the pastime of motoring had attained a modicum of decorum if not comfort.

The idea of a national highway designed for modern automobile travel did not come into its own until 1912. Carl Graham Fisher of Indianapolis had made his fortune manufacturing carbide headlights. He had also made a success of the Indianapolis Motor Speedway, a racetrack he had paved with brick for the running of the first Indianapolis 500 in 1911. Assessing the rapid advances in engines, brakes, steering, and tires, Fisher grasped that the biggest thing holding back automobiles was the surface they rode on, and the following year, he proposed building a Coast-to-Coast Rock Highway, the first paved road across America. He urged that it be completed in time for the opening of the Panama-Pacific Exposition in San Francisco in 1915. Fisher's deadline would prove impossible, as would his dream of paving the entire route, but his grand vision of a coast-to-coast highway was as unshakable as it was contagious. Almost overnight he received millions of dollars in pledges from auto manufacturers, and when Congress decided to fund the Lincoln Memorial in Washington—instead of a Lincoln memorial highway from Washington to Gettysburg—Fisher borrowed the name for his national road.

In 1914, which was also the first year that manufacture of motor vehicles exceeded that of horse-drawn wagons and carriages, the Lincoln Highway Association announced its route. The starting point was Times Square, New York City; the road then struck out across New Jersey, Pennsylvania, Ohio, Indiana, to Chicago. The western portion ran through the midriff of the nation, essentially following the original immigrant and rail routes—Omaha, Cheyenne, Salt Lake City, Reno, Sacramento—to San Francisco, a total distance of 3,300 miles.

The Lincoln Highway was hardly America's Appian Way. Portions of it were graded, surfaced, and groomed, but others, especially in the Midwest and West, were never much more than the horse and oxen tracks they had once been. The real innovation, the enduring contribution, of the Lincoln Highway was its recognition as *the* national road. America now had a designated automobile route across the entire continent—a path that one could follow on one's own, in one's own private car, a latter-day pioneer, but mechanized and much safer.

The overwhelming enthusiasm for the Lincoln Highway prompted the federal government to enter the highway age. In 1916, Congress passed the Federal Aid Road Act, appropriating $75 million in matching funds for state-by-state road improvement—the first tentative step toward a federal highway system. Better roads naturally made driving more appealing, although it is hard to imagine America's passion for the automobile growing any more fervent than it already was. In the five years that followed 1916, the year of the seminal federal highway act, the number of registered motor vehicles in the United States doubled, from four million to eight million. The proliferation would continue to accelerate; there were twenty-six million cars on the road by 1930.

Along with triggering government involvement in national roads, the Lincoln Highway spawned spin-offs. Cities and towns along the route were elated to have the transcontinental route wend through their main streets, much as towns had welcomed the commerce of the railroads a generation earlier. Towns not on the route tried to make their own luck, linking up with one another to establish their own memorial highways. A Rand McNally atlas of 1924 lists, in addition to the Lincoln Highway, the National Old Trails Road (Washington, D.C., to Los Angeles, along part of the old Santa Fe Trail); the Theodore Roosevelt International Highway (Portland, Maine, to Portland, Oregon); the Old Spanish Trail (Florida to California); and the Pikes Peak Ocean to Ocean Highway (along the fortieth parallel, via Pike's Peak). Other routes, both east-west and north-south, included the Dixie Highway, Jefferson Highway, National Parks Highway, Victory Highway, Meridian Highway, and Midland Trail. Still other towns, near but not actually on these roads, designated themselves as "laterals," endeavoring to siphon off a portion of the traffic and money that were now flowing across the country.

Since the days of Peter Norbeck's rugged journey from Pierre to Rapid City, South Dakota had attempted, somewhat haltingly, to befriend the automobile. By 1910, there were ten thousand cars registered in the state. A decade later, that number had increased tenfold. Most of South Dakota's roads, meanwhile, were still geared for wagons. The one exception was the Yellowstone Trail, the brainchild of Joe Parmley, a resident of Ipswich, in the north-central part of the state, who had grown tired of bogging down in the mud while driving to Aberdeen, the next town over. Soon Parmley's modest yearning for twenty-six miles of decent road expanded into a vision of "a Good Road from Plymouth Rock to Puget Sound." Parmley was wise enough to include Yellowstone National Park on the route he drew up, and he named it the Yellowstone Trail. While the Lincoln Highway designated its route with red-white-and-blue mileposts, Parmley chose yellow, and in the early going, he painted the roadside markers himself. On the treeless prairie, he made do with large stones, which he lugged in his car. To prove that the South Dakota portion of the road was viable, Parmley made a 340-mile "flying trip" in sixteen hours—at an average speed of 21 miles an hour.

The only problem with the Yellowstone Trail, from Doane Robinson's standpoint anyway, was that it only creased the northern brow of the state. (Today the trail is U.S. Highway 12.) It did not pass through the state's commercial centers of Yankton, Sioux Falls, Mitchell, or Brookings. Nor did it pass through Pierre, the capital. And the nearest it came to the Black Hills was Lemmon, more than two hundred miles north of Rapid City.

With all due respect to Parmley and his achievement, Robinson could not bear to see so much of his adopted state excluded from the new highway boom, so beneficial to inter- and intra-state business and, moreover, the biggest chance yet to bring tourists into South Dakota. Accordingly,

Robinson conceived a second road, the Black Hills and Yellowstone High-way—"the Black and Yellow Trail"—which mapped a sixteen-hundred-mile route from Chicago to Yellowstone National Park that passed through the heart of South Dakota and the Black Hills (present-day Highway 14, more or less). But even then, he had to have a gimmick. Compared to the grandeur of Yellowstone and the Rockies, the Black Hills were a little sister, attractive to be sure, but nowhere near as comely. For all the pride he had in South Dakota, Doane Robinson was also a pragmatist and, even though he would never admit as much, he must have harbored doubts about the drawing power of the hills. "Tourists soon get fed up on scenery, unless it has something of special interest connected with it to make it impressive," he remarked, adding, "They want the table spread before them and the exhibits labeled." The Black Hills had Custer State Park, but no Old Faithful. The answer, of course, was to build something. And once it was built, Robinson reasoned, the tourists would come, dropping crumbs along the Black and Yellow Trail.

The notion of the roadside attraction was nothing new. The Cardiff Giant had drawn thousands of curiosity seekers to an out-of-the-way hamlet in upstate New York. The extraordinary architecture of the Philadelphia, Chicago, Buffalo, St. Louis, and San Francisco World's Fairs, not to mention the phantasmagoria of Coney Island, had enchanted millions. And more recently, Robinson had read of a colossal Indian sculpted by artist Lorado Taft and erected on a bluff overlooking the Rock River near Oregon, Illinois. Why not something similar in the Black Hills?

On December 28, 1923, Robinson wrote to Taft:

> South Dakota has developed a wonderful state park in the Black Hills. I enclose a brochure illustrating some features of it. On the front cover you will observe some pinnacles—we call them needles—situated high upon the flank of Harney Peak. The tops of those shown are more than 6300 feet above sea level. These needles are of granite.

Having in mind your "Big Injun," it has occurred to me that some of these pinnacles would lend themselves to massive sculpture, and I write to ask if in your judgment human figures might be carved from some of them as they stand. I am thinking of some notable Sioux as Redcloud, who lived and died in the shadow of these peaks. If one was found practicable, perhaps others would ultimately follow.

Lorado Taft was one of the most prominent sculptors in America. He had received important commissions for the Chicago World's Fair in 1893, and his elaborate sculptural fountains graced several of Chicago's public gathering places. Those who had never visited Chicago or passed by his *Columbus Fountain* at the entrance of Washington's Union Station recognized him as the author of *The History of American Sculpture*, the first authoritative survey of its kind.

Doane Robinson, though, only had eyes for "the Big Injun." At the turn of the century, Taft and several artist friends had set up a summer retreat at Eagle's Nest Bluff on the Rock River, not far from the spot where the Sac and Fox Chief Black Hawk had fought and died defending his homeland seventy years earlier. Inspired by Black Hawk's spirit and no doubt impressed by Daniel Chester French's allegorical goddess, *The Republic*, which had been the centerpiece of the Chicago World's Fair, Taft erected a forty-eight-foot-tall concrete Indian two hundred feet above the river, where it could be seen for miles around. Taft did not intend his figure to represent a specific individual, but locals took to calling it Black Hawk. Taft sometimes referred to the piece as "our Colossus," after the Colossus of Rhodes, one of the Seven Wonders of the Ancient World. His creation was likewise a wonder of its day. People drove hundreds of miles to see it. Photos and sketches appeared in numerous publications—which is presumably how Doane Robinson made its acquaintance.

Taft wrote back to Robinson, explaining that, due to ill health, he could not undertake the Black Hills project. Robinson tried again anyway, this time expanding his offer: "Near the summit is a little park through which the highway passes. . . . It is studded with column after column of these pinnacles." On the pinnacles, Robinson envisioned "all the heroes of the old west peering out." He mentioned Meriwether Lewis and William Clark, John Fremont, Jedediah Smith, Jim Bridger, Sacagawea, Red Cloud, and Buffalo Bill Cody.

Despite the more tantalizing offer, Taft again declined, but by now Robinson was sold on his plan. In a speech entitled "The Pull of the Historic Place," he shared his idea with his fellow members of the Black and Yellow Trail Association on January 22, 1924. "It would add a lot to the pull of [the Black Hills] if one or more of [its] great monoliths should be converted into a memorial," he told his audience. In a newspaper interview the following week, Robinson reiterated, "I can think of nothing in America that would outrival such a spectacle, with the possible exception of Stone Mountain, near Atlanta, Georgia." The key word was "spectacle."

Strangely, though, Robinson was slow to contact Gutzon Borglum, who was then garnering so much favorable publicity for his immense Confederate memorial at Stone Mountain. Perhaps he assumed that Borglum had his hands full. With Taft unavailable as well, Robinson briefly considered Daniel Chester French, who had recently completed the Lincoln Memorial in Washington. Eventually, though, he came around to Borglum. As it happened, Robinson's timing could not have been more perfect.

On August 20, 1924, Robinson wrote to Borglum in Georgia. His pitch was more cautious, verging on obsequious: "In the vicinity of Harney Peak, in the Black Hills of South Dakota are opportunities for heroic sculpture of unusual character. Would it be possible for you to design and supervise a massive sculpture there[?] The proposal has not passed beyond the mere suggestion, but if it would be possible for you to undertake the matter I feel quite sure we could arrange to finance such an enterprise."

In fact, Robinson didn't have a clue how much his project would finally cost—he had told the Black and Yellow crowd $100,000—or how he would finance it. Borglum, for his part, didn't need a firm answer just then, for unbeknownst to Robinson and the greater public, things were beginning to fall apart at Stone Mountain. In January of that year, Borglum had celebrated the completion of the first figure, a twenty-one-foot-tall head of Robert E. Lee, with a grand dedication attended by thousands of grateful, tearful southerners. But in the months that followed, he had begun to clash with his backers—over money and politics and control—and although Stone Mountain was still years from completion, he was ready for a change of scenery. When Borglum's assistant opened the letter from Robinson, he jotted across the top, "Here it is, Borglum. Let's go."

On August 28, Borglum telegrammed Robinson: "Very much interested in your proposal. Great scheme you have. Hold to it."

As a historian and now a businessman, Robinson could have asked a number of questions about Borglum before inviting him to South Dakota, but his enthusiasm obviated any such diligence. The same month in which he had written Borglum, Scientific American had reported that Stone Mountain—"the largest piece of sculpture ever attempted in ancient or modern times"—might eventually cost $4 million, $2 million over the original estimate. Price notwithstanding, Stone Mountain was shaping up as a stupendous achievement, and its similarities to Mount Rushmore are worth noting.

Stone Mountain, like the core of the Black Hills, is an enormous, lichen-streaked upthrust of granite, 560 acres in all, rising 800 feet above the surrounding countryside, sixteen miles east of Atlanta. As with Mount Rushmore, its otherworldly uniqueness made it a sacred spot to Native Americans. Shortly after the Civil War, faithful Georgians had begun suggesting that the granite dome be consecrated as a memorial to those who had sacrificed for the Lost Cause. No one put forward a firm plan until 1913, and the job was not offered to Borglum for another two years. Lorado Taft was considered ahead of him, but even then Taft was too frail.

Borglum came to Georgia from his home in Connecticut and instead of agreeing to a bas-relief of Robert E. Lee, he proposed profiles of Lee, Stonewall Jackson, Jefferson Davis, and possibly others, followed by a cavalcade of Confederate troops that would cover the entire mountain. We shall investigate more fully the trials and tribulations of Stone Mountain in future chapters, but suffice it to say, Borglum encountered extraordinary logistical challenges, not the least of which was how to project and sketch an immense image on the side of slick granite hundreds of feet from the ground. And nobody had ever attempted stonecutting on this scale, under these conditions. To his great credit, Borglum overcame every technical and artistic obstacle, as he had done throughout his very busy career as a sculptor. But inevitably he became embroiled in a battle of egos—a pattern that was characteristic of all his professional relationships.

Doane Robinson knew nothing of these negatives when he invited Borglum to South Dakota. Nor would he have known that throughout his years at Stone Mountain, Borglum had been an avid and influential supporter of the Ku Klux Klan, the secret brotherhood that had been reborn at a ceremony at Stone Mountain in 1915. All of these proclivities of temperament, bias, and intrigue would come to light eventually, and they would all inform Borglum's role in the Mount Rushmore story.

Borglum stepped off the train in Rapid City on the morning of September 24, accompanied by his twelve-year-old son Lincoln; his superintendent from Stone Mountain, Jesse Tucker; and Robinson, who had joined them at Pierre. Borglum had requested that the trip be kept quiet; instead he was greeted at the station by a crowd of local business leaders, who bustled him off to a Rotary Club luncheon of prairie chicken, at which, according to the following day's front page, he was prevailed upon to recount in rich detail the wonders of Stone Mountain. Borglum was a veteran of hundreds of public speeches and took to his assignment with gusto. He was not a big man, no more than five-foot-nine, yet he always seemed to fill a much bigger space. With his bald head, bristling moustache, and burly build, he bore a slight resemblance to Ernest Hemingway, although his manners were more polished and his deep voice came across as vaguely continental, aristocratic even. Applying his customary brio, he promised that the Confederate monument would "give to the South a recognition in the way of permanent memorial art. It will give back to it some of its self-respect." The Rapid City sachems, in the midst of their own regional doldrums, greeted Borglum's words with thunderous applause.

After lunch, Borglum and company were driven by a roundabout route through the town of Custer and then to a lodge at Sylvan Lake, high in the hills within Custer State Park. The next morning, he was guided to the top of Harney Peak. Although fifty-eight years old, Borglum had the strength and energy of a man half his age and relished athletics of any type. A boxer, fencer, equestrian, and all-around outdoorsman, he was invigorated by the strenuous ascent, some of which demanded the use of hands as well as feet. The top of Harney Peak is a crow's nest; on a clear day, the prairie perimeter stretches fifty miles in every direction, and the granite brows of the immediate hills are like the rooftops of an ancient kingdom. "We walked through a veritable 'Garden of the Gods,'" Borglum said of the trip and the view from the top. "I know the West . . . yet I know of no grouping of rock formation that equals those found about this mountain in the Black Hills of South Dakota, nor do I know of any so near the center of our country that is so available to the nation or so suitable for colossal sculpture. . . . [T]he large ledges to the rear, near and to the south of Mount Harney are available and should be examined for definite historical portrait characters, preferably national in the largest sense."

If Borglum had thought big at Stone Mountain, he was thinking even bigger now. For all the national attention and federal support that the Confederate memorial was receiving, it was, in the end, still a southern monument. The canvas before him in South Dakota was remote, but it was, as he said, *central*. And judging from the apparent pliability and implicit neediness of his hosts, he could have his way here: He could carve a monument that was *national in the largest sense.*

For some reason, though, he held his tongue, something he was not in the habit of doing and would seldom do again. "[F]or the present," he told his hosts, "I would prefer to confine my statement to one of delight and approval in the opportunity and favorable to what is proposed." But before leaving for the East two days later, he did present to Doane Robinson a hasty sketch of a Continental soldier in a tricornered hat—a profile of George Washington.

Robinson was totally enthused—by the scheme for a national monument and by Borglum himself. "Borglum has come and gone," he wrote Peter Norbeck, by then a U.S. senator. "I count it one of the great experiences of my life to have spent two days with a man of his genius and high character. . . . I can hardly believe that this wonderful thing is to be handed to us."

In October, Borglum sent Robinson his further thoughts on the Black Hills project, warning that if it were not handled with the utmost care, "we will only wound the mountain, offend the Gods and deserve the condemnation of posterity." Instead of Washington alone, he now included a sketch and proposal for Washington and Abraham Lincoln. Whereas the heroes of Stone Mountain were being carved in relief, those intended for the Black Hills were to be carved in the round, emerging from the granite as columns, not unlike Lorado Taft's "Big Injun." In a speech Borglum gave years later, he referred to his early design as the "totem pole idea." The scale would be of men two hundred feet tall. (Ultimately, the Rushmore faces would be scaled to men more than four hundred feet tall.) Borglum also suggested adding Theodore Roosevelt—his friend and mentor who had died in 1919—and a secondary bas-relief of Custer and other western heroes. He estimated the job would take six years and cost $1.2 million. For preliminary surveys, retainer, and expenses, Borglum said he would need $10,000. "Financing of the main work offers no real difficulties," he assured. When Robinson wrote back, urging that they stick to Washington and Lincoln for the time being, Borglum quickly concurred: "Let us hold to that unbeatable thought of those two lone giants standing on top of America. That plan ... will arouse the nation."

Robinson took the thought and ran with it, giving speeches to civic groups across the state. For the most part, his descriptions of the proposed carving were greeted with great encouragement. An editorial writer for the *Sioux Falls Press* imagined a monument that "dwarfs the Sphinx of Egypt, the Lion of Lucerne in Switzerland, the ancient Colossus of Rhodes, and the Statue of Liberty in New York harbor." The writer pictured the Black Hills attracting "millions of visitors from the far corners of the earth. . . . In my mind's eye I can see great streams of traffic flowing year by year to the western shrine, greater streams even than have gone to Georgia, for South Dakota lies en route to the Pacific coast and motorists certainly would take that route. . . . Yes, in time the state might well become a tourist mecca for people of all lands."

Robinson and Borglum's plan was not without its critics, however. As the "tamers" of America's wilderness gave way to the industrialists of the modern era—with the know-how to build ever taller buildings, longer ships, broader dams, and deeper mines—groups like the Sierra Club, founded by John Muir, and the Boone and Crockett Club, founded by Theodore Roosevelt and George Bird Grinnell, warned that the nation's natural resources were limited and urgently in need of conservation. In 1925, at precisely the time that Doane Robinson was drumming up interest in a Black Hills carving, a nationwide campaign was under way to prevent logging in the forest surrounding the Old Man of the Mountain, an entirely natural, fifty-foot crag of granite in the White Mountains of New Hampshire that looks uncannily like a human profile. In the end, more than 15,000 people raised $400,000 to preserve the Old Man's sanctuary, a benchmark in the American conservation movement—and hardly a vote of confidence for Doane Robinson's proposal to reshape the Black Hills of South Dakota. "He seems to think that by making this radical alteration on nature's handiwork will please tourists and will add to the tourist traffic through the Black Hills country," frowned one Black Hills newspaper. "The famous [N]eedles region ... will attract attention and exclamations of wonderment so long as they continue to stand in their majestic grandeur.... To set the hand of man at work to improve on that of nature is a desecration which should not be permitted." And on a less idealistic note, the paper added: "If the Robinson suggestion means that the fund for this proposed transition is to be raised from taxation, it will not meet with a hearty response from a people already burdened to a heart-breaking point with constantly mounting taxes."

Robinson defended his position aggressively, insisting that nature had no better friend than he. "The suggestion that to bring the world's greatest Artist to South Dakota to create the world's most tremendous work of Art could be a desecration of nature is certainly a very mistaken view," he responded. Robinson's philosophy was that "God always leaves it to man to finish [His] work," and he had no patience for locals who welcomed mining but not sculpture. "[I]f the granite [of the Harney Peak region] should assay five cents a ton in gold," he chided, "they would unanimously subscribe to a machine to grind up the Needles and wipe them off the face of the earth. I do not want to harm the native beauty of the Needles at all, but I would find a bunch of them some where in a location that would be reached by a special side trip and there I would set Gutzon Borglum ... at work upon a great historic pageant, and when it is done the result will be worth a lot more in cash than would another Homestake, and it will not grind up its material and pass away, but for a thousand years would continue to bring its annual harvest of gold. With such a sculpture in the Hills[,] no eastern man would think of going west for pleasure without passing through the Hills enroute."

Despite his own conviction and Borglum's assurances, Robinson understood that securing public approval would be an uphill battle. The final site for the carving had not been determined; that would not come till Borglum's survey was funded and he was able to return to the Black Hills. But whether it was located on federal or state land, either would require official permission before work could proceed. Likewise, appropriation of the preliminary $10,000 would take an act of the South Dakota legislature. This would necessitate the support of the state's tightfisted governor, Carl Gunderson, and Senator Norbeck, the unofficial gatekeeper of all that transpired within Custer State Park.

At Robinson's urging, Borglum had visited Norbeck in Washington in early December and again in January, and the two can-do Scandinavians had hit it off. "He is a peculiar combination of a promoter, publicist, politician," Norbeck related to Robinson, "and, last but most important, he is one of the great artists of the world. The most remarkable trait . . . is probably the fact he refuses to be discouraged. He looks upon it as a weakness, and almost a disease. . . . Evidently he is not one of the artists who are going to die and wait a century or two for recognition. He is going to get a good deal of it as he goes along."

Norbeck was in favor of the Black Hills project from the start, though he was even more of a realist than Robinson. "I don't want to say anything to dampen your ardor," he wrote to Robinson after first meeting Borglum, but he warned his friend that setbacks were inevitable. "Even the Washington Monument stood half completed for nearly a half century, and there were no sectional complications involved in this." Norbeck also passed along some worrisome Washington intelligence on Stone Mountain: "The literature indicates the total cost of Stone Mountain Memorial at about three and one-half million dollars," and the association backing it was overdrawn and counting on a bail-out by the federal government. "I do not feel that any of these matters need change our plan," Norbeck concluded, "but I do feel that in the end South Dakota will be called upon to make up some substantial part of the cost."

Robinson listened to Norbeck's common sense, as he did to the grousing of conservationists, and was undeterred. In fact, he was so bent on beginning the mountain carving that he purported not to care if it were ever finished. To him, Borglum was the second coming of Michelangelo, and half a *David* was better than none at all. "I am first for the enterprise because of its wonderful artistic value," he lobbied Norbeck. "I tell you from that point of view it is unparalleled and it is doubtful if it ever could be surpassed. Secondarily it will 'sell' the Black Hills and [Custer State] Park as nothing else could. The moment Borglum sets chisel into the granite there we have accomplished a publicity. . . . Money cannot buy the good advertising this thing will give us. Like Stone Mountain, if he failed to finish the work, the wreck of it would bring the world running to see where he had left his mark."

In February 1925, Robinson and Norbeck, along with South Dakota congressman William Williamson, were pushing separate federal and state legislation to establish the Mount Harney Memorial Association, under the assumption that the carving would be located somewhere fairly near Harney Peak. The bills would allow a survey to be conducted in the state park and adjoining national forest and would dun the state $5,000 for the expenses required by Borglum. (Borglum had startled Robinson by suggesting out of the blue that they ask for an appropriation of $200,000 over three years. Given the mixed sentiments in the state capital, Robinson had ignored Borglum's outlandish request and reduced the original $10,000 request by half.) The South Dakota bill was expected to come to a vote by the end of the month.

However reasonable Robinson's request may have been or however persuasive his lobbying, nothing he could say or do would have overcome the news that hit South Dakota on February 26. "Borglum's Row With Stone Mountain Men Ends in His Release," blared the *Rapid City*

Journal, an avowed supporter of the Black Hills memorial. The front page quoted an Associated Press report from Atlanta the day before: "Warrants charging Gutzon Borglum, sculptor, and J. G. Tucker, his superintendent of construction, with malicious mischief in connection with destruction of working plans and models for carving the Confederate memorial at Stone Mountain near Atlanta, were sworn out today by Stone Mountain Memorial Association, which has dismissed Borglum as directing sculptor."

As more details filtered in from Georgia, the picture got only more sensational. Borglum had indeed feuded with the Stone Mountain Association and in a fit of proprietary rage had smashed his models of Robert E. Lee, Stonewall Jackson, and Jefferson Davis, asserting that if he was forbidden to work on the memorial, no one else would be allowed to follow his blueprint, either. Worse still, he had apparently raced from the state at high speed with the sheriff in hot pursuit. There were even rumors that shots had been fired. At any rate, Borglum was now a fugitive from justice, holed up in North Carolina.

On the morning of February 24, as Borglum was fleeing Georgia, the South Dakota senate defeated the Mount Harney appropriation bill, 14–19. The main objection was the money. Robinson dusted himself off and promptly reintroduced the legislation, this time asking for nothing except approval to proceed with the project on state land. Funding, he hoped, would come from private sources. All along, Borglum had hinted that he had friends who would step forward with large sums. Now even that seemed a stretch.

Once again, Norbeck's assessment of the situation was astute. "I suppose it all depends on how you tell the story," he wrote to Robinson in recapping the recent events in Georgia. "Borglum felt himself all-powerful and did things with a high hand. After all, he has not the business man's viewpoint. He is an artist, and a promoter. His plans are not all sound."

Still, Norbeck stressed in a follow-up letter, "This Stone Mountain fiasco may work decidedly to our advantage in South Dakota—who knows." By this he meant that with Borglum now apparently divorced from Stone Mountain, perhaps permanently, he would have more time and energy to devote to the Black Hills. As it turned out, Norbeck guessed correctly. Borglum was more motivated than ever to carve a memorial to Lincoln and Washington. Norbeck had also been dead right about Gutzon Borglum's nature: He was a lousy businessman. On the other hand, he was a consummate promoter, a shrewd politician, and a great artist. And when it came to high-handedness, nobody could touch him, although many tried.

4

GREAT MAN

G UTZON BORGLUM believed in the role of the Great Man in history. It was a notion impressed upon him by his father, an eccentric but persuasive patriarch. He focused on it intently in his art, devoting his career to sculpture of great men, climaxing with Mount Rushmore. And he demonstrated it in his bearing—by the way he treated people whom he perceived to be of meaner talent, intellect, or social station and especially by the way he strove to win the patronage and join the peerage of America's brightest, wealthiest, and most powerful men and women. In his heart of hearts, Borglum believed he was a Great Man himself.

The phrase "great men" crops up over and over again in his correspondence and public speeches. "We do not know our great men," he liked to tell audiences. Then he would name the great men of yesteryear, a list that varied according to venue and mood, but often included such disparate luminaries as Pericles, Christopher Columbus, Robert E. Lee, and, of course, the Rushmore foursome. Sometimes the list would include poets—Dante, for example. Sometimes it included women—Cleopatra, Joan of Arc. And when it included artists, he invariably mentioned Michelangelo and the Greek sculptor Phidias. As for the great men of his own time, Borglum lamented the shortage thereof. "We have not twelve great men in our one hundred ten millions," he told the *New York Times*. Pressed to give their names, he responded, "In a time of really great men is it likely that [the] question would be asked?"

Greatness has many interpreters, but in the nineteenth century, there really was a Great Man Theory, to which Borglum was an avid, if somewhat facile, subscriber. Most historians credit its genesis to Georg Hegel, the German philosopher whose discourse on another topic, dialectics, would eventually catch the attention of Karl Marx and Vladimir Lenin. "Such are all great historical men—whose own particular aims involve those larger issues which are the will of the World Spirit," Hegel wrote in his *Lectures on the Philosophy of History* (1833–1836). "They may be called Heroes, inasmuch as they have derived their purpose and their vocation, not from the calm, regular course of things ... but from ... that inner spirit, still hidden beneath the surface.... World-historical men—the Heroes of an epoch—must, therefore, be recognized as its clear-sighted ones; *their* deeds, *their* words are the best of that time." In short, not only is the Great Man an exemplar of his era; more significantly, he is one of the elite who, through action and insight, succeeds in changing his era.

The individual who deserves the most credit for popularizing the term "great men," however, is essayist and historian Thomas Carlyle, whose lectures *On Heroes, Hero-Worship, and the Heroic in History* were first published in 1841. It was Carlyle who wrote, "The History of the world is but the Biography of great men," adding that "what [the great man] says, all men ... were longing to say." The American transcendentalist Ralph Waldo Emerson was echoing Carlyle, a contemporary and correspondent, when he wrote that "there is properly no history; only biography." Like Carlyle, Emerson appreciated the role of the great man in history: "I count him a great man who inhabits a higher sphere of thought, into which other men rise with labor and difficulty; he has but to open his eyes to see things in a true light."

In 1913, when asked by the editor of the *New York Sun* to name his favorite authors, Borglum mentioned Shakespeare, Emerson, and Carlyle. Among Shakespeare's characters, he admired Hamlet, who, after all, was a fellow Dane. Of Emerson, he noted, "I have worn out several editions." And the stamp of Carlyle on his philosophy and behavior was no less evident, although not necessarily in perfect harmony with the Emersonian influence. Carlyle, the class-conscious European, essentially espoused that some men were born to greatness; Emerson, the homespun American, supposed that greatness was a quality that could be thrust upon the common citizen. In the manner in which Borglum lived his life, and like so many Progressives of his day, he demonstrated remarkable ambidexterity: As the mood and setting suited him, he could present himself as a bootstrapping commoner who made good; in the very next breath, he could posture as an extraordinary man, an artistic, intellectual, and social aristocrat who was simply fulfilling his birthright.

"The first thing I can remember was a Sioux Indian's face pressed closely against the window of our main room. I was sitting at my grandmother's knee, who had been telling me some Norse stories, and I have never been able to disentangle the Vikings of Denmark from the Sioux Indians." So wrote Borglum to an acquaintance in 1922. Two years later he expanded his recollection in the pages of *Famous Sculptors of America*:

> I was born in the Golden West, reared in the arms of the Church
> ... and suckled on Italian art: my slates were covered from end to
> end with portraits of Savonarola, Fra Angelico, and Wild Bill and
> Sitting Bull; I knew all equally well and admired them about alike.

... Into this were injected the legends of the Danes, poured into my ear by a Danish mother, while a father talked Socrates till the candles went out. I grew into manhood with this variety of ideals and of life from all the corners of the Old and New Worlds.

The most honest aspect of these statements is Borglum's acknowledgment that memories of his childhood had melded with myth. He didn't even get his age right. "I was born on the Oregon Trail in '71," he wrote to John Collier, Commissioner of Indian Affairs, in 1933. In fact, he was born four years earlier, on March 25, 1867, at Bear Lake, near Ovid, Idaho. His mother and father were Danish immigrants; that much was accurate. But there was more to it. Their church at the time was Mormon, and his father had not one wife but two.

In the years since Joseph Smith's first revelations and the establishment of the Church of Jesus Christ of Latter-day Saints, the Mormons had expanded their evangelical outreach to Europe, particularly England and Scandinavia. Jens Borglum, Gutzon's father, had joined in Copenhagen, one of thirty thousand Scandinavians to convert to Mormonism between 1850 and 1880. A man of voracious intellect and woodcarver's hands, he welcomed the call to the new Zion taking shape in the Great Basin of the American West. Gutzon Borglum would later applaud his father's "wild impulse to flee conventions." But in discarding one set of conventions, Jens Borglum agreed to a much stricter set of obligations, including an arranged marriage. On April 27, 1864, the day before his ship departed Liverpool for America, Jens Borglum married Ida Mikklesen in a Mormon ceremony that included numerous other couples. Jens was twenty-five, Ida twenty-two.

After a stormy crossing, they made their way by boat and train to Nebraska, the jumping-off point for the frontier. (The transcontinental railroad would not be completed for another five years.) Like thousands of determined Mormons before and after them, the Borglums could not afford their own wagon and were obliged to walk the final twelve hundred miles. Jens—his name now Anglicized as James—

worked for a while in Salt Lake City, possibly helping to build the Mormon Tabernacle, among other jobs. In March 1865, Ida bore a son, Miller. Later that year, Ida's younger sister, eighteen-year-old Christina, arrived from Denmark, and in keeping with the doctrine of the church, she became James Borglum's second wife. With his growing family, James moved north in 1866 to a new Mormon settlement at Bear Lake, in the Wasatch Mountains of southwestern Idaho Territory. There he built a sod and timber cabin, and within several months of each other, first Christina and then Ida gave birth to sons. Christina's son was named John Gutzon de la Mothe Borglum. (Ida's was named August.)

As an adult, Gutzon Borglum never mentioned his Mormon past, much less the polygamous circumstances of his birth. Instead he made up a story: His father, a promising medical student, had run away from Denmark with his sweetheart. They married in London, navigated the fierce Atlantic in a "fishing smack," and on the trek across America, James Borglum assumed command of the wagon train. At one point, they were attacked by Indians, but through James's valor, they kept the Indians at bay and reached their new home.

And then, conveniently, Gutzon has his mother die. "Not many years after [younger brother Solon, second son by Christina] was born she left us," Borglum related in *The One Man War*, his unfinished autobiography. "I was five. She turned to me as she lay ill. There were tears in her eyes and she was trembling as she took my hand. . . . And she told me to take care of little Solon. I never forgot it."

Nothing could have been further from the truth, save for the fact that his mother "left" him. Sioux faces pressed against the cabin windows? There were no Sioux within hundreds of miles of Bear Lake. The attack on the wagon train? Likely the stuff of dime novels. As for the death of Christina Borglum, she did not die; she was cast out—purged from the family. When Gutzon was five, James Borglum decided he'd had enough of Mormonism and moved his family to

Omaha, Nebraska. Ida, now mother of three sons, and Christina, mother of two sons, came along, but to avoid stigma and possibly even arrest, Christina presented herself as hired help.

Church founder Joseph Smith apparently had contemplated plural marriages for his flock as early as the 1830s, although God did not command him to direct his people to embrace polygamy until 1843. Even then, the church officially denied the existence of polygamy for another ten years—and for understandable reasons. As far as the Yankee establishment was concerned, two of the very worst evils in America were slavery and polygamy. The slavery issue eventually brought the nation to civil war, and polygamy led to widespread, often violent persecution of Mormons. It was one of the main reasons they were driven from Ohio, Illinois, and Missouri to the West, and it was one of the principal reasons Congress refused to admit Utah to the Union until 1896. To accept polygamy was difficult enough for European-born converts such as the Borglums. To live openly in a plural marriage outside of Mormon country was unthinkable.

The break came in 1871, when James Borglum enrolled in the Missouri Medical College in St. Louis. Christina, the second wife, was not invited to go along. How this decision was reached, and how the rupture was finessed, are not clear, but after 1871, Christina never saw her children by James Borglum again. She is said to have remarried, borne more children, and moved to California, where she later died of tuberculosis. The record is muddled further by Mary Borglum, Gutzon's second wife, who in her 1952 memoir, *Give the Man Room*, repeats the fiction of Christina's untimely death and states that only afterwards did the widowed James marry Ida. In a way, Mary Borglum was not dissembling, for Ida, whom she introduces as James's *second* wife, did in effect become Gutzon's (and Solon's) stepmother. Creating still more confusion, Gutzon occasionally mentioned that he had been raised by his *Aunt* Ida, which was much closer to the truth.

Regardless of which euphemism fit best, the experience must have been profoundly traumatic for young Gutzon. "It was a mutual separation of a second wife who did not really belong in that family," his brother August explained to Mary Borglum. "Whether Christine [*sic*] died or went out of our lives seems to have been about the same thing." Yet for Borglum to have his mother suddenly disappear, not by an act of God or even by the laws of man, but under such arbitrary circumstances, must have been especially difficult to fathom and to reconcile.

In later years, Borglum recalled with pride that as a child he had a predilection for running away from home—sure evidence of inchoate independence and adventurousness. On one occasion, he apparently wandered off and was taken in by a group of men who put him to bed on a table, bundled in their coats. In another reminiscence, he asks his father:

> "What is the moon?" And without waiting for him to answer I told him how beautiful she was and how I loved the moon better than the sun, better than anything in the world. He picked me up and said, "I'll give her to you if you promise never to take her away from the world." I wriggled out of his arms and ran toward her. I stumbled, fell, rose up, ran on, began to cry but kept on, faster and faster. . . . But the moon was retreating faster than I could move. And then the knowledge came to me—I could not have my moon. I stood weeping my heart out.

A child who runs away is often running toward something. Describing the moon as female suggests its maternal symbolism, although Borglum never quite put the two together. "I've often tried to analyze the motives that made me run away, but never found a real answer," he told *American Magazine*. "I guess it was just life surging up in me, the desire to get into the great drama all about me."

One aspect of his past that Borglum did explore thoroughly was his Norse heritage. In a 1938 memo submitted to a lecture agency for publicity purposes, Borglum described himself as "Western by birth," but "of North Danish, Viking and Crusader stock, which if heredity means anything, answers much."

To Borglum, heredity meant much indeed. He could recast his childhood to fit the all-American ideal, but in the end what mattered more was blood. In Borglum's lifetime, the population of the United States would triple, thanks largely to immigration. In the early years, many of the newcomers had originated in northern Europe—fair-skinned Germans, Scandinavians, British, and Irish. But beginning in 1892, the newer masses who funneled through Ellis Island were swarthy Eastern and Central Europeans, olive-skinned Mediterraneans, and Jews. To Borglum, it was crucial that he differentiate his own fore-bears from what he considered to be the lower castes. America was becoming "the scrap-heap of nomadic wanderers running away from their duties at home," he wrote to the *New York Times* in 1922 at the height of the country's anti-immigrant fervor, "and in this maelstrom of mediocrity there is little opportunity for greatness or recognition of it if it appears." Never mind that his own father, by joining the Mor-mons, had evaded military service in Denmark. Just as Borglum was able to repress the anxiety caused by his mother's banishment and his father's Mormonism, he was now able to distance himself from the great unwashed. In a separate letter on "the Jewish question," he stated bluntly, "All immigrants are undesirable." Borglums, after all, were not *immigrants*: they were seekers, crusaders, conquerors.

"I should like to begin this story with Eric the Red, the great warlike Dane," Borglum wrote in his aborted autobiography. Not only was this the stock from which he descended, but he regarded it as the stock that had spawned modern civilization as well. It was "our fellow Danes who invaded Greece and gave that people their heroic age, left in their blood-stream the blue in the eyes of Pericles, the gold of Helen's hair, the short nose of Socrates and the one blue eye of Alexander the Great," he posited. "I am as certain as I am of anything, the spirit and the ancient

Danish or Borglum blood were with and in the raiders of the Mediterranean." However far-fetched this sounds, the link was essential to
Borglum's self-identity. As he emerged as an artist and activist in his
twenties and thirties, he came to perceive that, in terms of art, philosophy, and government, nobody deserved higher marks than the Greeks.
He constantly compared himself to them and cast himself as a modern-
day Phidias, the Parthenon's sculptor of record. To be heir to the
Greeks, and also to be their progenitor, made for a sterling pedigree.

Not even the Mormons, in their obsession with genealogy, could
have traced Borglum back to Athens, however. His Danish roots were
much easier to uncover. The Borglums came from Jutland in northern
Denmark, where their name is still remembered. When Borglum was
in Europe in 1931, he visited the Borglum Kloster, a centuries-old retreat
for Danish clerics and nobility. Even more indelible is Borglum's middle
name, de la Mothe. Although he rarely used it (or his first name, John),
he knew everything about it. The Mothes, or Moths, were originally
Saxon, according to a letter written by James Moth, a Danish relative.
The name means "courage," "boldness," "mettle," "heart." During the
Christian crusades of the twelfth century, the story goes, one of Borglum's forebears saved the life of the king of Sweden—supposedly from
a charging goat—for which he was awarded the name "de la Mothe," a
coat of arms, and a passport to posterity. Thenceforth the family blood
mingled with only that of the wealthy, wise, and aristocratic. "Of such
stock is the Family," assured the Danish relation, "freeborn Patricians
... exhibiting the same original qualities in all the branches in continuous lines for so many Centuries. Almost all kinds of Offices in Church
and State have been honorably filled by members of the Family [—]
Authors, Dramatists, Professors, Physicians, Military Officers, States-
men, and many Ecclesiastics."

Gutzon Borglum's father was the sum of all that and more. After
breaking with Christina, James took the family to St. Louis, where at
age thirty, he took up the study of medicine. After he received his

diploma in 1874—medical degrees were *sui generis* in those days—he moved the family back to Omaha briefly and then to the town of Fremont on the Platte River, where he took over the practice of a doctor who had poisoned his wife and then himself. Although Fremont was only forty miles west of Omaha, to the Borglums it was raw frontier. When Dr. Borglum was not delivering babies, he was patching up gunshot wounds inflicted by outlaws and Indians.

Gutzon and his brothers, meanwhile, had the run of the Nebraska prairie. "[I]t is a fact, from six years old I began to buy ponies from the Indians.... I rode them all myself and did what they call 'broke them,'" he told an editor of *Britannica Junior*, the children's encyclopedia. Eventually the litany of Indian acquaintances expanded into a virtual Indian pantheon, tenderly embroidered. "I was born among you many winters ago," he elaborated in a radio address to Native Americans in 1934. "My father was a great medicine man and administered to your wounded and sick.... My father knew Chief Joseph [of the Nez Perce of Oregon and Idaho]; also the great Red Cloud.... He knew [the Lakota] Rain in the Face, Spotted Tail, and Crow Dog. He took me over to Crow Dog after he had killed [Spotted Tail].... [Crow Dog] pulled me off my pony and examined me. I was seven and riding a little grey mare I had bought for sixty cents from the Pawnees. Crow Dog said, as he put me back on my pony, 'Big boy.'"

Borglum's formal education was far more pedestrian, surprisingly so, given the extraordinary range of knowledge he displayed as a grown man. Most of his schooling came from his parents, who read to him incessantly. From Mormonism, James Borglum had progressed to Theosophy, the mystical rage of the day, and ultimately to Roman Catholicism. He had some familiarity with Greek and Latin and spoke both English and Danish. He raised his children to be bilingual as well. At some point during Borglum's teens, he and his brother August were sent to a Jesuit boarding school in St. Mary's, Kansas, although it is not clear for how long. Borglum had enjoyed drawing as a boy, and at St.

Mary's he was asked to paint images of saints and angels around one of the altars. For the first time, he recalled twenty-five years later, he learned that it was possible "to treat seriously what I had previously considered a delightful trick."

Ever quixotic, James Borglum decided in 1884 to transplant his family once more, this time to Los Angeles. Separate from James's own personal motives, the move was extremely fortuitous for seventeen-year-old Gutzon. Southern California in the 1880s was in the midst of one of its epic booms, thanks to a fare war between the Southern Pacific and Santa Fe Railroads, which made migration to the land of fruit groves and sunshine too affordable to resist. From 1880 to 1890, the population of Los Angeles more than doubled, from twenty thousand to fifty thousand.

Borglum's first job was as a lithographer's apprentice, a discipline that doubtless improved his drawing. Within a year, he was working as a "fresco painter," decorating the walls of houses with "scrolls and cherub heads." He also became absorbed in the city's fledgling art community. From the "wilderness of dabblers," commented the Los Angeles Times, Borglum emerged as a "genuine delight." His talent, the Times surmised, "will make the artist famous if he continues." One who agreed with this opinion was Elizabeth Jaynes Putnam, his teacher and, in short order, his lover as well.

Lisa Putnam was a divorcée eighteen years older than Borglum—approximately the same age as his banished mother. She had moved to California from New England, first studying art in San Francisco, then coming to Los Angeles in 1884. She was by then an accomplished landscape painter. Her oils of Spanish missions embodied the plein air romanticism of the day and California's self-image as the "American Mediterranean." Records do not mention just when student and teacher became more than that, but when Lisa decided to move back to San Francisco in 1888, Borglum accompanied her. In San Francisco, she introduced him to the circle of artists whose hub was the California

School of Design. There Borglum took instruction from two highly respected painters, Virgil Williams, the school's founder, and William Keith, Lisa's teacher. At this point, Borglum was beginning to do some sculpting, although his primary focus remained painting. "The walls of his atelier were hung with pictures of stage coaches and studies of horses," recalled one visitor.

Borglum and Lisa moved back to Los Angeles the following year and were married on September 10. He was twenty-two; she was forty, already too old to consider starting a family.

Borglum's attraction to Lisa was complex. She was intense and quite pretty, even in middle age. Beyond that, she opened his eyes to the notion that art could be more than just a way to make a living; it could be a way of life as well. And giving Oedipus his due, Lisa was the mother he had been yearning to catch for so many years.

By comparison, Borglum's appeal to her is much easier to assess. He was "sturdy, energetic, and interesting," recalled one acquaintance, and despite balding prematurely, strikingly handsome. He could not have been very sophisticated in those first years in California, although his European parents surely instilled in him a strict code of manners. And whatever he lacked in polish, he made up for with his western freshness and innate bravura. Also, his potential as an artist was quite obvious. Very quickly the youth and talent of Lisa's tutee reflected becomingly on her. He gave her a new lease on life, and she delighted in showing him off. The difference in their ages stirred a decidedly bohemian cachet.

What Lisa saw in Borglum, other women saw also. Throughout Borglum's life, he would strain the patience of his male friends and lose as many as he gained. On the other hand, his most loyal friends, his most steadfast patrons and defenders, were women. Unquestionably, Borglum exuded a sexual magnetism. He was not unseemly in the slightest, but he was *attentive* in a way that was both gentlemanly and intimate. (The female nudes that he sculpted in later years were always dignified but intrinsically sensuous.) When he turned his gray-blue eyes on women and listened to their words and feelings, they reciprocated with undying devotion. One of the first, after Lisa, was Jessie Benton Fremont, the doyenne of California society.

Jessie Fremont was the daughter of Thomas Hart Benton, the expansionist senator from Missouri (and great-grandfather of the artist of the same name). In 1841, she married John C. Fremont, the western explorer. In 1846, Fremont had led the wayward battalion that seized California from Mexico and had become the first military governor of the new American territory. His vaulting ambition earned him a court martial (later dismissed), and the gold rush made him a millionaire many times over. In 1856, he was the Republican Party's very first candidate for president, four years before Abraham Lincoln.

When Borglum met the Fremonts in 1888, General Fremont was seventy-five and brittle, his wife sixty-four and still a force to be reckoned with. She had admired Borglum's work and commissioned him to paint a portrait of her husband in full military dress. More important than the commission—no small feather in Borglum's cap—was the resounding endorsement Jessie Fremont bestowed on the young artist. Not only did she persuade him to travel to Europe to study; she also wrote letters of recommendation to high-placed friends in New York, urging them to buy paintings that would pay for his trip. "Mr. Borglum is . . . so affectionately connected with some of our latest happy days here," she enthused to one potential customer, "that for these I beseech your personal advice and friendly help. His works speak for themselves."

One recipient of Fremont's entreaty was New York's young police commissioner, Theodore Roosevelt. Roosevelt did not acquire one of Borglum's pieces—not yet—but the two hit it off just the same. Roosevelt had spent time ranching and hunting in the West, and the hale Knickerbocker recognized in Borglum a kindred champion of the strenuous life—good stock made stronger by the outdoors and vigorous labor. Their friendship, frequently volatile but always frank, lasted until Roosevelt's death. Of all the faces on Mount Rushmore, Roosevelt's is the one that, at first glance, seems most arbitrary. Yet for all the florid encomiums that Borglum would lavish on Washington, Lincoln, and Jefferson over the years, Roosevelt was the man with whom he identified most closely. In the end, it is impossible to imagine Borglum's life absent the influence of Theodore Roosevelt. In manner, words, and philosophy, they were virtually interchangeable.

On their way east, the Borglums had also stopped over in Omaha to visit Gutzon's father and Ida, who had given up on Los Angeles a year or so earlier. The local paper applauded Borglum's ambition, noting that "Europe, which has spoiled so many American artists, will not spoil him. He will not return to this country to paint French peasant girls and Swiss lakes. He stands pledged not to do it. He realizes that the natural beauties and the people of America are waiting for artistic expression. . . . He will gather the strength that only Europe can help him to, but he will not contract the weaknesses which are epidemic among the artists abroad."

Great changes and challenges lay ahead, but to Borglum's everlasting credit, he accomplished exactly what he had promised that day in Omaha.

With money earned from the sale of recent artwork, he and Lisa departed for Europe, where they lived eight of the next eleven years. During that period, Borglum became an even more accomplished painter, making his living by society portraits and commercial commissions. In England, he was inducted into the Royal Society of British Artists. Queen Victoria asked to see his work. He met George Bernard Shaw. Isadora Duncan, another transplanted Californian, gave one of her first dance performances at Borglum's studio in St. John's Wood. Yet despite this very legitimate acclaim and his new set of cultured friends, Borglum might easily have been remembered as just another passing talent if he had not gone to Paris. The difference, in a word, was Rodin.

Not that the French sculptor was the only influence on Borglum during his years in Europe, for he took classes at the École des Beaux-Arts and the Académie Julian and spent hundreds of hours roaming museums and galleries, absorbing thousands of years of art, from classical to Renaissance to Impressionist. But Auguste Rodin was the force that topped all others, so much so that Borglum, who had gone to Europe a painter, returned home a sculptor. "I hold Rodin to be one of the great individuals of history," Borglum testified (that word "great" again). He was "one of the rarest souls of whom we have record during the past three thousand years."

Borglum never became an intimate of Rodin, but they did meet on several occasions, and Borglum's sculpture at the time made enough of an impression on the French master that he later wrote several very warm letters of encouragement as Borglum was aspiring to become, in effect, the American Rodin. At the turn of the century and in the years that followed, to have garnered the approval of Rodin was a cherished credential indeed.

In 1884, Rodin had been approached by the city of Calais to sculpt a monument to the town's martyr, Eustache de Saint-Pierre, who during the Hundred Years' War had offered himself as a hostage in order to break the English siege of the city. Rodin instead proposed a group sculpture of the town fathers who, inspired by Eustache, had joined him in martyrdom and so saved Calais from starvation. In *The Burghers of Calais*, first exhibited in 1889, each of Rodin's figures expresses anguish, doubt, and, finally, commitment. While Rodin had ostensibly been commissioned to shape a tribute to medieval valor, *Burghers* delivers a very democratic message as well: The measure of humankind is the sum of every person's free will. Reviewers applauded Rodin's genius for capturing the essence of "the modern soul." Not since Michelangelo had a sculptor succeeded in expressing allegory with such specificity. Rodin, as has been noted so often, did not put life into bronze or stone; he released it.

Over the next decade, Rodin was commissioned to sculpt the three great men of modern French literature: Charles Baudelaire, Victor Hugo, and Honoré de Balzac. Each piece boldly defied the conventions of both classicism and the Beaux-Arts of the day, and all were eventually received as masterpieces. Then in 1900, the sixty-year-old Rodin staged one of the most extraordinary events in art history. The Exposition Universelle was intended as a celebration of the new century, and countries outdid one another showcasing their best artistry and invention. (For its first world's fair, eleven years earlier, France had erected the Eiffel Tower.) Rodin, forever at odds with the academy and the agencies that controlled public commissions, vowed not to be lost in the crowd. Rather than submit token works for consideration in one of the sanctioned French exhibitions, he rented his own pavilion and presented a tour de force of 165 sculptures. Astoundingly, the exhibition was the first-ever retrospective by a sculptor, a long-standing tradition among painters. Under one roof were nearly all of the masterpieces, including *The Thinker* and *The Kiss*—destined to be two of the most famous sculptures ever—and the stunning *Gates of Hell*.

Amidst the cumulative hubbub of the exposition, Rodin's exhibition was the talk of the town. "For the first time I have all of Rodin before my eyes ... the power, the life, the passion, reaching the extreme limits of expressive intensity," wrote one visitor. Oscar Wilde called Rodin "the greatest poet in France." A young Henri Matisse was so struck by Rodin's headless, armless figure, *The Walking Man*, that he asked Rodin if he would let him employ the model who had posed for it. Not everyone shared this enthusiasm—many regarded Rodin's stone and bronze as a "tumult of form"—but they came by the tens of thousands just the same. By the close of the exhibition in November, Rodin's name had become a household word. Without question, other sculptors before him—Michelangelo, Donatello, Bernini, Canova—and even Rodin's contemporary Jules Dalou had enjoyed comparable standing. But Rodin was a new sort of celebrity, uncompromising and independent—

"stormy and eccentric" in the words of one critic. To Borglum—who had visited the exhibition, presumably numerous times, and had marveled at the quantity and quality of sculpture, the phenomenon of the crowds, the reviews, and the sheer boldness of it all—Rodin was the embodiment of what an artist should be. To experience Rodin's work, Borglum wrote, is to be "in the presence, not of great effort, but of a great power."

Next to Rodin, the other crucial influence on Borglum's decision to focus exclusively on sculpture was his brother Solon. Solon Borglum was born a year after Gutzon, the only other child of James and Christina. Apparently not much of a student, he was not considered boarding-school material, as were Gutzon and brother August, and so he took the next most obvious path: He became a cowboy. The 1880s witnessed the height of the cattle boom in the West, when the big trail drives ascended from Texas to fatten and multiply on the plains so recently vacated by buffalo and Indians. While Gutzon was in California and Europe pursuing a career in art, Solon worked on the family ranch along the Loup River of Nebraska. In 1893, when Gutzon and Lisa returned from their first stint abroad, they passed through Omaha, and Gutzon encouraged his brother to come with them to California and try his hand at art.

There are many today who still insist that of the two Borglums, Solon is the better sculptor. If nothing else, he was the more natural, particularly when it came to depicting the movements of horses and the mannerisms of cowboys. Along with the "cowboy artists" Charles M. Russell and Edward Borein and the gifted poseur Frederic Remington, Solon captured the naïve and robust spirit of the Wild West and in doing so helped to found a genre of art that flourishes today—even as the more urbane art of his brother Gutzon inches toward archaism.

Unlike Gutzon, Solon's passion was always for sculpture, a medium

he seems to have chosen so as not to crowd his brother's already flour-
ishing career as a painter. Working alongside Gutzon in California,
Solon showed immediate promise. If there was sibling rivalry at this
point, neither brother displayed it overtly. The only friction, it seems,
was Lisa. She had brought Gutzon a long way, and she was not going to
share him with this semi-couth brother-in-law with his own set of
ambitions. Her cold shoulder and sharp tongue eventually drove Solon
from the studio. The brothers did not get together again until 1897,
when Lisa and Gutzon were back in England. Solon had spent the
interim in art school in Cincinnati and was stopping off in London on
his way to France for further study.

In Paris, Solon's rise was meteoric. The French, who cherished their
equestrian statues and honored the tradition of the *animalier*—and
more recently had been drawn to the Wild West shows imported from
America—were quick to embrace the work of the latest prairie savant.
Solon not only had a knack for the form, balance, and equipage of
horse and rider; he also conveyed the deep, inherently western devotion of the working cowboy to his closest companion. Solon's sculptures of cowboys getting the best and worst of violently bucking
broncos are on a par with any by Russell or Remington. Even better is
Night Hawking, of a cowboy and his horse serenely standing watch, or
The Blizzard, in which man and beast share each other's warmth during
a storm.

In 1898, Solon's *Lassoing Wild Horses* was accepted by the Paris
Salon. The following year, he took a French bride, and they honeymooned on the Sioux reservation—the first of the Borglums to set foot
in the Dakotas. Back in Paris, his *Stampede of Wild Horses* was selected
by the dean of American sculpture, Augustus Saint-Gaudens, to grace
the entrance of the United States pavilion at the Exposition Universelle,
where it was admired by thousands of passersby. He received two
medals at the exposition. By all measures, Solon had arrived in the
ranks of the "significant and important," according to Lorado Taft,

who would soon single out Solon—but not Gutzon—in his landmark *History of American Sculpture*.

Now it was Gutzon's turn to catch up. Several years later, when both he and Solon were in consideration for a monument of George Armstrong Custer, Gutzon wrote to an intermediary that in Paris his brother had done "work of the same character as mine." In fact, Borglum's sculpture, while improving, was at that time still a sidelight. One of his few pieces of real competence—and the first piece he ever exhibited publicly—was *Death of a Chief*. Its depiction of an Indian fallen beside his horse was very much in keeping with the "vanishing American" motif echoed by so many artists at the end of the century. Much to Borglum's surprise, it won a medal from France's Société Nationale des Beaux-Arts in 1891. But despite this early honor, over the next decade Borglum produced only two or three sculptures of note. One, *Apaches Pursued*, of two Indians astride galloping horses, may well have been inspired by Solon. Another, *Return of the Boer*, was a reflection of Borglum's dissatisfaction with the way his life was unfolding.

Return of the Boer is a small bronze of a bearded, hatless rider slumped in the saddle in a posture of utter dejection. His horse is gaunt, its head hung low. In 1899, Gutzon was mired in his own slough of despond. Despite ample work and stimulating friends, he was overcome by "gloom and mediocrity." Once a prodigy, he was now thirty-two and hardly a lion of the arts. "I feel an unformed and unpracticed student," he confided to his journal. He and Lisa were living beyond their means, behind on their bills. Perhaps it was purely coincidental, but when the Boer War broke out in October 1899, he sided not with the English gentry, whose favor he had courted so intently, but with the underdog Afrikaners.

"Society I do not want," he wrote in his journal while in England, laying bare the other side of his personality. "How I hate so many of its leaders ... cold, flippant, immoral in everything." His belief in Great Men was matched only by his disappointment in those who purported

to be great but fell short. In such instances, he transferred his sympathies to the common man and championed the populist cause. Over
the ensuing years, this tendency would lead to his involvement in such
organizations as the farmer-based Nonpartisan League and even the Ku
Klux Klan. Under a different title, *Return of the Boer* could easily have
been the return of the war-torn Confederate soldier, whose memory
Borglum would salute at Stone Mountain.

In this respect, *Return of the Boer* is a successful piece. Like the work
of Rodin, it is at once allegorical and personal. It won no particular
acclaim, but it was an indication of things to come. Then, too, the mood
of the Boer sculpture was not to be shrugged off easily. In addition to
Borglum's professional gloominess and his bitterness over British aggres-
sion in South Africa, he and Lisa were nearing the end of their tether.

Again the issue was age. Lisa was by now past fifty, and Borglum
himself was bracing against middle age. "I feel ripe," he wrote in his
journal, then admitted that "the parent in me fairly weeps at times."
Lisa was no longer his mother figure, nor was there any chance that
she would ever be the mother of his children.

The story of the Borglums' breakup is no more reliable than the
accounts of his parentage and early childhood. Just as we are without
Christina's take on the Mormon years, we shall never have Lisa's perspective on the endgame in Paris. What seems plain, however, is that
the peculiar bond of love, admiration, and ambition that had knit Borglum and Lisa together was frayed beyond repair. Even so, he insisted
the decision to leave was entirely whimsical:

> I was standing on the Rue de Rivoli ... a French cabby asked if I
> wanted a cab, and without further reflection, I told him I did. I had
> a small bag with me, six or seven hundred dollars in my pocket, [so
> I told him] you have just 30 minutes to catch the train to Cher-
> bourg. ... Every block I had to increase my tip. ... I caught the
> train. ... I ordered passage for New York, reservations on the boat,
> caught onto the train just as it was moving out. ... That is about all

the thinking, and all the preparations that were made for my return to America.

Borglum's second wife, Mary, repeats essentially the same story in her memoir: "Suddenly there came to him an irresistible urge to return to the United States—to go home. All his pent-up irritation over spiritual repressions and his grievance over decadent art conditions in Europe [Rodin excepted!] surged over him at once. . . . This ended an era in his life and marked, definitely, the beginning of another."

What the book neglects to mention is that the trip marked the end of Lisa and the beginning of Mary. For it was aboard the steamer SS *Ryndam* that the two met—an uncanny reprise of James and Ida Borglum's voyage thirty-seven years earlier. But if James and Christina Borglum had been thrown together by their church, Mary Williams Montgomery was the answer to a very different prayer.

Borglum would always be drawn to strong women—Jessie Fremont, Lisa Putnam, Isadora Duncan—whose talent and bearing complemented his own. His subliminal yearning for his lost mother was doubtless part of the attraction, but he also possessed a progressive attitude toward women. He admired their minds as well as their figures. In the 1930s, when prominent members of the women's movement, including Eleanor Roosevelt, lobbied him to add the face of Susan B. Anthony to Mount Rushmore, he listened patiently. To be sure, he did not believe that Anthony belonged with the four presidents—Great Men all—and he remained adamant that there was no room for any more figures, but the tone of his refusal, while dismissive of Anthony, was not patently insensitive of her gender.

Yet while it is true that women loved Borglum and he loved women, and despite the fact that he had been married to Lisa for twelve years, it seems quite likely that he had never been *in* love. That is, not until he met Mary Montgomery on board the *Ryndam*. She was slim and brunette, with eyes even bluer than his. She had just turned twenty-seven and was without chaperon, unless one counts the brother of an old college friend who happened to be on board.

The ship's steward seated Mary next to Borglum in the dining room, and by the time the *Ryndam* docked in New York, the two had spent dozens of uninterrupted hours together. Presumably she knew that Borglum had a wife in Paris, but she was far too charmed to concern herself with Victorian convention. If anything, she was the more worldly of the two. Her father had served as a Congregationalist missionary in Turkey, and the Montgomery family members were seasoned travelers of the Middle East and Europe. By the time Mary encountered Borglum, she could read or speak a half-dozen languages, including Turkish, German, Hebrew, Arabic, and Sanskrit. She had graduated from Wellesley College in 1896 and had just earned her doctorate from the University of Berlin—reportedly the second woman ever to earn a Ph.D. from that institution. Now she was on her way home to tackle what few American women had ever considered in 1901: a career—in her case, one that involved writing, editing, and translation.

Borglum likewise was about to take a radical step. Although he would remain married to Lisa for another eight years, they would never share the same address again. She had helped him to become a very good artist, and he had enjoyed an enviable amount of success. But the vigorous thirty-four-year-old who strode down the Manhattan wharf in November 1901 was a husband only nominally and a painter no more. From here on out he would be a sculptor, and an uninhibited one at that.

Not long after seeing the Rodin exhibition at the Exposition Universelle—and shortly after meeting Mary—Borglum had submitted for publication a gushing appreciation of his French mentor: "His creations throb with a life that enjoys or suffers with the passions of the earth.... And he is still in his prime. I believe that the best is yet to come; he has not yet rounded his circle; his road is still leading to new fields. Whither he will go his work does not help us even to guess."

Borglum could just as easily have been talking about himself.

chapter 5

ART FOR AMERICA

B ORGLUM RETURNED home to a bright new world. Sculptors of the previous century, as a rule, had been regarded as artisans, turning out lachrymose headstones, architectural filigree, and cold statuary in churches, parks, and squares. The sculptor as fine artist was the exception, even though the nation was blessed with a number of superb exceptions, most notably John Quincy Adams Ward, Augustus Saint-Gaudens, Daniel Chester French, and Frederick Macmonnies. Ward was the leading American sculptor throughout most of the latter half of the nineteenth century. In New York, his statues were everywhere—*George Washington* on the steps of the Subtreasury, *The Indian Hunter* in Central Park, and *Horace Greeley* in City Hall Park. His memorial to assassinated president James Garfield stands below the Capitol at the east end of the Mall in Washington.

But if Ward was the man to beat, Saint-Gaudens dethroned him handily. Like Borglum, Saint-Gaudens was born of European parents, raised in America, then immersed in the Beaux-Arts salons of Paris. His

1881 memorial to Civil War hero David Glasgow Farragut in New York's Madison Square changed American sculpture forever. The Civil War had prompted countless memorials across the country, but Saint-Gaudens's eight-foot-tall *Farragut* was significantly more than just another roost for pigeons. Admiral Farragut stands in military dress. (Saint-Gaudens had sculpted the figure naked, then added clothes, a method also used by Rodin.) His feet are set wide apart as if he were balancing on a rolling deck. (The ship is a graceful pedestal designed by architect Stanford White.) Farragut's coat is blown back, and his left hand grasps neither scepter nor sword but naval binoculars. His gaze is alert, expressing, as one reviewer noted, "the spontaneity of a specific moment." With *Farragut*, Saint-Gaudens had brought new life to a moribund genre, and in the coming years, he produced one triumph after another: an eleven-foot *Abraham Lincoln* in Chicago; a naked *Diana* atop Madison Square Garden; and the splendid *Shaw Memorial* in Boston, immortalizing Robert Shaw, the white colonel who died leading black troops against Charleston.

Daniel Chester French and Frederick Macmonnies expressed a similar naturalism in their work—French with his intrepid *Minute Man* in Concord, Massachusetts, and sage *John Harvard* in Harvard Yard; Macmonnies with his fey *Nathan Hale* in New York's City Hall Park and elaborate *Soldiers' and Sailors' Memorial Arch* in Brooklyn's Grand Army Plaza. Clearly influenced by both Saint-Gaudens and the Beaux-Arts, the sculpture was unmistakably heroic but very human, not unlike Rodin's *Burghers of Calais* in the balance struck between strength and vulnerability, allegory and intimacy.

Any lingering doubts that a new era in American sculpture was in full bloom evaporated in 1893 with the opening of the World's Columbian Exposition in Chicago. Saint-Gaudens was put in charge of sculpture for the fair, whereupon he commissioned French and Macmonnies to do the two most prominent outdoor pieces. Plainly inspired by the Statue of Liberty, which had been erected seven years earlier, French crafted his colossal *Republic*, a sixty-five-foot gowned goddess at the fair's entrance. Macmonnies's *Columbian Fountain* featured his elaborate *Barge of State* in which fair Columbia is rowed by Art, Science, Industry, and Agriculture. Everywhere one looked was more sculpture, some fresh and inspired, some ghastly and baroque. But regardless of the mixed quality of the work at the fair, one message came through loud and clear: If you were a sculptor, there were opportunities galore.

Archives are vague on whether Borglum was among the ten million who attended the Chicago World's Fair, but we do know that he was living in the United States in 1893 and that he submitted at least one painting and one of his very first sculptures: a small bronze, *Tribal Sentinels* (also called *Indian Scouts*), of two Indians peeking from behind a rock in a pose very reminiscent of a work by Frederic Remington. Without knowing for sure whether Borglum visited the fair, one can only guess at the additional impact Chicago had on his decision to concentrate on sculpting. Yet it seems reasonable to say that his awareness of the bull market for sculpture in America, combined with his new-found insight into what sculpture should and could be, made his career adjustment both inspired and shrewd.

In 1901, eight years after the World's Columbian Exposition, sculpture commissions were more available than ever. The barons of railroads, steel, publishing, and finance were the new Medici; the estates of the Vanderbilts, Fricks, Pulitzers, and Morgans were palaces, and the neoclassical creations of society architects Richard Morris Hunt and the firm of McKim, Mead, and White called for sculpture high and low—poets and nymphs in the gardens, *putti* on facades, and great men in the grand rooms. What is more, the new American plutocracy recognized a duty to impose order and dignity on the increasingly chaotic urban landscape. *Richesse oblige* took the form of the City Beautiful movement, which began around the time of the Chicago fair and did not lose momentum until America's entrance into the First World War.

The unspoken message of the movement, above all, was of a republic undivided, regardless of its increasingly dappled demography. And nothing communicated this message more graphically than public sculptures. They announced: Here are our heroes—heroes common to all Americans—and here are our common virtues of courage, industry, and creativity.

The tone of idealism set by the Statue of Liberty in New York Harbor was soon echoed by a skein of other sculptures, both freestanding and architectural, throughout New York. In 1892, Saint-Gaudens was commissioned to sculpt an equestrian statue of General William Tecumseh Sherman led by a winged Nike, goddess of peace. Daniel Chester French carved allegorical images of Justice, Power, and Study on the Appellate Courthouse and humanized *The Four Continents* for the U.S. Customs House. The list of new buildings for New York, each with its abundance of opulent, didactic sculpture, seemed without end: the Hall of Records, the Public Library, the Brooklyn Institute. Hardly a park or plaza was not slated for some sort of memorial.

And New York was only part of the sculptural boom. Boston needed sculptural ornamentation for its new public library. Buffalo, with the Pan-American Exposition of 1901, strove to pick up where Chicago (and Paris) had left off. That same year, a congressional commission had determined to fulfill architect Pierre Charles L'Enfant's century-old vision for the nation's capital. Alarmed that the Pennsylvania Railroad was about to commandeer a hefty portion of the Mall—imagine a rail yard in front of the Smithsonian—the commission intervened with a master plan for public buildings and parks that was faithful to L'Enfant and very much influenced by the Columbian Exposition. (The commission included Daniel Burnham, chief architect of the Chicago fair, along with Saint-Gaudens, architect Charles McKim, and Frederick Law Olmsted Jr., son of the country's most venerated landscape architect.) Among other things, the blueprint called for extending the axis formed by the Capitol and the Washington Monument to include a new memorial to Abraham Lincoln and a bridge across the Potomac to Arlington Cemetery. (The railroad problem was solved by appropriating the land for present-day Union Station.)

To Borglum, the flurry of public art and architecture must have seemed a sumptuous smorgasbord. He had arrived in the United States too late to participate in the Buffalo World's Fair, but he was just in time to enter the competition for the first big commission under the new Washington plan. Earlier that year, Congress had authorized $250,000 for a memorial to Ulysses S. Grant, at the time the largest public sculpture commission in U.S. history. The jury, like so many juries of the period, was headed by Augustus Saint-Gaudens and Daniel Chester French.

Borglum, with only a few small bronzes to his credit but nonetheless emboldened by the spirit of Rodin, believed he had as good a chance as anyone, even his more experienced and celebrated brother Solon, who was also entering the competition. In the end, twenty-three sculptors submitted models, which were put on display in the basement of the Corcoran Gallery. Sorting through the distinguished entrants, the Washington Star gave special attention to Borglum: "[His Grant] is firmly seated upon a spirited horse, held in check by a steady rein, as he turns to address one of the two mounted aid[e]s who are pressing close to him. The attitude is excellent, full of motion and character.... This is indeed one of the finest works of sculpture and one of the most dignified compositions of all those shown in the exhibition."

At the same time, the Star, while complimenting Solon Borglum generally for his past successes with "spirited and admirable bronzes of animals," chose to damn his Grant submission with faint praise, calling it "elaborate and complicated." More significantly, the paper reported that Solon's model had been "very seriously damaged in shipping."

Neither of the Borglum brothers won first prize, and to hear Gutzon tell it, the entire deliberation had been a travesty of aesthetics and ethics. The Grant commission had been awarded to Henry Merwin Shrady, a young artist from a well-to-do New York family who had recently won acclaim for animal sculptures at the Buffalo World's Fair and for a George Washington equestrian at the Brooklyn approach to the Williamsburg Bridge. Despite these achievements, and despite the fact that Shrady's father had been the attending physician at the death of Grant, he was regarded as an unworthy long shot. The award was protested by a number of Shrady's rivals, among them Charles Niehaus, the second-place finisher and a sculptor of much loftier repute. The jury deliberated a second time and again gave the prize to Shrady.

Nobody, not even Niehaus, felt as burned as Borglum. In a letter written many years later, he recalled the excruciating outrage of the Grant affair. "I entered but the one model.... I had just arrived from Europe and it was thrown out of the competition, although allowed to remain in the [exhibition] hall, by a ruling from Mr. St. Gaudens that it had not been made by anybody in America and could not have been made by anybody in America, but was evidently produced by some European employed for the purpose of the competition. That disposed of me."

This analysis seems patently fishy and characteristically self-serving. After all, the Borglum name was not exactly unfamiliar to Saint-Gaudens and his fellow jurors, even if they had not heard of *Gutzon* Borglum until now. They knew Solon Borglum to be 100 percent American. Furthermore, Saint-Gaudens and French had both studied in Europe themselves; they harbored no bias against European-trained artists.

Borglum's recap of the Grant commission grows more curious. In the same letter, he chose not to mention that Solon had submitted a model for the competition. Instead he asserted that his brother had been in the employ of Niehaus at the time and had secretly worked on two of the three models Niehaus had submitted. Stranger still, Borglum insisted that in the second round of submissions, Solon had switched horses, figuratively and literally, and gone to work for Shrady, who, according to Borglum, "could not model anything that I had ever seen worthy of placing in a public square." Borglum apologized for his brother, explaining that Solon was broke at the time and that Shrady had offered him five hundred dollars to redo his model. "Solon's model was enlarged and that is the model which is in Washington."

Today, the Grant memorial is one of the most prominent and magnificent sculptures in the capital, and, for that matter, the entire country. Located at the east end of the Mall, just below the Capitol (and not far from Ward's Garfield memorial), Shrady's seventeen-foot statue is a study in ferocity and resolve. Grant—there was no question whether he would be depicted as general or president—sits astride his bruising charger Cincinnatus, collar turned against the winds of war. He does not so much survey the field of battle from under the brim of his hat as he does command it. Flanking Grant on either side, and offsetting his mood of Old Testament obduracy, are two breathtakingly kinetic compositions: one of charging, plunging cavalry, the other of a pivoting, horse-drawn caisson ridden by three artillerymen. To stand before the Grant memorial is to be captured by history. The postures and expressions of the cavalry and artillerymen are at once haunting and inspirational. The anatomy and balance of the horses are entirely natural, their motion headlong and violent. In sum, the Grant memorial is both a visual and visceral appreciation of *who* fought the Civil War (on the Union side, of course), *how* they fought it, and *what* it took to restore unity to the republic. It does for the Civil War what the *Marine Corps Memorial*—of four soldiers planting the flag on Iwo Jima—does for World War II, and what, arguably, can never be done so conventionally for Vietnam. Shrady took twenty years to complete his masterpiece, and either he had inspired helpers—Solon Borglum not among them—or else he rose to the heroic task heroically.

Borglum's account of the Grant competition tells any number of truths about the one man who believed it. First, one has to wonder about his code of honesty and his capacity for self-delusion. His assertion that he had been mistaken for "some European"—backhandedly boasting that his work was too good for the competition—is shrill egotism poorly disguised as sour grapes. Even more transparent is his trashing of his brother: While ostensibly praising Solon, Borglum in fact had relegated him to the role of pickpocket's apprentice.

Last but not least, the Grant affair marked the onset of Borglum's chronic annoyance with the art world in general. Within six months of arriving in the United States—within six months of declaring his new ambition as a sculptor—Borglum was disgusted, bitter, cynical, self-righteous, and more than a bit defensive. After his experience with the Grant commission, he vowed never again to stoop to public competitions. The establishment, to which he so dearly wanted entrée, was not to be trusted. For the rest of his life he would expect special treatment, meanwhile waging a dogged campaign against what he perceived to be an elaborate conspiracy of fraud and mediocrity in the world around him. Art was only the initial target; soon he would level his disapproval at government, business, and nearly every other aspect of human endeavor. It went without saying that he himself, and in many instances he alone, was good enough for the job.

Perhaps it was coincidence, but in the months following the Grant episode, Borglum fell seriously ill. Dr. James Borglum, who came from Omaha to attend his son, diagnosed "brain fever"—typhoid. Others have suggested that he may have suffered a nervous breakdown. Whatever the name and regardless of the cause, Borglum slipped in and out of delirium for several weeks. Mary Montgomery, who had been living with a brother in Connecticut, moved to New York to help speed his recovery. When she was not working at her own fledgling career as a freelance editor, she was pitching in at Borglum's studio on 38th Street. With his permission, and doubtless acting as his shield, she wrote to Daniel Chester French, inquiring about admission to the National Sculpture Society. Borglum may have been too sick to make the overture himself, but apparently he had not been so chapped by the Grant experience that he had lost his appetite for acceptance. His bronze *Apaches Pursued* drew compliments at the society's show of 1902, and the following year he was welcomed as a member.

Still, Borglum had yet to receive a major commission. The Grant memorial had already slipped away. And on Memorial Day of 1903, he had to swallow his jealousy as Saint-Gaudens's gilded equestrian statue of Sherman was installed with great fanfare at the southeast corner of Central Park. Later that year, Borglum took the initiative of writing Cass Gilbert, the architect of so many of New York's finest buildings, soliciting sculpture work. Gilbert had none to offer.

His next big chance was yet another world's fair, the Louisiana Purchase Exposition in St. Louis, which had been scheduled for the centennial of the Lewis and Clark Expedition in 1903, only to be put back a year due to construction delays. Borglum submitted three paintings, a pastel, and seven sculptures. Two of his bronzes—one of the Roman emperor Nero, the other of John Ruskin, whom Borglum had met and sketched in England—show the strong influence of Rodin and demonstrate just how much he had improved since *The Boer*, which he also submitted to St. Louis. Two other pieces made an unwitting pair: a bronze of his model for the Grant memorial and a recent carving of a female musician in the company of an impassive Pan, listed on the application as *I Have Piped to You and You Have Not Danced*. The latter piece could easily be construed as a metaphor for the rude reception given the former by the Washington jury.

The most important piece in the St. Louis group, however, was a nine-foot-long plaster of stampeding horses, a naked rider clinging to the neck of one of the leaders. The piece would eventually be called *Mares of Diomedes*, but while its execution was Greek in the best sense, its genesis was not so classical.

My first sketch of 'The Mares of Diomedes' was a couple of gun[slingers] in stampede," Borglum informed a fellow artist ten years later. "The horses had charged into each other and were wrecking everything. The debris they created annoyed me, and the harness covered the horses too much, so I removed all of that. The lone rider who was in charge of one team I converted into a cowboy, but I found that he had too much clothes. I converted him into an Indian, and that did not seem satisfactory, so I finally pulled the feather and the G string off, and had a nude man riding a savage nude horse and leading a stampede. For the sake of the public, the great lay mind, I had to find a name for it, and in my rummagings I came upon the "Seventh Labor of Hercules." My rider is Hercules. It was his job to get the Mares of Diomedes away from the King, and my group fitted it well enough, and so was named.

Solon Borglum's biographer (his son-in-law) insists that Gutzon appropriated the composition for *Mares of Diomedes* from Solon's *Stampede of Wild Horses*, which had been exhibited at the Exposition Universelle in Paris. This was a plausible indictment, but on the other hand, in 1903 no single artist had a monopoly on wild-horse sculpture. Frederick Macmonnies had shown *The Horse Tamers* in Paris, and Frederic Remington's exuberant cowboy and cavalry images now saturated America. Indeed, what is remarkable about *Mares of Diomedes* is that Borglum chose to swap its western motif for one of Greek mythology, particularly because he had created it expressly for the St. Louis fair, whose prevailing theme was the West and western expansion. A more likely interpretation, given how prickly Borglum had become of late, is that he was trying to set himself apart from, or even above, the madding crowd—the "great lay mind." He had not been one of the commissioned artists of the fair. He well knew that Solon had been commissioned (by Saint-Gaudens and French once again) to install four major sculptures in the Monument Court, all with cowboy or Indian themes. Remington's equestrian *Cowboys on a Tear* welcomed visitors to the Midway, and the rest of the fairgrounds was a virtual Wild West show of sculpted pioneers and padres, generals and chiefs.

Regardless of the originality of *Mares of Diomedes*, it stands out as one of the very best pieces of Borglum's entire career. The stampeding horses are as natural and fluid as any by Macmonnies, Remington, Shrady, or brother Solon. Moreover, *Mares* evidenced just how much progress Borglum had made as a sculptor in the course of just a few months. The leaps and bounds of his horses were the leaps and bounds of his own talent. Strangely, *Mares* stirred no special acclaim at St. Louis. But two years later, a bronze version of *Mares* was purchased by New York banker James Stillman for $12,500 and donated to the Metropolitan Museum of Art. Whereas Solon's pieces at the fair had been made of straw and plaster and soon disintegrated, Borglum's *Mares* was one of the Metropolitan's first acquisitions under a new campaign—directed by the ubiquitous Daniel Chester French—to bolster the museum's collection of American sculpture. (Apparently Borglum's original western intent for *Mares* was not entirely erased, for eventually the Metropolitan decided to pasture the horses at the Buffalo Bill Historical Center in Cody, Wyoming.)

Whenever Borglum began to hit a good stride, he invariably found a way to throw a hitch in it. This would be the case during the Mount Rushmore years, and it was certainly so in the early New York years. Within five months of his acceptance as a member of the National Sculpture Society, he had charged several members, including the society's president and founder, the venerable John Quincy Adams Ward, with "insult and slander." The source of the disagreement is difficult to pinpoint, but with Borglum, conflicts typically had as much to do with style as with substance. Although a newcomer, he had apparently challenged the professional worthiness of some of the older members and had tried to rewrite the society's constitution, offending the old guard even further. Inevitably, push came to shove, and with Borglum there were no shades of gray—you were either for him or against him. "I am sorry to say [that] the measures I worked for were not as successful as they should have been," he told a prominent New York art critic, "and the evils that I spoke of were not corrected as far as they should have been." And so he quit in a huff. It was classic Borglum: demand control, ruffle feathers, allege conspiracy, exaggerate evil, throw down the gauntlet, burn the bridge—and lastly, foul the nest. The pattern would repeat pitifully at Stone Mountain and would come close to ruining Mount Rushmore more times than anyone cared to count.

Yet Borglum seemed to thrive on adversity. He admired Hercules, but he also had a bit of Antaeus in him. Divorced from the National Sculpture Society, but now settled into his studio on 38th Street, he bore down on an ambitious range of commissions. In 1904, he completed a series of gargoyles for Class of 1879 Hall at Princeton University. Gargoyles were a signature of Princeton architecture, and Borglum distinguished himself by carving a monkey with a camera and another of monkeys crawling on a tiger (Princeton's mascot). The Princeton job was noteworthy for two reasons. First, it was one of Borglum's earliest successes at carving stone, rather than modeling in clay. Second, the class of 1879 happened to be the graduating class of Princeton's current president, Woodrow Wilson. A decade later, during the First World War, Borglum would renew the acquaintance first made in 1904, quickly becoming, from Wilson's point of view, a troublesome gargoyle in his administration.

Shortly after finishing the Princeton work, Borglum stretched for an even bigger commission. Reading in the paper that Congress had decided at last to complete the frieze in the United States Capitol, work on which had been halted since 1889, he submitted a ten-page proposal on how he would execute both sculpture and painting. At the same time, he made a bid to complete the sculpture on the pediment above the House of Representatives portico, another commission that had been awarded years earlier but never completed. He did not get either assignment, but it was a measure of his self-confidence and growing reputation that he even made a stab at them.

Borglum did some fine work over the next few years, including some very lovely smaller sculptures of women, but the reputation he made for himself was based as much on controversy as on pure talent. A prime example was an incident involving the Cathedral of St. John the Divine in New York. In addition to the Princeton gargoyles, Borglum had won a commission to sculpt a series of angels for St. John's. When he gave his angels female faces—God's iconographic flock was traditionally male—the church objected. By now, the entire New York art community knew of Borglum's short fuse. "It was only necessary to point a finger at the Sculptor to draw a spark," reported the art journal *Brush and Pencil*. On cue, Borglum fanned the spark into a flame—lopping off the faces of his clay models and spitefully replacing them with male features, including pronounced Adam's apples and, according to *Brush and Pencil*, "Jewish-looking beards." The newspapers made hay of this harmless holy war, and Borglum's reputation was further enlarged. If he had accomplished nothing else at St. John the Divine, he had learned how much could be gained by taking his case to the press.

To Borglum, the pen was the staunch ally of the sculptor's chisel and knife, and quite often mightier. In January 1907, incensed by a news item about another juried sculpture competition in which the runner-up had been judged, this time by President Roosevelt, to be better than the sculpture awarded first prize, Borglum fired off a scalding letter to the editor of the *New York Sun*: "[T]he abominable method of competition that has become a practice in this country for obtaining the best mental efforts of artists and architects has not been more ludicrously demonstrated than in this competition. We are spending in America hundreds of thousands of dollars annually on 'monuments,' effigies of people few of us know anything about, but ... artists are called upon to give weeks and months of time and much money to competitions that, like this one, end in confusion and dissension. Competitions were made for bulls and bears.... Mental efforts are wholly unfitted for [this sort of] struggle."

Borglum may have frowned upon the game of open competitions—they were risky and too often rigged—but he hardly played fair in his own quest for commissions. What he had failed to mention in his letter to the *Sun* was that over the previous year, he had made several attempts to circumvent competitions for a variety of sculpture commissions, mostly of Civil War heroes, both Yankee and Confederate. And in the ensuing months, he would wage a shamelessly Machiavellian campaign to claim the lucrative commission for a memorial to General Philip Sheridan—along the way trampling his old nemesis from the National Sculpture Society, John Quincy Adams Ward.

In 1891, Ward had been commissioned by the Society of the Army of the Cumberland to make a bronze equestrian statue of Sheridan, the decorated Civil War veteran and ruthless frontier fighter. (It was Sheridan who is said to have commented that "the only good Indian is a dead Indian.") Later Congress took over the project and appropriated $37,500 for its completion. Ward did not finish his model until 1906, only to have it rejected by Sheridan's widow. Borglum saw his chance. Stung by the Grant competition, he seized the opportunity to win a public commission without having to run the public gauntlet. Through mutual friends, he arranged a dinner with Mrs. Sheridan, and with the charm that had previously won Jessie Fremont, he persuaded Mrs. Sheridan to visit his studio in New York. By July he had the contract; the fee was raised to $49,000. At long last, Borglum had finagled a major monument.

Borglum got busy immediately on his model for the Sheridan memorial, making sketches of Sheridan's horse, which was still alive, and using Sheridan's son Philip as a model for the general. Meanwhile, he had his eye on an even more famous general, whose widow was also notoriously hard to please. And this time his rival was his brother Solon.

Within weeks after the death of George Armstrong Custer at Little Bighorn, there had arisen a public cry for a national monument to the flamboyant warrior. Elizabeth Bacon Custer, who would devote the remaining fifty-seven years of her life to promoting (and defending) her husband's honor, favored something at West Point, from which Custer had graduated at the bottom of his class and where his ashes were finally interred. But when a statue (by the forgettable J. Wilson Mac-Donald) was unveiled in 1879, Mrs. Custer hated it and eventually succeeded in having it removed in 1884. Another twenty-three years passed before she finally allowed the state of Michigan, whose troops Custer had led in the Civil War, to erect another monument.

As with the Sheridan commission, it was a mutual friend who urged Mrs. Custer to pay a visit to Borglum's studio, where she was wooed by her debonair host and likewise by his model of Sheridan, who had been her husband's commanding officer. Borglum was confident that he had won the commission—that is, until he learned that Solon was also in the running. Initially, Mrs. Custer was unaware that there were two Borglum sculptors, believing that the Borglum whose Sheridan she had admired was the same Borglum whose work she had seen at the Paris Exposition in 1900.

Solon had added to his success since then and had recently completed two major commissions, a Rough Rider memorial in Arizona and a Civil War memorial in Atlanta. He was in such demand, in fact, that he had agreed to let a granite company do business for him—an arrangement that Gutzon chose to use against his brother. On December 4, 1907, Gutzon's friend C. H. Davis sent a "confidential" letter to Mrs. Custer, doubtless with Gutzon's consent, in which he advised, "Borglum's brother approaches [the Custer monument] entirely from a commercial side. He is hand-in-glove with the monument building concern." Gutzon, on the other hand, "is a doer of big things, and he is as careless of the financial side as the other one is eager for it. That is the whole case in a nut shell. I have known Gutzon Borglum to spend his own money to make a thing approach his ideal."

On this occasion, however, Borglum's back-channeling did not work in his favor. Once Mrs. Custer realized that she was dealing with two Borglums instead of one, she eschewed controversy in favor of a trip abroad, turning the decision over to the Michigan committee. When Gutzon learned that he had lost the inside track, he dropped out of the running and endorsed Solon. By then, the race was lost for either brother, and the committee awarded the commission to someone else entirely. Yet so deft was Gutzon in his approach and retreat that Solon felt only the pats and none of the cuts of his older brother.

Borglum might have been less diplomatic if his career weren't going so well in 1907. Due in large part to the Sheridan commission, more monument work had begun to come his way, most notably a statue of Nevada mining tycoon John Mackay in Reno and a statue of Mary Magdalene for a burial plot in Washington's Rock Creek Cemetery. His most important sculpture of the year was a piece he did ostensibly for himself.

Before the Civil War, the icon of American icons had been George Washington, but after the assassination of Abraham Lincoln in 1865, commissions to carve the martyred president became the choicest plums in the land. One of the first commissions, for the Capitol, was awarded to nineteen-year-old Vinnie Reams. The best by far was Saint-Gaudens's *Lincoln* of 1887 for Chicago's Lincoln Park. Since then, dozens more sculptors had thrown themselves at the task, although, in Borglum's opinion, none had done full justice to the subject.

Borglum became obsessed with Lincoln, surely seeing shades of his own youth in Lincoln's backwoods beginnings. "Lincoln was the first real product of our poor to gain the Presidency," Borglum jotted in his notebook. "He was born on the very frontier of life; his people led an almost nomadic existence." In addition, Borglum was moved by the story of Lincoln's long-suffering mother, Nancy Hanks, who, as biographies had recently revealed, may have been illegitimate—a stigma for which Borglum had great sympathy, given his own confused parentage.

In a 1910 essay entitled "The Beauty of Lincoln," Borglum elaborated on his fixation, beginning with a quote by one of his favorite authors, Thomas Carlyle. "'I'm only a poor man,'" Carlyle begins the excerpt, "'but I would give one third of what I possess for a veritable, contemporaneous representation of Jesus Christ. Had those carvers of marble chiseled a faithful statue of the Son of Man ... and shown us what manner of man he was like, what his height, what his build, and what the features of his sorrow-marked face were, I for one would have thanked the sculptor with all the gratitude of my heart for that portrait.'" In citing this passage from Carlyle, Borglum did not necessarily mean that he regarded Lincoln as the American Savior (although much has been made of the fact that Lincoln was slain on Good Friday). Rather, he meant that, for all the images of Lincoln spread across the land, none depicted him genuinely. "Lincoln, one of the greatest of observers," Borglum explained, "was himself the least truly observed. God had built him in the back-yard of the nation, and there, wrapped in homely guise, had preserved and matured his true humanity. He was heard, but seems rarely, if ever, to have been truly seen."

Perhaps not, but Lincoln was photographed scores of times, most famously by Mathew Brady. A mask of Lincoln's face was molded twice during his life, and his likeness was imprinted on all manner of memorabilia and more than one postage stamp (although not on a coin until the Lincoln penny in 1909 or on the five-dollar bill until 1914). By 1907, Lincoln had even been portrayed in a motion-picture adaptation of *Uncle Tom's Cabin*, produced by the Edison Film Company. Without question, Lincoln became the most recognizable face in American history. Shaven or bearded, with his thatched hair, hewn cheeks, jug ears, and dark, asymmetrical eyes, his was the most *American* face in American history.

Nevertheless, Borglum insisted, no photographer, portrait painter, or sculptor had quite captured the heart and soul of the man. "A great portrait ... is always full of compelling presence," he wrote, "more even than is at times seen in the original; for a great portrait depicts great moments, and carries the life record of the whole man. It is, therefore, not sufficient to draw a mask. If this were enough, the life-less, bloodless state-paper to which [George] Washington has been reduced would be a great portrait. . . . No mask will satisfy *us; we* want to see what we care for; *we* want to feel the private conscience that became public content."

Borglum's criteria for great portraiture echoed Rodin and compli-mented Saint-Gaudens, both of whom had succeeded exceptionally in conveying the "private conscience" of their subjects. Borglum too was looking for the inner man, and Lincoln was the ultimate challenge. He read everything he could by and about Lincoln, including presumably Ida Tarbell's probing two-volume *Life of Abraham Lincoln.* Even though he had decried artistic overdependence on life masks, he acquired a copy of the mask of Lincoln done by Leonard Volk in 1860 (as had Saint-Gaudens). With the greatest care and dedication, he set to work on a large block of Greek marble, which had been in his studio for sev-eral years awaiting just such a noble enterprise. Borglum had drawn and painted many portraits in his career, and in his early sculptures, he had paid close attention to facial features. But his bust of Lincoln would be his first fully realized sculptural portrait. There is no question that it is a masterpiece.

Borglum studied every aspect of Lincoln's bearing—his posture, the way he stood, sat, walked, swung his arms—and where others had seen ungainliness, Borglum saw something approaching grace. "I did not believe there was ever a grotesque Lincoln," he said. "No, Lincoln was not an awkward man." To get the face right, Borglum took careful measurements of the Volk mask and internalized them the way a blind person might memorize features by touch. And in the end, his instincts were as much geologic as artistic. "[Lincoln's] face was large in its sim-ple masses," he observed. "Nature seems to have intended him to be ten or twelve feet in height, and as he failed to grow to that, the free skin settled back to fit the natural man. . . . He was wide through the temples; his brow projected like a cliff. The hollow of the eye was large and deep, and the eye seemed to lie in a kind of ravine...." (And to think that Mount Rushmore was still two decades in the future.)

As Borglum continued to work on Lincoln's head, he came to focus—as all who stare at Lincoln long enough must do—on Lincoln's eyes, specifically their irregularity. Lincoln's eyebrows were of different contour, making the "laziness" of his left eye that much more noticeable. And because the two eyes were so different, Lincoln came across as a man of facets. For Borglum, "the storm center of Lincoln's face was about his right eye." By contrast,

> The left eye was open, noncommittal, dreamy.... I believe he knew this and ... it explains why he managed so often to get the photographer to the right side of him. This right side was as cautious as Cassius, and in profile remarkably like that of Keats.... Briefly, the right side of this wonderful face is the key to his life. Here you will find the record of his development.... All [that] the man grew to seemed engraved on this side. It guards his plan—watches the world, and shows no more of his light than his wisdom deems wise. The left side is immature ... long drawn and indecisive; and this brow is anxious, ever slightly elevated and concerned.

And so in reading Lincoln's eyes, Borglum also read the man. Surprisingly, the scale of the bust—forty inches in height (if a full figure, it would have been twenty-eight feet tall)—does not strike the viewer as colossally heroic. Instead, by making Lincoln larger, Borglum managed to magnify his humanity—his sorrow, his weariness, his wizened humility. An even more impressive aspect of Borglum's creation is the fact that Lincoln's face, the most chiseled face imaginable, does not in this case appear chiseled at all. The pouches of worry under his eyes are tender, the furrows on his brow are fragile, like slightly crinkled wrapping paper, and the mole on his cheek seems somehow to have grown quietly from the granite *after* Borglum finished the bust. Two other things: By separating Lincoln from his body—those distracting elbows and knees and disheveled suits—Borglum, as promised, succeeded in isolating the man within. And by carving Lincoln in white marble, he rendered him that much more fathomable. Photos of Lincoln stress the darkness of his hair, eyes, and clothes. The opposite is true of Borglum's Lincoln. Never mind its opacity; the exchange of black for white makes it as revealing as an X-ray.

In 1927, as Borglum was beginning work on Mount Rushmore, he was invited to immortalize his sense of humor in *The Favorite Jokes of Famous People*. Instead of a joke per se, he chose to tell the following anecdote, which, although of questionable taste, nonetheless reveals his profound pride in the Lincoln bust:

> The Negro woman cleaning my studio had noticed [the block of marble intended for Lincoln] and dusted it a great many times. Suddenly I began to work upon it, and [in] the course of a month's time the face of Abraham Lincoln appeared. One morning the Negro woman jumped back in great amazement as she was dusting the marble, rushed over to the secretary [Mary Montgomery?] ...in a state of anxiety and fright and whispered to her, "Ain' dat Abraham Lincoln?" "Yes," the secretary said. "Well, how'd Mister Borglum know he's in deah?'"

Borglum's rendering of the Great Emancipator had stirred other fans besides his cleaning lady. Eugene Meyer was a thirty-two-year-old New York investment banker who in recent years had developed a passion for Lincolniana. Another collector, knowing of Borglum's own infatuation with Lincoln, arranged a meeting. Meyer was immediately spellbound by Borglum's bust and astonished to learn that, as yet, it had no home beyond Borglum's studio. Meyer and Borglum struck a deal: Meyer would pay Borglum $8,500 for the piece, provided that it would then be given as a gift to the U.S. government.

Here was yet another instance of Borglum slipping in the side door. For two years, he had been hearing rumors of a possible congressional commission to explore ideas for a Lincoln memorial. The centennial of Lincoln's birth was coming up in 1909, and even though the commission would not be officially appointed until 1911, Borglum understood that adroit anticipation surely beat waiting in line. And now came Eugene Meyer, an ambitious young banker who also had an eye on Washington; he would eventually serve in the Wilson and Hoover administrations, and in 1933, he purchased the *Washington Post*. With Meyer backing him financially, Borglum played his final card.

Borglum had known Theodore Roosevelt since Roosevelt's days as police commissioner in New York. He had already carved a set of eagles for Roosevelt's house at Oyster Bay, Long Island. So when Borglum asked President Roosevelt if he would display the Lincoln bust in the White House on the occasion of Lincoln's ninety-ninth birthday, February 12, Roosevelt was only too happy to oblige. "That head grows upon me more and more," Roosevelt wrote to Borglum after the sculpture was delivered at the end of January. "I think it one of the finest things I have seen." Lincoln's only surviving son, Robert, now president of the Pullman Company in Chicago (the country's largest employer of African Americans), concurred, calling it "the most extraordinarily good portrait" of his father to date. With such resounding and impressive endorsements—not to mention Meyer's underwriting—Congress quickly passed a joint resolution placing the Borglum Lincoln in the Capitol Rotunda in perpetuity.

Perhaps it would be too harsh to say that Borglum had beaten the system once again, for one could also argue that the Lincoln sculpture could have earned its honored place on merit alone. Nevertheless, Borglum had finally found a way to insinuate his work into the Capitol without having to compete directly against his contemporaries. And certainly he now had the advantage—or at least he felt that he deserved preferential treatment—when it came to future Lincoln commissions. From here on out, he contended adamantly, Lincoln belonged to him.

The installation of the Sheridan monument later in 1908 did not come off as smoothly as that of the Lincoln. On January 30, just before the Lincoln bust arrived at the White House, the *Washington Times* printed a letter from a J. M. Dunbar slamming Borglum's "freakish-looking statue of Sheridan." Dunbar, who had seen only the model (the full-size bronze was not yet installed), objected most of all to the untraditional "jumping-jack" pose of Sheridan's horse.

The observation was not entirely groundless, but Borglum's rendering was anything but irreverent. In place of the typical, overstuffed general on a horse—any number of ossified Revolutionary and Civil War immortals, not to mention Shrady's glowering Grant, already dominated Washington's squares—Borglum had chosen to depict Sheridan as the vigorous leader who had turned his routed troops at Cedar Creek, Virginia, with the battle cry, "You'll sleep in your tents tonight or you'll sleep in Hell!" Borglum sculpted a bareheaded Sheridan violently swiveling his horse. At the jerk of the rein in Sheridan's left hand, the stallion coils on its hindquarters and fights the bit. Sheridan twists in the saddle; his right arm swings backward, hat bunched in his hand, beckoning those behind him to follow. The effect is elastic, explosive, and, as Dunbar aptly observed, Borglum had borrowed more from cowboy art than from the formal equestrians that had come before. "Some have said my [sculpture] is 'most unusual' and 'without precedent,'" Borglum rebutted his critics in a letter to the rival *Washington Post*. "Where can I find a precedent on which to model Sheridan? Surely none exists in Washington nor in New York."

Indeed, if there was a precedent, it was his own. We recall that six years earlier the *Star* had described Borglum's model of Grant as "firmly seated upon a spirited horse held in check by a steady rein, as he turns to address one of the two mounted aid[e]s." By hook or by crook, Borglum had finally gotten his way in Washington. The result was well worth the wait, and refreshingly good art besides.

The Sheridan memorial was dedicated on November 25, 1908. Set upon a stone pedestal, the fifteen-foot-tall bronze monument stands in the center of comparatively intimate Sheridan Circle. Without a doubt, Congress's acceptance of the Lincoln bust had been a great achievement for Borglum, but not until the Sheridan ceremony was he received as a full-fledged celebrity. Before the festivities, he lunched with President Roosevelt at the White House. At the unveiling later that afternoon, he was seated among generals, cabinet members, Supreme Court justices, senators, ambassadors, and the president and first lady—all of whom, it seemed, were there to honor him as much as the memory of Sheridan. "Before I begin talking to you about Sheridan," Roosevelt said to the gathered dignitaries, "I want to show you the man who made the statue; for next to the hero ... I place the man who created that bronze."

But too quickly fortune's pendulum swung the other way, and as usual it got an extra shove from Borglum. Success had gone to his head, and once again his mouth got him in trouble. In the October 1908 issue of *The Craftsman*, a journal of the Arts and Crafts movement published by furniture designer Gustav Stickley, Borglum ripped the art establishment from top to bottom. The essence of his jeremiad was that American art was "cribbed" from the Old World. The result was a "musty, pseudo-antique aestheticism that makes the atmosphere in this green land of ours all but intolerable." Two of the most egregious examples were the Washington Monument—a knockoff of an Egyptian obelisk—and Horatio Greenough's august statue of George Washington wearing a toga, which had stood for fifty years in front of the Capitol. Nor could Borglum abide that libraries, public buildings, and "counting houses" were now fashioned after "the old temples." "[We] hawk our wares from the windows of buildings redrawn after the old palaces," he growled.

He had a point: Neoclassicism had gone mad in America, and Borglum's essay might have been received more sympathetically if he had not also gone out of his way to deprecate America's most beloved sculptor, Saint-Gaudens, who had died the year before. "He gave us Farragut and one or two other great statues," Borglum allowed, but then his "sense of refinement led to conventions, and his lack of imagination to a repetition of these conventions." Having knocked Saint-Gaudens from his pedestal, Borglum then put the boots to him and his offspring:

"Saint-Gaudens, master that he was, was a master workman—he was not a creator, and it is but natural his following should, in their effort to catch his spirit, acquire his style. His reserve becomes in their hands more reserved, his architectural and impersonal manner more mannered, and we have a pseudo-classic school which for dull mediocrity is without a rival in the whole field of art." Thanks to Saint-Gaudens's example, Borglum concluded, most of the recent sculpture in America, through its "commonplaceness," would look "quite at home as a soup advertisement." The title of Borglum's article was "Individuality, Sincerity and Reverence in Art"—his point being that the country lacked all three.

Needless to say, the art establishment seethed. "Sincerity, reverence and individuality in American art!—Borglum doesn't know the meaning of any of those three words," spat painter Everett Shinn. "Mr. Borglum himself has never done any really original work—and thank God that he hasn't," seconded Hugo Ballin, another painter. Although not everyone disagreed with Borglum's statements, and despite his protest that the attack on Saint-Gaudens had been taken out of context, he had now established himself as one of the art world's loosest cannons, a role he actually seemed to relish.

What is also apparent from the *Craftsman* article is that Borglum had now codified a philosophy of art, a philosophy that wavered little, and in fact grew more strident, over the next thirty years. Its roots are worth tracing. We have already touched on the Great Man Theory and Rodin's imprint upon Borglum. Now to the list of Borglum's influences we must add two more names: John Ruskin and the less famous but no less relevant William Ordway Partridge.

Ruskin, the son of a wealthy English sherry merchant, was the most influential critic of art and architecture of the nineteenth century. Borglum called him "[t]he most marvelous, magnificent . . . genius the world has ever known." Ruskin was a champion of naturalism in all its forms, from the misty landscape paintings of J. M. W. Turner to the

Gothic cathedrals of Europe. What set him apart from his peers, besides the elegance and sheer prolificness of his writing, was his underlying message that aesthetics are much more than an expression of whimsy; they are a measure of morality: Taste in art and architecture says who we are, influences who we will become. Especially worrisome to Ruskin was the trend toward increased mechanization and industrialization. "Division of labour" was replacing "ennobling labour." The machined surface was replacing the nuance of the handmade. "Choose whether you will pay for the lovely or the perfect finish," Ruskin lectured in *The Stones of Venice*, "and choose at the same moment whether you will make the worker a man or a grindstone. . . . [I]f we are to have great men [that term once more!] working at all . . . the work will be imperfect, however beautiful."

From the teachings of Ruskin and then from his disciple William Morris sprang the Arts and Crafts movement, a cottage rebellion against the machine age. Borglum undoubtedly was well steeped in its tenets and expressions by the time he met and sketched Ruskin in England, probably only months before the esteemed author's death. And in both his art and rhetoric, Borglum continued to reflect the Arts and Crafts sensibility after his return to America. Like Ruskin, he lamented the depersonalizing effect of modern manufacturing and mourned the demise of the "artisan" in the twentieth century. "The end and aim of the United States is the production of the 'machine,'" he wrote in his 1908 *Craftsman* piece. "The end and aim of the 'machine' is that nothing shall live not 'machine made.'" He fulminated further in a speech entitled "Municipal Art": "We live on canned food. We dream on canned music. . . . We sit for hours and watch canned drama. . . . There is nothing made for any of us; we make nothing for anybody: our productions are soulless."

Here, however, Borglum goes Ruskin one step further, along the way exposing the deeply ingrained populist/elitist polarity in his own personality. For Borglum, it was one thing to champion the cause of the artisan, quite another to elevate the artisan to the rank of artist. In 1908, Borglum had taught classes at the Art Students League in New York, an experience that soured him on art education in general. "I am opposed to art schools . . . they should be closed," he declared in *The Craftsman*. In Borglum's view, to be an artisan or craftsman was a job, a skill learned and improved. Artists, on the other hand, were a cut above—born, not made, members of an exclusive fraternity. "This idea of going into a school to become a genius, to become a great painter or a great sculptor is as foolish as it has proven utterly unsuccessful," he contended. "There are today hundreds of . . . graduates from our art schools [who are] not capable, useful craftsmen, but 'artists.' . . . Anyone who has had experience with these young people knows how useless, practically worthless, they are." Eventually, he predicted, the vast majority of art-school graduates would forgo their "hopeless puttering [and] drop back to a layman existence, without a craft, without an art of value enough to wring from the world a living, with nothing to recommend them but a certain amount of taste, and that taste impractical."

Most striking about Borglum's posturing against art schools was not that he was right—in fact, he probably was—but that he had chosen to take a tone of such righteous superiority. More than didactic, he was dogmatic. More than angry, he was growing downright mean-spirited.

If Ruskin had steered Borglum to the moral high ground with respect to the overall role of art in society, William Ordway Partridge helped to fine-tune his vision of what distinctly American art should be. Partridge, a New Englander six years Borglum's senior, was a prolific, if second-tier, sculptor; his subjects included Shakespeare, Pocahontas, Alexander Hamilton, and his own Grant equestrian in Brooklyn. Borglum likely first made Partridge's acquaintance during his brief membership in the National Sculpture Society. There is no record of how

Borglum felt about his colleague's work—although privately he must have thought it mainstream and lackluster. What impressed Borglum about Partridge was his writing.

In 1894, Partridge had published a series of essays under the title *Art for America*, and subsequent articles on a similar theme appeared in journals throughout the next decade. Above all, Partridge was a nativist. "Of one thing I am sure," he sermonized, "and that is that the men who are to mould the destiny of this nation in art or politics must be nurtured and developed upon its soil.... I have no sympathy whatever with the Americans who give up their native land and become pseudo-French or pseudo-Italian.... In the name of the lives that make this ground holy, let us be American or give up meddling in art, and take to something that is worthy of our forefathers."

Partridge believed that America was a country of destiny, but like the great civilizations of history, America would not arrive at true greatness until it had produced truly great—and by great, he meant homegrown—art. "Art is not to be borrowed or stolen or invented," he explained. "It comes only by evolution." Then, he added, "Our people are ready for their great sculpture.... [T]he conditions of life [today] are in the main those necessary to the production of a great art."

Borglum loved the idea of a nation waiting for its artistic prince to come, just as he loved Partridge's slant on world history. The first great civilization, according to Partridge, had been ancient Greece, where men were prosperous, free, brave, and strong, and the "producing of fine physical form was a chief art," whether at the Olympic games, in poetry, or on the pediments of the Parthenon. Phidias, the sculptor in charge of the Parthenon pediments—nowadays better known as the Elgin Marbles—was a friend and virtual peer of Pericles, the king. Indeed, Partridge explains, "To be a great artist in Greece was to be the equal of the greatest in the land." He lavishes no such praise on the Phoenicians—"When a nation has no ideas worthy to be perpetuated,

no sculptor arises to put them in enduring form"—or the Romans—
"whose chief art was warfare" and who "never had a native artist
because the calling was thought to be undignified and effeminate."

Partridge then races forward to the next cultural high water mark,
the Italian Renaissance, when "[l]ife became once more normal, intelligent, and free; and art, corresponding to these conditions, arose and
was developed to a marvelous degree of perfection." Michelangelo is
the standout of this era, in which the "greatest sculptor ... was unquestionably one of the greatest men of his time."

And finally, Partridge comes to America. "We, like the Greeks, are
free men. The conditions of our life, the new life that is beginning everywhere, are much the same as those which existed in Athens in her palmy
days of art.... We are the heirs, more than any other people ... of the
past history of the world.... We may never reach the height attained by
Greece in the days of Phidias ... but even that is not impossible."

If imitation is the sincerest form of flattery, Borglum paid Partridge
the ultimate compliment. In *Art for America*, Partridge identifies "dignity, reverence, and self-control" as the essential criteria for good art.
Borglum, for his part, stresses "individuality, sincerity, and reverence"—
not exactly the same, but surely inspired by Partridge's trinity. The
overlap with Partridge is even more blatant when Borglum takes his
own tour of world history. Here, for example, are snippets from an article that Borglum wrote in the early 1920s, "America in Bronze." He
begins with Greece and faithfully follows Partridge's itinerary: "Little
Greece alone in the Periclean age sought what was good and just....
Rome, red Rome, whose imperial heel ground the heart blood out of
the world she enslaved, contributed and left little more than a glorious
and drunken gesture.... 'Twas not until the Renaissance that the great
dawn broke.... Out of it all ... America, alone and in the forefront,
rides the crest of the great modern awakening."

Throughout Borglum's writing and speaking career—which began
in earnest with the *Craftsman* article—he would repeat, time and again,
the chronology originally laid out by Partridge, although as best we

can tell, he apparently never credited his source. Sometimes Borglum would add Carthage to his presentation as an example of a civilization with no cultural value; sometimes he would make a plug for his Norse forebears as the blue-eyed antecedents of Greece; and unlike Partridge, he gave Rodin his due.

The individual from Partridge's parade whom Borglum latched onto most ardently was Phidias, who had served, in effect, as Pericles's artistic director, a position of broad authority that Borglum especially admired. (Borglum once suggested the appointment of a cabinet-level Secretary of Fine Arts, urging President Warren G. Harding to become the "Yankee Pericles.") In addition to the extraordinary accomplishment of the Parthenon, Phidias is remembered for three monuments. Two were of goddess Athena, thirty and thirty-eight feet tall, respectively. The third, a statue of Zeus at Olympus, was more than forty feet tall and considered one of the Seven Wonders of the Ancient World. "When you stand before this statue," wrote the Roman historian Pliny, "you forget every misfortune of our earthly life, even though you have been broken by adversities and grief and sleep shuns your eyes—so great is the splendor and beauty of the artist's creation."

Given the colossal scale of these sculptures, their placement atop mountains, and the strong response they elicited from everyone who viewed them—could there be a more vivid precedent for Stone Mountain and Mount Rushmore?

Yet the parallels between Phidias and Borglum get snugger still. Through his artistic deeds, Phidias joined the privileged ranks of politicians, poets, philosophers, and military leaders. But with fame also came jealousy. He was accused of embezzling gold from the Athena at the Parthenon (he got off, thanks to assiduous record keeping). Then he was charged with the much more grievous crime of impiety. His detractors claimed that he had included an image of himself (also one of Pericles) on the shield in Athena's hand—a blasphemous vanity that is said to have led to Phidias's imprisonment and eventual death.

During Borglum's career, he likewise would be accused of mismanaging money, cozying up to big shots, and various other sins of arrogance and grandstanding. When persecuted, he liked to invoke the name of Phidias, who, he was quick to point out, had been exonerated by history. "Phidias," he lectured, "had the insight, the training ... and the opportunity as superintendent of public works of Athens to build for that great people the story of their religion into their public gathering places." As for America, "We have our own life, our own civilization, our own emotions, our own religion; and we will write these into our monuments, for that is what we want the future to know.... There never has been a greater story than has been lived in this wonderful country." America, in short, could be "the Greece of to-day."

When invited on another occasion to define the term *artist*, Borglum again did not mince words: "Artist means to me, and it will mean one day to mankind, the master of men, the master of civilization." The job was big, he admitted, and only a truly Great Man could get it done.

CHAPTER

6

INSURGENT AMONG INSURGENTS

I NEVITABLY THE POLITICS of art and the art of politics merged. The big sculpture commissions were of politicians and public figures. To win commissions required political skill. And the subject matter and style of public sculpture expressed our national character in much the same way our politics did. No American artist understood this equation more instinctively or applied it more ambitiously than Gutzon Borglum, who in 1909 was forty-two years old and just entering the prime of his career. "We have been born—many of us—under heroic conditions," he told the *New York Times.* "This land of promise ... has given the adventurous offspring of the great peoples of the past a new world to play within."

Without question, Borglum was now a player. The only step remaining was to immerse himself directly in politics, art this time serving not as an end but as a springboard.

Borglum was in the habit of dashing off letters to newspaper editors, usually protesting the latest misstep by an artist, author, or civic leader. But with increasing frequency, the papers now came to him, a gadfly good for a column or two of incendiary repartee. "[D]o you glory in the title of arch-enemy of the academicians?" asked a reporter. "Not at all," Borglum demurred. "But I do love a good, honest, open argument." One paper described him as "a Sphinx in a sandstorm" who has "not only caused the storm, but he has also guided its direction. And when it's all over there is apt to be a considerable amount of dead-wood strewn about the landscape."

Borglum's propensity for vituperation did not keep him from making friends, however. He was an active Mason, and he had been admitted to two of New York's most prestigious clubs, the Players and the Century, as well as the Metropolitan Club in Washington. He was a popular and always scintillating dinner guest in New York society, rode horseback regularly in Central Park, and took a keen interest in boxing, a sport just beginning to attract a broader range of practitioner and spectator.

And finally he was able to marry Mary Montgomery. After leaving Europe in 1901, Borglum had little to do with his wife, Lisa. She had remained in England a short while, then returned to California, where she lived alone. Still, it wasn't until 1908 that Borglum finally succeeded in negotiating a divorce. In the meantime, he and Mary had been inseparable. Between stints as a teacher, literary agent, translator, and editor—including significant work on the formidable *Jewish Encyclopedia*—she helped manage Borglum's affairs. At last, in June 1909, they were married by her minister brother in Connecticut. They honeymooned at a fishing camp in Canada and then in Colorado.

These were heady times professionally as well. In May, a month before his wedding, Borglum was awarded an honorary master's degree from Princeton by Woodrow Wilson. And then came an even bigger coup: a $25,000 commission to sculpt another Lincoln, this time for the city of Newark, New Jersey.

In recent months, Borglum had been vying for two other Lincoln commissions, one in Lincoln, Nebraska, another in Cincinnati. He dropped out of the Nebraska competition, ostensibly because his brother Solon was also in the running, and he eventually withdrew from the Cincinnati job after being asked to compete head-to-head with other artists. He had hoped—assumed—that his Lincoln in the Rotunda would obviate any such formality. Finally, the Lincoln bust did pay off in Newark, and this time Borglum was the only candidate seriously considered. Amos Van Horn, a wealthy Newark manufacturer and Civil War veteran, had died in 1908, leaving money for three memorials: one to Lincoln, one to George Washington, and a third to a soldiers' and sailors' war memorial. The executor of Van Horn's estate, Ralph Lum, had admired the Lincoln bust in Washington and greased the wheels for Borglum. (Twelve years later, Lum would also give Borglum the war memorial.) It was a windfall indeed. When the *New York World* published a short item written by Borglum in January 1910, it gave his byline as "Gutzon Borglum (The Famous New York Sculptor)."

New York had been Borglum's home and workplace since 1901. But now with a wife, a great deal of work, and too many distractions, he decided to seek the peace and expanse of the Connecticut countryside. In March, Borglum borrowed $40,000 from his patron and friend Eugene Meyer, and bought 400 acres along the Rippowan River near Stamford. He set to work refurbishing the rundown cottage and stables, damming the river, rerouting the road, planting gardens, and building an immense studio out of granite quarried on the property. A profile of him in the journal *The Guide to Nature*, published the following year, depicts Paradise Regained: "One thing Mr. Borglum has not done; he has not cut and slashed and cleared away the beauties of the roadsides; he has not felled the trees and 'reclaimed' the land, but he has tried in every possible way to develop the natural beauties of the four hundred acres that he has collectively named 'Borgland.'" The article, entitled "Beauty in the Life of the Portrayer of Beauty," follows Borglum as he fishes for trout with barbless flies, stalks native orchids, and exercises his Arabian stallion.

But if life at Borgland was an Arts and Crafts idyll, Borglum was scarcely the typical country laird. Between his labors on his buildings and grounds and his work on the Newark Lincoln, he still found time to raise Cain. In the fall of 1910, he began lobbying for the position of director of sculpture for the Panama-Pacific Exposition, the world's fair celebrating the completion of the Panama Canal, scheduled for five years hence in San Francisco. One of the chief qualifications Borglum gave for the job was that he was "a Pacific Coaster, born and bred out there." His vision for the fair, as outlined in numerous letters to those who might pull strings for him, was to avoid repetition of the neoclassical excesses of Chicago, Buffalo, and St. Louis—expositions that had "bargained for an hour of revelry and got little else." World's fairs, he groused, had degenerated into a "bunco game," and he worried that California would fall victim to "the counterfeits of the East."

His worst fears were confirmed when the job of sculptural director went to Karl Bitter, a highly regarded New York artist who had figured prominently in the previous three world's fairs. (Today Bitter's most visible work is a nude atop the *Pulitzer Fountain* in front of the Plaza Hotel in New York.) More galling still, Bitter wasn't even an American; he had emigrated from Vienna at the age of twenty-one. "Nothing has hurt me in twenty years like this," Borglum confided to a friend who had been campaigning for his appointment. "Turned down for the poorest professional quack in all America." With Bitter in charge, he ranted, "the deadest group of professional 'artificers' left over in the East have settled on the thigh of [the] Fair."

Borglum's friend had a much simpler explanation for why Borglum was rejected by San Francisco: "It seems the report is that you are a very difficult person to get along with."

Borglum was testy, to be sure, but as always he backed up his rhetoric with his art. On Memorial Day 1911, his Newark Lincoln was dedicated in a grand ceremony presided over by Theodore Roosevelt. For his first full Lincoln figure, he chose to seat the president on a plain bench, and unlike so many previous Lincoln sculptures, in which Lincoln appears poised to speak, Borglum created a mood of somber reflection. In studying Lincoln's life, Borglum had noted the president's habit of slipping away to the White House garden whenever he felt especially overwhelmed by dispatches from the war. For Borglum, this was Lincoln's Garden of Gethsemane—with a lot of help from Rodin's *The Thinker*. "The Lincoln I have endeavored to portray is not thinking about himself or about anything that will be of advantage to himself," he explained. "His mind is engrossed with the vast responsibilities that have weighed him down."

Unlike Borglum's earlier bust of Lincoln, his *Seated Lincoln*, as the piece would eventually be called, reveals less of the inner man and more of the gravity that weighed on Lincoln's soul and lineaments. The bags under his eyes are like scar tissue. His bow tie is out of kilter. His left hand drapes across his left knee; his right hand lies flat on the bench—not the hands of a rail-splitter or even an orator, but those of a man whose once-strong arms are now heavy. For the second time, Borglum had done justice to the ultimate American subject and produced a deeply evocative work of art.

The unveiling was the most important day in Borglum's life so far. He and Mary picked up Theodore Roosevelt, now a civilian and recently returned from a yearlong safari in Africa, at the Hudson ferry. They drove to Newark in an open car, crowds lining much of the route. When the car reached the Essex County Courthouse in Newark, in front of which the *Seated Lincoln* was positioned facing the downtown business district, the crowd was enormous; Borglum, probably exaggerating, estimated one hundred thousand. They were on hand to see Teddy, the most beloved president since Lincoln, but the event meant something much more to Borglum. No audience of this size had ever applauded a sculptor before—not Phidias, not Michelangelo, not Rodin.

"I want to thank you for yesterday and all it brought, and all it meant," Borglum wrote Roosevelt after the event. Then he shared some anecdotes from the Memorial Day ceremony: "The story has just come to me that an old lady climbed onto the seat and embraced the figure, and had to be taken away by a policeman. And one of my workmen last night, working through the crowd about the statue, heard a mother tell her children that Lincoln was sitting down on a bench so that he could tell children stories. These are the first sproutings of the folk lore that will build around that bronze."

The folklore that followed sprang from the accessibility of the *Seated Lincoln*. Unlike most monuments of prominent men, this one does not surmount an Olympian pedestal, exalted but removed. Instead, Lincoln sits at almost street level on a bench similar to one found in most parks. Lincoln's scale is one-and-a-half times normal human size—heroic but not so huge that one cannot sit beside him as a fellow human being. His right hand, outstretched upon the open bench, invites holding. And as thousands of children would soon attest, his angular bronze knee is more welcoming than that of the most benevolent Santa. When a priggish Newark pastor alerted Borglum that "[d]irty, ragged street Arabs" were in the habit of playing on the Lincoln, Borglum made it clear that he didn't wish to have the kids shooed away. In August 1912, *The Masses* ran on its cover a photograph of two young black children perched on Lincoln, one on his knee, the other in the fold of his right arm. A more touching testimonial to Lincoln—and his sculptor—is hard to imagine.

(In recent years, the *Seated Lincoln* has continued to symbolize Lincoln's legacy. The old courthouse is condemned, girded by a chain-link fence, leaving Lincoln isolated in a small triangle formed by the confluence of busy Springfield and Market Streets. Traffic pulses by indifferently, car stereos thumping hip-hop. Cigarettes are stubbed out in

Lincoln's right hand. Graffiti tattoos his forehead. The businesses Lincoln now surveys from his bench are named Dunkin Donuts, Dr. Jay's Sneakers, Sin City, and they are patronized almost exclusively by descendants of the people whom Lincoln emancipated in 1864.)

After the glory of the Newark dedication, the news out of Washington concerning its Lincoln Memorial grabbed Borglum's full attention. In March 1911, two months before the unveiling of the *Seated Lincoln*, the Lincoln Memorial Commission (President William Howard Taft, chairman) met for the first time. By August, the commission had selected an architect, Henry Bacon of New York. By Christmas, Bacon was able to present his design for a building that, with only a few minor changes, is the neoclassical Lincoln Memorial we recognize today. The site already selected was Potomac Park, on the axis with the Capitol and Washington Monument. The cost was estimated at $2 million.

Although the actual sculptor of the Lincoln to be placed within the memorial would not be chosen for another four years, Borglum was not shy in advertising his interest in the job. In January 1912, he sent a letter to the *New York Sun*: "It is proposed to erect a Greek or Greco-Roman temple on the Potomac as the Nation's Lincoln Monument. . . . The great question before the country's commissions regarding this matter is, what is the nation's conception of Lincoln?" As background, Borglum reminded his readers of Horatio Greenough's sculpture of a toga-draped George Washington—the father of the country mocked by "emasculated, soulless aesthetics." Having seen Bacon's drawings and models for the Lincoln Memorial *structure*, Borglum warned against a similar humiliation for the Lincoln *sculpture* that would be placed within it: "Is there no one who feels enough . . . to stop this vulgar, unfelt, boughten taste that is steering . . . a great nation's tenderest of memories into a cold meaningless pile of imported garments of the past . . . ? In heaven's name, in Abraham Lincoln's name, don't ask the American people . . . to associate a Greek temple with the first great

American.... [H]ow long must we erect and re-erect memorials to peoples thousands of years past?"

Over the following months, Borglum continued to berate the Lincoln commission's plan to use "pilfered, out-worn forms." He underscored that he wasn't against classicism per se. Indeed, he had high praise for the Greeks: "The Periclean period of Greek art appeals to me as a period when understanding of form and beauty, and the fitting use of it, almost reached perfection." But, he hastened to add, the Greeks' "sincerity, their taste, their craft, their gods and myths and religious rites were *their own*." Borglum asked one of his audiences how they would feel about "taking Mr. Lincoln ... over to the Acropolis and putting [him] there in bronze? Of course the idea is grotesque and ridiculous."

Worn down by Borglum's sniping, the commission finally agreed to consider his ideas. He proposed a series of bas-reliefs and friezes on the interior walls that told the story of the period before the Civil War, the war itself, and the "restoration of peace" afterward. "In the center of it all," he offered, "I would put Lincoln alone, deep in thought, absorbed, conscious of all that was passing about him but sitting alone." The commissioners listened attentively, but they did not give Borglum the job. Four years later, in May 1916, the Lincoln commission approved the model of another seated Lincoln—this one by Borglum's erstwhile friend and lifelong competitor, Daniel Chester French.

French's Lincoln, not completed until 1922, rivals Mount Rushmore as the best-known sculpture in America. And like Rushmore, it is gigantic. Two years into the project, the memorial commission gave French permission to increase the height from thirteen feet to nineteen feet (including the base) to better fit the scale of the Greek temple Bacon was erecting. French seated Lincoln on a ten-foot throne, godlike. Lincoln's coat drapes open like a robe (or toga); his arms rest imperiously on the arms of his chair, which themselves are ornamented with bundled fasces, the traditional symbol of Roman authority. Engraved on the marble walls are the Gettysburg Address ("Four score and seven years ago . . . ") and Lincoln's Second Inaugural Address ("With malice toward none; with charity for all . . .").

Many who contemplate French's Lincoln describe his mood as one of contemplation. Others suggest that its size, elevation, and posture create a Lincoln more judgmental than gentle. The final determination, as always, is in the eyes. Working on such a scale and striving for realism, French realized that he could not sculpt typical monumental eyeballs, with their hollow—dead—pupils. Instead he accomplished with a chisel what portrait painters achieve with a dab of paint: He carved small rectangular protrusions—tiny spikes of marble—in the center of Lincoln's eyes. The ambient light catches these small chips of stone and reflects off of them very much as light does in the lens of a flesh-and-blood eye. The effect is dramatic. Ask the squirmiest child on the most unruly class trip to the Lincoln Memorial: It's impossible to look at Abraham Lincoln and not feel the focused force of his magisterial gaze.

Borglum insisted lamely that he didn't really care who had designed the Lincoln Memorial or who had sculpted the Lincoln statue. It was strictly the style he objected to. But even his most principled criticisms were a poor mask for his tremendous frustration, and in the years that followed he could not resist deprecating French's Lincoln—and, for that matter, every other Lincoln that was not his own. "I found [that] statues of Lincoln were either awkward or crude, intending to be natural, or else they were artificial and mannered," he wrote in the early 1920s, before he had become involved in Mount Rushmore, "and two of the most important statues, made by the two most important sculptors [Saint-Gaudens's in Chicago and French's in Washington], are perhaps the most false and artificial. One [Saint-Gaudens's] makes him look like an actor, like a Hamlet; and the other [French's] looks like a Sunday school teacher. Neither one gives any idea of the weight of responsibility that bore on this large, sincere nature." Borglum was even harsher toward George Grey Barnard's statue of Lincoln in Cincinnati, damning it as "an abortion." Reading between the lines, it is difficult not to hear Borglum promising to himself that if he ever got the chance to do another major memorial to Lincoln, he would do it with weight, on a large scale—and with individuality, sincerity, and reverence.

In the meantime, Borglum had plenty else to keep him busy. Besides the ongoing work at Borgland, sculpture commissions continued to come his way. Arrogance and suspicion kept him from entering a $50,000 Lincoln competition for Springfield, Illinois, but he did a fountain in Bridgeport, Connecticut; a Civil War memorial in Raleigh, North Carolina; a statue of railroad baron Collis P. Huntington in the West Virginia town named for him; and one of abolitionist minister Henry Ward Beecher in Brooklyn. In January 1913, he was offered $10,000 to sculpt a memorial to "The First Flight of Man" in honor of the Wright brothers in Dayton, Ohio. He was two months into it when a flood ravaged Dayton and put the project on hold.

At about this same time, Borglum articulated a bold proposition in a letter to U.S. Senator Francis Newlands, the powerful chairman of the Interstate Commerce Committee: "I have been thinking a great deal about properly finishing the shores and entrances of the [soon to be completed] Panama Canal. . . . I suggest that a proper appearance of a gateway be made on the Atlantic side, marking definitely the entrance to the Canal; that it be some kind of monument; that some form of a gate or entrance be marked on the Pacific side. . . . The monuments might simply be shafts in some form to be hereafter agreed upon or they might be colossal allegorical devices of some sort. If sculpture is used, some evidence should appear in the monument that the Anglo-Saxon built it, together with the date and other records of interest. There is also a nice idea of the Union of two great Oceans, of the West and the East, and the greater union of the North and the South or of the two Americas."

The concept hearkened back to the legendary Colossus of Rhodes, the wonder of the ancient world that had guarded the harbor of the Mediterranean island of Rhodes, and more recently to Frédéric

Auguste Bartholdi's colossal female figure *Egypt Passing the Light to Asia*, holding aloft a lamp, intended for the entrance to the Suez Canal—a design that never came to fruition in Suez but eventually evolved into Bartholdi's *Liberty Enlightening the World*, better known as the Statue of Liberty, in New York Harbor. Borglum's pitch for Panama fell on deaf ears, but it was significant nonetheless, for it provides the first glimmer of his Phidian ambition to sculpt truly colossal monuments. What is more, the message of Mount Rushmore, fifteen years later, would be the same as he had urged for Panama: the triumph of manifest destiny; the unity of east and west, of north and south; and of course the glory of Anglo-Saxon achievement.

Yet none of Borglum's various projects and proposals distracted him from his war against the sorry state of art in America. In a speech to the National Arts Club in February 1912, he called fine arts schools "humbug" and again urged that they be padlocked. The presumption that any more than one in a hundred art students might emerge as a worthy, self-sufficient artist was a "betrayal of the people by a false democracy," he wrote in *The Craftsman*.

He was just getting warmed up. Alienated from any number of art societies already, Borglum joined with a group of fellow iconoclasts to form the Association of American Painters and Sculptors. The group's first big venture was to be an exhibition of Modernism and its precedents at the 69th Regiment Armory in Manhattan. Borglum pitched in $500 of his own money toward rent of the building, and he was named chairman of the sculptural selection committee.

The Armory Show, as it came to be known, was the most controversial event in American art history up to that point. For the first time, America came face-to-face with the cutting edge. The exhibition also included pleasing morsels by European stalwarts Goya, Delacroix, Daumier, Corot, and Manet, not to mention the cream of the Impressionists and Fauves. America's best included Ryder, Henri, Hassam, Inness, and Whistler, plus the topical Ashcan School. But all of these esteemed artists were knocked for a loop by the startling presence of the Cubists: Léger, Braque, Picasso. Seventy thousand people took in the Armory Show, and a good many found it so unpalatable that they recoiled in disgust. Theodore Roosevelt, who was sufficiently aroused to review the exhibition for *The Outlook*, warned that a "lunatic fringe" had breached the gates of the republic. Those less aghast were simply amused. Critics outdid one another ribbing Marcel Duchamp's frenetic, multifaceted *Nude Descending a Staircase*—"explosion in a shingle factory" the phrase that tickled the deepest.

Borglum, as can be expected, plunged into the thick of the tempest—or rather, he jumped in, then withdrew in a huff, and wound up taking potshots from the perimeter, making himself, as one paper quipped, "an insurgent among the insurgents." On February 1, two weeks before the Armory Show was scheduled to open, he resigned from the Association of American Painters and Sculptors via a letter that he also distributed to the press. He charged that sculpture had been given short shrift in favor of oil paintings and works on paper (sculpture made up only 10 percent of the exhibition), that European sculptors had been given too great a presence, and that association members had bypassed his authority and selected friends over artists of greater merit. "Sculpture as it really exists in America will not be shown," he scolded. The association called his accusations "absurd," and the *New York Sun* called his letter of resignation "pompous." The *Globe* took him to task for "sympathies [that] predispose him to attack those who sit in authority.... [W]e wish Mr. Borglum walked to the battlefield on ankles not quite so thick, and struck his adversary with a lighter hand." (Solon Borglum, who had several sculptures slated for the show, defended his brother's protest but in the end did not withdraw his work.)

Today, it is difficult to get to the heart of the Armory Show imbroglio, but one suspects that Borglum, who purported to be at the forefront of American sculpture, had received a sneak preview of the

future and had felt personally and professionally outraged, not to mention challenged. Sculptors who had been weaned on the Beaux-Arts and
the Impressionism of Rodin were now venturing into distorted, even
abstract, forms. Constantin Brancusi was shaping elegant, egg-shaped
heads. Alexander Archipenko was punching holes in faces and torsos.
William Lehmbruck's nudes were radically elongated. ("[T]hough mam-
malian, it is not especially human," Roosevelt said of Lehmbruck's *Kneel-
ing Woman*.) Not only did Borglum resent the inclusion of these artists in
the Armory Show; more to the point, he had received his first inkling
that the brave new world of art might not necessarily be reserving a
front-row seat for him. Sculpture had always been a turf war to Borglum,
and rather than make accommodation—or undertake his own
evolution—he pitched a fit. "That farcical and foolish exhibition [was]
made up largely of paranoiacs," he fulminated. The Armory Show "has
not suggested a new order. It has wallowed in riot—or worse, indirection.
It has not added color, it has tipped a pot of paint in the public's eye."

Once Borglum got on his high horse, he could not resist riding
roughshod over anything else that got in his way. After the uproar over
the Armory Show died down, he took on all comers, still waving the
banner of "insurgency." In 1913, he was at work on his first commission
for Statuary Hall in the Capitol, a portrait of North Carolina's Civil
War governor Zebulon Vance. Each state was allotted two figures in
the hall. Sizing up the other sculptures already installed, Borglum
declared a number of them "fraudulent"; sculptors whose names were
on the work had farmed out the actual carving "to struggling young
geniuses working for a pittance." Going further, Borglum asserted in a
series of speeches, interviews, and bylined articles that 40, perhaps as
much as 60, percent of the statues in the United States are "not made
by the man whose name is signed to it." (Borglum used assistants himself over the years, including Marian Bell, daughter of Alexander Graham Bell, and Malvina Hoffman and Isamu Noguchi, both of whom
went on to have illustrious careers of their own.)

Nor could he resist taking a few whacks at the most recent outdoor sculpture. The elaborate, allegorical *Maine Memorial* had just been completed, at long last, in New York's Columbus Circle. The sculptor was Italian-born Attilio Piccirilli, a protégé of Daniel Chester French. (Piccirilli and his brothers would also assist French in the carving of the Lincoln Memorial.) Borglum deemed the monument to sailors killed in Havana Harbor during the Spanish-American War a gross waste of time and money: "The Maine Memorial should never have been built. A great catastrophe, and nothing more, forms not fitting subject for commemoration in art.... Nowadays we are building monuments for anybody, everybody, and nobody." Asked by the *New York World* what, hypothetically, he would do with $10 million, Borglum said that he would "clean house," knocking down the "graveyard sculpture" of "impostors and artistic prostitutes." With the money left over, he would fund a "real" national art academy and erect proper monuments to Washington and Lincoln. So far, neither one existed, he adjudged.

Borglum presented a gentler face to the public in 1914 with his first major one-man exhibition of sculpture. The assemblage arrayed in the gallery of the Avery Library at Columbia University included *The Return of the Boer*; *Mares of Diomedes*; and a series of small, very sensuous and sensitive tributes to womanhood: *Conception, Wonderment of Motherhood, The Martyr,* and a female Atlas holding up the Earth. "My Atlas is a woman," he explained, "because the burden of the world is not borne on the backs of men.... It is borne in the arms, in the breasts, of women; and they reach up and receive it—on their knees, crushing them though it does, with a kind of benediction." His appreciation of womanly virtues was doubtless inspired by the manifest strength, intelligence, beauty, and graciousness of his wife, Mary. As hinted by the titles to some of the pieces, Mary had further enriched his life by presenting him with a son, Lincoln, on April 9, 1912. Asked several months later to name his best work of art, Borglum answered cheerily, "Why there it is," and pointed to the baby named for his hero.

But even with the birth of a child, life at Borgland was far from bucolic. Borglum was forever dashing off to job sites and meetings in New York and beyond, every one urgent and of paramount consequence. And despite the steady flow of sculpture commissions, his finances were anything but flush. When it came to money, Borglum was pathetic. He was delinquent on his mortgage payments almost the minute Eugene Meyer had loaned him the money to buy Borgland. Meyer was cordial with his friend but insistent, and when Borglum sent checks, he was always dollars short and many days late. Even to creditors as understanding as Meyer, Borglum appeared negligent and irresponsible. Mostly, though, he was simply oblivious. Money wasn't a distraction; it was an abstraction. He had no clue how much anything cost. He spent more than he earned on a sculpture, most recently the *Seated Lincoln*. He never scrimped on his lifestyle and ordered up dinners, hotels, houses, horses, and motorcars without any notion of how he would pay for them. When he had no cash, which was often, he ran a tab. When he borrowed from friends, as was his preference, they were the last to be paid back. And when the bills and foreclosure notices did arrive, he was usually absent, leaving his wife to face the music as best she could.

Throughout 1915, as Eugene Meyer was pressing Borglum for his tardy mortgage payments, Borglum kept him at bay with assurances that a number of lucrative jobs had just come his way. He had been offered $54,000 to sculpt a twelve-foot monument of General Daniel Butterfield, one of the heroes of Gettysburg. He had just submitted a model for a Stonewall Jackson memorial for Richmond. The flight memorial in Dayton was still pending, and he was just finishing up a $25,000 monument to Governor John Peter Altgeld of Illinois. His plate was full, and soon his purse would be, too—or so he promised.

As bad luck would have it, he never got the Jackson job; the Dayton job remained a washout; and although he completed the Butterfield monument, the general's estate, like Borglum, was a slow pay. As for the Altgeld memorial, politics nearly scuttled that, too.

Altgeld was a German immigrant who had fought in the Civil War at sixteen, studied law, risen to Superior Court judge, earned a fortune in Chicago real estate, and served a single term as Illinois governor, from 1893 to 1897. A friend of labor and the poor, he was best known for pardoning three of the convicted Haymarket bombers. On May 4, 1886, amid a season of violent labor strikes, armed police had attempted to disperse a crowd of protesters in Chicago's Haymarket Square. A bomb was thrown into the ranks of the police, fifty-nine of whom were wounded; eight died. Although the bomb thrower was never identified, eight anarchists were brought to trial and found guilty of the crime. Four were hanged in 1887; a fifth committed suicide. The three who survived rotted in prison until Altgeld pardoned them in 1893. When Altgeld died nine years later, his body lay in state at the Chicago Public Library; thousands of mourners waited patiently in the Chicago wind for a chance to pay their respects to this "man of the people."

Borglum saw Altgeld as an Illinoisan cut from the same cloth as Lincoln. Both, he said, were reformers who had waged a "battle against oppression." Accordingly, Borglum sculpted Altgeld standing tall with helping hands outstretched. At his feet he positioned a man, woman, and child—symbols of the disenfranchised and downtrodden whom Altgeld had protected. Similar statues of Lincoln had placed grateful blacks at the feet of the Emancipator.

But before the Altgeld memorial could be installed in Lincoln Park, the city arts commission raised a shriek of protest, asserting that the sponsors of the memorial had not gone through proper channels before awarding the commission to Borglum. An even shriller objection came from organized labor. To the unions, the supplicants in Borglum's sculpture were not just bowing; they were scraping. "This is a slap in the face of labor," charged a spokesman. "Labor does not kiss the hem of any garment. Nor does it stand bareheaded in the presence of any man. Labor is dignified. Labor is majestic.... And Governor Altgeld would not allow such a statue of himself to be erected if he were alive—he'd kick it into the lake."

In the end, Borglum's sculpture was not kicked into Lake Michigan. Mayor William "Big Bill" Thompson interceded, summarily disbanding the municipal arts commission, and the dedication, on Labor Day 1915, went off without a hitch. The keynote speaker of the day was another of America's great populists, William Jennings Bryan—whose statue Borglum had carved two years earlier.

Borglum had not been particularly fazed by the arts commission's attack. He was used to that sort of bureaucratic harassment. He called the commission "incompetent" and compared Chicago to Carthage, known more for "trade" than for "culture and art." What did wound him, however, was the accusation that he had been insensitive to the common man. Three years earlier, Borglum had become a founding member of the National Progressive Party, committed to correcting the social, economic, and moral imbalances of the modern era.

His decision to join had hardly been an about-face. He could still be an insufferable snob. Artisans and artists would always be of different classes; some men were great, and some would never be. But lately he had broadened his definition of greatness to include those men who "with their backs to fate, fight other men's fight." In particular, he cited those who advocated "a shorter day, a lighter load ... easier taxes, [and a] safer community." And increasingly he expressed bitter disdain for Americans spoiled by wealth and privilege—those who couldn't be bothered to venture far from "the [Stock] Exchange or comfort resorts." The Progressive credo called for the haves to help the have-nots, and also for the haves to shake some sense into those among them who had disgraced their station and were spoiling the nation. It was a political movement tailor-made for Borglum.

The patriarch of Progressivism was Borglum's good friend and mentor, Theodore Roosevelt. Roosevelt had become vice president on the strength of his initiative and gallantry under fire during the Spanish-American War. Then, after the murder of President McKinley in September 1901, he had marched into the White House with the same bravado that had carried him to the summit of San Juan Hill. At forty-two, he was the youngest president in U.S. history, and as such, the hyperactive poster child for the new Age of Energy. The government he inherited was, in his view, the corrupt and craven handmaiden of big business, an inequity that Roosevelt sought to correct in a series of bold strokes. He made it clear that he was not against capitalism or entrepreneurship outright, merely their excesses. His enemies were the gargantuan trusts and other so-called malefactors of great wealth. He challenged the sacred tenets of the tariff, demanded better conditions for workers, made food and drugs safer. He favored conservation of natural resources, women's suffrage, welfare reform, and a graduated income tax. The Roosevelt way to achieve these goals was to tighten federal control over business and state and local governments—using, somewhat paradoxically, "Hamiltonian means for Jeffersonian ends." The name he gave to his agenda and approach was "New Nationalism."

One of the primary differences between Roosevelt's progressivism and the populism of Bryan, which had thrived at the end of the previous century, was that Bryan's base had been predominately rural; Roosevelt, too, was backed by the nation's yeoman farmers and small-town citizenry, but additionally he had succeeded in mobilizing urban progressives and convincing Old Guard conservatives that reform was not revolutionary, but simply a matter of reapplying traditional values to modern conditions. Like Bryan, Roosevelt was an inspirational orator. His message, invariably delivered in a lion's roar from a "bully pulpit"—Roosevelt's coinage—was one of moral regeneration and social justice.

Roosevelt preached the power of the presidency, yet in 1908, he declared that he would not seek a third term, honoring the tradition of antimonarchy begun by George Washington. Instead, he gave his blessing to William Howard Taft, his secretary of war. The corpulent, arch-conservative Taft, as would soon become evident, had no intention of filling Roosevelt's shoes. On the contrary, the new president seemed bent on trampling everything his predecessor had mapped out. To Roosevelt's mind, Taft had reverted to business as usual, and business of the worst kind.

There was no question that Taft had to go, even less of a question of who should succeed him: Roosevelt—affectionately called "the Colonel" by his loyalists—wanted his old job back. But in the notorious Republican civil war of 1912, which climaxed at the national convention in Chicago in June, Taft drubbed his former boss by a margin of five to one, thanks largely to the lockstep of southern delegates who Roosevelt's men claimed were bought, stolen, or steamrolled. In high dudgeon, the Roosevelt righteous repaired to nearby Orchestra Hall and proceeded to form the National Progressive Party, soon nicknamed the Bull Moose Party in honor of Roosevelt's hearty assurance that he felt "as fit as a bull moose."

The army that rallied around Roosevelt's was an unlikely hodgepodge. "Everyone who had a cherished *ism* had gone running to Roosevelt," recalled Amos Pinchot, one of the Colonel's key lieutenants. The ranks included Wall Street bankers and organized labor, western ranchers and skid-row settlement workers. H. L. Mencken called the Progressives "the most tatterdemalion party ever seen in American politics"; their agenda was "a cocktail made up of all the elixirs hawked among the boobery."

Roosevelt himself was a bundle of contradictions. When he had been president, he could not decide whether to call himself a "progressive Conservative" or a "conservative Progressive." Ironically, in stressing the dignity and responsibility of the individual (the Jeffersonian paradigm), he had pumped up the muscle of big government (the Hamiltonian). He had offered a "Square Deal" at home and waved an imperialist stick abroad. His views on immigration were more enlightened than those of most of his Republican peers, yet his record on race was spotty at best. He had welcomed Booker T. Washington to the White House but publicly regretted passage of the Fifteenth Amendment, which in 1869 had ensured blacks' right to vote.

Regardless of Roosevelt's philosophical inconsistencies, it was his character that galvanized and energized the Progressives. His detractors called him a "stunt man," an updated Napoleon, or "Achilles in his tent." To his proponents, he was "the big-game hunter who tamed [the GOP] elephant" or "Superman . . . striding the world like the colossus he is." No one, however, doubted his innate talent for bringing people together. "This nondescript army," wrote Pinchot, "with aims as far apart as the poles from the equator, was miraculously kept united by the magnetism of one electric personality."

Like hundreds of thousands of other Americans, Gutzon Borglum was entirely enamored of the image, the force, and the substance of Theodore Roosevelt. Borglum attended neither the Republican nor the Progressive convention in Chicago, but he leapt aboard the Bull Moose train soon thereafter and quickly became one of the Colonel's most tireless warriors. And once politics got into his bloodstream, it became a consuming passion—not eclipsing art, but equaling it, and informing it absolutely. Even four years later, when Roosevelt no longer wished to be the Progressive standard-bearer, Borglum battled on a little longer, beseeching Roosevelt to stay in the fight.

The links between Borglum and Roosevelt—the similarities, the compatibility—were, as has already been mentioned, uncanny. Both were solidly built and vigorous, and both grew bristly moustaches. As a younger man, after early setbacks in politics and the death of his first wife, Roosevelt had refreshed and, on some level, reinvented himself on a ranch in the Dakotas. Borglum, nine years younger, was also the product of his own reinvention. His movement had been from West to East, and he too had married a second time. Even without Jessie Fremont's letter of introduction, the possibility that the two men's paths would not somehow have crossed seems remote. One thing, though, is certain: By the time Roosevelt and his followers bolted the convention and formed their own party, he and Borglum were boon allies.

Borglum was perfectly suited to the melodramatic posturing and high moral stakes of Roosevelt's Bull Moose campaign. Roosevelt had elevated his credo of "applied idealism" to the level of religious crusade. "[I]f they melted Roosevelt down, they'd find a preacher militant," remarked author Owen Wister, who had dedicated his western romance, *The Virginian*, to his good friend. At the hijacked Republican Convention in June 1912, Roosevelt had exhorted his brethren to join him in a holy war: "We stand at Armageddon," he trumpeted, "and we battle for the Lord!" To join the Progressives called for "a confession of faith," Roosevelt announced, and the only way to fight "evil"—a term he used frequently—was through "insurgency"—a term Borglum soon appropriated for his own use. At Progressive rallies, crowds sang "Onward, Christian Soldiers."

Borglum had been a crusader in his own field for years, calling for banishment of the effete past and warning against the undisciplined future. Like Roosevelt, he was a man of means and security who bucked the establishment. In February 1912, four months before the Progressives had broken with the Republican "stand-pats," Borglum had fired his own salvo at the conspiracy of questionable taste and slick commerce that he perceived was choking the fine arts in America: "The opportunities [for recognition and sales] are in the hands of a few. Art is machine controlled, just as politics is machine controlled, although fewer people know it."

"Machine" was a loaded term in the Borglum lexicon. In the factory, the machine had supplanted craftsmanship, made men into grindstones, sacrificed "the best for the good enough." In politics, the machine meant spoils and bossism. And in art, it meant the clubby favoritism that had stolen the Panama-Pacific Exposition, ruined the Armory Show, ramrodded the Lincoln Memorial. Borglum was nothing if not idealistic, but invariably his idealism could be traced to a more personal animus. It followed, then, that his politics were usually personal as well, one more characteristic he shared with Roosevelt. "Mr. Roosevelt is so constituted," confided William Howard Taft, "that it is impossible for him to get into controversy without becoming personal.... Each blow he strikes is a hard one because it calls attention to some defect in his enemy's armor, or some great claim to right on his part."

Borglum had made his first forays into the trenches of politics and government shortly after he had moved to Connecticut. "In Stamford," Mary Borglum related in an early draft of her memoir, "he came at once into contact with the civic life of a small town and was introduced to the famous Connecticut town meeting. This opened his eyes to the part an individual could play in the political existence of his country, first in his town, next in his state and finally in his whole native land. In his diary, as a young man, he had written: 'A man's first love is his mother; his second, his sweetheart; his third is his art; his fourth, *all*.' And in a letter he says: 'No individual's life is worthy the immortality he seeks, unless he articulates the voice of his tribe or his people.'"

Borglum, as it happened, spoke first for himself and then for his people. One of his first civic projects was the rerouting of the public road that ran through his own property in Stamford. After he accomplished that, he lobbied the town to improve other roads and ultimately organized a rural bus system for Stamford, even directing the conversion of trucks to buses himself. Inevitably he locked horns with the town fathers, accusing them of corruption, "falsehood," and "gross misrepresentation."

Less than a month after the birth of the National Progressive Party in Chicago, Borglum and several others formed the National Progressive Party of Connecticut. The eight founders were a fitting microcosm of the national organization. Chairman Joseph Alsop was a wealthy tobacco grower married to Roosevelt's niece. Herbert Knox Smith had been Roosevelt's Commissioner of Corporations, a "trust buster." Joining them were a college president, a professor, a doctor, a minister, and a merchant. All were well-to-do, hardworking, respected in their communities, and committed to social justice and cleaning up local government. "Evil is to be beaten at last," promised Flavel Luther, president of Trinity College in Hartford. "[G]reed ... masquerading as individualism" must be eradicated, chimed Yandell Henderson of the Yale medical school. Yet for all their professed outrage over society's decay, none of the Connecticut leaders had ever suffered serious hardship themselves. Nor did they adopt an agenda much beyond calling for general reform. For Borglum, the main objective was to elect "honorable, clean, upright men whose character for reliability and efficiency is above reproach [and who] place patriotism and the interests of the state, city and town above private advancement." Mostly, the Connecticut Progressives were strong for Roosevelt.

Borglum campaigned hard for the Colonel throughout the state during the summer and fall of 1912, giving speeches, organizing rallies, and backing a slate of Progressive candidates in local races. He led a torchlight parade through Stamford, fitting an elephant head on the rear of the family donkey—a jocular, two-headed expression of the Progressives' third-party independence. Along the way, needless to say, he made plenty of enemies. When the Stamford mayor tried to coerce him on some political matter. Borglum flatly refused, according to Mary Borglum. The mayor purportedly responded: "Then it's a fight, a fight to the finish."

"Yes," Mary has her husband answering à la D'Artagnan, "and the sword to the hilt."

The campaign nearly did have a storybook ending—tragic, but not as tragic as it might have been. On October 14, with just three weeks left in the campaign, Roosevelt arrived in Milwaukee, where he was to give a speech. While Roosevelt was driving from his hotel to the auditorium, John Schrank, a tavern owner from New York, pushed through the crowd, drew a .38 revolver, and at close range shot the former president in the chest. (Schrank later testified that the ghost of President McKinley, another victim of an assassin's bullet, had come to him and demanded, "Avenge my death.")

Roosevelt was saved by his own words. The bullet passed through his suit coat but then struck the folded manuscript of the evening's speech as well as the case carrying the eyeglasses he would use to read it. The slug did enter his body finally, but at such reduced speed that it did no vital harm. Roosevelt shrugged off his worried doctors and continued on to the auditorium. "I don't know whether you fully understand that I have just been shot, but it takes more than that to kill a Bull Moose," he told the crowd, unbuttoning his vest to reveal his bloody shirt. "The bullet is in me now, so that I cannot make a very long speech, but I will try my best."

The speech in his pocket had been destroyed, but Roosevelt substituted oratory far superior: "I have altogether too important things to think of to feel any concern over my own death. . . . I am telling you the literal truth when I say that my concern is for many other things. It is not in the least for my own life. I want you to understand that I am ahead of the game, anyway. No man has had a happier life than I have had . . . I can tell you with absolute truthfulness that I am very much uninterested in whether I am shot or not."

To Borglum, who already worshipped Roosevelt, it was as if the Colonel had rolled away the stone and stepped from his own tomb. "Thank God you are safely back home again," he wrote from Stamford ten days later. "No one has watched you from the time of your attack in Milwaukee more than your friends here. Now that it is so nearly over we are thankful that you have been saved for the country."

The rest of America, while unquestionably happy to have Roosevelt go on living, did not want him to go on to the White House for a third term. On election day, Roosevelt had the satisfaction of burying his Brutus, the incumbent Taft, by a million votes, but lost by two million to the Democrat, the progressive-minded ex–college president and governor of

New Jersey, Woodrow Wilson. If there was a silver lining for Borglum, it was the knowledge that he would still have a friend in the White House.

Not that he considered deserting Roosevelt even for a minute. Three months after the election, Borglum announced to the *New York Herald*: "I have been thinking ... of attempting what should be the masterpiece of my life. I am planning a heroic statue of Theodore Roosevelt. When that work shall be completed, I will be willing to let posterity assign my rank as a sculptor.... What an inspiration the life of Roosevelt affords me! To put into stone a great man—a typical American! My ambition will certainly be satisfied when I have executed in the 'imperishable' the features and figure of the greatest man of his time!"

The Roosevelt monument would have to wait, but over the next four years, Borglum stuck to the Progressive cause in general and to the Colonel especially. In October 1913, he was one of the sponsors of a farewell dinner in New York that launched Roosevelt on his harrowing journey down the *Río Dúvida*—River of Doubt, later named *Río Téodoro*—in South America. Roosevelt nearly died of fever on the trip and returned home uncharacteristically frail. Convalescing at his home at Oyster Bay, Long Island, he had no choice but to look on passively while President Wilson appropriated much of his New Nationalism under the name "New Freedom." Meanwhile, the Progressive Party soldiered on, but without Roosevelt as its lodestar, the center would not hold. The Connecticut branch of the party took to infighting, a game at which Borglum now enjoyed considerable proficiency. After the 1914 midterm elections—in which Borglum bucked the party's national headquarters and persuaded his Connecticut Progressives to endorse a number of Republican candidates—he became a sworn enemy of George Perkins, the former partner of J. P. Morgan who now chaired the Progressives' executive committee. "It is useless to talk about the water that has gone over the falls," he castigated Perkins, "but if ever power misused itself, the Progressive power [at the national level] did so last fall." In his own state of Connecticut, he complained to Perkins, "ignorance, selfishness, and, in petty ways, corruption never flourished in so brief a time as in the Progressive ranks." The only salvation was to coax the Bull Moose to make one more charge.

Very few people thought that Roosevelt had a chance of winning reelection in 1916, as either a Progressive or a Republican candidate. He had not helped his case by first defending, then becoming increasingly bellicose toward, Germany—at a time when most Americans detested the kaiser but were nevertheless eager to keep out of the war already raging in Europe. Nor did Roosevelt engender optimism with pronouncements such as "I will not be a candidate for President. Even if I am nominated unanimously I will not be a candidate." Still, something about his denial was less than persuasive. It was well-known that he regarded Wilson as a "prize jackass" and that he craved nothing more than to remove the Democratic administration from power. Then, too, the Progressive and the Republican conventions were scheduled, quite intentionally, to overlap each other in Chicago in June.

If anybody believed that the Colonel had a prayer, it was Borglum. "You can be the next nominee for the presidency of the United States, if you wish," he wrote to Roosevelt in January, "but it will be wrung from the covetous grip of powerful forces.... However, if the stars are so set, I shall be in the field fighting for you until the polls close, in every way my power and ingenuity can devise."

As the convention neared and Roosevelt still had not acted, Borglum promoted, and even claimed authorship of, a shrewd, side-door strategy. According to Borglum, the scheme was to unfold as follows: Roosevelt would remain at home in Long Island, which he had pledged to do all along. Leaders of both the Republicans and the Progressives would caucus over cigars and liquor in the back rooms of Chicago. There was no question whom the Progressives wanted as *their* nominee. But Roosevelt had made it known that he would not allow them to put forward his name until the Republicans gave some sign that they too would embrace him. It was a desperate ploy. The Progressives understood that their only chance for survival as a party was with Roosevelt as their candidate, and they suggested to the Republican Old Guard that the only way that Republicans could defeat Wilson was by joining with the Progressives behind Roosevelt. The catch-22 was that Roosevelt vowed that he was not a Progressive candidate until he was a Republican candidate—meaning the Progressives had nothing to offer if the Republicans had nothing to offer. Although the dickering lasted through the night for several nights, the Republicans would not budge in favor of Roosevelt. And as time ran out, the Progressive rank and file, who had agreed not to proffer Roosevelt's nomination, grew increasingly restive and obstreperous.

There was, it seems, one last card in the deck, and in Borglum's version of the story, he was the one man whom Roosevelt trusted to play it. In his January letter to the Colonel, he had advised, "If the conditions are not favorable for you ... I think you should boldly and frankly name a man [to take your place]." Borglum mentioned General Leonard Wood, Roosevelt's longtime comrade from the Spanish-American War, believing that Roosevelt wanted Wood as the fallback nominee as well. "[W]e all understood [we] were [actually] working for the nomination of Theodore Roosevelt," Borglum told Wood's biographer, Hermann Hagedorn, years later. "But in the event of his failure, he would throw his entire support to General Leonard Wood." By doing so, he explained, Roosevelt would provide "the Conservatives and the Irreconcilables ... the key to the deadlock."

Borglum arrived in Chicago and positioned himself to "confidentially communicate the wishes of the inside leaders, each to the other." His telegrams to Roosevelt over the final three days of the convention reveal, among other things, his deep loyalty to the Colonel, his penchant for breathless melodrama, and a sense that he was not the kingmaker that his ego had made him out to be.

Wednesday, June 7: "Crisis reached. If anything but pulling the temple down on our own heads is to be done, it must be done now.

Immeasurable consequences to our country and vast, inevitable adjustments facing America hanging in the balance and await you. Delay means suicide...."

"Wood seems now the only candidate who can prevent the return of the Democrats. Fight terrible and little quarter given.... My early predictions have come true so far...."

Thursday, June 8: "Please send me a line confirming approval of Wood...."

"No reply found to my telegram. Demand that you name him [Wood] yourself openly and frankly."

"There should be something done to save us.... Die is set tonight."

And finally, this to Leonard Wood himself: "Nothing but power the Col no longer commands can save the situation.... He seems ... determined to be completely ruined."

By daylight Saturday, the battle was lost. Within minutes of each other, the Republicans nominated Charles Evans Hughes, former governor of New York and a Taft appointee to the United States Supreme Court, and the Progressives at last cleared their throats and cheered the name of Theodore Roosevelt—and in so doing both parties fell on their own swords. Woodrow Wilson defeated Hughes in November, and with a deflated Roosevelt as its figurehead, the National Progressive Party was for all intents and purposes dead.

What is *not* evident in Borglum's telegrams is that on Saturday morning Roosevelt *had* submitted a name: U.S. Senator Henry Cabot Lodge and *not* Leonard Wood. In his later correspondence with Hermann Hagedorn, Borglum did acknowledge that Roosevelt had ultimately given the nod to Lodge, but he insisted that the Republican leadership had confided to him that they didn't want either Lodge or Hughes but in fact preferred Wood. The rest of the story is too Byzantine to iterate in full—involving secret, wee-hour phone calls between Borglum and Roosevelt and then between Borglum and Wood; an alleged phone tap by Chairman Perkins, Borglum's Progressive nemesis; and a larger conspiracy by Perkins to undercut Borglum's credibility and keep both Roosevelt and Wood out of the running. Only after much sleuthing, Borglum contended, did he finally discover that "the Colonel himself had been utterly and grossly deceived in the whole matter and that the entire situation in Chicago was executed by Perkins himself." With Borglum, there was always a bad guy.

When Hagedorn checked Borglum's recollections of 1916 with others who had been on the scene, both in Chicago and in Oyster Bay, he turned up numerous incongruities. The Republican leadership, Hagedorn informed Borglum, in fact had not preferred Wood. Roosevelt, for his part, had named "Lodge and no one else." And on the night that Borglum claimed he had spoken to Wood at Oyster Bay, setting up the whole transfer of power, Wood had actually been giving a speech at the Harvard Club in New York. "Can you give me any light on these discrepancies?" Hagedorn queried. To which Borglum replied: "There is nothing that I can add."

Regardless of what really happened on those long, muggy nights in June, Borglum came away from the convention not with the feeling that he had in any way let his party or the Colonel down, but the opposite, that they had let him down. "I have left the Progressive Party and am behind Hughes," he told a friend the week after returning to Stamford. He even lost confidence in Roosevelt temporarily, believing that the Colonel had played a "contemptible trick" on both Wood and himself. But then, two years later, he was back in servant's harness, urging Roosevelt to run for Congress. "It will be the most wonderful campaign since [Lincoln's for president] in 1860." And once Roosevelt was elected, he would be acclaimed Speaker of the House—and the nation would be saved.

Roosevelt, we know, did no such thing.

chapter 7

SIZE MATTERS

N OW MORE THAN EVER, Borglum could see the big picture. He no longer thought just in terms of the potholes and primaries of Stamford but also grasped the entire panorama of American politics. And increasingly, he had come to view art on a grand scale, too. Bronzes in the park, a bust in the Rotunda—these were first steps toward national monuments. The American canvas was huge, and he, perhaps he alone, possessed the unique blend of vision, talent, and tenacity to fill it to its limits.

His vantage point improved further still in the fall of 1916. On November 8, the day after Woodrow Wilson defeated Charles Evans Hughes, Borglum wrote to the chief engineer of General Electric's National Lamp Works, accepting an invitation to design new lights for the torch of the Statue of Liberty. France's gift to America was thirty years old in 1916, and in all that time, *Liberty Enlightening the World* had done so only metaphorically; the torch that *Liberty* lifted three hundred feet above New York Harbor, for all its swirling elegance, had been so poorly engineered that it cast hardly any light whatsoever. With clouds of war now darkening Europe and rolling toward the United States, America's pride in its tallest monument swelled commensurately. Liberty—and *Liberty*—must not be taken for granted.

Moreover, both needed protecting, as had become all too evident on July 30, 1916. In the middle of the night, a suspicious fire broke out on the docks of Black Tom Island, a narrow peninsula jutting into New York Harbor near Jersey City and less than half a mile from the Statue of Liberty. The fire spread rapidly to a half-dozen rail cars loaded with dynamite and munitions en route to the European front. The ensuing explosion jolted northern New Jersey, Manhattan, and Brooklyn and was heard halfway to Philadelphia. At least a dozen people close to the blast lost their lives. Countless windows were shattered, including those in most of the elevated trains, the New York Public Library on Fifth Avenue, and J. P. Morgan's Wall Street headquarters. Thousands of hotel guests along Broadway were shaken from their beds and rushed into the streets of midtown, "scantily clad," observed the *Times*. Burning warehouses of wheat, sugar, and tobacco on Black Tom Island sent flames hundreds of feet into the sky. Shrapnel from the piers rained down till dawn, and black smoke hung in the air for days. It was as if the entire region had been seized by the neck and shaken. Even though the United States would not enter the war for another seven months, German sabotage was immediately suspected and never entirely dispelled, despite persuasive reports that the cause of the conflagration had been accidental.

Miraculously, *Liberty* escaped with only minor bruises: broken glass, several bent struts, dings from flying shrapnel, and scores of iron bolts loosened or sheared off. Still, the threat had been too close for comfort. During a different national crisis a century earlier, Francis Scott Key had endured an evening in Baltimore Harbor, fretting over the fate of the star-spangled banner, which he had spied waving intrepidly above Fort McHenry. Echoing the anthem Key had written on that harrowing night, a committee of twentieth-century patriots now pledged to keep the Statue of Liberty shining brighter than ever. Money was raised to install two hundred floodlights around the base so that *Liberty*'s copper-gowned figure could be admired at night from miles around. Additionally, her flame needed brightening. With Bartholdi long dead, General Electric called on Borglum.

Borglum decided that Bartholdi's original mesh of copper had to be removed from the torch. He replaced it with amber-tinted glass, behind which he installed fifteen 500-candlepower lamps. For his service, most of it advisory, he was thanked profusely by the restoration committee and invited to a special banquet with President Wilson. Even more important than the honor and acclaim were the intimate interludes he was granted with the *grande dame* of American monuments.

True, he didn't think much of her beauty. "The figure is squat, overloaded with unnecessary drapery, rooted to her post," he criticized. Nonetheless, *Liberty* moved him, as it does nearly all who are ever in her presence. In 1886, when the Statue of Liberty was first erected, few people had ever seen, much less been inside, a structure so tall. (Until the development of steel-frame construction and the passenger elevator in the 1880s, buildings rarely exceeded five or six stories, although by 1915, the tallest skyscraper in the world, New York's Woolworth Building, was fifty-five stories, 760 feet tall.) Borglum was one of the exceptions. He had climbed the 984-foot-tall Eiffel Tower in Paris and likely ridden the 260-foot-tall Ferris wheel at the Chicago World's Fair. He was an early enthusiast of aviation and had been aloft in balloons and airplanes. But *Liberty* was something quite different. Here was a work of *art* that, by the combination of its sheer enormity and symbolic potency, had become an integral part of the nation's visual, cultural, and now political vocabulary. As a more recent observer has noted, *Liberty* had entered our consciousness "like words of a native tongue."

And there was so much she could teach Borglum, not the least of which was the history of colossal sculpture.

★

There have been "giants in the earth" since Genesis, and they have commanded a conspicuous place in folklore and mythology since the beginning of time: David's Goliath was ... a goliath. Rabelais's Gargantua was gargantuan. The one-eyed Cyclops towered over Odysseus, as did Gulliver over the Lilliputians. The behemoth at the end of Jack's beanstalk was no slouch, either.

Closer to home, folk hulk Paul Bunyan strode the woodlands of America in seven-league boots. His camp stove was so great that cooks greased it by skating across its griddle with hams strapped to their feet. Bunyan's beloved blue ox, Babe, was so big that its hoofprints formed the Great Lakes; its appetite was so insatiable that one day it swallowed its master's stove and died from the world's most enormous attack of heartburn. When Bunyan found the carcass sprawled on the prairie, he simply covered it with dirt and rocks, forming a mound, which, according to legend, became the Black Hills. (And Bunyan's funereal tears became the source of the Cheyenne and Belle Fourche Rivers.)

Colossal sculpture has enjoyed an equally robust life span. The word *colossal* grows from the ancient root, *col*, meaning "a vertical statue." Some of these statues evolved into *col*ossal figures, others into *col*umns to hold up buildings. The sixty-six-foot Sphinx of Giza and the seventy-foot carved guardians of Memnon's temple on the upper Nile are perhaps the most readily recognized colossi. Gone but not forgotten are the oversized statues of Zeus and Athena created by Phidias; the Colossus of Rhodes; and the ancient Buddhas of Bamiyan, Afghanistan—one 175 feet tall, the other 120—demolished in March 2001 by Taliban artillery and scorn. Numerous other colossal Buddhas survive, including a 230-foot Buddha etched into a bluff overlooking the Min River of China, surely the world's largest stone carving. Its head alone is fifty feet; a single, sacred toenail is the length of a grown man. Also of note are the forty-foot-tall bas-reliefs of Bisitun, carved in the fifth century B.C. by Babylonian King Darius I on an escarpment in western Iran, complete with large-print captions in three languages.

And let us not overlook the monolithic heads of Easter Island in the South Pacific or the jumbo topknots of Apollo, Fortuna, Zeus, and Hercules, congregated on a mountainside in eastern Turkey.

The Romans likewise had a tendency to go to extremes, in sculpture as in everything else. They erected a 120-foot-tall statue of Nero near the renowned Coliseum. (Hadrian required twenty-four elephants to tear it down.) The massive stone remnants of imperial figures found in Rome's Capitoline are said to have been the inspiration for Michelangelo's Renaissance *David*, which itself is three times normal human size. Michelangelo also contemplated carving a figure, Rushmore-like, out of an entire Italian mountainside of Carrara marble—an extravaganza that not only anticipated Borglum's Black Hills impulse but fulfilled a much older dream as well: In the fourth century B.C., the Greek sculptor Dinocrates had proposed to Alexander the Great that he whittle Mount Athos into a likeness of his patron on a scale so immense that Alexander could hold a city of ten thousand in one hand and a bowl from which would pour all the rivers of the land in the other.

The emerging nationalism of the eighteenth and nineteenth centuries, along with increased technical know-how, spurred a brand new binge of bigness. Borglum was well aware of sculptor Bertel Thorvaldsen, not only because Thorvaldsen was the first internationally acclaimed Danish artist, but also because in 1821 he had chiseled into the face of a cliff the *Lion of Lucerne*, a thirty-foot memorial to Swiss Guards killed in battle. Fifty years later, France's Bartholdi topped Thorvaldsen, carving a lion forty feet tall at Belfort. By the time Bartholdi got around to designing the Statue of Liberty, he was responding not just to ancient colossi but also to contemporary monuments such as the *Elephant de la Bastille* in Paris, whose size was thrice elephantine, and the *Bavaria* in Munich, a female figure whose swollen head held a room large enough for a half-dozen people.

The first American Dinocrates was Senator Thomas Hart Benton, father of Jessie Benton Fremont, who in 1849 proposed that a towering statue of the New World's Alexander, Christopher Columbus, be carved on a peak somewhere in the Rocky Mountains. Like Dinocrates, Benton never got his wish, and the monumental torch was not officially passed until 1886, when France freighted *Liberty* to New York and lifted her neoclassical lamp "beside the golden door" of her sister republic. It was only fitting that Emma Lazarus entitled her 1888 poem to *Liberty* ("Give me your tired, your poor, / Your huddled masses yearning to breathe free . . . ") "The New Colossus."

Size mattered for a number of reasons. In the days before we came to respect the authority of the atom, the microchip, and DNA's double helix, bigger was unquestionably better. Just as most cultures strive to set their kings atop thrones, they also labor to erect temples to high heaven, from Machu Picchu to Angkor Wat. "There is in the colossal an attraction, a particular charm, to which the theories of ordinary art are hardly applicable," observed Gustave Eiffel, designer of *Liberty*'s trusswork as well as his eponymous tower. "Does one suppose that it is by their *aesthetic* value that the Pyramids have struck man's imagination so strongly?" The sixteenth-century art historian Vasari called the essence of colossalism *gran maniera*—the harmonious marriage of grandness and grandeur.

And that which applied to temples and tombs, obelisks and steeples, also applied to statues. The larger the rendering of god or goddess, Buddha or Christ, the more exalted the tribute. The metaphor is one of ubiquity, omnipotence: God is great because He is great. And the same is true secularly: The might and majesty of princes or their people is proportionate to the size of the monuments honoring them. Alexander, when teased about his lack of stature by the Amazons, purportedly ordered large statues of himself erected. (Hence, we assume, the Dinocratic mountain.) The Romans drove home their imperial message by forging a colossal statue of Jupiter from the armor of their enemies. Size meant triumph; it also implied supernatural qualities and conferred immortality, or at the very least, enduring remembrance. Larger meant larger than life.

And not all the attention was directed at the patron or the subject of the colossus, either. History tends to remember the names of those who execute the big jobs. The case of Phidias is an example of just how bigheaded sculptors of big heads could become. (In Borglum's time, the lesson of colossal hubris resonated emphatically on April 14, 1912, when the Royal Mail Steamer *Titanic*, the humongous, unsinkable ship named for the imposing Titans of Greek mythology, struck an iceberg in the North Atlantic and was swallowed by the waves within three hours, taking fifteen hundred passengers with it.)

Borglum regarded America as colossalism's most deserving heir. "The amazing and expanding character of [American] civilization clearly demand[s] an enlarged dimension—a new scale," he wrote in 1927. With buildings and planes now scraping the sky, canals cleaving continents, and cables tying them back together, he declared with stentorian confidence that "ours will be called the Colossal Age."

In 1916, however, such visions were only just taking shape. To be sure, Borglum had gained a heightened appreciation of the Statue of Liberty's place in history, and he fully comprehended its powerful hold on the American imagination. Even so, on the days he worked on *Liberty*'s lights, he seemed to get a much greater charge from looking *out* of the Statue of Liberty than from itemizing her external virtues or flaws. "I shall never forget ... the strong feelings that came over me as I sat in that hand. That great arm swayed in the wind. The whole panorama of American civilization swept past."

Not long before, he had written a one-sentence letter to influential publisher H. H. McClure: "My one great desire as a boy was to rebuild the world—and I have never outgrown it." Now the world was at his feet, and if he squinted intently, he might just discern, a thousand miles to the south, the bald crown of Stone Mountain, which he had pledged to reshape into the largest sculpture anyone had ever seen.

*

The history of Stone Mountain is in many ways the history of the South. General Sherman had camped near the flank of Stone Mountain on his heartless march to the sea in 1864. Almost as soon as the smoke of his unsparing fires had cleared, Georgians began discussing the installation of some sort of Confederate memorial on Stone Mountain's summit or side. "May we not mate the mountain and the man...?" implored an 1869 verse honoring Vice President of the Confederacy Alexander Stephens, a Georgian. In 1914, William Terrell, an Atlanta attorney, wrote a letter to the *Atlanta Constitution* calling for a Confederate museum in the form of a Greek temple on the top of Stone Mountain and a series of statues set in niches on the mountain's face—a sort of Rebel rendition of Thorvaldsen's *Lion of Lucerne*. Three weeks later, John Temple Graves, editor of the *New York American* and a transplanted Atlantan, suggested that Lorado Taft (creator of Illinois's "Big Injun," *Black Hawk*) sculpt a sixty-foot likeness of Robert E. Lee on the mountain's side. In the end, though, it took the unrivaled champions of southern memorials, the United Daughters of the Confederacy, to get the rock rolling.

In the decades following Appomattox, while the South mended, the North had embarked on an orgy of Civil War monument building. One of the primary missions of the Daughters, founded in 1894, was to even the score. They erected a sixty-foot-tall monument to Jefferson Davis in Richmond, followed by monuments at Shiloh, Arlington, and a second Jefferson Davis monument, this one an immense obelisk near Davis's home in Fairview, Kentucky. A memorial to "faithful slaves," proposed in 1907, took twenty-four years to install at Harper's Ferry, West Virginia. The Daughters even conceived their own version of the Lincoln Highway: the Jefferson Davis National Highway, a commemorative sash across the South from Virginia to San Diego.

The founder and honorary life president of the Atlanta chapter of the United Daughters of the Confederacy was a force of nature by the name of Helen Plane. When she received news that her husband had been killed at Sharpsburg (Antietam) in 1862, she traveled north and searched the battlefield till she found his body, then carried it home for proper burial beneath southern soil. Moved by the suggestions of Terrell and Graves in 1914, Plane, by then eighty-five years old, had written, "Now the time has arrived for us to cease the erection of small and perishable local monuments ... and to concentrate our efforts on one which shall be a shrine for the South and of which all Americans may be justly proud."

There is still some conjecture whether Plane intended to contact Gutzon Borglum or his brother Solon; she had been on the committee that had selected Solon to sculpt a statue of General John Gordon, now on the grounds of the Georgia capitol. Regardless, it was Gutzon who received the letter. He agreed to come to Atlanta in August 1915. Plane greeted him cordially—although she would not shake his hand; by her reckoning, he was a Yankee—and by the time they reached Stone Mountain, she had joined the legion of well-to-do women who hung on the sculptor's every word.

In a speech to the Atlanta Daughters two years later, Borglum described his first encounter with Stone Mountain:

> I was immediately asked, "What are you going to do with it?" I said, "My dear ladies, let me get acquainted with this monster before I suggest anything." The result was I spent a couple of days and a night, climbing over the mountain, walking all around it, and seeing it from all angles.... In the North a sculptor thinks about Lincoln; he thinks about Grant; he thinks about Sheridan. [He] thinks about great individuals; but there is not yet formed in the North one single sentiment that unites the whole people and makes it possible for poet, or sculptor, or artist to conceive a great epic that applies to them all as it applies to one. You have got that in the South.... [W]hen I began to feel this and see that great canvas, the virgin stone ... I saw the thing I had been dreaming of as a sculptor all my life.

Borglum quickly rejected Terrell's idea of a temple with sculpture niches, and likewise Graves's idea of Lee on top. Anything less than colossal would be "like pigmies," he said. Even a twenty-foot head on the side of the mountain would be "like pasting a postage stamp on a barn door."

The plan he presented to Plane and her fellow Daughters several weeks later blew the door right off the barn. He proposed five groups of figures carved in deep relief across a twelve-hundred-foot span of the mountain's eastern face. "There will be hundreds of them," he elaborated. "In the front of the main group will ride the principal figures of the South—Lee, 'Stonewall' Jackson, Jefferson Davis, [Albert Sidney] Johns[t]on and 'Jeb' Stewart. . . . To their right, coming over the crest of the mountain, will appear the main army—cavalry, artillery, and infantry. As the sloping sides of the mountain grow steeper the horses will be shown collected, and finally sliding . . . with hind legs tucked under them." The largest of the figures—Lee, Jackson, and company—would be fifty feet tall.

But he wasn't done yet. In addition to the mountain sculpture, Borglum intended to carve a gallery deep into the base of the mountain. It would be fronted by thirteen columns, one for each Confederate state, and contain a memorial hall to honor the women of the Confederacy and to house Confederate records.

When Sam Venable, the cigar-chomping owner of both the mountain and the granite quarry at its base, asked Borglum how much of Stone Mountain he would use up by the time he was finished, Borglum replied: "The whole of it. . . . I want the sky, too." And when someone asked him to guess the price, he estimated $2 million, the same cost as the Lincoln Memorial—a monument which, in his view, would never be more than "an empty Greek shell."

The Lincoln Memorial, which would not be completed until 1922, was a chronic sore point. Borglum would have loved to have been its sculptor, but now he had to be satisfied with a tribute to the opposition—a consolation prize that he vowed would dwarf all comers. "[A] new Acropolis is about to rise in the southern states," he wrote a friend after returning to Connecticut. But unlike Pope and French's collaboration taking shape in Washington, Borglum's extravaganza in Georgia would convey "all of the fineness, freedom and freshness of the new, Western world." Long before chisels had taken their first bites of Stone Mountain, Borglum was calling it "the eighth wonder," although he predicted it would last longer than the previous seven: "Here is a piece of work that will outlive the Republic, outlive present-day civilization; that will be standing there a million years from now, telling people its story—if there are any people then!"

It took quite a leap of faith to believe that the Confederate memorial would ever be received as a fully accredited *national* memorial. Nevertheless, over the ensuing years, until Mount Rushmore came into sight, Borglum continued to make the case for Stone Mountain's universal appeal, and never once did he contemplate the irony of worshiping both Lincoln *and* the rebel who had bedeviled his beloved president. "The reasons for this war have passed, and the justice of the Southern cause belongs to an earlier time," he explained. "But the character, the high principle of these great men, should not be ignored." Between Lincoln and Lee, he wondered, "who shall say which of them was more sincere? . . . We are simply happy that America can give us a Lincoln and a Lee, and we are thrice happier that we have reached an hour and a day when we can all honor each, all glory in the purity of purpose of each."

Borglum expressed comparable reverence for the Stone Mountain setting. As a rule, mountain sculptors of the past had simply blocked out convenient quadrants of stone and commenced chiseling. By contrast, Borglum took into account the mountain's unique form and scale. "My reason for composing this subject in this manner," he told the *New York Times*, "was to respect the granite mountain as much as possible, both for economy's sake and to maintain its wonderful contour. . . . To the spectator, suddenly coming upon the mountain in dusk or a soft light . . . the general appearance will be that of the natural mountain, over which, silently, this great gray army moves."

Today, many art historians tend to underestimate the sheer organic boldness of Borglum's scheme. More recent (and more voguish) artists, including Michael Heizer, Robert Smithson, and Christo, have gouged mile-long trenches in the Nevada desert, shoveled a spiraling jetty into the Great Salt Lake, and draped colorful curtains across a Colorado canyon. They too are heirs to the ancient tradition of colossalism. But their link to the past is Borglum. Let us not forget that, long before the term "earthwork" entered the artistic lexicon, it was Borglum who reawakened the potency and glory of using not a canvas, not a single block of rock, but *geography* as a medium. Stone Mountain—in concept, if not in final execution—is America's first modern earthwork, an achievement that, in and of itself, warrants a place for Borglum in the first rank of American artists.

From the very start, Stone Mountain engendered conflicting opinions. "The desire of humanity for self-commemoration is insatiable and indefatigable," gibed *The Nation*, a historically northern voice.

> Down near Atlanta stands, and has stood for some million or more years, a monument to the unimaginable forces that drove it upward through the pie-crust of our then debutante mother-earth, a great granite cliff ... which might have gone on in unblemished security brooding over its secrets had not a committee of patriotic Southerners recently called in an eminent Northern sculptor.... No one will quarrel with Mr. Borglum's audacity in seizing the opportunity to sign his name in letters fifty feet high.... [T]he passion of ordinary men, as of geniuses, for immortality must be sated.

As a final swipe, *The Nation* predicted that Stone Mountain would become less of a shrine and more of a tourist trap, Coney Island style. "One wonders," the magazine asked, "did the Pharoahs erect roadhouses furnishing excellent chicken dinners at the feet of their pyramids to attract camel-touring parties?"

(As it turned out, *The Nation* was right on the money. Stone Mountain is now a three-thousand-acre state park visited by four million peo-

ple annually. The rock can be scaled by tram or trail, or admired from
below by train or paddlewheel riverboat on manmade Stone Mountain
Lake. The grounds include an antebellum mansion, waterslide, thirty-
six holes of golf, sundry museums, and a surfeit of gift shops. Its 732-
bell carillon was acquired from the 1964 New York World's Fair as a gift
from Dixie's own Medici, Coca-Cola. Most of Stone Mountain's special
events have a decidedly Confederate, if postmodern, twist—for example, a recent display of costumes from the movie *Gone with the Wind*
and annual Civil War reenactments on Plantation Meadow. Not to be
outdone, the park's Lasershow Spectacular fires a "Liquid Flame Can-
non" nightly during summer months. As for those pharaonic feasts,
today's visitor to Stone Mountain can sup on a three-piece fried-
chicken dinner for six dollars. For the snack-minded, there are Depot
Funnel Cakes and Peachtree Pork Rinds.)

In general, though, public taste was not offended by Stone Mountain's bombast. The more pressing question in the public mind was not
whether Stone Mountain should undergo a face job, but *how* Borglum
would accomplish it. Separate from the extraordinary logistics of building stairs, suspending scaffolding and catwalks, hooking up hoists and
electricity, hauling air compressors (for pneumatic drills), and hiring
skilled carvers was the more basic problem of how to enlarge the original design and transfer it to the side of the mountain. Borglum thought
he knew, but really he didn't. His initial methodology was akin to the
old plainsman's technique of squatting beneath a horse's belly and
measuring a mile as the amount of horizon bracketed by the horse's
fore- and hind legs. "I shall build a studio about a hundred feet long,
squarely on the axis on the face of the mountain, and from three quarters of a mile to one mile from its base," Borglum explained to the *New
York Times.* "In the side of this studio I shall have a window of such
length as will cover that portion of the mountain which I can see standing comfortably against the opposite inner wall. . . . I shall then lay the
window out to scale . . . and I shall draw in my entire work on the win-

dow itself. Then, by a little imagination, force it back on the mountain. . . . By moving towards the window I can increase it in scale, or moving away from it, reduce it." Needless to say, he was a long way from a solid solution. Nevertheless, the Daughters were taken with his scheme and his optimism and gave their approval.

Money, though, came more slowly. The Daughters had raised a few thousand dollars, and Borglum was so sanguine about the project that he agreed to pay his own expenses for a while. But the net would have to be cast wide and deep if they were ever going to raise two million.

One of the early fundraising schemes was both innovative and portentous. In December 1915, Helen Plane wrote to Borglum, "The 'Birth of a Nation' will give us a percentage of next Monday's matinee." *Birth of a Nation* was D. W. Griffith's sprawling silent film of the Civil War and Reconstruction. Based on *The Clansman*, a novel and then stage play by Thomas Dixon, it was arguably the very first epic film. "It is like writing history with lightning," President Wilson exclaimed after a screening at the White House—the first movie ever shown at that address—and his remark was no exaggeration. *Birth of a Nation* not only altered the medium of motion pictures forever; its message sparked a world of controversy.

"[W]e demand as a right the liberty to show the dark side of wrong, that we may illuminate the bright side of virtue." These introductory words frame a tale of two families, one southern, one northern, as they weather the Civil War. The first half of *Birth* presents the battle of Petersburg, the assassination of Lincoln, and Lee's surrender at Appomattox. What most viewers remember, however, is the second part, "Reconstruction," in which white carpetbaggers and freed slaves band together to turn the South into Sodom. Drunkenness, miscegenation, mob rule, and a general lack of chivalry prevail—that is, until the Ku Klux Klan rides to the rescue, routs the northern scalawags, burns a few crosses, and lynches an uppity Negro.

Birth of a Nation, which opened in January 1915, grossed an unprecedented $60 million in its first run. After the NAACP sought an injunction against the film on the grounds that its inflammatory content threatened public safety, black safety in particular (to allege anything so obvious as racial slander would have been a waste of time), director Griffith, whose father had been a Confederate colonel, dressed actors in Klan robes and paraded them on horseback in front of a Los Angeles theater.

The hoopla surrounding *Birth of a Nation*, not to mention its polemical plot, was not lost on thirty-five-year-old Joe Simmons, a former Methodist minister turned garter salesman turned "colonel" in the benign Woodmen of the World. On Thanksgiving 1915, three months after Borglum's initial visit to Georgia, Simmons and a dozen like-minded friends lugged a sixteen-foot wooden cross to the top of Stone Mountain. They built a crude altar of granite boulders, draped it with an American (not Confederate) flag, and opened the Bible to the twelfth chapter of Romans ("So we, being many, are one body. . . . "). By the light of a "fiery cross," Simmons, having already minted the honorific of Imperial Wizard for himself, swore in the charter members of the revived Knights of the Ku Klux Klan, a name that had lain dormant since Reconstruction.

Birth of a Nation opened in Atlanta the following week, accompanied by a thirty-piece orchestra. "The picture is vindicated by historical facts," professed the *Constitution*, "and does not attempt to misinterpret or warp these facts for the purpose of dragging from their graves prejudices that have been dead long since." Maybe so, but the film was sensational just the same, and on opening night, the sold-out house exploded. "Never before . . . has an Atlanta audience so freely given vent to its emotions," observed the *Constitution*'s man on the aisle. Toward the end of the film, when a mounted Klansman brandishes a burning cross, the Atlantans lost all restraint. "Many rise from their seats," the paper reported. "With the roar of [orchestral] thunder a shout goes up. Freedom is here. Justice is at hand! Retribution has arrived!"

In Helen Plane's cheery letter to Borglum, announcing that the local theater had agreed to donate a percentage of its *Birth* box office, she had added: "Since seeing this wonderful and beautiful picture of Reconstruction in the South I feel that it is due to the Ku-Klux Klan which saved us from negro domination and carpet-bag rule, that it be immortalized on Stone Mountain. Why not represent a small group of them in their *nightly* uniform approaching in the distance?"

Whether Borglum had seen the film at this point is unclear, and even though he surely must have had at least passing knowledge of the Klan's historic canon of white supremacy and racial purity, it seems unlikely that he was aware of the recent second coming of "the Invisible Empire." And so, needing all the help he could get and not wishing to hurt the feelings of his dedicated and remarkably spry patroness, he added a Klan altar to his plans for the base of Stone Mountain.

In 1916, Borglum spent a great deal of time at the mountain, working on his design and drumming up interest among southern business leaders, politicians, and anyone else with a soft spot for the Lost Cause. He put nearly all of his other sculpture work on the back burner and eventually brought his family to live in a donated house several miles from the mountain. It was here that his second child was born, a daughter, Mary Ellis, named for her mother and the doctor who delivered her on March 25—Borglum's forty-ninth birthday.

The ceremony to mark the start of work on the Confederate National Memorial at Stone Mountain was scheduled for May 20, 1916. A brave assistant had been lowered over the side of the mountain in a harness and had pounded iron spikes into the granite, from which was then hung a twenty-by-thirty-foot flag—Confederate this time. The ceremony culminated with the presentation of a warranty deed by the Venable family, granting the Stone Mountain Confederate Monumental Association use of the mountain and ten acres at the base. The deed generously gave the association twelve years to finish the memorial, or else the land would revert back to the Venables.

Three weeks later, Borglum was off to Chicago on his quixotic mission to engineer Theodore Roosevelt's nomination for president. While he was away and throughout the summer and fall, workers clambered over the mountain, erecting stairways and platforms in preparation for actual carving the following year. That November and December, Borglum revamped the lamp of *Liberty*. And then, just as he was preparing to throw himself into the project of a lifetime, the bottom dropped out. On April 6, 1917, the United States declared war on Germany, and the nation, once divided, now pulled together to save Europe and the world. Work at Stone Mountain was put on hold. Borglum and his family returned to Connecticut.

Ever the warrior, but never a soldier, Borglum was keen to see action. A year earlier, in the spring of 1916, when Theodore Roosevelt had talked of mustering an independent force of Americans to quell raids by Pancho Villa and his Mexican rebels along the Texas and New Mexico borders, Borglum had volunteered for duty. "I have spent half of my life in the open," he told the Colonel, "and can do anything that falls to the lot of the Rough Rider." In fact, both Roosevelt and Borglum were too old for combat, and both were turned down when they put in for service in Europe. In his place, Roosevelt sent four sons, one of whom was killed, two more wounded. Borglum, for his part, decided to mount a war of his own creation at home.

Short of actually fighting, he thought that the best way to contribute was to share his knowledge of flying. In 1906, only three years after the Wright brothers had made their famous flight at Kitty Hawk, North Carolina, Borglum had joined the Aero Club of New York. Two years later, in September 1908, he had represented the club at Fort Myer, outside Washington, when Orville Wright demonstrated his newest plane for the army. "Nothing I have ever seen is comparable," Borglum wrote at the time. "There is no action of the 'wings,' so you do not think of birds. . . . It is inconceivable, yet having seen it, it now seems the most natural thing in the air." On the day of the visit to Fort Myer, Wright had remained airborne for more than an hour, a new record that was clocked in bold strokes of white paint—fifty, fifty-five, then sixty minutes—on a nearby roof so Wright could read the time from above. "Man has put safely and forever his shod heel into the blue heavens, and glides about as on ice," Borglum exulted that evening. "Wright . . . will rub out the boundaries of the world."

After his unforgettable day at Fort Myer and throughout his continuing involvement with the Aero Club, Borglum came to fancy himself an expert on aviation and airplane design. "There are no principles related to flying heavier-than-air machines that I am not thoroughly familiar with," he once bragged, adding, "I feel as Da Vinci did." Between 1908 and 1917, he found time to work up a number of designs for propellers, fuselages, something called an "air brake," and an improved engine that funneled air through the nose of the plane and out the tail. Even so, his technical know-how was sketchy at best, and, if anything, he relied on his talent as an artist—with a little help from his experience as fisherman and frontiersman. Airplanes, he explained in a long letter to the Smithsonian Institution, should look more like fish than kites. Specifically, Borglum suggested salmon or trout, species with "the ability to live in conditions similar to air moving at the rate of 60 or 70 or 80 miles an hour." Mixing metaphors, or role models anyway, he then advised that the fins of his airborne fish should imitate the feathers of an arrow: "As a boy I aided the Indians in making arrows and learned . . . that three feathers were necessary"—a flighty notion, perhaps, but one that would soon become flight gospel. Borglum was very much in earnest, and he filed patent applications for a number of his designs—none of which were approved. In November 1917, he even considered opening his own propeller factory to boost war production, a scheme that never got off the ground either.

That same month, Borglum made a trip to Ohio, ostensibly to meet with Lester Barlow, owner of a company that was building a hoist for Stone Mountain. Barlow was not your ordinary industrialist. He too was a flying fanatic, a free spirit with an inventor's brain and bravado. He had flown and galloped about Mexico with Pancho Villa's rebels for a year and a half. Then, with the help of his brother and the blessing of the U.S. government, he had developed a series of bombs; up till then, the military had regarded airplanes merely as aids to observation and communication, not as killing machines, and no one knew anything about aerial bombardment. Barlow's greatest hits included the wickedly effective Barlow Bomb, which exploded five feet above the ground, and the India Rubber Bomb, which bounced diabolically before detonation. Barlow and Borglum became fast friends, initially through the Stone Mountain connection, then through their common interest in airplanes, and ultimately through their mutual penchant for political rabble-rousing.

After visiting Barlow in Cleveland, Borglum then dropped down to Dayton to tour the factory of the Dayton Wright Airplane Company, which was busy meeting orders for thousands of war planes. Borglum no doubt had entrée through his connection with the Wrights. In addition, he knew Colonel Edward A. Deeds, one of the founders of Dayton Wright and a member of the government's powerful Aircraft Production Board, which oversaw all wartime procurement and manufacturing. It was Deeds who had commissioned Borglum to sculpt the ill-fated Wright brothers memorial in 1912, for which Borglum had been only partially paid. He and Deeds had renewed their acquaintance earlier in 1917, when Borglum had carved a marble bust of Deeds's deceased son. Borglum had also discussed designing an elaborate mausoleum for the boy.

We do not know if Borglum pitched any of his own aviation ideas to the Dayton Wright staff on this particular trip; we don't even know if Deeds was present. But we do know that Borglum was given a thorough tour of the aircraft factory. And while the details of the inspection are now lost, judging from Borglum's extreme reaction to what he observed that day, he might as well have been dropped behind enemy lines.

He was so alarmed by what he had seen, in fact, that he rushed to Washington and proceeded directly to the White House, where he demanded, without prior appointment, to meet with President Wilson immediately. Wilson was a friend, but he was busy prosecuting a war, and Borglum was turned away with the advice that he state his business in writing. On November 22, he wrote to Wilson's secretary Joseph Tumulty, alleging that "self-interested groups," through "cheap, grandiose projects," were steering the aircraft industry toward inevitable "disaster and scandal." Details would have to wait until he talked to the president in person.

Depending on whose point of view one adopts, the events of the next ten months cast Borglum in the role of either Horatio at the Bridge or Alice in Wonderland. The so-called aircraft scandal of 1918 was not a fiction, to be sure, but it had all the elements of a nickelodeon whodunit—except, of course, that tens of thousands of lives were at stake, and by war's end, the government's appropriation for aircraft had exceeded one-and-a-half billion dollars. And regardless of how Borglum was listed in the credits, he became the central character in a drama with a global audience.

The plot thickened this way: Wilson, who had spent so much of his presidency trying to keep America out of war, soon became frustrated by the aircraft industry's sluggishness in delivering planes. Accordingly, on January 2, 1918, he invited Borglum to Washington "to lay the whole matter frankly and fully before the Secretary [of War, Newton Baker], and *by your own investigation* discover the facts. . . . The Secretary of War assures me that he will be delighted to *clothe you with full authority* to get to the bottom of every situation." (Emphasis added.)

Borglum interpreted Wilson's letter as carte blanche to poke his nose and point his finger anywhere he pleased. By January 21, he had toured several more aircraft factories, interviewed scores of public officials and private experts, and claimed to have uncovered a "distinct conspiracy" of "profiteering and graft" perpetrated by the "Aircraft Trust" and condoned by an administration "benumbed by some frightful poison." The United States, he warned, was facing the gravest danger in its history.

At the beginning of the war, America's airpower had been virtually nonexistent. Within a month the Aircraft Production Board had been formed, answering to the Army Signal Corps (planes as messengers still), and because no one in the country had any experience mass-producing high-performance aircraft of any sort, the job logically fell to the manufacturers of automobiles, who, needless to say, were only too willing to serve their country and meanwhile grab a slice of the billion-dollar pie. The decision was made to import the actual planes from Europe—most notably Britain's De Havilland 4—but the production board deemed European-made engines unsatisfactory. The board decided that if America was going to rule the air, it had to have an engine of its own design and manufacture. On May 29, two engineers, one from the Packard Motor Company in Detroit, the other from a smaller aircraft shop in San Francisco, closeted themselves in the Willard Hotel in Washington. Five days later, they emerged, bloodshot, with designs for an eight- and twelve-cylinder engine, promptly dubbed the "Liberty."

The production board, which was stacked with auto executives, promptly awarded contracts to Packard, Lincoln, Ford, and General Motors, among others. Dayton Wright would do a major portion of the assembly and testing, and the ignition systems would be built by Dayton Engineering Laboratories Company (Delco)—whose presidency Colonel Deeds had recently resigned (transferring his stock to his wife's name). The modern era of multimillion-dollar defense contracting had dawned.

Borglum thought the whole arrangement stunk mightily. He dismissed the Liberty engine's immaculate birth as a "fairy tale." On the contrary, he insisted, America's planes were "flaming coffins." Manufacturing was "floundering in ignorance and incompetency." Worse than the misfeasance and malfeasance was the nonfeasance. Factories were lying to the government about productivity, willfully deceiving the public by shipping empty crates to Europe to boost morale and cover up their abject inability to turn out finished, reliable planes.

Borglum brought to bear his full repertoire of saber-rattling and name-calling. He fought hard, and he also fought sly and dirty, never equivocating, never backing down. All his evidence was anecdotal, and for reasons of security, he refused to disclose any details to anyone but the president. He was not so secretive, however, that the gist of his allegations did not leak to a thirsty press. The Roosevelt in him had blamed the aviation "saturnalia" on the "air monopoly." The Ruskin in him had identified the "disease of America" as "quantity production."

Going one step further, he soon identified the enemy as a criminal "ring" and called for "immediate seizure of the manufactories." (He also asked for authority to issue his own subpoenas.) He excoriated Secretary of War Baker and General George Squier, chief of the Signal Corps, but reserved most of his calumny for Colonel Deeds. At a time when the nation's jingoism conjured Hun spies and sympathizers at every beer hall and Lutheran supper, Borglum announced that Deeds's real name was actually Dietz. "He is of German extraction," he informed Wilson, confident that he had uncovered a double agent. Naturally, he explained, "[I]t is unfair to ask German blood, though born in America, to be as prompt as war demands in the execution of their orders against their Fatherland." Deeds's "powerful Teutonic personality" had turned Dayton into "the center of evil in the aircraft program." While raking in huge profits through personal investments—recently divested, but only nominally—Deeds was simultaneously scuttling the war effort by impeding airplane production, or so Borglum alleged.

It got zanier still. Borglum claimed that he was being "dogged by agents" who had tapped his phone, stolen his letters, and threatened his sources. Later he would state that someone had fired a shot at him—whether to scare or kill, he could not say—while he sat at an outdoor café. He typed up tell-all memoranda and locked them in safe deposit boxes in three different cities. He even hired his own private detective for a short while.

By April, Wilson had pulled the plug, perturbed by Borglum's grandstanding and below-the-belt tactics. "I am afraid that you have for some time been under a serious misapprehension," Wilson advised. "I never at any time constituted you an official investigator. I merely gave you the right to look into the matter on your own motion. . . . [W]e have at no time regarded you as the official representative of the administration." Without Wilson's imprimatur, Borglum was effectively declawed, although he would never be silenced. The newspapers continued to give him all the attention he wanted until finally Congress had no choice but to conduct its own inquiry into the charges now being chorused by thousands of overwrought Americans in every state.

Borglum was elated, believing that public hearings would vanquish doubters and treasonous profiteers in one stroke. The papers still referred to him as "Borglum the artist," but it was clear, to him at least, that he was much more than that.

Too quickly, however, he discovered that he was the one in the cross hairs. Appearing before the Senate Military Affairs Committee, Borglum refused to reveal the damning details of his confidential report to the president, citing reasons of security but also exposing himself to suggestions that his attack had been all thunder, no lightning. Meanwhile, his skeptics, including several senators aligned with Deeds, Baker, and Squier, produced a sheaf of affidavits that endeavored to gut Borglum's credibility and shame his motives. His charges against Deeds were discounted as a personal vendetta that dated back to the 1912 Dayton sculpture commission. Borglum was portrayed as a spurned suitor, whose various aircraft designs had been brushed aside by the Production Board. Further, the Senate produced witnesses who claimed that Borglum's true intent was to discredit the manufacturers in order to make room for an aircraft company that he hoped to found.

When it came Deeds's turn to testify, he shrugged off the aspersions against his name and heritage. His great grandfather, also named Deeds, had emigrated from England to Pennsylvania. Borglum could only wriggle and fume as Deeds told the Senate and an attentive gallery that the artist had approached Deeds the previous summer with yet another of his harebrained schemes for a new aircraft. What sort of aircraft, Deeds was asked. Suppressing a grin, he recalled something about a "fish plane."

"Drop Air Bomb on Borglum Now" bellowed that evening's *New York Telegram*. The next morning's *Globe* was only slightly more humane: "Thus far [Borglum], although shouting graft charges against the aviation management, has furnished no specific evidence comparable to that exploded in his own vicinity. . . . The public will be indisposed to believe that Mr. Borglum is a deliberate and designing villain. It prefers to hold the theory that he is a fool, or even a lunatic. The way he compares himself to Phidias, Michel Angelo, and da Vinci must raise among his friends gloomy apprehensions concerning his mental future."

The headline above the *Globe* editorial had spelled "The End of Gutzon," but the press jackals had underestimated their prey. Borglum called the campaign to shoot the messenger a "scurrilous frame-up" and vowed to battle on. "Nothing will stop me but the firing squad," he wrote an ally in New York. And, in a way, it was he who fired the last shot. On May 15, while the Senate was preparing to issue a report on Borglum's charges and the countercharges against him—a report that, when finally released in August, managed to inflame the public further while distilling little useful truth from the aircraft mess—President Wilson announced that he had requested the attorney general's office to open its own investigation "in order that the guilty, if there be any such, may be promptly and vigorously prosecuted and that the reputations of those who have been attacked may be protected in case the charges are groundless."

To head the probe, Wilson appointed his defeated rival, Charles Evans Hughes, who, before becoming governor of New York and associate justice of the Supreme Court, had proven his Progressive mettle by ferreting out corruption in public utilities and the insurance industry. Borglum was chapped that Hughes had usurped his pulpit, but thrilled when it was leaked that Hughes was on the verge of corroborating many of Borglum's accusations. Finally, on October 31, just eleven days before Armistice, Hughes dropped his own bomb. His 180-page report exonerated the Liberty engine, Baker of the War Department, and Squier of the Signal Corps, but painted Deeds as a fox in the henhouse. Reciting a litany of lying, logrolling, and profiteering, Hughes recommended that Deeds be court-martialed.

Although the Army Board of Review ultimately declined to follow through on Hughes's suggestion, Borglum felt exonerated. He may have wished that the Hughes investigation had gone further, deeper, and that its recommendations had been harsher, but the proof was in the open at last: The American aircraft industry, which before the war had been in the hands of daring entrepreneurs and artful inventors, was now in the clutches of huge, plodding corporations. And if there was any poetic justice, it came in 1919, when Borglum's sculpture of a winged man, originally intended as the Wright brothers monument in Dayton, was installed at the University of Virginia as a memorial to James McConnell, the first American flyer killed in the war.

Looking back, the one thing that cut Borglum to the quick during the aircraft investigation was the doubt cast on his loyalty. In his initial letter to Woodrow Wilson, he had stated, "My reason for wishing to discuss aeronautics with the President was and remains because of a desire deeper than any I have outside my immediate family's happiness, that of helping the country at this hour." But as patriotic as Borglum plainly was, once again he had left himself open to attack by blurring his high-minded ideals with personal grudges. A similar conflict of interest arose over Borgland, the mortgage for which was still held by Eugene Meyer.

Since donating Borglum's Lincoln bust to the Capitol, Meyer had become an important player in Washington. A multimillionaire, he had left investment banking, moved to Washington, and volunteered his services to the Wilson administration. Meyer turned down a position on the Aircraft Production Board because he owned stock in Fisher Body, which had gone into the manufacture of plane fuselages, and instead accepted the newly created position of Assistant Secretary of War for Air—another of Wilson's dollar-a-year men and a strange stroke of kismet indeed.

Borglum, too, was paying his own way in Washington. He estimated that he had spent $17,000 of his own money on the aircraft investigation. But unlike Meyer, he had little savings to fall back on, and he had yet to be paid for his preliminary work at Stone Mountain. His wallet was pinched further when he invited two hundred Czechoslovak freedom fighters to camp and train on his property before heading to the European front. Since acquiring Borgland in 1910, Borglum had fallen behind on his mortgage. Now he gave up paying altogether.

When Meyer pressed him for money, Borglum jumped to the basest conclusion. He asserted that a vengeful Secretary Baker had sicced Meyer on him. "[Meyer] came to me ... and demanded all my papers and records, and with that demand told me I would have to pay my mortgage," Borglum cursed. "I will not compromise with what I know to be evil." Meyer, the wealthy philanthropist, ascendant power broker, and former friend, was now simply "that Shylock."

Mary Borglum wrote to Meyer, attempting to make peace between the two men, but to no avail. Meyer's reply to her chastised Borglum for "running around in his harum scarum way" when he should have been concentrating on his art. Borglum's recent meddling in public affairs had only put him "out of joint with the world and you think it is the world's fault." And then came the sternest blow of all, one that would resonate far into the future: "Gutzon has failed to hold a single one of the many sincere friends he has had at one time or another.... Your letter appears to be written under the impression that I care for Gutzon; I would be deluding you if I left you under that impression. He has alienated my friendship with a long series of acts and ... attitudes toward me which have not failed to render me entirely indifferent, to say the least." When Mary asked for Meyer's forbearance with the delinquent mortgage, he declined: "Even if I were to do the best that could be done, and even do very well for him, I have no confidence that I would receive his thanks or fail to be victim of new abuses with regards to actions intended to be friendly."

After the war, Borglum did not return to Stone Mountain immediately. For one thing, the money was not yet in place to fund a full-scale operation, and Borglum desperately needed money himself. The $12,000 for the McConnell commission helped, and over the next year, he contracted to reprise two of his other works. He carved another Lincoln bust, a mate to the one in the Capitol, for Samuel Colt, chairman of United States Rubber, but when Colt would not meet Borglum's $10,000 asking price, Borglum settled for $5,000, then borrowed an additional $5,000 from Colt, leaving three smaller sculptures for collateral. He needed the loan to finance a trip to Havana, where, against his sworn policy, he entered a competition for a monument to Cuban revolutionary hero Máximo Gómez. Armed with a letter from General Leonard Wood, another hero of the 1898 war, Borglum spent several weeks pursuing the $200,000 prize, only to lose out in the end.

His fortunes reversed dramatically the following year. He was offered $50,000 to carve a second Sheridan equestrian to be placed in Lincoln Park in Chicago. And then the Van Horn estate, which had commissioned the *Seated Lincoln* in 1910, awarded him the contract for another monument in Newark, an enormous memorial to "the military life of the Soldiers and Sailors of the United States." Payment, in installments, would be $100,000. "Thank God," Borglum said with an exultant sigh, "I am [finally] squaring myself with the world."

Another major distraction—this one sad, but not without its own silver lining—was the death of Theodore Roosevelt. Roosevelt had never fully recovered from the illness he had contracted in South America, and his heart still ached from the loss of his youngest son, Quentin. Roosevelt died at Oyster Bay on January 6, 1919. He was sixty years old. Although his popularity had waned in his later years—H. L. Mencken had written him off as "blatant, crude, overly confidential, devious, tyrannical, vainglorious, sometimes quite childish"—Roosevelt still retained a broad retinue of loyal, if nostalgic, supporters. "Roosevelt was the Man of Action," eulogized educator John Dewey in the February issue of *The Dial*, "in that he incarnated his time. He preached the strenuous life and practiced what he taught. The age was delirious with activity. It wanted not only action but action done with such a resounding thump and boom that all men should sit up and take notice. . . . He endued the cause of the reformer with the glamour of virility and vitality."

Within weeks of Roosevelt's death, a memorial association had been formed. Within months, it had raised more than a million dollars for the threefold purpose of perpetuating Roosevelt's "spirit of Americanism"; creating a memorial park at Oyster Bay; and last but not least, erecting "a monumental memorial in Washington which will rank with the Washington Monument and the Lincoln Memorial."

Borglum had long ago forgiven Roosevelt for the "betrayal" of 1916, and Roosevelt had vouched for Borglum's character during the aircraft scandal. "What? Borglum a traitor?" Roosevelt had reportedly scoffed. "If he isn't a patriot, there aren't any." Borglum responded in kind. "[N]o man in the past century so inspired and will continue to inspire his countrymen," he wrote in the *Stamford Advocate*. "Roosevelt stands [as] the symbol father, public servant and a model of individual responsibility. As a citizen to the state, few men have appeared who will be missed more profoundly; because even those who resisted him admired the fine lone citizen and soldier he remained to the end." In a separate letter to the *New York Herald*, written two days after Roosevelt's death, Borglum proposed carving a colossal equestrian sculpture of Roosevelt on the Palisades of the Hudson River, north of New York City. "Could a more stately or yet a more peaceful spot be found?" he implored.

Location, though, was not a critical issue. More important to Borglum was making sure that he was included in any plans for a Roosevelt monument. When the Roosevelt Memorial Association announced its preference for Washington, D.C., he rallied quickly to the cause. He carved and cast an edition of small Roosevelt busts, donating the proceeds to the association. Meanwhile, he promoted himself as a candidate for the larger memorial. To bolster his bona fides, he reminded the association just how deeply Roosevelt had admired the Lincolns in Newark and the Capitol and passed along a remark Roosevelt had made to him a few years earlier. "I don't want a statue of me until I'm gone," Borglum had the Colonel saying, "and then I want *you* to make it."

Borglum had yet another reason for not hurrying back to Stone Mountain: His blood was still up. The aircraft investigation had deepened his antipathy toward the "entrenched political privilege" of the eastern machine. And it wasn't simply a case of old Progressive principles dying hard. Borglum's enemies now had faces—crooked, bloated, villainous faces—and he nursed an abiding passion to get even with those who had ignored, defied, and humiliated him during the war. The Bull Moose Party had faltered long before the Bull Moose himself, but Borglum's newest chum, the adventurous bombardier, Lester Barlow, was urging him to sniff the latest breeze of reform coming out of the West.

If nothing else, it was a way to get back into national politics, a cruel arena, but one he sorely loved.

Progressivism would take different forms over the years. Born in the farm states in the late nineteenth century, it had moved into the cities. Then, after the splintering of Roosevelt's national crusade, agrarian Progressivism had withdrawn westward again, reseeding itself in the heartland, awaiting another season. In the years leading up to the war, a group of North Dakota wheat farmers had become fed up with the hegemony of out-of-state brokers, bankers, and railroaders who, they judged, were guilty of systematically downgrading and underweighing their grain, fixing prices, and gouging them on shipping and elevator storage. Eight out of ten North Dakotans lived on farms or in small towns; nearly all were no-nonsense, first- or second-generation immigrants—Scandinavian mostly—who could stand harsh weather and hard work but would not suffer the tread of another man's boot on their necks.

The story is told that when a delegation of frustrated farmers sought redress from the state legislature, they were ordered to "go home and slop the hogs." The farmers huffed from the capital only to storm back in 1915 as the Nonpartisan League, choiring a new slogan, "The Goat That Can't Be Got." The NPL was no barnyard joke, however. Within a year, it had seized control of virtually every branch of state government. The strategy was to remain *non*partisan and support candidates of the two dominant parties who concurred, or, through the promise of NPL block votes, could be persuaded to concur, with the League's pro-producer, anti–"Big Biz" agenda. In the November 1916 election, League candidates won every state office but treasurer, including three state supreme court judgeships and ninety-nine of 138 legislative seats. In 1918, the NPL collected even more seats and added the state's three congressmen to its fold. Through efficient collection of dues, the League funded a newspaper to keep far-flung members informed and mobilized. A platoon of hot-blooded speakers crisscrossed the plains in League-owned Fords, spreading the Nonpartisan word at picnics and town meetings.

The message was heard in other states as well. By 1919, the League boasted two hundred thousand members, mostly in the sparsely populated Dakotas, Minnesota, Montana, Nebraska, and other breadbasket states. (Charles A. Lindbergh, congressman, farmer, and father of the soon-to-be-famous aviator, ran as the League's candidate for governor of Minnesota in 1918. He lost, one of the few disappointments of that otherwise stunning year.) The rest of the country paid close attention to this prairie storm, wondering if, like the Greenback, Granger, and Populist movements of an earlier day, it had the makings of a national juggernaut.

The Nonpartisan League was just what Borglum was looking for in 1919. As a native of the West, he idealized its wide-open landscape and high principles as the antidote to eastern grime and venality. Nor did it hurt that Dakotans were Norse before they were Nonpartisan. And the image of a prowling, growling underdog evoked the old fighting spirit of the Progressive Party. If Borglum had doubts, all he had to do was listen to the League's rhetoric. Take, for instance, a speech given by the NPL's demagogic president Arthur Townley at the opening of the 1919 North Dakota legislative session. "For the first time in the history of the United States," Townley proclaimed, "the lawmaking power of a sovereign state has been taken away from the exploiters and devourers, the beasts that prey, and has been placed in the hands of white men—men who have a noble purpose, who are raised from out themselves."

Borglum's files do not reveal the precise details of when and how he first joined the NPL, other than the fact that Lester Barlow was becoming active in the league at about the time the two met. At any rate, by the summer of 1920, Borglum was barnstorming North Dakota as one of the league's speakers. On and off over the next two years, he dedicated weeks and perhaps months of his time stumping for NPL candidates and causes. And while his speeches are lost to us, he did author a series of articles that melded, somewhat haphazardly, his early philippics on craftsmanship ("Nothing in America is now made for anybody, nor is it the product of personal taste") and his shriller Deeds-era tirades against the "big-bellied, red-necked plutocrats." At times he slid perilously close to Socialist dogma ("In itself, capital boasts no soul"), but more often he held to the safer ground of regional righteousness ("The West has risen again ... and the South will help!").

Mostly, though, he seemed happy to be back in the rough-and-tumble of the hustings, and he undoubtedly relished playing big frog in a comparatively small pond. As the league's chairman in the East (where it had numerous allies but few members), he was proud to hand-deliver the league's endorsement of Senator Warren G. Harding, the Republican candidate for president in 1920. And to some extent he got to count coup on Congress, which had treated him so rudely during the aircraft scandal. "I did more to elect [reformist] Senator [Robert] Howell of Nebraska than any other living man," he bragged of those years. "I had the honor and pleasure of driving [George] Chamberlain of Oregon out of office, as I had the pleasure of driving out [Porter] McCumber of [North] Dakota."

Hyperbole aside, whatever political cockiness he had lost during the war, he regained during his Nonpartisan filibustering. And by the time the Nonpartisan League faltered in the mid-1920s—tarred (in some cases, literally) by the Red Scare and sapped by the unrelenting dominance of urban life over rural—Borglum had already moved on to other things, taking with him a renewed appreciation of the West as not just the grassroots, but the very bedrock, of American democracy. He would return sooner than he knew.

At last, time had come to turn his full attention to Stone Mountain. His assistant, Jesse Tucker, had been on the job since the summer of 1919, rebuilding stairs and scaffolding that had fallen into disrepair. Borglum arrived in the autumn of 1922. Over the next two years, he accomplished some astonishing feats, the first of which was figuring out how to transfer his image from model to mountain. He came up with the notion of projecting a stereopticon slide onto the rock face at night, allowing men who hung from the mountain in harnesses to trace the shapes with white paint. The only catch was that the maximum range of existing projectors was three hundred feet. Borglum needed to throw his image, with clarity, one thousand feet. With the help of a Connecticut photographer, he designed his own projector, then took the specifications to Edward S. Porter in New York.

Porter was already a bit of a legend. He had worked for Thomas Edison for fifteen years, developing the first motion-picture cameras, and in 1903, he had made *The Great Train Robbery*, one of the first westerns and the first movie to use close-ups and pan shots. Happily for Borglum, Porter had quit moviemaking in 1915 to focus once again on technology. The projector that Porter made for Borglum weighed nearly a ton. Borglum set it up a quarter mile from the face of Stone Mountain. From that distance, a drawing on a two-inch-square slide covered an acre of granite. Thirty gallons of white paint and a few dizzy spells later, Borglum's untrained trapeze artists had delineated the three central figures, Lee, Jackson, and Davis. (Jeb Stuart and Albert Sidney Johnston had been dropped.) The plan was to complete these before undertaking the rest of the cavalcade. Lee rode in the middle of the three. The distance from the top of his hat to the hoof of his horse was 120 feet—two Sphinxes tall. His head alone was twenty-one feet; his noble nostril, three. The total width, from the ear of Jackson's horse to the tail of Davis's, was 240 feet. Borglum anticipated carving a relief twenty feet deep, which would require removing an estimated three hundred thousand cubic feet of stubborn granite. All this while suspended four hundred feet above the ground.

To remove the stone, Borglum set men to drilling with jackhammers. The work required strength, courage, and a good degree of finesse. The method was to drill a honeycomb of holes, then apply wedges to break off the perforated rock, not unlike tearing a coupon from a mammoth magazine. Despite the availability of experienced rock men—the Venable quarry had been a going concern since slave days—Borglum quickly realized that it would take an Egypt's worth of slaves to complete this modern colossus in his lifetime. His thoughts turned to dynamite. "The general idea is that high explosives can be used only to destroy," he explained. But if a gun could explode a shell without ruining the gun, why couldn't he explode rock without ruining the entire mountain? He consulted an engineer who happened to be visiting from Belgium and who had recently used dynamite to enlarge a tunnel's diameter by mere inches. Following the Belgian's instructions, Borglum discovered that he could remove rock by as much as a ton or as little as an inch at a time—in the latter instance, employing charges as small as half an ounce. Never before had anyone attempted to sculpt with dynamite.

One final technical hurdle remained: Working on such a grand scale, hugging the cliff, it was hard to get perspective, even harder to get the rock to honor the nuance of the model. Borglum worked out a system of "pointing" not unlike the system of enlargement worked out by artists in ancient Greece. For Lee, he molded a one-quarter-size model of the central group and then a model of Lee's head alone, which he hauled up the mountain. When it came time to carve the general's features, it was a relatively simple matter of measuring the model and doing the math. At one point, he even contemplated developing a "pantograph," a sort of Rube Goldberg puppet show, whereby a worker could place a pointer on the model and, through a system of pulleys and cables, make a corresponding mark on the face of Stone Mountain.

But despite all these innovative shortcuts, the final details still demanded an artist's touch. For this phase of the work, Borglum had to be present on the mountain, either to wield hammer and chisel himself or, as was more often the case, to direct the hand of his talented under-study, Hugo Villa, an Italian stone carver by way of Mexico. Borglum could be an unstinting disciplinarian—a tendency that would become even more evident at Mount Rushmore—but he was never reluctant to get dust in his eye and scrapes on his knuckles and knees. Indeed, at times he seemed to be half goat, clambering over the mountain in his knickers and high-top gym shoes. "I went over the mountain myself to [draw] the martingale on Lee's horse," he related blithely. "After going down 200 feet . . . I slipped and fell, it seemed to me about two feet but it was only about ten inches. I was not afraid but in slipping I spilled a bucketful of paint. . . . I was mad and next day I tried to find it, suppos-ing it would be a great big daub but could hardly find the small spot, showing the hugeness of the horse's leg. . . . This fall was due to the cable catching for a moment."

Such slips were rare, however. Borglum was a stickler for safety, and he never lost a man during the work at either Stone Mountain or Mount Rushmore. "I take every precaution," he assured. "We con-stantly inspect our machinery. If the windlass breaks there is a safety clutch and if that breaks they can stop it quickly by using a second break. . . . If the cable breaks of course the man would go to the bottom but the cables hold 4000 pounds."

Borglum's sense of balance was put to the test in December 1923. He had promised to finish the head of Lee by January 19, the hun-dredth anniversary of the general's birth. To meet the deadline, he ran three shifts around the clock. To ward off the inclement weather, he hung tarps and installed stoves on the side of the mountain. At night, the men worked by electric light.

On January 18, the day before the Lee unveiling, Borglum threw a luncheon for thirty VIPs. It made sense to have the event at Stone Mountain, but Borglum went one giant step farther: He set up tables and white tablecloths on Lee's shoulder. Among the honorees to descend the three-hundred-foot stairway from the top of the mountain were three southern governors. The menu was fried chicken and bis-cuits—for those still able to swallow. Lincoln Borglum, the sculptor's eleven-year-old son, perched jauntily on a ledge, waving a drumstick.

The following afternoon, ten thousand people overcame muddy roads, drizzle, and a stiff north wind to gather at the foot of the moun-tain. Ninety-four-year-old Helen Plane, carried to the rostrum in Borg-lum's arms, waved a small Confederate flag, and with that, two enormous American flags were lifted away from the face of the cliff. "The silence of the spectators was long," recalled Mary Borglum, who was at her husband's side that day. "Then suddenly out of the stillness spoke a voice clear though quavering—an old man's voice: 'It's General Lee! It's the general!' . . . Applause—cheers, screams and the shrill rebel yell—crashed across the valley and came echoing back again." More than a few of the men present that day dressed in their gray uniforms, sixty years saved. Borglum too swelled with pride, although of a slightly different sort. "I'd rather do that piece of work than be President of the United States for the rest of my life," he told *American Magazine*.

The rest should have been relatively easy. Borglum had his staff and infrastructure in place. He had proven he could carve, and carve well, on a colossal scale. And the public was behind the memorial. But as usual, there was a stumbling block: politics. More accurately, money and politics, but the two were hopelessly intertwined. The Daughters of the Confederacy had long since relinquished the reins of the project to the Stone Mountain Confederate Monumental Association, whose executive committee was dominated by Atlanta business leaders. After much deliberation, Borglum had agreed to complete the job for $250,000, with a guaranteed monthly payment of $3,000. He was also repaid the $20,000 he had spent of his own money in the early going. The association had received generous donations from the city of Atlanta, Fulton County, and the state of Georgia, but these gifts were only drops in a bottomless bucket. Originally, Borglum had estimated that the entire monument would cost $2 million; now it was looking more like $4 million. Asked on the eve of the Lee unveiling how long it would take to finish, he admitted, "They say about five years, but ten would be nearer right."

The Stone Mountain Association had explored a number of different strategies for raising money. It had hired a professional fundraiser, called on the former Confederate states to do their part, even established a Children's Founders Role that solicited schoolchildren to send in a dollar apiece, for which they would be given a souvenir medal. Borglum, predictably, had insisted on playing a much broader role than that of sculptor. When he wasn't on the mountain, he was giving speeches at women's and men's clubs, drumming up support and whatever contributions he could. He eventually persuaded Lester Barlow to pledge $100,000 in patent royalties from one of his wartime bombs—when and if the federal government ever released them. A more promising scheme was for Borglum to design a Stone Mountain commemorative fifty-cent coin, which, if all went as planned, would be approved by Congress, issued by the U.S. Mint, and sold as a souvenir for a dollar. Five million coins would reap an estimated $2 million in profit. But as 1924 wore on, the coin was not forthcoming, and payrolls and expenses at the mountain were getting harder to meet.

It was only a matter of time before Borglum and the association took to bickering. How often had he broken with a group he had initially tried to bend to his will? On this occasion, however, the rift had unusually dark undertones. For in the pursuit of his dream to create the next wonder of the world, Borglum had finally thrown in with the wrong crowd.

CHAPTER 8

A ROCK AND A HARD PLACE

A N OLD AXIOM of journalism stipulates that when cannibals crop up in a story, however incidentally, they deserve a front-row seat. The story might be about a new cancer medicine derived from a rare moss discovered on a jungle island where natives are rumored to have practiced cannibalism sometime in the gloomy past. Editorial triage says cure cancer, by all means; but be sure to mention cannibalism in the first paragraph. A similar protocol applies to the Ku Klux Klan. A person who consorts with the Klan, even for a short while, can never expect to rub it from his résumé, regardless of what else is accomplished in his life. It becomes its own topic sentence, invariably set in boldface.

Such is the case of Gutzon Borglum, despite the best efforts at stigma control by family members, historians, and the National Park Service, who prefer to characterize Borglum's Klan participation as a) the whimsical indulgence of a compulsive joiner, or b) an unfortunate application of ill-chosen means to otherwise honorable ends. Two texts underwritten by the Mount Rushmore Memorial Society—Gilbert C. Fite's *Mount Rushmore* and Rex Alan Smith's *The Carving of Mount Rushmore*—choose to overlook this awkward chapter in Borglum's past altogether, as does Mary Borglum in her memoir *Give the Man Room.* Slightly less demure is granddaughter Robin Borglum Carter, who in *Gutzon Borglum: His Life and Work* suggests that Borglum merely "misunderstood the nature of the KKK." Only Howard and Audrey Karl Shaff, in their independently published *Six Wars at a Time: The Life and Times of Gutzon Borglum*, explore the Klan connection with any measure of frankness, but even they underrate the intensity of Borglum's Klan convictions during the Stone Mountain years.

The following statements are fair and true: The Ku Klux Klan was reborn on Stone Mountain in 1915, at virtually the same time that the Confederate memorial was conceived. Sam Venable, owner of the mountain and a founding member of the new Klan, granted the Klan permission to hold meetings on the mountain, and hooded Klansmen continued to conduct ceremonies on the summit throughout the time Borglum was at work there. After the United Daughters of the Confederacy announced a plan to carve a Confederate memorial at Stone Mountain, the Klan supported the project wholeheartedly. In the early going, the Klan contributed money directly to the Stone Mountain Confederate Monumental Association, a number of whose members were active Klansmen. While there seems to be no extant proof that Borglum officially joined the Klan himself—that he took the secret oath or donned a hooded robe—he nonetheless became deeply involved in Klan politics, as they related to Stone Mountain and on a national scale as well. He attended Klan rallies, served on Klan committees, and endeavored to play peacemaker in several Klan leadership disputes (with mixed results). On a strictly mercenary level, he saw the Klan's burgeoning, highly organized network throughout the South and the Midwest as a source of funds for his expensive undertaking. More than that, however, he came to view the Klan as the next Nonpartisan

League, a promising grassroots movement with the potential to reshape the political map of the nation.

Membership in the Klan had increased steadily but somewhat lackadaisically since Joe Simmons first carried his cross up Stone Mountain in 1915. Simmons, it turned out, was strong on ritual, but weak on message and organization. His Klan owed as much to the hocus-pocus of the local fraternal lodge as it did to the strident dogma of the original post–Civil War Klan or even the Klan of *Birth of a Nation*. The first Klan had taken its name from the Greek word for circle, *kuklos*, from which Simmons had extrapolated a lexicon of alliterative nomenclature. In addition to its royalty of Imperial Wizard, Grand Dragons, and Exalted Cyclops, Klan peerage included the titles of klaliff, kludd, kligrapp, and klexter. Klansmen joined klaverns and gathered at klonvocations and klonklaves, where they exchanged greetings such as "Ayak" (Are you a Klansman?) and "Kigy" (Klansman, I greet you).

To be sure, the Klan was not just another brotherhood of Odd Fellows or Woodmen of the World. The Kloran, the Klan's book of rules, demanded that members be native born, white, male, and Gentile. And after World War I, the Klan's Kreed became increasingly white supremacist, anti-Catholic, anti-Semitic, anti-labor, anti-alien. A series of articles in the *New York World* in 1921 documented a horrifying skein of Klan lynchings, burnings, floggings, tar-and-featherings, and kidnappings. "Ku Kluxism," the *World* pronounced, "has become a menace to the peace and security of every section of the United States. Its evil and vicious possibilities are boundless." The exposé prompted congressional hearings, at which Simmons attempted to soft-pedal his organization by comparing it to the Knights of Columbus, his robe to a Mardi Gras costume.

If anything, the publicity seemed only to stimulate the growth of the Klan. The year before the congressional investigation, Simmons had enlisted Atlanta wunderkind Edward Young Clarke of the Southern Publicity Association to help solicit membership. Clarke had a gift for snaring money and members for organizations as diverse as the Anti-Saloon League, Near East Relief, and the Theodore Roosevelt Memorial Association. He shrewdly divided the nation into realms, hired one thousand professional salesmen, or kleagles, to recruit members; primary targets were Masons (Borglum was one) and other lodge men. Klan membership was ten dollars, of which the kleagle kept four. More middlemen—king kleagles, grand goblins—skimmed another dollar and a half, and the remaining $4.50 went to Imperial Kleagle Clarke in Atlanta, who pocketed two for himself. Robes were an additional six dollars.

Within a year, Clarke had upped the Klan ranks from three thousand to more than one hundred thousand. Klan headquarters in Atlanta moved from a modest downtown office to a new Imperial Palace on Peachtree Road. Simmons, who owned the rights to the Klan name, Klan costume, the Kloran, and other materials, moved into his own estate, Klan Krest. Even those who condemned the Klan's doctrine as morally bankrupt could not deny that its methodology was solid gold.

By the time Borglum came on the scene in Atlanta, the Klan had expanded another tenfold. In November 1922, Hiram Wesley Evans, a former Dallas dentist and Great Titan of the Realm of Texas, had ousted Simmons from his throne as Imperial Wizard. The most stubborn myth about the twentieth-century Klan is that it was strictly an organization of southern brutes. This was only partly true, and less so once Evans took over. Evans strove to clean up the Klan's unsavory image of violence and vigilantism. He directed his klaverns to exhort police and lawmakers to enforce the Klan agenda, rather than harassing "hyphenated" Americans directly. "Don't Rant. . . . Don't Abuse the 'Enemy,'" Evans instructed his minions. Instead he tailored a more civil, more euphemistic strain of nativist rhetoric to fit the middle-class majority of Americans who were becoming increasingly unnerved by immigration, industrialization, and the generally decadent roar of the twenties. The strategy worked. In 1922, before Evans took charge of the

Klan, 70 percent of Klansmen had been from the South (and South-west). A year later, the Klan could boast well over a million members, 80 percent of whom lived somewhere other than the South. More than half lived in the Midwest. Evans had succeeded as the Populists and Nonpartisan League had not. He had turned a fly-by-night society of regional rednecks into a national force—an accomplishment not lost on Borglum. "I have too much experience in life ... to waste time over speculative fraternities," Borglum said in June 1923. But by then the Klan was well beyond the speculative phase and thus worthy of his full attention.

Still, Borglum was far more discreet in his approach to the Klan than he had been with the Progressives or the Nonpartisans. After initially encouraging direct donations by the Klan to Stone Mountain, he ultimately saw the wisdom of hiring Clarke's Southern Publicity Association to do the soliciting. The Monumental Association had been careful to present the most wholesome, ecumenical face possible, even inviting an Atlanta rabbi to speak at the Lee dedication, and if there was to be any hope of raising money outside the South, it was crucial that the Klan's involvement be kept under wraps. With Clarke acting as a fundraising foil, Borglum now felt free to assert that "the Klan has nothing to do with the Memorial." Clearly, though, he was not telling the whole truth. At the same time that he was disavowing the memorial's connection with the Klan, his letters reveal that he was serving on the Klan Kloncilium, a committee charged with drafting, among other things, a national political platform. A series of telegrams suggests that sometime in mid-1923, he may even have brokered a meeting in Washington between Evans and President Harding. (At least one source suspects that at some point Harding may have taken the Klan oath in the Green Room of the White House.)

Borglum's own decision *not* to take the Klan oath provided him with a hood of deniability, which he could lift and lower as he saw fit. When the *World* included his name on a list of Klansmen, he bristled: "I am not a member of the kl[o]ncilium; not a Knight of the Ku Klux Klan and

I say this as a matter of fact." But when Ralph Lum, who had awarded him the sculpture commissions in Newark, inquired about a recent Klan altercation in nearby Perth Amboy, Borglum was less quick to distance himself: "[Klansmen] have been very friendly in Atlanta, and while I am under no obligation to them as an organization, I am under the obligation of deep friendship to many of their most prominent leaders and would do anything I could, publicly or privately, to serve them." To another New Jersey friend, he wrote, "Is it true you joined the Ku Klux Klan? I hope so. They are a fine lot of fellows as far as I can learn and if they elect the next President, by gosh, I'm going to join 'em."

The possibility of a Klan-sympathetic president was not that far-fetched. By 1924, the not so Invisible Empire was vowing that it could deliver five million voters to the polls. Individual Klan klaverns had backed local legislators and initiatives in recent years, and in May, the Klan claimed a major portion of the credit for a new federal law setting the stiffest quotas on immigration in U.S. history. Next on the Klan calendar was the Democratic National Convention in June. Officially the Klan was nonpartisan—although practically speaking, it was Democrat in the South, Republican in the North. Borglum had always leaned toward the Republicans, but, like so many Americans, he was outraged by the odor of corruption then beginning to leak from the Harding administration. Harding himself was off the hook, having died in August 1923 of mysterious causes (some said bad heart; some said food poisoning; some even said his wife did him in as punishment for taking a mistress), but the Teapot Dome scandal continued to hiss while Calvin Coolidge served out Harding's term and prepared to run for reelection. Democrats figured their chances of unseating Coolidge were good but could stand to be even better. And so they courted the Klan millions, and vice versa. The leading Democratic candidate going into the June convention was New York governor Al Smith, a Catholic and thus anathema to the Klan. That left Georgia native William Gibbs McAdoo, former Secretary of the Treasury and Woodrow Wilson's

son-in-law. In no time at all, press wags had stuck him with the nickname "Ku Ku" McAdoo.

But even as Evans and his Atlanta cronies were pushing their noses
into the McAdoo tent, Borglum was quietly backing away from the
Imperial Wizard, leaning toward Evans's most able and ambitious lieutenant, David C. "Steve" Stephenson of Indianapolis. Stephenson's title
was Grand Dragon of the Realm of Indiana. He deserved much of the
credit for delivering the Midwest to the Klan, and ultimately he was
awarded authority over the Klan in twenty-two states besides Indiana.
His induction as Grand Dragon in Kokomo, Indiana, on July 4, 1923,
was the largest Klan rally in U.S. history; estimates of the crowd ranged
as high as one hundred thousand.

Stephenson lived like a king. With the millions he had earned in the
coal business and through TWK ("Trade with Klan") deals, he could
easily afford to ride in a Cadillac chauffeured by armed bodyguards. He
kept a large yacht on the Great Lakes. His mansion in Indianapolis was
modeled after the original Klan Krest. Ignoring Prohibition and the
Klan's own code of moral constraint, he drank wantonly; nor was his
reputation as a womanizer a secret. Above all, though, the greatest of
his appetites was for power. He strove to put judges, legislators, the
mayor of Indianapolis, and the governor of Indiana in his profound
debt. Not surprisingly, he had designs on the Klan's Imperial Palace in
Atlanta, and surely much beyond that.

Borglum never spelled out just what drew him to Stephenson, but
almost immediately after meeting the energetic, smooth-talking
Dragon in 1923, he pledged his allegiance with more than his usual
abandon. Of all the acquaintances Borglum maintained during the
Stone Mountain years—except possibly Lester Barlow, who shared
Borglum's enthusiasm for the Klan—Stephenson was the individual
who won Borglum's greatest trust and admiration. Borglum typically
closed his letters to Stephenson with "Affectionately yours," "More
power to you!" and "Love to you my dear friend." And it was to

Stephenson that Borglum confided the depth of his Klanish convictions. The most extreme of his epistles was composed on September 4, 1923. "Before I went to bed last night," Borglum begins, "I wrote 2500 to 3000 words on the evils of alien races." He had apparently just been reading Madison Grant's *The Passing of the Great Race*, an alarmist, pseudo-scientific tract that became a sacred text for eugenicists, the Klan, and proto-Nazis everywhere. Here are excerpts of Borglum's remarks to Stephenson.

On Anglo-Saxons and African-Americans: "[W]hile Anglo-Saxons have themselves sinned grievously against the principle of pure nationalism by illicit slave and alien servant traffic, it has been the character of the cargo that has eaten into the very moral fiber or our race character, rather than the moral depravity of Anglo-Saxon traders...."

On Catholic immigrants: "[O]ld world wanderers ... have grown from hamlet through suburb to the heart of our great cities, and through church and sinister leadership ... have sold Anglo-Saxon American freedom ... into the slavery of south Europe Romanism."

On Jews and eugenics: "If you cross a thorough-bred with a jackass you get a mule.... [T]he lowest race in civilization is the strongest physically and breeding (crossed) is always down. A Negro and a Jew will produce Negro, but Hindu and Jew—Jew; Chinese and Jew, offspring Jew; Italian and Jew, offspring Jew; and European race and Jew, offspring Jew."

Borglum's biases were not born of convenience and delivered simply to win favor from his friends in the Klan. He labeled immigrants "slippered assassins," and well before his arrival in Atlanta, he had warned that America was becoming an alien "scrap heap." If the Klan is to be blamed for anything, it is guilty of hardening Borglum's already active prejudices. Careful review of his personal papers reveals that the shrillness and frequency of his long-festering anti-"isms" increased markedly once he embraced the Klan in 1923. It is also worth noting, in light of future developments, that the animosities Borglum gave rein to in Georgia did not subside once he left the South and moved to the West. In 1939, with the Holocaust under way in Europe (and Mount Rushmore nearly complete), he lashed out at Eugene Meyer, to whom he still owed money. Never mind that Meyer now owned the *Washington Post*. To Borglum he would always be Shylock: "There is no question that ... you have for some years punished me or the Borglum family ... in a manner that cannot be called anything under the sun except the ultra-Jew method." In a letter to Isidor Singer, editor of the *Jewish Encyclopedia*, he chided Jews for their reluctance to assimilate. Jews, he said—and it is difficult to tell if his spelling was accidental or simply ironic—were "most klanish."

Despite his ideological vehemence, Borglum did not have any discernible success in shaping the Klan's overall political agenda. In a rambling letter to Stephenson, he outlined a set of goals that were half Klan, half holdovers from the Nonpartisan League manifesto: "We [the Klan] are in truth the great non-partisan amalgam that will reunite and rebuild the broken course of our original Nationalism." Of all Americans, he opined, farmers were the most threatened by "Alien manned city industries ... and the mongrel hoard [*sic*] that is ... bringing disease, ignorance, immorality and contempt for our laws, our language and our customs.... Immigration from the slums ... of Europe must cease if America is to continue a free peaceful protestant people."

But once again, Borglum's reach had exceeded his grasp. There would be no reprise of the Nonpartisan League glory, however limited and short-lived that had been. For one thing, Borglum had sided with Stephenson, who, just weeks before the Democratic Convention, had been frozen out by a wary Evans. At a gathering of his supporters on May 12, 1924—a meeting that Borglum had made a point of attending—Stephenson reportedly responded to his ostracism by calling Evans "an ignorant, uneducated, uncouth individual who picks his nose at the table and eats peas with his knife. He has neither courage nor culture." Borglum, while doing his best to stay on good terms with Evans and the Atlanta bosses, was treated with growing suspicion and denied any special voice or privilege.

Then, at the Democratic convention at Madison Square Garden in June (which Borglum did not attend), Evans's ambassadors were given an unexpectedly rude reception. Instead of welcoming the Klan, as Evans had anticipated, a determined group of moderate Democrats entered a motion to condemn it. The motion was defeated by barely a whisker, but party wounds healed slowly. Evans and his white knights had become the Democrats' dirty laundry, and for all intents and purposes, the Klan's hopes of becoming a national presence were dashed. The Klan did succeed in keeping the nomination from the Catholic Al Smith. But Ku Ku McAdoo was a marked man in his own right, and the nomination finally went to Charles Davis, a compromise candidate who made the bland Coolidge, the eventual victor in November, seem like a man about town. Never again would the Klan enjoy the collective clout that it had in the summer of 1924.

By fall, Borglum's bond with Stephenson had cooled markedly. Klan factionalism deserved some of the blame. But the real sore point was money. Once again, Borglum had taken advantage of a friendship, borrowed from Stephenson (amount unknown), and then ignored his debt. Stephenson had been a fair-weather ally, and now that the election season was over and Borglum was beginning to inch away from the Klan, he withdrew from Stephenson, too. The endgame was not pretty. The following year, Stephenson would be arrested for forcing himself on a female office worker, who, in shame, drank poison and died—but not before describing the grisly details of her assault, in which Stephenson had not only raped her, but also savagely bitten her dozens of times in unspeakable places. Stephenson spent everything he had made defending himself, but was convicted of second-degree murder and sent to Indiana State Prison. Desperate for dollars and moral support, he corresponded with Borglum for years. In return, Borglum barely gave "My dear Steve" the time of day.

By late 1924, Borglum was having his own problems. The chairman of the Stone Mountain executive committee was Hollins Randolph, a prominent Atlanta attorney with an impeccable Old South pedigree and strong ties to the Klan. Like Evans, Randolph had been an ardent supporter of McAdoo, and if McAdoo had won the Democratic nomination and then the White House, Randolph figured to benefit personally. Instead he was back in Atlanta, saddled with Stone Mountain and its increasingly prickly sculptor. Borglum did not like the cavalier way in which Randolph had taken over the Stone Mountain executive committee and stacked it with his friends. Randolph, for his part, resented that Borglum had volubly rejected the McAdoo candidacy in favor of Progressive Robert LaFollette. In addition, Borglum had made friends with the editor of the *Constitution*, who was in the midst of a vitriolic feud with Randolph. Lastly, Borglum felt he was not being paid enough, or on time.

Much as Randolph had bet his future on McAdoo, the association had bet the future of Stone Mountain on the commemorative coin, which, if five million were minted, could net two million dollars, maybe more. Commemorative coins had become a bonanza of late. In 1920, Congress had allowed Maine, Missouri, and Alabama to issue half dollars marking the centennial of their respective statehoods. All had sold well for a dollar apiece. Fortunately for Stone Mountain, Congress had already authorized the Confederate memorial coin by the time the Klan had come under such conspicuous fire at the Democratic convention. (Public relations to the contrary, most northerners still regarded Stone Mountain as a Klan-tainted project. This was the main reason the Klan altar had been quietly scratched from the plans.)

But even after the coin was approved in concept, Borglum was having a devil of a time getting a specific design past the Fine Arts Commission and the U.S. Mint. The Mint had become notoriously proprietary about the look and origin of coin designs ever since President Roosevelt had spurned the Mint's chief engraver and commissioned Augustus Saint-Gaudens to design new ten- and twenty-dollar gold pieces. Roosevelt had also pushed for sculptor Victor Brenner, artist of a recent Roosevelt–Panama Canal medal, to design the first Lincoln penny, issued in 1909. Then in 1913, James Fraser, famous for his nostalgic Indian sculpture *The End of the Trail*, had carved the most American of coins, the buffalo nickel. (For the coin's "tail," Fraser copied Black Diamond, a dowdy bison in the Central Park Zoo. The "head" was actually a composite of several faces, including Iron Tail, a Lakota who had fought Custer at Little Bighorn, and John Big Tree, an Iroquois whom Fraser discovered working at Coney Island.)

Borglum welcomed the chance to join such an exclusive club. But admission was not as easy as he had first imagined. The Fine Arts Commission appreciated the wording, "In God We Trust," on the coin. It tolerated the thirteen stars of the Confederacy, which could just as easily stand for the thirteen colonies. But the image of Jefferson Davis had to go. It was one thing for a congressionally sanctioned coin to honor valiant warriors, Lee and Jackson; quite another for the republic to celebrate the Confederate most liable for splitting *pluribus* and *unum*. Besides, there simply wasn't enough room for three riders on a half dollar. All told, Borglum had to make nine revisions before the coin finally won approval in October, by which time he and Randolph were at each other's throats.

Randolph accused Borglum of procrastinating, of diverting his attention to other projects when he should have been focusing solely on Stone Mountain. Work on the Confederate memorial, which appeared to have gone so quickly the previous winter, now seemed to have slowed to an almost glacial pace. At the end of June, just as Randolph, McAdoo, and the Democrats were disappointing one another in New York, a much more tangible fault was discovered along the bridge of Stonewall Jackson's nose. There was no choice but to reposition Jackson's head so that, instead of gazing at Lee, the martyr of Chancellorsville now faced the opposite direction. Needless to say, the task of flipping a fifty-foot slab of granite was immensely more difficult than doing the same to a fifty-cent piece of silver.

Randolph was right about Borglum's splintered attention. To Randolph's disgust, Borglum took to the road, stumping for LaFollette. He also used time that he could have been spending on the Confederate coin to design LaFollette's campaign medal. In July, Borglum had gone off to Chicago for the dedication of his second Sheridan monument, a ten-foot colossus that he had somehow managed to complete in his Stamford studio between stints in Georgia. And throughout the summer, he was under tremendous strain to complete his war memorial for Newark, which was already a full year behind schedule.

Wars of America, as the piece would eventually be titled, was clearly influenced by Stone Mountain. If Stone Mountain was to be the world's largest stone carving, then *Wars* would be the largest bronze. Borglum conceived a sprawling tableau, more than forty figures in all—forty-two feet long, eighteen feet wide, and seventeen feet tall, including pedestal. As with Stone Mountain, the focal point was a central group of officers, followed by their loyal troops. Borglum's initial notion was to place Washington and Lincoln at the fore—an idea he discarded in Newark but later revived in South Dakota. In the end, he fronted the group with four nameless officers, one dressed in the uniform of the Revolution, one from the Union army, one from World War I, and a fourth representing the navy. Behind them come thirty-eight more full-size figures, plus two very restive horses.

Only a half dozen of the men carry weapons, and only the Revolutionary officer carries a sword, yet the composition still manages to evoke, in Borglum's words, "an entire nation mobilizing under great pressure of war." The group is leaning forward en masse, a concerted thrust of citizen soldiers. Borglum wanted to express the "indignation, fear . . . physical distress, and pathos" of war. He achieved all of these and more. Some men are in the act of throwing off their coats or shirts—stripping for action, baring their breasts to an unseen enemy.

Some have their mouths open in cries of alarm or exhortation. Some clench their fists; some seem to be praying. Still others, as with Rodin's *Burghers of Calais*, are more reluctant heroes, needing the nudge of comrades. The horses, Borglum explained, provide "the allegro of the symphony ... the power and movement and irresistible forward plunge of impetuous anger."

Wars of America is a brilliant sculpture, the complement of all Borglum's talent and experience. Like Stone Mountain, the various pieces add up to a kinetic, organic whole. Like Shrady's Grant memorial in Washington, *Wars* is sober yet raucous, part anthem, part dirge. And like the free-willed *Burghers*, each of Borglum's figures is, on one hand, a distinct personality and, on the other, a compelling embodiment of a universal truth. Many of the forty-two warriors of America were actually Borglum's friends and acquaintances. Easiest to spot are the sculptor and his son Lincoln, depicted halfway down the left flank of the sculpture as the anxious father sending his callow son off to battle. Another figure is John Mitchell, a friend and former mayor of New York. And records suggest that another might be Madison Grant, author of *The Passing of the Great Race*.

The model for *Wars of America* took forty tons of clay to complete. It was so enormous that Borglum had to sculpt it under an awning of tarps outside the Stamford studio. According to the terms of his contract, the piece was supposed to be finished and installed by April 1923. But Borglum had let himself get carried away. By fall of 1924, the model was finished but still not cast. Several American foundries quoted prices that nearly equaled Borglum's $100,000 fee. Finally, an Italian firm agreed to take the job but demanded a significant down payment. The cost of shipping the plaster molds of a forty-two-foot sculpture was astronomical. Borglum, who had already spent the money due him, had no choice but to plunge deeper into debt.

Yet as great as the pressure was in the North, it scarcely compared to the storm that was brewing at Stone Mountain. When things were not going precisely Borglum's way, his usual response was to single out one person and assign him all the blame. He had done it with George Perkins in the Progressive campaigns, with Edward Deeds during the aircraft investigation, and the pattern would repeat again at Mount Rushmore. In Georgia, he aimed his enmity at Randolph, saving a punch or two for Eretus Rivers, the association's business manager and yet another Klansman. On August 25, Rivers wrote Borglum from the safety of his office that, quite understandably, the executive committee had "completely lost patience" with him. "[G]rown men don't do business [this] way. And you are dealing with grown men. And they're not going to let you run any wild horse performance with them and get away with it.... [Y]ou don't know friendship when you meet it in the middle of the road in broad daylight."

And then out of the blue, a letter arrived from South Dakota historian Doane Robinson, asking Borglum if he might consider carving a mountain in the Black Hills. Robinson's letter was dated August 20, sent to Stone Mountain, and then forwarded to Borglum in Stamford. Taking such a roundabout route, it probably reached Borglum at just about the same time as Rivers's admonitory "wild horse" letter. With his affairs on the home front so snarled, no wonder Borglum telegrammed Robinson enthusiastically on the 28th: "Great scheme.... Hold to it." More telling was Borglum's remark: "Am two years ahead in my Southern work. Can get to the Black Hills during September."

He couldn't help himself. The following day, he wrote Lester Barlow: "My own big plan ... for a great Northern National Memorial in the center of the nation is finally materializing.... [T]he conditions that are offered to me ... make me believe that a Memorial equal in proportions to the Southern Memorial can be secured for the principle of the Union. I consider this the most important political thought that has been contributed to ... modern government—I mean the principle of an unbreakable union.... I beg of you to hold yourself in readiness to accompany me."

The events of the next six months seem, if not scripted, then almost inevitable. Borglum had asked the South Dakota committee to keep his September visit quiet, but to no avail. His presence and purpose splashed across the front page of the *Rapid City Journal* and weren't long in reaching the executive committee of the Stone Mountain Association, whose members were already miffed that Borglum had spent the summer "here, there, and yonder." In Borglum's defense, when he was not in Georgia (or Connecticut), he was often in Washington, negotiating the coin legislation and design and assisting with Lester Barlow's claim on his bomb patent. Borglum had an extra incentive for securing the Barlow royalty: Not only would the award bring Stone Mountain a windfall of $100,000; in addition, Barlow had announced that he would give another $100,000 to the recently organized Mount Harney Memorial Association in South Dakota.

The Stone Mountain committeemen were outwardly pleased but privately peeved by Barlow's largesse. It was bad enough that Borglum was about to divide his time and energy between Stone Mountain and the Black Hills. Even more irritating was the knowledge that a large sum of money that could just as easily have gone to Stone Mountain was now being earmarked for a *northern* site, which, if reports were correct, would honor George Washington and—more galling—Abraham Lincoln.

Several things happened in fairly quick succession that pushed Borglum and Randolph over the edge. On December 1, Borglum delivered an ultimatum to the executive committee that he be paid all that was due him—approximately $40,000—within forty-eight hours, or else "I shall be compelled to suspend my work on the mountain." The committee placated him by agreeing to arbitrate his claim and by voting him onto the executive committee—in exchange for a promise that he would continue carving.

Borglum was not mollified for long. Two months later, on January 21, 1925, he wrote to President Coolidge, urging him to form a national committee of "big men" to take control of Stone Mountain. Coolidge wisely declined to participate in Borglum's coup, but Borglum kept pressing. His latest gripe was that the commemorative coin, which had finally been issued, was not producing the revenue hoped for. Instead of five million, barely more than one million had been minted, and distribution was chaotic at best. Borglum suspected that whatever money was coming in was winding up in Randolph's pocket—the aircraft scandal all over again. At a meeting of the executive committee on February 10, Borglum blew up. The details are recorded in the diary of Rogers Winter, the association's publicist: "Borglum without provocation launches bitter attack on [business manager] Rivers, who replies in a speech flaying Borglum. The sculptor then called Rivers a liar and Rivers has to be pulled off of him. Thus is created the most serious internal situation the memorial has ever faced."

Back in Washington a week later, Borglum received more upsetting news: Congress had deferred its decision on the Barlow bomb royalty until at least the next session, perhaps indefinitely. Borglum's frustration boiled over again. The following day, he told the Associated Press that, despite the issuance of one million commemorative half dollars, he still had not received a dime of the money he believed was overdue him. The Stone Mountain Association, he charged, "has shrunk into a local habitation with scarcely a name."

Randolph and company didn't bother to figure out what exactly Borglum meant by "local habitation." They had had enough. Two days later, Randolph issued his own statement to the press, accusing Borglum of loafing, grandstanding, and brinksmanship. "It has been extremely difficult to get [Borglum] to do any work at all on the mountain, notwithstanding the large amounts of money paid him. His main desire seems to be to get his name in the newspapers as often as possible." Randolph asserted that Borglum had already received 40 percent of the $250,000 owed him under contract, while estimating that the sculpture was no more than 20 percent complete. "This association is not endeavoring to erect a monument to Borglum, but to the soldiers and sailors of the Confederacy," Randolph added, "and we will bend every effort to carry it to completion"—including hiring another sculptor, if need be. The headline on the front page of the *Atlanta Journal* announced Borglum's "imminent" dismissal—a likelihood that became even more certain when the association at last got hold of a copy of Borglum's insurrectional letter to Coolidge.

On Wednesday morning, February 25, the executive committee fired Borglum, citing, among many other things, "offensive egotism and delusions of grandeur." Another affidavit attached to the official minutes of the meeting remarked: "It is difficult for a sane, sound mind to fathom the depths of a neurotic temperament. If anything is clear, however, in the whole muddled situation, it is that Borglum is consumed by two desires: first, for money, and secondly, for notoriety, and that back of this he has little sense of the obligation of a contract, no ethics, and that he is treacherous and disloyal. . . . The sooner we break with him the better. When a growth is thoroughly diagnosed as cancer, it is best to cut it out entirely." To drive their point home, that same morning the executive committee sought an injunction barring Borglum and contractor Jesse Tucker from Stone Mountain.

Borglum had already arrived at the mountain earlier that morning, and when word reached him of the committee's actions, he reacted impulsively. He strode into his studio, and with the help of a black quarryman named Homer, demolished the models of Lee, Jackson, and Davis with an ax, leaving only a "wreck of crumbling plaster and wire," according to witnesses. Bad news traveled fast, and by the end of the day, the memorial association had filed a $50,000 damage suit and had sworn out a warrant for his arrest, charging malicious mischief—a felony in this instance because the models were valued at more than fifty dollars.

But Borglum was nowhere to be found. Minutes before the sheriff arrived, Tucker and the sculptor had jumped into a car and sped away.

Accounts of their flight to the Georgia state line would grow more colorful with passing years, the best versions borrowing from the time-honored southern genre of moonshiners racing madly along back roads with revenuers in hot pursuit. Were shots fired? No more than during the aircraft investigation, but why smother a good yarn? Borglum and Tucker arrived safely in Durham, North Carolina, late that night and awaited the consequences. Defending his decision to flee, he explained, "[H]ad I been a single man . . . I would have plunged headlong into it. . . . If I had gone to Atlanta and met with any kind of violence I should certainly have killed somebody." The inference was that Klan thugs were out to get him.

Meanwhile, back at Stone Mountain, Mary Borglum, ever stalwart, issued her own statement: "This design belonged absolutely to Mr. Borglum. . . . Therefore Mr. Borglum has a perfect legal right to destroy his own property." She also put a classical spin on the day's events that Borglum himself could not have improved upon: "It was the Hollins N. Randolph of Greece who passed a law making it a crime for a sculptor to sign his work, yet the name of Phidias has outlived the ages, while the names of those who drove him into exile have been forgotten."

The war of words continued for months, years even. Borglum moved to a hotel in Raleigh, where soon he was joined by his family. He announced that he would "rot in jail" before bending to the will of the Stone Mountain Association. Charges against him were soon dropped, but the broadsides continued, with allies and adversaries piling on with their own accusations and appeals for justice. The invective in the newspapers got so turgid that both camps eventually published their own "true records" of the affair. Borglum, as always, thrived on the attention and his role as the aggrieved party. "My . . . heart has wounds that will bleed until it is dust," he wrote to North Carolina governor Angus McLean. "After nine of the best years of my life and of my work, to be called a loafer!" He insisted that he had destroyed the models "to prevent their use by inexperienced hands and minds without knowledge or vision." But his detractors stressed his history of irrationality, comparing his behavior at Stone Mountain to the defacement of the angels at the Cathedral of St. John the Divine.

As in the past, Borglum's actions may have seemed rash, but he had not lost his mind entirely. Independent audits of the memorial association's books soon revealed that from the beginning of his contract in 1923 until the time of his dismissal, the association had paid Borglum approximately $113,000, from which he had to cover all labor and materials at the mountain. In that same period, the association had spent $116,000 in general expenses. "In other words," Borglum lectured, "it cost $116,936.79 to collect and spend $113,922.61." To him, the real villain was obvious.

Right or wrong, though, he was still in exile. While Borglum lingered in Raleigh, Randolph and the association searched for a new sculptor to complete Stone Mountain, which at that point revealed only the head of Lee and the roughed-in profile of Stonewall Jackson. On April 16, the committee announced its choice. Augustus Lukeman, a native Virginian living in New York, was a respected, if second-tier, sculptor with dozens of commissions to his credit, including several war memorials and work at two different world's fairs. Borglum was not impressed. "[N]o sculptor of standing would take the position," he vented to Doane Robinson. "[E]very able man in America refused it, and thank God every Christian. They got a Jew."

Robinson and his colleagues at the Mount Harney Memorial Association didn't care who Borglum's successor was, much less his religion. They were, however, deeply anxious about the impact Borglum's newest notoriety might have on their own project. On February 22, the South Dakota papers picked up the Associated Press report out of Washington in which Borglum blasted the Stone Mountain Association. Of particular interest to South Dakota readers was Borglum's claim that the money to finish Stone Mountain had dried up. South Dakota, in the midst of its own fiscal crisis, was loath to adopt a similarly bloated tar baby. Two days later—and the day before the blowup at Stone Mountain—the state senate voted against authorizing and funding the Mount Harney monument. "It does beat all how unfortunately things break for us," Senator Norbeck tried to console Robinson. "Mr. Borglum gets himself in trouble just at the time you are trying to get the appropriation."

The only recourse was to draft a new bill, this time leaving out any request for money. The revised bill passed the state legislature several days later, leaving Robinson wondering where he might find "some malefactor of great wealth" to underwrite the project. "From your exalted position as United States Senator," he asked Norbeck half-jokingly, "can you not interest some gentleman who would like in this way to perpetuate his name in American history?"

Borglum, meanwhile, exuded characteristic confidence. "Get your heads together and let us take up this work vigorously," he exhorted Robinson. "I shall give you all the heart and experience I have, and will take special pride in leaving on Mount Harney two or three GREAT figures." But, he beseeched, "[D]on't put Real estate speculators and bankers who are thinking of possible opportunities for theft and graft on your Board. What I mean is that it should be made up of men like yourself—men of ideas and largeness of mind who can see the real purpose of everything."

Funding, he assured, would take care of itself. "I am not worried about the money—whether it costs half a million or a million and a half will really not matter in the least. The only question is to determine upon the right thing to do and doing that . . . in a manner that places it above criticism and keeps it entirely out of a vaudeville class. That sculpture has got to be of the kind that will cause it to be seriously discussed as an art production in itself if we want to attract the critical attention of the critical minds in the country."

Precisely when he could come to the Black Hills and settle on a final location for the memorial he did not say. Nor had he decided exactly whom he would carve when he got there. The legislation specified Washington and Lincoln, but lately Borglum was thinking of replacing Washington with Roosevelt. "Teddy and Lincoln ... belong so much more to the West," he reasoned. Norbeck, who had backed the Progressive ticket in years past, also liked the switch to Roosevelt, and some sources have even asserted that Roosevelt was Norbeck's notion to begin with. But given Borglum's well-documented desire to memorialize his mentor in stone, the inspiration had to have been mutual at the very least.

In the meantime, South Dakota was not so far away that it could escape the spite of the Stone Mountain Association. "Your enemies in Georgia have simply plastered the state with propaganda against you," Robinson notified Borglum in May. "Last week the Women's Club of the Black Hills met at Deadwood and protested against [the mountain carving]." Cora Johnson, whose husband published the *Hot Springs Star*, summarized the opposition's view most succinctly: "Man makes statues but God made the Needles," referring to the distinctive spires near Harney Peak, southwest of Mount Rushmore. "Let them alone." Borglum deflected this sort of criticism with a promise "not to injure any of the tall needles.... [N]or will I deface any of those great granite pillars [nearby]. The Monument I propose will be simple, dignified, and if these honest plainsmen will have confidence in me, we can ... come to an understanding of what is best and wisest." By midsummer, the public attitude was "somewhat better," Norbeck allowed, and he and Robinson thought the time was right for Borglum to visit the hills again.

Borglum's mood was improving steadily, too. He took perverse pleasure in accounts of the backbiting and second-guessing that were crippling the factions in Atlanta. The commemorative coin was selling poorly, and Randolph had apparently begun to fall into disfavor. Borglum even held out the prospect of eventually returning to Stone Mountain—Napoleon home from Elba. And while his personal finances were still a mess—the Italian foundry was screaming for payment for *Wars*, and various creditors in the North were threatening suit or foreclosure as well—he saw lucrative commissions on the horizon. A group in North Carolina had approached him about another Confederate memorial on Chimney Rock in the western part of the state, at best a pipe dream, but one that boosted Borglum's morale, if nothing else. In June, he had gone to San Antonio to meet with the Trail Drivers Association, an organization of Texas's ranching aristocracy. After seeing photos of the model of *Wars of America*, the Texans envisioned a comparable bronze capturing the heroic spirit of the great Texas cattle drives of the previous century. Borglum, too, thought in epic terms. "Texas is an empire," he exclaimed, and the Texas cowboy symbolized the triumph of Anglo-Saxon civilization over the Spanish. Despite having lost money on *Wars*, which was *still* not done, Borglum agreed to do the Trail Drivers monument for the same price, $100,000.

Leaving San Antonio, he proceeded to Omaha to discuss a proposed World War I memorial. "Things are picking up in splendid shape," he wrote Doane Robinson upon his return to Raleigh. "I shall soon be free and 'forking a good horse' again. I have some excellent work in Texas which involves me with a powerful set of real men, not the 'left over' kind; and I have something in Omaha which seems to be developing very strongly and will run into possibl[y] a quarter of a million." Several weeks later he was approached by a New York man interested in commissioning a monument to American Revolutionary author Thomas Paine. Borglum informed the man that he would take the job for $100,000 and requested an immediate deposit of $1,000—to test the man's resolve, no doubt, but also to keep himself alive until one of his other patrons started paying. For the time being, he still had no income to speak of.

There was no point in returning to Connecticut. Borgland was ringed by bill collectors. Borglum needed to go where the money was, and so in August he moved from Raleigh to San Antonio, with his family soon following, and they took a suite of rooms at the Menger Hotel. Leaving his wife and daughter to settle into their new home, he and Lincoln Borglum, now thirteen, traveled north to survey the Black Hills. For the next fifteen years, the Borglums would migrate back and forth between Texas and South Dakota. Although they would continue to own Borgland (heavily mortgaged always) and regard it as home, they would never spend any appreciable time there again.

Borglum and Lincoln arrived in Rapid City on August 11, accompanied by Senator Norbeck. After lunching at the Lions Club, Borglum repaired to a nearby Baptist church, where he spelled out his plans for the Black Hills to a large audience. He began by again assuring that he would not mar the Needles. "I wouldn't touch them at any price, and there never has been any intention of ... trying to improve these works of nature." Instead, he would find another worthy but less controversial location. For the first time, he articulated his "empire builder" concept. Over the past few months, he had been debating whether to carve two or three presidents; now he said he would carve four. Washington and Lincoln were guaranteed spots as the nation's "founder" and "savior," respectively. They would be joined by Roosevelt, who had "thrust himself upon the western plains" as a young man, plus as president had established "commercial control by securing Panama." To this trio, Borglum finally added Thomas Jefferson, "the first great expansionist." Jefferson, he elaborated, "is particularly associated with this region because he brought about the Louisiana Purchase through which the Central West became part of the United States." (No mention, at this point, of Jefferson's authorship of the Declaration of Independence, the Bill of Rights, or other intellectual achievements.)

Borglum wrapped up his remarks with a pep talk: "If you carve ... these empire-builders, the whole world will speak of South Dakota." He pointed out that Stone Mountain already drew as many as two thousand visitors a day. "Three highways have diverted their routes so as to pass by this world-famous work." The same could happen to the

Black Hills, he declared. What was more, he told the Rapid City crowd, "You're not asked to spend a dollar on the project. You're asked only to understand." Borglum, Lincoln, and Norbeck stayed that night at the Game Lodge at Custer State Park and the next morning drove to the tourist hotel at Sylvan Lake, with its magnificent views of the nearby Needles and Harney Peak.

Borglum needed only three days to select the site for his next mountain carving. The morning after arriving at Sylvan Lake, he and Lincoln rode horseback through the jumbled mountains, guided by state forester Theodore Shoemaker. Climbing Harney Peak, as they had done the previous year, they again were able to take in the exhilarating scope of the Black Hills and surrounding prairie. With the Needles now off-limits, Shoemaker suggested they examine several peaks to the northeast. Two days later, they motored up a rugged track to the moribund mining town of Keystone. Horseback again, they ascended Grizzly Gulch to the base of Old Baldy, Sugarloaf, and a third peak, which, Shoemaker explained, had been named almost in jest for a New York attorney, Charles Rushmore, who had come west some time back with the modest objective of inspecting a tin mine. Rushmore had learned two things during his brief western sojourn. One was that tin mining in the hills had a desultory future. Another was that, while most local mines had names—Holy Terror, Holy Smoke, Golden Slipper—not all the mountains did. Mount Rushmore was his for the asking.

The Mount Rushmore that Borglum beheld on August 15, 1925, was not classic in any postcard sense. Rather, it was a five-hundred-foot knot of ungainly granite surrounded by barn-sized boulders and tenacious pines. Still, it was not without character. For one thing, Rushmore, like Stone Mountain, turned its best face south and east, the ideal orientation for Borglum's purposes. And there was something coyly suggestive about the rock. Viewed in the right light and shadow, its faults seemed to divide the mountain into wizened torsos. If Stone Mountain was a drive-in movie screen, awaiting the artist's projection, then Mount Rushmore was an immense formation of petrified mummies, begging reincarnation. Borglum made some rough sketches of the rock, fitting anatomy to geology. That night he arrived in Rapid City, exulting to the *Journal* that he had found a superb location for "the Great American Memorial."

From here, the story of Gutzon Borglum and Mount Rushmore can be spun two ways. One would be to view Mount Rushmore as simply the continuation, or repetition, of all that had gone before, as indeed it was. The Lincoln bust, the *Seated Lincoln*, the Sheridan equestrians, *Wars of America*, and the Confederate memorial were indispensable rehearsals for the grand performance at Mount Rushmore. The galloping ego, political truculence, and penchant for paranoia that infected and ultimately enabled Mount Rushmore all gestated (and metastasized) during Borglum's immersions in the Progressive Party, the aircraft investigation, the Nonpartisan League, the Ku Klux Klan, and Stone Mountain. And most especially, Borglum's determination to meld American art and patriotism into a mountain-sized monument— Great Men carved by a Great Man—is the sum of every second and cell of his existence, from his pure Danish heritage to his breached Mormon upbringing, from his Old World elitism to his Old West outsiderness.

A better way to look at Mount Rushmore, however, is as a rebirth. Beneath all his operatic posturing, Borglum had been genuinely bruised by his dismissal from Stone Mountain, not to mention the frustrations of the Nonpartisan League and aircraft years. He had resigned from organizations before, but not until Stone Mountain had he walked away from a major sculpture without finishing. ("A true mother never abandons her child," he remarked later.) More's the pity because, notwithstanding nagging environmental concerns, the specter of the Klan, and the inherent sectionalism of the subject matter, Stone Mountain, fully executed, would have been a stupendously effective work of art—more so even than Mount Rushmore.

Borglum turned fifty-eight in 1925 and could easily have retreated to a respectable career of more modest commissions (not that there was anything remotely modest about the Trail Drivers memorial). But his pride and drive would not allow him to slacken the pace. He was sincere in his belief that America owed itself a major monument in the center of the nation. He truly felt that "eastern money-kings" would step forward to finance it. And in his own mind, there was no question that he would get the job done this time. He wanted Mount Rushmore much more dearly than he had Stone Mountain—because of his disappointment with the latter and the national significance of the former. A man who should have been demoralized and exhausted instead redoubled his energy and enthusiasm. And while some might say that he stumbled from Stone Mountain only to be crushed under the weight of Rushmore, given that he died in 1941 before it was complete, more accurately, Rushmore gave him a new lease on life. True, his bad habits died hard, too. He would always be his own worst enemy. But no one else could have accomplished what he did, much less dreamed it, and for that reason alone, Mount Rushmore must be regarded as a colossal triumph.

After announcing he had found the spot for his monument, Borglum returned to the hills and set up camp at the foot of Rushmore. He soon discovered that the mountain, while appearing so massive and formidable from the front, is actually a crescent-shaped formation, with a narrow, sixty-foot-deep canyon wrapping around its north side. Hiking up the canyon was strenuous, but not as difficult as the final scramble to the top, even for Borglum and Lincoln, who had been spidering across the slick face of Stone Mountain for years. Various slots on the granite offered lanes of ascent, but there were vertical stretches that required a brave heart and a sure grip. Over the next ten days, Borglum circled and climbed the mountain numerous times, probing and inspecting it from every possible angle. He even spent one night on the summit to observe the way light struck the mountain at dawn.

The granite itself was as good as he could have hoped for. Not flawless, like the almost creamy complexion of Stone Mountain. More like the figure of a well-kept dowager, streaked by the odd strand of gaudy jewelry—intrusions of bright, unstable pegmatite—but generally even-grained and firm. The cap of the mountain was a smooth, fairly flat plane, approximately 400 feet broad and 100 feet deep—much smaller than Stone Mountain, but ideally suited for sculpting in the round, from the top down. The most immediate logistical problem was not how to get men and equipment *up* the mountain—lifts and stairs could take care of that—but how to get them to the bottom. The nearest road ended at Keystone, three miles away, more than a thousand vertical feet below the base of Rushmore.

Borglum left the Black Hills on August 27, bubbling with ideas and energy. Before leaving Rapid City, he proposed, in addition to the figures of the four presidents, a tablet bearing the names of other nation builders: Lewis and Clark, Sam Houston, John C. Fremont, Thomas Hart Benton, and William H. Seward. "I am sure," he wrote to Norbeck from Nebraska, "that the world will recognize in this the first step that has ever been taken to collect at one point in the Union the record of its growth, and that makes it the first really national memorial."

Norbeck had his own reason for liking the foursome: "[I]t makes it possible to divide the work into several units and [to] accept contributions for any one of these units." Borglum may not have been worried about how to pay for Mount Rushmore, but Senator Norbeck, the pragmatist, knew how tough the task would be. "I met several men who said the monument should be Sitting Bull," he quipped to Robinson shortly after Borglum's departure. "I said to each one of them that I had no objection to a Sitting Bull monument, but that the friends of Sitting Bull would have to raise the money."

Borglum had vowed to return to the Black Hills in two or three weeks with his crew from Stone Mountain: superintendent Jesse Tucker, carver Hugo Villa, photographer Charles D'Emery, and Cliff "Dynamite" Davis, his explosives man. Together they would take careful measurements from which Borglum would make a scale model. Earlier he had told the *Rapid City Journal* that the memorial might cost as much as a million dollars. (Norbeck and Robinson were hoping they could get it done for half that.) But to get started, all he would need was five thousand dollars. "Personally [I] have no intention of making any charges as sculptor," he wired Robinson, "but initial actual expense must be born[e] by South Dakotans or I can't do anything for you."

Robinson and Norbeck were nonplussed. Borglum had been so blasé about the money, first saying it was not an issue, then recommending that Rushmore be financed by a commemorative coin, and then boasting that his "eastern money-kings"—he dropped the names of John D. Rockefeller of Standard Oil and Elbert H. Gary of U.S. Steel—were on the verge of writing $100,000 checks. But now, after promising that South Dakotans would not have to contribute a dime, he was putting the onus squarely on their shoulders. Under the circumstances, the most Robinson could raise was $1,000, donated begrudgingly by the Commercial Club of Rapid City.

Borglum returned to Rapid City on September 24, accompanied by Lincoln and photographer D'Emery, but without the entourage he had promised. For the next week, rather than taking measurements of Mount Rushmore, he directed preparations for an elaborate dedication ceremony, reminiscent, he hoped, of the one he had staged at Stone Mountain. Thirty women were enlisted to stitch enormous, thirty-by-eighteen-foot flags. Fort Meade in Sturgis promised to send a troop of cavalry; Rapid City offered its military band. Borglum himself shot an elk at Custer State Park to feed the expected crowd.

On October 1, an estimated three thousand celebrants and curiosity-seekers converged on tiny Keystone, probably more people than had ever set foot in the knockabout town in its entire half century of existence. Most walked the final three miles to the base of Rushmore, although a number of less cautious souls tested their flivvers against the new road scraped, just barely, into the flank of Grizzly Gulch. The band played, Lakota from Pine Ridge danced (to their own drums), and politicians dusted off their best Fourth of July oratory. Then Borglum, Norbeck, an Indian identified as Chief Black Horse, and several others in colonial and frontier costumes climbed to the top of the mountain. With the crowd arrayed below, they raised and lowered flags of France and Spain, the two nations that had previously held title to Rushmore. (The Indians didn't warrant a flag, but Black Horse got to stand on the summit alone for a minute or so.) For the grand finale, Borglum's men raised Old Glory atop Mount Rushmore, saluted by the singing of "The Star-Spangled Banner" and a volley from the Fort Meade soldiers. All in all, Borglum had put on a splendid and convincing show. "The hand of Providence is seen decreeing that a national memorial shall be erected," he declared when it was his turn to talk. He pledged that the statue of Washington would be completed in twelve months. "Meet me here a year from today," he dared.

The spirit of goodwill and great expectations waned considerably later that evening at a post-dedication banquet at the A&F Café in Rapid City. Norbeck, who heard the story secondhand, related the details to Doane Robinson. After dinner, the Rapid City men reportedly had pressed Borglum about finances. "I guess they were in hopes he would tell them about the million dollars he was so sure of," Norbeck said. "His replies were rather clever, but absolutely disclosed the fact that he had no money in sight and that it would be impossible to get money from the outside unless substantial progress was first made on the monument. In fact, he said at one time that if he had George Washington's head carved, the rest would be easy. They tried to pin him down to the cost of getting this done and then he showed his weakness, for he gave ill-considered estimates that were partly conflicting." What most in the group gathered, though, was that Borglum expected the citizens of the Black Hills to pitch in another $50,000 to pay for the surveys, models, and feasibility. "In other words," Norbeck concluded, "I feel that Borglum rather bungled the matter."

When Borglum got wind of the controversy, he flatly denied that he had made any such demand. "The story that $50,000 had to be raised before the memorial can be started is not true," he told the Sioux Falls *Argus Leader*. "I never made that statement." But when invited to set the record straight, he answered evasively: "Plans for financing the project as a shrine of interest to the nation are not in a state to be ... discussed at this time."

The truth was, he had no surefire strategy, and for the next two years, although Borglum, Robinson, and Norbeck cast about bravely for money to begin Mount Rushmore, they reaped only meager returns. The names of Rockefeller and Gary faded as benefactors, to be replaced by others. William Randolph Hearst was rich enough to pay for the entire monument (though of course he didn't). Then, as Norbeck had proposed, specific men from specific states were assigned specific presidents. In Illinois, perhaps someone from the Pullman family or W. G. Edens of the Central Trust could underwrite Lincoln. In Pennsylvania, Andrew Mellon of U.S. Steel or Arthur Humphrey from Westinghouse could claim Washington. Someone from Virginia would step forward on behalf of Jefferson. And Roosevelt's champions now had fresh incentive to enshrine their hero.

Since Roosevelt's death in 1919, the Roosevelt Memorial Association had raised nearly two million dollars. In February 1925, Congress had given the association permission to locate a memorial between the Washington Monument and the Potomac River, effectively awarding Roosevelt the last great site in the capital layout. Architect Henry Bacon's plans were submitted to Congress for approval the following year, only to hit an unexpected impasse. All along, many people, including some of Roosevelt's friends, had felt uneasy about erecting a memorial so soon after his death. "Give the grass time to grow on his grave before we pile up the marble," urged naturalist John Burroughs.

Still, the memorial might well have been authorized had 1926 not also been the centennial of Jefferson's death and the sesquicentennial of his masterwork, the Declaration of Independence. How could Roosevelt be more deserving of a monument than Jefferson? Congress, overcome by an acute case of Jefferson reappreciation, quashed the Roosevelt proposal and instead reserved the site for Jefferson. "Time will award to Roosevelt his proper place in history," remarked Representative John Boylan of New York. For now, however, it was Jefferson's turn "at the top of the list." (The Jefferson Memorial, while conceived in the 1920s, was not begun until 1939; it was dedicated in 1943.) Suddenly Roosevelt was in need of a new Acropolis. And while we have no record of Borglum's reaction to this abrupt turn of events, we can be sure that he relished the prospect of finally claiming Roosevelt for his own.

At any rate, the time seemed ripe for making monuments. Even Doane Robinson, the most provincial of the key Rushmore fundraisers, was convinced that sooner or later patrons would step forward. "I think," he confided to Borglum, "that 'John Smith' would be mighty glad to have inscribed on the base of the Sphinx 'Erected by John Smith B.C. 2000.'"

In his travels around the country, paid for somehow from his own pocket, Borglum called on every plutocrat and patriot he could think of. He was hardly shy about his solicitations—nobody liked buttonholing big shots better than Borglum—and experience had taught him that bluffing was part of the game. "So we are pretty well financed," he wrote to a wealthy San Antonio acquaintance. But, just in case, he added, "Why don't you be one of two men who will put up $25,000 apiece to begin the work immediately." Although he received universal encouragement and any number of verbal pledges, by early 1927 the Mount Harney Memorial Association, as the Rushmore organization was still called, had yet to raise its first $10,000. Senator Norbeck tried to look on the bright side. Mount Rushmore, he allowed, "has given South Dakota about the only favorable advertising it has had ... during the last eighteen months and has already brought many visitors to the state." Beyond that, the picture looked bleak.

Finally, the association decided to do just what Borglum had done at Stone Mountain: It would start carving and pray that the work in progress would somehow make its own rain. "[T]here is nothing so fatal to a monument," Borglum wrote to a wealthy Michigan prospect, "as to delay its building until you have got all the money in." The plan was to begin in May. At the last minute, the burghers of Black Hills commerce were enticed into committing $25,000, although not for reasons of art or patriotism, Robinson observed. "[C]hiefly they are hard boiled business men who have an eye only for the material side of it." Similar motives also led the region's three leading railroads to pledge $15,000. Herbert Myrick, publisher of several agricultural journals, including *Dakota Farmer*, donated $2,500 simply out of loyalty to his friend Borglum, who had accepted $1,000 of Myrick's gift in advance just to make ends meet. And finally, Charles Rushmore, who had prospered amply in the years since his tin-mining days, donated $5,000, presumably for the same reason that had prompted him to stick his name on an anonymous peak in the first place. On the other hand, Theodore Roosevelt Jr., son of the Colonel, had neither the ego nor the resources to contribute even a token sum.

As late as April, Borglum was still clinging to the hope that friends with "a couple of million dollars in idle money" would underwrite all or part of the memorial, and despite everything, Doane Robinson remained vulnerable to Borglum's wishful thinking. On May 19, with the work still not begun, Robinson noted: "We have an adequate pledge for the Roosevelt statue. We have a conditional pledge for Jefferson. We have tentative provision for Lincoln." But George Washington, he had to admit, "does not have a friend in the world."

All was a mirage, and Mount Rushmore might never have material-
ized if an extraordinary visitor had not arrived in the Black Hills in the
summer of 1927. President Calvin Coolidge, whose apparent goal was
to have as little impact on American history as possible, chose the Black
Hills, of all places, for his vacation, and in doing so, ensured, if not the
future of Mount Rushmore, then at least its birth. Over the ensuing
decades, various interests would advocate the addition of one president
or another to the four faces of the memorial. But if there ever was a
president who deserved cordial admission to the Rushmore elite, it was
Silent Cal Coolidge.

chapter 9

CLIFF NOTES

C ALVIN COOLIDGE could be a very eloquent orator when he wished. Still, he was never accused of being long-winded. Someone with nothing better to do once calculated that Abraham Lincoln's sentences averaged 26.6 words, Woodrow Wilson's 31.8, and Theodore Roosevelt's 41. Coolidge managed a frugal 18. When a pushy hostess bet that she could coax him to say more than two words to her, he replied, "You lose." And though he was said to have a handsome smile, the cameras never seemed to catch it. He told frequent jokes, but never laughed at them. One observer claimed that on the occasions when Coolidge did open his mouth, only moths flew out. While his contemporaries blamed his taciturnity on his "imprisoned soul" and "bitter self-control," Alice Roosevelt Longworth, unbridled daughter of America's verbose Rough Rider, figured that "Silent Cal" had simply been "weaned on a pickle."

Given Coolidge's profound, at times painful, reserve, politics seemed an unlikely calling. His own succinct explanation was that he wished to be "of some public service." There was nothing flamboyant, or even twentieth-century, about him. He refused to eat packaged breakfast cereal and never danced a step. Yet beneath his shyness and his old-fashioned fustiness ticked a precise, incremental ambition. In America, any man could be president. By most reckonings, Calvin Coolidge was pretty close to that.

He was born in Plymouth Notch, Vermont, on the Fourth of July, 1872. His family was Yankee, although Coolidge allowed that there might have been an Indian in one of the early woodpiles. When he was not attending the local one-room schoolhouse, he did chores on the family farm, where the virtue of thrift applied to speech and emotions as readily as to field and orchard. For college, he chose Amherst in Massachusetts, after which he read the law in nearby Northampton. His first elected office was that of town councilman. Soon he was mayor, then state assemblyman, state senator, lieutenant governor, and at last governor—the party of Lincoln all the way. In breaking the Boston police strike of 1919, he stated to the American Federation of Labor's Samuel Gompers, "There is no right to strike against the public safety by anyone, anytime, anywhere." With the nation in the midst of widespread upheaval—economic, social, spiritual—Coolidge's dispassion and deliberateness were received as comforting throwbacks.

In this respect, he was the ideal running mate for Warren G. Harding, the backslapping booster from Ohio. When Harding died on August 2, 1923, Coolidge was on the family farm in Vermont, riding a horse-drawn hay rake and pruning one of his cherished maple trees. His father, a notary, issued the presidential oath by the light of a kerosene lamp. If this was the Jazz Age, no one bothered to tell the new president. Harding had been America's soiled Babbitt—corrupt, besotted, adulterous. By the starkest of contrasts, Coolidge was perhaps the soberest, most moral president since Lincoln. William Allan White, the Midwest's Mencken, called him "a Puritan in Babylon."

Coolidge was even more laconic than Lincoln, although he too had

little difficulty getting his message across. His most memorable statement, "The business of America is business," said all that needed to be
said about his laissez-faire administration. Less talking also meant less
governing. His workday rarely lasted longer than four hours. On after-
noons, once his desk was clean, as it often was, he would take a long
nap, or if the weather was nice, pull his rocking chair onto the White
House porch and rock away in full view of Pennsylvania Avenue.
Asked by Will Rogers how he kept so healthy, Coolidge replied, "By
avoiding the big problems." With the stock market apparently robust
and self-sustaining (the crash wasn't until October 1929, on Herbert
Hoover's watch), Coolidge identified few matters deserving of his
intervention, which gave him plenty of time to pick out his sons'
clothes each morning and to count the apples in the White House
kitchen.

Coolidge won easy reelection in 1924, thanks to his primordial
calm, not to mention the disarray of the Democrats. But despite
Coolidge's two-to-one trouncing of John Davis, he and his wife, Grace,
were in no mood to celebrate. In late June, just two weeks after the
Republican Convention, their sixteen-year-old son Calvin Jr. had
rubbed a blister on his toe while playing tennis on the South Lawn of
the White House. The toe became infected, and on July 7, the boy died.
(For decades afterward, parents would admonish their children against
wearing sneakers without socks.) Coolidge, notoriously stoic, broke
down. "When [Calvin Jr.] went the power and the glory of the Presidency went with him," Coolidge confessed in his *Autobiography*. "I did
not know why such a price was exacted for occupying the White
House." Thenceforth, he could not look out at the White House
grounds without imagining Calvin Jr. at play there.

Nor could the Coolidges bear to spend another summer at the
White House. In 1925, Coolidge, his wife, and their other son, John,
took a beach house on the Massachusetts shore. The following year,
they tried the Adirondacks, which Coolidge loathed. In 1927, the

GREAT WHITE FATHERS

Coolidges had an additional reason to get out of town. The White House was undergoing major renovation, obliging them to take up temporary residence at Dupont Circle. Knowing that the first family would be seeking yet another summer retreat, numerous states fell over one another, extending welcomes. The Coolidges hardly cut a glamorous figure, but to win the presence of the president was still an honor, not to mention a considerable public-relations coup.

South Dakota's congressman William Williamson was delegated to make the case for his state, specifically the Black Hills. "The climate is all that could be desired," he touted, "and the scenery is unsurpassed. It is not so massive as to be overawing and oppressive, but it is sufficiently rugged to possess the charms of the best mountain landscape." Sensitive to the Wild West image of the hills fostered by movies and pulps—and mindful of the president's New England rectitude—the South Dakota legislature drafted a resolution informing Coolidge that "[t]he population in and about the mountains are intelligent and moral, with whom neighborly relations are most safe and pleasurable."

By March, the rumor reached Borglum that, miraculously, Coolidge was leaning toward the Black Hills. "It means everything to [the] monument," he telegraphed Doane Robinson. "Roads must be improved, work on monument must be rushed." Coolidge did not make his final decision until May 31, waiting until his advance man had checked out the accommodations thoroughly. For one thing, the president had never been so far from home. For another, he had an irrational fear of snakes, which he perceived to be coiled under every western rock. And he had one more reason to be nervous about his choice of South Dakota. Despite having grown up among farmers, as president he had not proven to be a steadfast friend of agriculture. The farm belt was still suffering in 1927 due to continuing overproduction and the rising cost of manufactured goods. Reminded that farmers across the country were struggling to make ends meet, Coolidge responded, "Well, farmers never have made money. I don't believe we can do much about it." Twice in the past year he had vetoed the McNary-Haugen bill, an immensely popular initiative of agricultural price supports. Washington pundits suggested that Coolidge's ulterior motive for selecting the Black Hills as his summer destination was to appease the disgruntled farm bloc, rattlers in their own right.

But finally the Coolidges did arrive in the Black Hills on June 13, establishing the summer White House in the folksy, twenty-room Game Lodge in Custer State Park. Rapid City High School, thirty miles away by freshly graveled road, became his executive office building. The hills reminded the Coolidges a lot of Vermont: austere, cool, attractive, but not "overawing," as Representative Williamson had assured. South Dakota did its best to roll out the red carpet, honoring President and Mrs. Coolidge in every way imaginable. They were presented with horses, sheep, a buffalo robe, a peace pipe, moccasins, fishing gear, agate jewelry, a twenty-five-pound tub of butter, and a ninety-pound watermelon. The president was given a ten-gallon hat, calf-high cowboy boots, spurs, and batwing chaps emblazoned with bucking horses and "Cal" in large letters. The Coolidges were feted at parades, fairs, rodeos, powwows, mines, the state fish hatchery, and an irrigation station. Mount Lookout was formally renamed Mount Coolidge, and in a precocious expression of political correctness, Squaw Creek, which ran past the Game Lodge, was renamed Grace Coolidge Creek.

In a somewhat less progressive ceremony during the Days of '76 rodeo at Deadwood, a delegation of Lakota inducted Coolidge into the tribe, presenting him with a dashing headdress and the Indian name "Leading Eagle." "We have nothing to give but our national respect," tribal spokesman Henry Standing Bear told Coolidge. "Our fathers and chiefs, Sitting Bull, Spotted Tail and Red Cloud, may have made mistakes; but their hearts were brave and strong, their purposes honest and noble. They have gone to their Happy Hunting Ground, and we call on you, as our new High Chief, to take up their leadership."

Even before the Coolidges had arrived in the Black Hills, Borglum had calculated how to lure the president into his web of granite. He had in mind a second dedication ceremony, this one marking the beginning of actual carving on Rushmore. "[T]he president should present to me the drills that I shall use," he elaborated to Doane Robinson, "and then I will go up on the mountain and start the work. We will have three drills and we will take them away that evening and have them properly inscribed; one of them given to the President, one to the Governor to be kept in the archives of the State, and one I shall keep myself.... They should be silver plated.... [T]hat is the kind of stuff that the morons of the world feed upon, and we must not overlook their human interest in these events."

One thing that Borglum hadn't figured on was Coolidge's guarded schedule. Between stints at the office in Rapid City and all the other touring about, Coolidge was, after all, supposed to be on vacation. Neither he nor his wife was a zealot for recreation, but the president did have a passing interest in fishing. Anticipating his every whim, his hosts had stocked Grace Coolidge Creek with sluggish trout fattened at the state hatchery in Spearfish. "[T]hey were so tame that they would swim right up to you and eat ground liver or ground horse meat out of your hand," recalled South Dakota governor William Bulow with a chuckle. "Those trout would fight and battle one another to see which could grab the President's hook. He became the nation's foremost trout fisherman." Unfortunately for Bulow, who had approved the secret stocking, he was obliged to join the Coolidges for a trout dinner. "The first bite I took," Bulow rued, "I could plainly taste the ground liver and the ground horse meat upon which that trout had lived for years. I never did like liver or horse meat either."

One other event intervened that summer. On August 2, Coolidge motored routinely to his office in Rapid City, handed a one-sentence message to his stenographer, and asked him to run it off several times on sheets of legal-sized paper. The president then cut the pages into two-inch strips, and at the stroke of noon, on the fourth anniversary of first taking the oath of office, he summoned the press corps and handed each reporter a slip on which was typed, "I do not choose to run for President in nineteen twenty eight." Coolidge offered no elaboration to his stunned audience, and instead put on his hat and drove home to lunch at the Game Lodge, where he had to be reminded to share the day's astonishing revelation with his wife.

Coolidge's terse announcement was not good news for Borglum—in neither the short run nor the long. As always, he had been counting on a friend in the White House to protect and promote his interests. Now Coolidge would be gone in a year and a half. More immediately, the press was totally absorbed with speculation over why Coolidge had made his decision and what it would mean for the country. The inauguration of work at Rushmore, scheduled for August 10, just eight days after the president's twelve-word bombshell, was suddenly a sidebar.

Coolidge of course knew Borglum, as had every president since Roosevelt had succeeded McKinley in 1901. The Stone Mountain coin and controversy were still fresh in Coolidge's mind, and he would have been fully briefed on Borglum's latest endeavor. Yet it was not automatic that the president would be party to the ceremony Borglum had planned. Coolidge had said that he would make no formal speeches while in South Dakota, and the brevity of his "I do not choose" announcement did not bode well for a sermon on the mount at Rushmore.

But Borglum was not to be denied. On May 27, a shy, gangly flyer from Minnesota, Charles Lindbergh, had stunned the world by completing the first-ever nonstop crossing of the Atlantic. Borglum called the flight "the act of a super man . . . the apogee of courage in our Colossal Age," and took inspiration from Lucky Lindy's triumph. On June 23, Borglum, no stranger to planes himself—or to theatrics, for that matter—hired a local pilot with the splendid name of Clyde Ice to swoop low over the Game Lodge, where the Coolidges were entertaining another of Borglum's heroes, General Leonard Wood. Mount Coolidge had been dedicated the day before, prompting Borglum to airdrop a wreath of flowers, weighted by two moccasins, bearing the felicitations, "Greetings from Mt. Rushmore to Mt. Coolidge." Grace Coolidge, whose vivacity was the antidote to her husband's starch, jotted a prompt thank-you: "Your greeting from the air found glad welcome and we echo it back to you."

The courtship worked, and the president consented to make a speech at Rushmore. On the morning of August 10, he was driven by limousine as far as Keystone. Then, dressed in his new cowboy boots, hat, and fringed gloves, he rode horseback up the hill to the reviewing stand at the foot of Mount Rushmore. His arrival was saluted not by bugle fanfare or rifle volley, but by the concussion of twenty-one stumps dynamited from the new Rushmore roadway. When the dust settled, Coolidge presented Borglum with six (not three) steel (not silver) drill bits. The crowd was then asked to wait while Borglum, wearing his mountaineer knickers and sneakers, lugged the ceremonial bits to the summit and was lowered over the side in a boatswain's chair. Wielding a cumbersome jackhammer, he drilled the first six holes in Mount Rushmore, one with each drill bit.

In his remarks before scaling the mountain, Borglum explained that he intended to add a grand entablature to the four faces—a Rosetta stone of sorts, on which would be recorded the high points of "the founding, preservation and expansion" of the United States. (Specifically, he jotted to Doane Robinson several days later: "the Declaration of Independence, the Revolution, the Constitution, the Louisiana Purchase 1803–4, the Florida annexation 1821, the Texas admission 1846, the Oregon assumption 1846, the California accession 1850, the Alaska Session 1867, the Panama Republic 1904.") Ad-libbing, he invited Coolidge to be the inscription's author. He even hinted that he might add

Coolidge's face to the mountain. Coolidge reciprocated by assuring Borglum that he would favor federal funding of Rushmore.

Coolidge was full of surprises that day. His speech, delivered under a bright sun to a crowd of more than a thousand, was longer and more florid than anyone had dared to expect. "We have come here to dedicate a corner stone that was laid by the hand of the Almighty," he began. More apple pie followed:

> Here in the heart of the continent, on the side of a mountain which probably no white man had ever beheld in the days of Washington, in territory which was acquired by the action of Jefferson, which remained an almost unbroken wilderness beyond the days of Lincoln, which was especially beloved by Roosevelt, the people of the future will see history and art combined to portray the spirit of patriotism. . . . If coming generations are to maintain a like spirit, it will be because they continue to study the lives and times of the great men who have been the leaders in our history, and continue to support the principles which those men represented. It is for that purpose that we erect memorials. . . . This memorial will be another national shrine to which future generations will repair to declare their continuing allegiance to independence, to self government, to freedom and to economic justice.

Afterward, Coolidge mounted his horse, rode back down the mountain, returned to the Game Lodge—and that same day matter-of-factly denied clemency for Nicola Sacco and Bartolomeo Vanzetti, convicted (many said unfairly) of murder and robbery, but demonized as well for their pro-labor politics and Italian nativity. The president's decision triggered riots around the world that climaxed thirteen days later when Sacco and Vanzetti were executed in Coolidge's adopted state of Massachusetts.

Coolidge remained in the West several more weeks, touring Yellowstone Park, dedicating a Boy Scout camp, and meeting with the local Temperance League. By far the biggest excitement of the final days came on September 2, when the Game Lodge was buzzed from the air again, this time by Lindbergh himself, who was on a victory tour across the continent. All in all, Coolidge seemed to have enjoyed the summer. Indeed, to the extent that the public remembers Silent Cal at all, it pictures him in war bonnet or cowboy hat, trying his level best to be jaunty.

For the next two months, the six holes Borglum had drilled at Rushmore were, for all intents and purposes, the only marks on the mountainside. Preparations that should have been completed in the spring and summer had been delayed for lack of money. The Homestake Mine in Lead and U.S. Senator Coleman DuPont of Delaware, a friend of Borglum's and an advocate of national roadways, had kicked in $5,000 each, and Samuel Insull, the millionaire utility magnate of Chicago, had donated a used 275-horsepower diesel power plant. But even with these additions, the Mount Harney Memorial Association was not yet flush enough to finish the year, much less the entire job.

But at least it had money enough to get started. Jesse Tucker was hired at an annual salary of $10,000. The contract awarded to Borglum called for him to be paid 25 percent of whatever money was spent on construction. The entire project—four presidents and the entablature— was expected to take five years and cost $437,000. Yet even if it took longer and cost more, the contract stipulated that Borglum's share would not exceed $87,500. Clearly, Borglum had an incentive to complete the work on schedule and on budget. Then again, given his track record at Stone Mountain and with *Wars of America*, the implicit optimism and self-inflicted parsimony of the contract seemed more like a formula for disaster.

For now, there was nothing to do but get busy. Tucker erected sheds, set up his power plant, air compressors, hoists, and winches. He strung air hoses and a 1,300-foot tram, for gear only. The crew, whom Tucker hired from the local populace of hard-rock miners, would have to walk to work—a climb of more than 700 wooden steps and forty-some ramps.

The lumpiness of Mount Rushmore, and the decision to carve in the round (three-quarter round, actually), precluded the possibility of employing the projector method that had worked so well at Stone Mountain. And because the true character of the granite could not be determined until Tucker began "peeling off" the worn and fissured outer layers, Borglum had decided to sculpt one figure at a time. Already he had tinkered with his composition, shifting Jefferson to Washington's right and snugging Lincoln up to Washington's left, leaving Roosevelt on his far left—a configuration that would change twice more before the memorial was completed.

All sculpture, regardless of scale, needs a Greenwich Mean Time that anchors and orients all the parts of the composition. As his ground zero, Borglum chose the dead center of the top of Washington's head. From here he would determine the position of all the other heads. His intention was to point Washington's nose due south, his ears east-west. "I'm building everything according to compass and sun," he explained to Robinson. He envisioned morning light catching Washington "as a footlight does the face of an actor," and he hoped that "the gold of the setting sun, now clear to the southwest, [would] touch his right cheek." With a steel plate marking the starting spot, he instructed Tucker to rough out an immense, egg-shaped mass of granite. Further study of light and shadow would tell him whether the head needed to be tilted up or down or pivoted left or right.

Crucial to these adjustments was the ability to "point," a skill perfected by Borglum and Tucker at Stone Mountain. At Mount Rushmore, they installed their pointing gear on the crown of Washington's soon-to-be head. The instrument was a thirty-foot boom that could be rotated horizontally with exactitude. Suspended vertically from the tip of the boom was a plumb line, which could be lowered or shortened with like precision. Meanwhile, a similar, much smaller pointing machine was mounted atop the plaster model of Washington's head. Borglum sculpted his model on a scale of one to twelve—one inch on the model translated as one foot on the mountain. Because he wanted the Rushmore faces to be sixty feet tall from chin to pate, he made the head of the model six feet tall. Honoring this golden ratio, the task of determining where to carve on the mountain—say, the tip of Washington's nose—was accomplished by carefully pivoting the boom on the model till it hung directly over its respective nose and then by lowering the plumb bob. By noting the degrees of rotation and the length of drop, this information could then be passed along to the "pointer" on the mountain, who, having converted inches to feet, could direct the carvers where to place their drills. Simple enough?

Hardly. On the mountain, geology had a way of confounding geometry. Moving men about on a 400-foot wall of granite was far more difficult than calibrating inches and degrees. A mountain carver began by cinching himself into a leather boatswain's chair attached to a three-quarter-inch steel cable. Also attached to the cable was a seventy-five-pound jackhammer, which had its own separate umbilical, a stiff air hose. The carver was required to walk backward over the side of the cliff, hefting his ungainly gear, and then allow himself to be lowered, one step at a time, by the operator of a hand-cranked windlass. The winch man sat in a shack located well back from the precipice and out of view of the carver. He had to depend on the eyes and voice of a "call boy," a youngster who perched on the brow of the mountain and relayed signals between the man with the crank and the man with the jackhammer—"down six inches," "up a foot," and so on.

Needless to say, a man who had drilled in a mine was not a guaranteed master of mountain carving. Even if he was able to adjust to the height and exposure—no small feat—there was still the matter of balance and leverage. If he lost his footing, he was in no danger of falling (the cable was plenty strong). Instead he merely smacked up against the side of the unforgiving cliff with an angry steel bit chattering between his legs. To get a decent purchase on the granite, carvers learned to lean back, wedge the drill bit between their boots, and brace the hammer against their stomachs. One of the drillers who got the hang of it was Norman "Hap" Anderson, who worked on Rushmore six years. "My belly was so hard in those days," he recalled, "that my wife could dance on my stomach in high-heeled shoes."

Actual carving did not begin until October 4. Until he better understood the rock, Borglum gave strict orders to use only the lightest explosive charges. "The crushing effect ... stuns too much," he cautioned Tucker. He was worried about the seams of fragile pegmatite and the mountain's overall "float block" dynamic. Geologists had informed him that Rushmore was not one single mass of granite but numerous gigantic lobes of rock—float blocks—pressed tightly together like mutant cloves of garlic. And so Tucker and his men proceeded gingerly at first, feeling out the mountain and one another. Fortunately, the initial work of removing large chunks of the outer rock required the least finesse. Dynamite, carefully measured and judiciously placed, could peel the granite down to within six or eight inches of the rock that would actually be "carved." The final layer would be removed by the same honeycombing method developed at Stone Mountain, and the finishing would consist of a "bumping" process, in which a lighter, four-pointed bit was bounced methodically across the granite, creating a surface that appeared quite smooth.

It was one thing for Borglum to expect prudence from others, quite another for him to be patient himself. One of his priorities had been construction of a studio near the mountain in which he could fine-tune his models. By the end of summer, it still had not been built. On August 31, he vented his frustration to Robinson: "I have been here now for more than seven weeks and except for securing the power plant from my friends, installing my models in a little log cabin, getting the President to make the inscription, giving Mr. Tucker a few measurements to keep him going, I have idled most of that time because I have no place to work in."

For the first time, Robinson got a taste of the acid that had stained Stone Mountain. He did his best to placate Borglum, but the normally congenial historian did not roll over entirely. "There is a vulgar expression much in vogue, called bellyaching," Robinson replied to Borglum. "You will excuse me if I say that your conduct and attitude very much savors of that complaint." Borglum, for the time being, seemed to welcome such frankness. "God bless you," he wired Robinson. "If it were not for you we never would have been on this great work. Perfection however must necessarily be my goal. In that alone lies the immortality of our race and in its accomplishment an artist becomes a kind of priest and posterity and civilization never forgives in him any compromise." To which, Robinson could only answer, "I will lift mine eyes unto the hills."

But there wasn't much to see. The weather grew so unmercifully awful that at the beginning of December, Tucker was obliged to shut down for the winter. Borglum was dismayed to learn that, due to lack of funds from the Mount Harney Memorial Association, Tucker had had to pay his men out of his own pocket. And the way things were going, there wouldn't be enough money in the association's account to rehire the crew the following spring, much less reimburse Tucker.

Borglum returned to San Antonio for the winter, where he had plenty of other work to keep him occupied. *Wars of America* was done, having finally been installed in Newark's Military Park on Memorial Day 1926. He had lost money on the project, but he had the satisfaction of knowing that the monument was a resounding success. The Trail Drivers memorial, his next *Wars*, was coming along, too. He completed an eight-foot model in clay (one-quarter the size of the proposed monument) and toured it around Texas, eliciting praise and soliciting contributions. And through the Trail Drivers, he met Lorine Spoonts, daughter of wealthy Texas cattle- and oilman William Whitby Jones. In

1919, Corpus Christi, on the Gulf Coast, had been thrashed by a hurricane, killing nearly three hundred people, and Spoonts, president of the Chamber of Commerce (and a recent widow), was predictably charmed by Borglum's sweeping vision of how to rebuild the Corpus Christi waterfront with a seawall, boulevard, and of course plenty of sculpture. Their friendship would last through thick and thin, and in 1937, Borglum's son Lincoln would marry Spoonts's niece Louella.

Nor did the Confederacy abandon Borglum. A group in Fort Worth approached him about carving a monument to Robert E. Lee and the "Mothers of the Confederacy." North Carolina wanted him to memorialize its sons killed during Pickett's heroic but fruitless charge at Gettysburg. The previous year, patrons in Atlanta—those of the faction chagrined over the Stone Mountain fiasco—had commissioned him to carve a marble portrait of Confederate vice president Alexander Stephens for the National Statuary Hall in Washington.

To Borglum, the Stephens monument was a tiny bandage on the still tender wound of Stone Mountain. Augustus Lukeman, the sculptor whom Randolph had hired to replace Borglum, had blasted Borglum's head of Lee off the mountain and proceeded with his own design. (Lukeman's Lee, Jackson, and Davis carried their hats in their hands, doffed in the presence of women visitors to Stone Mountain.) Yet Lukeman's luck was not much better than that of his predecessor. The Confederate coin never caught on, and money for carving was chronically in short supply. In 1928, Sam Venable, who detested Randolph and his cronies, took back Stone Mountain once the lease with the association had expired. For the next twenty-five years, the mountain sat idle, not so much unfaced as defaced, until finally the state of Georgia decided to pick up where Lukeman had left off. Crews used state-of-the-art thermo-jet torches that blasted away granite as a match melts ice, accomplishing in a day what fifty men could scarcely manage in a week. When the Vietnam War, specifically the American bombing of Cambodia and the subsequent public outrage, prevented President

Richard Nixon from appearing at the dedication of Stone Mountain in May 1970, he sent Vice President Spiro Agnew in his place, an unsatisfactory ending to an unsavory saga.

All hope of resuming work on Mount Rushmore in 1928 rested on approval of federal funding, which Coolidge had endorsed while in the Black Hills the previous summer. In an early meeting with Secretary of the Treasury Andrew Mellon, Borglum had stated that $500,000 would be sufficient to complete the job. Moreover, he had assured Mellon that he could raise half that amount from private donors. Accordingly, Mellon had endorsed legislation calling for an appropriation of $250,000 in *matching funds*. In other words, the government would not spend a dollar till Rushmore had raised a dollar. The legislation—one bill in the Senate, one in the House—also called for formation of a Mount Rushmore National Memorial Commission to oversee the federal appropriation (and to replace the Mount Harney Memorial Association).

Senator Norbeck and Representative Williamson both succeeded in passing their respective bills in May. Williamson had more trouble than Norbeck due to a misconception among House members that Coolidge was to be included on Rushmore. "The statue of the other patriots would fall off their pedestals laughing at Cal in a Tom Mix suit," sneered Representative Loring Black of New York. "Or perhaps there should be a frieze (freeze) of Cal, couchant a la Big Chief Pain-in-the-Neck." Borglum, who, for all his talk, still had not landed any big donors, ought to have been elated by the news from Washington, but instead he tasted only sour grapes. "Have a disposition not to help if federal government takes charge," he wired Norbeck from Texas. Only upon further reflection, plus some stern chiding from Norbeck, did Borglum come around, affirming that the appropriation had "solved everything."

But it hadn't. Minor discrepancies between the two bills had to be ironed out, and until then, work could not commence. Summer spun into fall, and soon there was no point in gearing up at all. In November, Herbert Hoover, Secretary of Commerce and a no-nonsense engineer, defeated Democrat Al Smith for president, and Coolidge, Rushmore's self-avowed champion, prepared to slip quietly from the White House. At the eleventh hour, on February 22, 1929, the Rushmore bill finally cleared Congress. Coolidge signed it three days later, just a week before leaving office. Borglum gave credit where it was due, but kept a hefty portion for himself, too, still boasting that he was about to pick the pocket of one Rockefeller or another. "I have a plan to get all of the [matching funds] within the next sixty to ninety days," he assured Robinson, "and I'm going to get the head of Washington finished this year."

While Borglum continued to make promises he couldn't keep, Norbeck and Coolidge put together the Mount Rushmore National Memorial Commission. Norbeck had declined an appointment for himself, partly because he believed he could be more useful outside the loop and partly because his friend Doane Robinson had been left off the list as well. Robinson, while the true father of Rushmore, was not a man of means or national clout, the preferred criteria for membership on this sort of board. Instead, the chairmanship went to Joseph Cullinan, a Houston oilman and friend of Borglum. The rest of the commissioners were railroad men; newspaper and radio station owners; and the chairman of Sears, Roebuck. Lorine Spoonts was also appointed, the only woman. All told, Borglum figured, the Rushmore commission had an aggregate worth of more than a billion dollars.

The logical choice for chairman of the commission's executive committee, which would handle the week-to-week responsibilities, was John Boland, former mayor of Rapid City, leader of the Commercial Club, and owner of the Rapid City Implement Company, the region's largest purveyor of farm machinery and supplies. As a boy, Boland had lived in Keystone, down the hill from Mount Rushmore, where he had worked in the mines until he could save enough to buy a feed and grocery store. He went to work for the Implement Company in 1917 and within a year had taken control. Boland was exactly what the Rushmore commission needed to balance Borglum's impetuousness. Yet it was only a matter of time before Borglum would pronounce the dutiful, thorough Boland "stupid," "uncultured," and "meddlesome." In Borglum's eyes, this mild-mannered merchant of the Black Hills—known universally for extending credit to farmers whose only collateral was a couple of hundred acres of blown-out prairie and a motley herd of livestock—soon metamorphosed into a fiendish "racketeer."

In reality, though, the only thing meddlesome about Boland was that he paid the Rushmore bills and tried his best to clean up Borglum's messes. The only thing conspiratorial about him was that he kept Norbeck and the commission informed of the goings-on at Mount Rushmore. Never mind—Borglum needed a nemesis, and Boland was the man for the job. Most prophetic was the letter that Borglum wrote to Norbeck shortly after Boland's appointment. "Boland has a fine, just mind [and an] even temper," Borglum offered, "and if I could not get along with him, I'd know there was something wrong with me."

One man who would never be rattled by Borglum was Herbert Hoover. Despite Borglum's polished pestering, which had worked so effectively with previous presidents, Hoover did not consent to convene the Mount Rushmore National Memorial Commission until June 6. The next day, Treasury Secretary Mellon released $54,000 to match the amount already spent on Rushmore. Borglum immediately wired Tucker that they were back in business, after a nineteen-month hiatus. At the end of the year, when weather and lack of funding again drove the crew from the mountain, Borglum was able to report that the head of Washington was complete "to within an average of 8 inches of the finished work" and that the head of Jefferson, located to Washington's right, was beginning to take shape. "It is contemplated," he said, "that the heads of Washington and Jefferson will be finished for unveiling on Independence Day, 1930."

News this sunny was especially welcome, given the prevailing gloom of that fall. In September, Jesse Tucker, Borglum's dedicated and knowledgeable supervisor, had walked off the job and sued the Memorial Commission, claiming that he was owed nearly two years in back pay. Borglum, who had not been paid his full salary either, received Tucker's exit as an act of utter betrayal, and instead of trying to woo back his most capable lieutenant, he bid him good riddance.

And as usual, Borglum's doctrinaire posturing put him in a real bind. His plan had always been to work on Mount Rushmore part-time, leaving Tucker to rough out his designs. Now he had no choice but to promote two inexperienced underlings, Calvin Denison and William Tallman, to oversee the carving and pointing. For all their eagerness to take on more responsibility, Denison and Tallman could not be left alone for very long. If the work was to be done right, Borglum had no other choice but to spend more time on the mountain. So in September, within days of Tucker's departure, he somehow finagled a loan and bought a twelve-hundred-acre ranch near the town of Hermosa on Grace Coolidge Creek, downstream from the Game Lodge and twenty miles from Mount Rushmore. Thenceforth, he would continue to spend winters in Texas, but from early spring until ice and snow evicted his crew from the mountain at the start of winter, he would function as both sculptor and supervisor of Rushmore, a commitment that put a significant crimp in his ability to undertake other sculptural endeavors.

Borglum wasn't the only one in debt that autumn. In October, the stock market crashed, and the Great Depression began to erode the will and wherewithal of the nation. Everyone lost something in those hungry years. What Mount Rushmore lost, almost immediately, was any chance of significant private funding. The "malefactors of great wealth" who hadn't gone entirely broke were guarding what they had left. That included the formerly flush Rushmore commissioners. In the future, Mount Rushmore would be a public project, or it would be nothing at all.

In later years, Borglum would call the stock market crash a "blessed thing." "I am glad that the bankers have squandered our money, and I wish things were worse," he told the Newark Art Club in 1932. "We need lessons like this to drive home the fact that joy of living lies beyond the pot of gold at the rainbow's end." And he was right to the extent that hard times may even have helped Mount Rushmore. As the Depression deepened, many Americans began to wonder whether the nation's economic model wasn't fatally flawed. All the while, socialism was gaining momentum abroad, as evidenced so graphically by the oversized monuments to Lenin and his comrades springing up across the Soviet Union and magnificent, propagandistic murals by artists such as Diego Rivera plastered so prominently on the public walls of Mexico and elsewhere.

The way to break the cycle of uncertainty was to keep the faith. Americans needed to stiffen their resolve, to stand strong, like the Rock of Gibraltar. Better yet, like Mount Rushmore, the immense monument taking shape at the center of the nation. George Washington, Father of the Country, had always been our bedrock. In this context, the dedication of Washington's unmistakable profile on Rushmore, scheduled for the Fourth of July 1930, loomed as more than just another occasion for patriotic prattle. It was shaping up as an earnest and overdue reaffirmation of America's character. During the First World War, the Statue of Liberty had shed its status as a white elephant, a garish gift from well-meaning friends. With her chin thrust toward war-torn Europe, *Liberty* became our Athena, the radiant hood ornament of an unswerving republic. Similarly, during the Depression and the Second World War, Mount Rushmore would emerge as the nation's vivid new icon of strength and stability.

And the fact that Rushmore was carved from the earth, that a mountain could also be a monument, made a strong impression on a nation whose self-image was so closely tied to its spectacular landscape. A century earlier, explorers who had discovered an enormous cruciform on the side of a remote mountain in the Colorado Rockies (now named Mount of the Holy Cross) took it as proof that America was God's chosen land. At about the same time, Nathaniel Hawthorne had written a parable, "The Great Stone Face," about New Hampshire's Old Man of the Mountain. "[A]ll the features were noble," Hawthorne observed, and the surrounding land "owed much of its fertility to this benign aspect that was continually beaming over it." Rushmore, because of its setting as much as its size, was every bit as talismanic. And while it still had its skeptics, those who doubted that Borglum could finish the job, those who disparaged its fundamental conceit, were becoming harder to find. Indeed, to suggest that Mount Rushmore was a spendthrift exercise in vainglory suddenly sounded almost sacrilegious.

Colossalism, Borglum stated repeatedly, was simply the appropriate scale for American public art, the proper-sized organ for the American tabernacle. "The amazing and expanding character of [our] civilization clearly demanded an enlarged dimension," he wrote in 1927. In his eyes, America's empire builders were larger-than-life characters. (Christopher Columbus, he once averred, was "the most important individual since Christ.") So he had designed Washington, Jefferson, Lincoln, and Roosevelt with sixty-foot heads, on bodies that, if finished, would have been more than 400 feet tall. "If they stood in the Falls of Niagara they would block the great cataract," he expounded in his best Paul Bunyan hyperbole. "If they should walk down the East River to the Hudson, they could barely creep under the great bridges ... and when they reached the Statue of Liberty, they would have to stoop to read by her dimming light." If this sort of swagger amounted to propaganda, if the American voice carried farther than any other, then so be it.

Borglum had always possessed a gift for playing his audience, and now with the Depression, he adjusted his tone to suit the times. More and more, he chose to downplay the image of the Rushmore presidents as conquerors. They remained Great Men, to be sure, but now he stressed the principles they embodied over their cult of personality. America's "Puritan chrysalis," he told a radio audience, had given birth to an immaculate, inalienable truth: "Man has a right to be free and to be happy." With this in mind, he concluded, "We are not creating a monument to Washington, Jefferson, Lincoln, and Roosevelt, but to the meaning of these eleven words." In March, the Rushmore commission channeled this heightened idealism into a new fund-raising campaign. The commission established an auxiliary, the Mount Rushmore Memorial Society, "to provide in part the funds for the carving ... [and] to aid in appropriate landscaping, parking ... and protecting the grounds." Chairman Cullinan suggested sprucing up the society's letterhead with the slogan, "America's Shrine for Political Democracy." In the economic drought of the 1930s, the society didn't raise a great deal of money, but Cullinan's moniker, soon shortened to "The Shrine of Democracy," caught on immediately. In principle at least, Mount Rushmore now held the highest ground possible.

Other attempts at sloganeering did not come off so well. On the eve of the Washington dedication, Borglum had pursued his plan to have Calvin Coolidge, now president emeritus, write the inscription for the Rushmore entablature. Borglum had already begun preparing the granite a hundred feet or so to Washington's left (roughly where Lincoln's head is positioned today). His aim was to reveal the text, if not the actual carved inscription, during the Washington dedication. "[F]or the first time, improbably, in the history of America[,] a monument is being erected for the purpose of making a record of great national accomplishments," he told the *New York Herald Tribune* in February. The three most important accomplishments cited no longer pertained to territorial expansion; instead Borglum listed the Declaration of Independence, the Constitution, and the Bill of Rights. Old urges died hard, however. Regardless of the final words and events chosen for the inscription, Borglum still intended to carve the entablature in the shape of the Louisiana Purchase.

Coolidge, the monumental minimalist, was the perfect choice as author of the entablature. Borglum calculated that if he used letters three feet high, he would have room for 375 words, averaging six letters per word. Coolidge's first two entries—synopses of the Declaration of Independence and the Constitution—were the quintessence of brevity. Even so, Borglum was congenitally unable to leave well enough alone, and so he decided to make minor changes in the text, an initiative that nettled both Coolidge and the press. Coolidge's reduction of the Declaration of Independence read as follows: "In the year of our Lord 1776, the people declared the eternal right to seek happiness, self government and the divine duty to defend that right at any sacrifice." All Borglum changed was one phrase: "the eternal right to seek happiness *through* self government . . ." (emphasis added). The *Boston Transcript* declared the alteration "a presumptuous act," and other papers soon joined in the hairsplitting. "Sculptor Borglum is an artist before he is a respecter of ex-Presidents," *Time* magazine jabbed. Coolidge, as usual, kept his thoughts to himself and simply withdrew from the project—even though the Rushmore legislation distinctly specified that he be the author of the inscription.

Borglum hated to lose the entablature. As a student of ancient civilizations and their artifacts, he knew that none lasted forever. Nor was there any guarantee that our own civilization would fare much better; the stock market crash of 1929 gave sober warning of that. One of the inspirations for the Rushmore entablature had been Darius the Great's two-and-a-half-thousand-year-old inscription on a mountainside near Bisitun, in present-day Iran, which enabled archaeologists to recall the high points of Darius's reign. (Because he was king, and not just president, Darius was allowed five thousand words, in three languages.) Borglum had intended Mount Rushmore to convey the message of America thousands of millennia into the future, long past the time when "every other government on earth has melted into fine clay and blown away." Indeed, he calculated that in ten thousand years, George

Washington's nose would not have eroded even one inch. But now, without its accompanying entablature, the monument seemed doomed to the enigmatic fate of Stonehenge or the animal designs of Nazca, scrawled across miles and miles of Peruvian desert. "You might as well drop a letter into the World's Postal Service without an address or signature as to send that carved Mountain into history without identification," he lamented.

George Washington, meanwhile, was coming along nicely, with or without the entablature. Given Borglum's intimate knowledge of the features and personality of Abraham Lincoln, he might just as easily have started with him, deferring Washington until he had gained more confidence on the mountain. Yet he had any number of reasons for tackling Washington first. Not only was Washington the First American; he was also the most familiar. Washington's face had appeared on postage stamps since 1847, on the dollar bill since 1869. His portrait had been painted numerous times, from the famous unfinished oil of Gilbert Stuart—Washington tightlipped with cotton stuffed in his cheeks to pad his false teeth—to Emanuel Leutze's more heroic (and often lampooned) *Washington Crossing the Delaware*. Popular prints, whiskey bottles, and tobacco cans bore his likeness. Even more conspicuous was Washington's name: 121 cities and towns, including the nation's capital, thirty-three counties, ten lakes, nine colleges, seven mountains, and one state are named after him, not to mention thousands of citizens. By 1900, forty-five states celebrated Washington's birthday as a legal holiday (compared to eight for Lincoln).

Countless scholars have tried to explain the special resonance of George Washington. His very stature—he was more than six feet tall, a rarity in his day—made him a man above most. His leadership and courage clearly helped win the Revolutionary War. And once the war was won, the new United States, having shed its monarch, needed a new symbol of stability, and so George the president replaced George the king. By turns of the patriotic zodiac, Washington also became America's Moses (and later God, to Lincoln's Christ), leading the chosen through the wilderness. He was Cincinnatus, the citizen soldier who rescues Rome, then returns to his fields. He stood as a standard of virility, undaunted amid the ice of the Delaware. And he was a paragon of humility (leaving office voluntarily), piety (praying at Valley Forge), and honesty (*not* lying about the cherry tree). These latter two characterizations owe their dissemination to Parson Mason Locke Weems, whose *The Life of George Washington; With Curious Anecdotes, Equally Honourable to Himself and Exemplary to His Young Countrymen* functioned as a sort of secular catechism for American youth throughout the nineteenth and early twentieth centuries. (Mark Twain was one of the few who claimed superiority to Washington, noting that while Washington could not tell a lie, Twain could, but wouldn't.) All in all, had Washington not existed, someone would have had to invent him.

And they apparently did, at least according to a torrent of articles and books that appeared in the 1920s, just as Borglum was getting started on Mount Rushmore. The leader of the pack was William E. Woodward, who had previously coined the term "debunking" (a play on the World War I procedure of "delousing") and was now keen to put it to good use. In his 1926 biography, *George Washington: The Image and the Man*, Woodward endeavored to humanize Washington—legend taking the hindmost. "Did any body ever see Washington nude?" Nathaniel Hawthorne had wondered in 1853. "It is inconceivable. He had no nakedness, but I imagine was born with his clothes on, and his hair powdered." By the Roaring Twenties, the wig was off and so was the halo. "He was the American common denominator, the average man deified and raised to the nth power," Woodward opined. Quick to praise Washington for his courage and honesty, Woodward also made sure to sketch his subject as a vain, pompous martinet of average intelligence and compromised morals. "Although he was a man of gentility and breeding," Woodward remarked in a subsequent essay, "he did not have much aesthetic taste, and beneath his gentility—very close to the surface—was a substratum of burly roughness."

The rest of the chorus was just as cheeky. Rupert Hughes, who completed his three-volume biography of Washington in 1930, dismissed Weems's accounts of the cherry tree and the prayer at Valley Forge as a "slush of plagiarism" perpetuated by a "priestcraft of suppression." With further help from Washington's diaries, the first volumes of which were published in 1925, and articles bearing titles such as "The George Washington Scandals" and "Washington—Man or Waxwork?" the public learned that Washington whipped his slaves and evicted his tenants. He played cards, bet the horses, danced madly, drank profusely, swore like a flatboatman, and scribbled smutty letters. He is accused of having an affair with an octoroon and a married Tory, and, according to gossip, may have taken ill and died after a cold ride home from the bed of an employee's wife. He is said to have chosen his own wife Martha (whom Woodward calls "dumpy") for her money. Some accounts assert that the Father of the Country was sterile (from a boyhood case of mumps), while others surmise that Alexander Hamilton was his illegitimate son. And by the way, Washington's false teeth were reportedly made from hippopotamus ivory.

Whether these recent investigations fell into the category of humanizing or simply scandal-mongering, the result was a heightened familiarity. "I have been peculiarly delighted," Rupert Hughes wrote in the afterword to his trilogy, "to find that many children who have somehow got hold of my book have said that it taught them to love Washington for the first time, by ridding him of the offensive handicaps of the cherry tree and other priggish inventions." Adults, no doubt, while titillated, were not necessarily shocked by the new warts-and-all Washington. His love of liquor could be forgiven. After all, Prohibition was a joke by 1930. Jazz had blurred the line between music and sex, and everybody knew that President Harding had kept a mistress. Even

Coolidge, immune to debunking himself, had called Washington "the first commercial American," an endorsement that qualified the Father of the Country for Rotary lunches, if not Olympus.

Borglum, who knew Rupert Hughes well, could not have missed the trend in Washingtonia. In December 1924, only three months after Borglum's initial trip to the Black Hills, Congress had created the Commission for the Celebration of the Two Hundredth Anniversary of the Birth of George Washington, to be held eight years hence. Borglum, attuned to every major commission coming out of the capital, including the recent tug-of-war between the Jefferson and Roosevelt Memorials, surely appreciated that Washington was now in play as well. He had no desire to join in the debunking, but when it came time to depict Washington on Mount Rushmore, he seized the opportunity to put fresh life in the ossified iconography of the previous two centuries.

While Borglum did not examine Washington as thoroughly as he had Lincoln, he did his share of homework. Besides studying the painted portraits by Gilbert Stuart, Rembrandt Peale, and John Trumbull, he had familiarized himself with most of the major Washington sculptures, including John Quincy Adams Ward's Washington on the steps of the Subtreasury in Manhattan and equestrian Washingtons in New York and the nation's capital. And he was well aware that the same estate that had commissioned Borglum's *Seated Lincoln* and *Wars of America* had also commissioned a major Washington bronze for Newark.

Quantity was not quality, however, and Borglum had very little nice to say about these stiff depictions of America's preeminent hero. They "buried that sound rugged man of the world under the make-believe of the periwig and powdered age," he complained. The more classical the treatment, the less Borglum liked it. He hated that the Washington Monument was no better than a plagiarized Egyptian obelisk and bore a similar resentment against the neoclassical Washington Arch in New York's Washington Square Park, as well as the nation's very first Washington monument, a 160-foot Doric column in downtown Baltimore, topped by a sixteen-foot marble by Italian Henrico Causici that looked nothing like Washington, to the extent that its features were discernible at all. (Woodrow Wilson, who lived across the square from the monument while attending Johns Hopkins University, once quipped, "That's the only time anybody ever got George Washington up a tree!")

Borglum's favorite whipping boy, however, was Horatio Greenough's neoclassical rendering of Washington. Greenough, an American, had lived and worked in Rome and chose to depict the hero of Valley Forge bare-chested, sandaled, and draped in a toga. When Greenough's Washington was placed in the Capitol Rotunda in 1841, it became an immediate target of ridicule. One pundit of the day ignored the obvious ancient overtones of Greenough's creation and instead chose to regard Washington's toga as "a huge napkin lying across his lap," surmising that he must be "in the act of consigning his sword to the care of the attendant until he shall come out of the bath." The piece was eventually exiled to the Capitol grounds and then to the entranceway of an out-of-the-way federal building.

Yet there was one sculptor of Washington who did meet with Borglum's approval: the Frenchman Jean-Antoine Houdon. In 1782, Houdon had sculpted the bust of Europe's illustrious general, Napoleon Bonaparte. Two years later, the General Assembly of Virginia commissioned him to carve a portrait of Washington. At the urging of Thomas Jefferson and Benjamin Franklin, Houdon journeyed to America to study his subject firsthand. Washington, no longer a general and not yet a president, was at the time absorbed in the daily rhythms of crops and livestock at Mount Vernon. For two weeks, Houdon accompanied Washington around the estate, observing his movements and expressions. One day he happened to witness an incident between Washington and a man who was endeavoring to sell him horses. Negotiations soured abruptly: Washington suspected the man of dishonesty and sent him packing with a steely resolve that Houdon promptly captured in the form of a clay bust, crafted on the premises. (We know the image well, for this noble, glaring Washington is the source of the profile that now appears on the twenty-five-cent coin, first issued in 1932.) Before leaving America, Houdon also made a life mask of Washington's face and took numerous measurements of his physiognomy—by far the best records we have of the real man.

Houdon completed his commission in 1788, a lifelike, life-size Washington carved from Carrara marble. Much has been written about the symbolic accessories of the piece, which now stands in the rotunda of the state capitol in Richmond. Like Cincinnatus, Washington has set aside his general's sword in favor of the walking stick of a gentleman farmer; his military cloak is draped over classical fasces, a bundle of thirteen rods representing the colonies he led to independence. But what is most remarkable about Houdon's Washington is its authenticity. Washington's clothes and boots are the garb of the day. Washington is his exact height, six-foot-two, and his long arms, narrow shoulders, and protruding rib cage are his and his alone. Houdon's thoroughness with molds and models was worth the extra effort: Washington's face is strong, robust, and a window on the inner man.

Borglum probably never saw the Washington statue in Richmond, but he did make a careful study of a plaster mask made from the original bust carved by Houdon at Mount Vernon. (The same plaster, in the collection of the Corcoran Gallery of Art in Washington, also guided Emanuel Leutze in his rendering of *Washington Crossing the Delaware*.) "This mask," Borglum wrote, "is the most valuable document extant of [Washington] ... and I have followed it more than any or all others. ... His face, definitely masculine, takes on a more rugged form, and reminds one of Cromwell at 45."

And indeed, the Washington that Borglum presents on Mount Rushmore depicts a man not yet over the hill. No need to hide the false teeth or powder the wig. Despite its scale, the Rushmore Washington is the essential Washington, a man of pride without pretense, a citizen who would not suffer horse thieves gladly.

The dedication of the Washington head on Mount Rushmore took place on July 4, 1930, as promised. Borglum had ordered a gigantic American flag, seventy feet by forty, which he draped over Washington's face. More than two thousand people turned out for the unveiling, but this time no presidents, governors, or congressmen were present. And when the flag was lifted, the face of Washington was plainly recognizable, although his mouth and other features still lacked detail and his head was still hemmed in by solid rock, far short of the dramatic relief we admire today. Still, Borglum had reached a major milestone, similar to the one reached when he had unveiled the head of Lee at Stone Mountain. He had proven to his public, his workers, his commission, and his patrons that the job was doable and well worth doing.

Yet the extra effort expended to meet the Fourth of July deadline had taken its toll. Borglum had employed two shifts a day throughout the spring and early summer, and now the money had run out once again. Even though it galled him to do so, he had no choice but to shut down the mountain from July 26 till August 15. And when work resumed, he had to carry on without the help of Calvin Denison. Denison was an able worker and had managed the men well, but he had no feel for the artistic nuances of the project. On July 16, Borglum had announced that he was bringing in Hugo Villa, his assistant from Stone Mountain and San Antonio, to be "in absolute charge of all sculpture work." In a less than diplomatic letter, Borglum advised Denison that his work had been "careless" and "slipshod." The next day Denison resigned, and Borglum was again without an experienced supervisor. The addition of Villa was some recompense, and the carving was able to proceed till snow fell in the fall. Next year they would begin on Thomas Jefferson—a colossal disaster in the making.

WORTHY OF IMMORTALITY

T HOMAS JEFFERSON has always been hard to pin down, and his placement on Mount Rushmore was no different. Compared to Washington, Lincoln, or Theodore Roosevelt, Jefferson is more of an idea than a person, and like a planet in the night sky, he shines brightly, but drifts according to the calendar of historical interpretation. Of all the presidents, he is without a doubt our most mercurial.

In 1825, the year before his death, Jefferson, who had earlier directed Jean-Antoine Houdon to sculpt George Washington, agreed to have his own life mask made. But legend has it that American sculptor John Henri Browere botched the plaster job, inflicting considerable pain on his subject, and the mask had to be removed from Jefferson's face with a mallet. The reassembled pieces make Jefferson look like a cracked egg. Discomfort to Jefferson aside, it seems fitting that the flesh-and-blood man should elude objectification. In that sense, he is more like Crazy Horse, whose shadow was never stolen by the camera.

Even painted portraits of Jefferson suggest a gathering of cousins more than representations of a single individual. Jefferson sat for the best artists of the day—John Trumbull, Charles Wilson Peale, Rembrandt Peale, Gilbert Stuart, and Thomas Sully—and while most succeeded in conveying the force and refinement of his intellect, along with his sandy hair, papery skin, and bold but graceful (Alexander Hamilton said "womanish") bearing, the collective effect is no more conclusive than the smile of the *Mona Lisa*. "A few broad strokes of the brush would paint the portraits of all the early Presidents," Henry Adams observed, "but Jefferson could be painted only touch by touch, with a fine pencil, and the perfection of the likeness depended upon the uncertain flicker of its semi-transcendent shadows."

By shifting the light and the direction from which he was viewed, Jefferson could be all things to all people. He was both populist and aristocrat. He was a romantic and a rationalist, a bold author but shy orator, revolutionary writer but reluctant warrior. He was a slave owner who favored abolition. He was a man of the soil who seldom soiled his hands. Urbane in his appetites, he saw salvation in the frontier. These protean paradoxes made Jefferson a magnet for all manner of political agendas throughout American history. Conservatives applauded him for keeping government off their backs; liberals saw him as a champion of the little guy. He was forever being "trotted out . . . like a trick mule at a circus," observed one pundit, "and made to perform all kinds of tricks for the entertainment of those present."

If there was a low point for Jefferson, it came in the late nineteenth century. In the decades following the Civil War, big government and big business ran roughshod over the Jeffersonian (and Jacksonian) notion of a live-and-let-live, agrarian-based democracy. The Populist insurgency, Jeffersonian at its core, proved to be frustratingly naïve in its supposition that the yeoman's worn plow could make a dent in the firm pastures of corporate plutocracy. Even during the Progressive era, when reform finally grew teeth, Jeffersonian liberalism—now clearly identified as a Democratic trait—remained largely in disfavor. The perceived trouble with America was abuse of freedom, and in the political shorthand of the day, individual liberty was a distinctly Jeffersonian principle. (Accordingly, regulation of it was Hamiltonian.) In hindsight, Jefferson was regarded as too soft (and by extension, so were the Democrats). On the other hand, Alexander Hamilton had been firm in his belief that a responsible, centralized government could direct America's best interests. Privilege (the domain of Republicans) was not something to be eradicated; it was something to be put to judicious use. Not surprisingly, Progressive crusader Theodore Roosevelt, whose New Nationalism was Hamiltonian in all but name, regarded Jefferson as "infinitely below Hamilton." In Roosevelt's opinion, Jefferson was "the most incompetent chief executive we ever had."

Under such disparagement, it is no wonder that Jefferson had become hard to recognize. His image was neither widely disseminated nor well received. It had appeared on postage stamps, although not on denominations that were used regularly. In 1929, a Republican administration permitted Jefferson on the two-dollar bill, a lukewarm honor at best. And even when the Democrats finally put his profile on the nickel in 1938, many people resented the fact that he had bounced the beloved buffalo.

Yet Jefferson had not been without his moments of posthumous tribute. The Louisiana Purchase Exposition, which opened in St. Louis in 1904, was a celebration of the centennial of Jefferson's daring doubling of the nation. With profits from the fair, the state of Missouri (whose capital is Jefferson City) commissioned Karl Bitter to sculpt a major statue of Jefferson in St. Louis. In 1923, the newly minted Thomas Jefferson Memorial Foundation purchased Monticello, Jefferson's Virginia home, with the aim of making it a national shrine. And then in 1926, Congressman John Boylan derailed the juggernaut to erect a Theodore Roosevelt memorial in Washington and introduced the notion of a Jefferson memorial in its stead. A reappreciation of Jefferson was long overdue, Boylan insisted in his speech before the House. So far, the only major statue of Jefferson in Washington—

sculpted by David D'Angers in 1833—was off "the beaten track of the tourists," Boylan lamented. "[T]he only way you can see it—and when you do see it you regret it—is to go down in the basement [of the Capitol] and then retrace your steps upward. If the light happens to be right you can gain a glimpse of this ancient statue of the author of the Declaration of Independence."

"It is time to honor Jefferson," Boylan concluded. "I am glad that all signs are that the honor will be not very much longer delayed."

Without question, Boylan's resurgent enthusiasm for Jefferson was blatantly partisan. A Tammany Democrat, Boylan saw 1926, the sesquicentennial of the Declaration of Independence as well as the centennial of Jefferson's death, as an opportune moment to rally his party, in disarray and disgrace after its poor showings in recent national elections. To Boylan and his brethren, Jefferson was the Democratic Party personified—not just a man for all seasons, but a man of the hour.

This was precisely how Jefferson had been characterized in a provocative 1925 book, *Jefferson and Hamilton: The Struggle for Democracy in America*, by Claude G. Bowers. A staunch Democrat himself, Bowers began his narrative by politely praising Hamilton for his brains and tenacity. Quickly, however, he stressed Hamilton's fundamental shortcomings: his impatience, intolerance, "flamboyant egotism," elitism, and above all, "his lack of sympathy for, and understanding of, the American spirit." By vivid contrast, Jefferson was modest and tolerant, resourceful and tireless; a humanitarian and a "master of diplomacy"; a "creator and leader of a party" who "never sought to overshadow or overawe"; "a psychologist [who] could easily probe the minds and hearts of those he met." Moreover, Bowers dispelled the notion of Jefferson as a wimp: "He was hard-headed and looked clear-eyed at the realities about him.... He never rested on his arms or went into winter quarters. His fight was endless."

In other words, Jefferson embodied all the essential qualities of a modern political leader. For those yearning to rehabilitate the Democratic Party, Bowers's depiction was an inspiration and a manifesto. "I have a breathless feeling," wrote Franklin Roosevelt, who had read the book while convalescing from polio in Hyde Park. "Is a [new] Jefferson on the horizon?" Indeed one was, and Gutzon Borglum was his usher.

Initially, Jefferson had qualified for a spot on Mount Rushmore due to his sterling credentials as an empire builder. "Jefferson's place in this memorial is more important even than Washington's," Borglum exaggerated in a fundraising letter to an affluent Democrat. "By that I don't mean that he eclipsed Washington one iota, but Jefferson purchased the Louisiana Territory, in the center of which, on a spur of the Rocky Mountains, this memorial is located." But as time went by and Rushmore became more of a Shrine of Democracy, Borglum expanded his appreciation of Jefferson. Although still "an old Republican of the Roosevelt brand," Borglum was in many ways a bit of a Jeffersonian, in the sense that he was capable of wearing the hats of both highbrow and populist as the whim struck him. And it took one Renaissance man to appreciate another. In another of his letters to Democrats, Borglum pointed out that Jefferson, in addition to his political achievements, was "easily the most influential factor . . . in shaping the city of Washington. . . . He was the inventor of the ploughshare and much else. . . . [He made] contributions to horticulture, . . . to our foreign relations, to literature, architecture. . . . And I might keep on for another page."

Borglum had another incentive for embracing Jefferson. While outwardly backing Herbert Hoover's reelection in 1932, Borglum harbored growing misgivings about the character of the Republicans and their leader. Hoover had never warmed to him, and Borglum compared the president to a "bogged elephant" whose party prejudices were impeding recovery from the Depression. "He is incapable of friendship, he is incapable of leadership," Borglum griped. Finally, just weeks before the 1932 election, he shifted his support to Franklin Roosevelt, who, although a Democrat, was nonetheless a Roosevelt. "I believe that [a] Rooseveltian national consciousness alone will save this republic,"

Borglum announced in a public statement, "and it is every man's duty to turn all he has of ability, property and mind into saving the republic and in this election [to] abandon politics!"

This dramatic shift in political alignment affected the way Borglum went about selling Jefferson. "It is not an idle statement to say had it not been for Jefferson there would have been no republic," Borglum wrote to Marvin Traylor, president of the First National Bank of Chicago and a prominent Democrat. "Jefferson was responsible for some, if not most, of the revolutionary political creed incorporated into our national creed. . . . We are facing a logical 'Democratic year' and for that reason Jefferson should not suffer eclipse. . . . [I]t is little short of scandalous that Thomas Jefferson is not sufficiently known to be genuinely cared for more as he merits." Opportunely, Borglum urged "big Democrats" to "jump right in and grab Jefferson," whom he called "their God." He asked Traylor to help raise $40,000. Nothing came of it, but there was now no question that Borglum had grown to appreciate the complete Jefferson.

Separate from how Jefferson would be financed was the matter of what he would look like. There was no public agreement on which likeness was the quintessential, iconic Jefferson. Borglum's intent at Rushmore was to portray Jefferson at thirty-three, the age at which he wrote the Declaration of Independence. "He was then a handsome man . . . full of life, initiative, and energy," Borglum explained to Franklin Roosevelt several years later. Unfortunately, no portraits had been done of Jefferson at that age. The earliest extant image was painted ten years later, in 1786, and a bust by Houdon, noble to be sure, was not completed until three years after that. Borglum apparently never saw Houdon's effort firsthand and so applied his own artistic license, vastly more than he had applied to Washington or to previous sculptures of Lincoln and Roosevelt. He tinkered incessantly with his models of Jefferson—the basic physiognomy, the expression, the hair, the inner spirit that kept eluding him in that Jeffersonian way.

The problem of actually carving the true Jefferson on the rock of Rushmore was even more difficult. The original plan had been to bracket Washington with Lincoln on his left (north) and Jefferson on his right (south), with Roosevelt flanking Lincoln. But it was not to be. In the summer of 1931, Borglum had made plans to travel to Europe for the installation and dedication of a statue he had made of Woodrow Wilson for Poznan, Poland. (Borglum was willing to amend his hard feelings toward Wilson for the sake of this eight-foot international commission.) On the way, he intended to visit his family's ancestral home of Denmark, where he was to be knighted by the king. It was an invitation too good to pass up, and he felt that the mountain was still at a stage at which it could be overseen by assistants William Tallman and Hugo Villa. Leaving behind detailed instructions on how the work was to proceed, he departed for Europe. Returning at the end of August, he was pleased to report to the memorial commission that carving had "progressed excellently" in his absence and that work on Jefferson had been "carried out as planned."

But within two weeks, he was singing a less congratulatory tune. Villa, a talented stone carver and a passionate artist, was also known to have a weakness for women and wine. With his taskmaster away, he had adopted a more sybaritic lifestyle and may well have taken certain liberties in the shaping of Jefferson's head. The upshot was that on September 11, Villa and Borglum had a row during which Borglum fired his chief carver. Villa claimed that of the $1,200 owed to him, Borglum had paid only $300. Borglum, who only two weeks earlier had been pleased with Villa's work, now accused him of "gross errors," "lack of watchfulness," and "disobedience." Specifically, he accused Villa of flattening Jefferson's forehead and cutting Jefferson's nose six inches too deep. Borglum even insisted that he had been able to spot Villa's mistakes from a mile away as he drove up to the mountain on his first morning back from Europe. Villa rebutted the charges in a letter to South Dakota governor Warren Green, insisting that there had never been sufficient granite to carve Jefferson, at least not the Jefferson indicated by Borglum's latest model. Borglum dismissed Villa's letter as "false and slanderous."

In the final analysis, both men were partially right. Villa had removed more granite than he should have, although not drastically so. Not that it really mattered, for as Villa had contended, there never had been enough good stone on Washington's right with which to carve Jefferson. Borglum would not admit as much—and certainly never apologized to Villa—but he cut his losses and reconfigured the composition, moving Jefferson to Washington's left (and shuffling Lincoln and Roosevelt). Then in 1934, he blasted the original Jefferson from the mountain like so much dandruff from Washington's continental collar.

The Jefferson head was mostly done by 1936, although, like the other three faces, it was not fully completed until 1941. Even then, Borglum never did succeed entirely in imprinting the face of Jefferson in the American consciousness. (Early tourists even mistook Jefferson for Martha Washington.) In the end, Jefferson simply defied iconic treatment. Shaping a mountain to resemble Washington, Lincoln, and Roosevelt was challenging enough, but at least the faces of these three presidents rang a bell. With Jefferson, Borglum had to introduce viewers to a visual stranger—and have them warm to him. "In the Jefferson I must approach [him] as a man of the world stirring everything about him," Borglum explained to an easterner who had not yet seen Rushmore. And so he carved Jefferson as Jefferson, but he also carved Jefferson as an incarnate ideal—like one of Rodin's sculptures, and like the democratic exemplar Jefferson truly was.

Perhaps it is unfair to say that Borglum took greater care with the figure of Jefferson, but it does seem that way. Some people single out Roosevelt's eyeglasses or Lincoln's beard as favorite details, and both features are indeed ingenious and convincing. But from the standpoint of fine art, the best, most expressive bit of carving on the mountain surely has to be the mouth of Jefferson. We can actually see the muscles in Jefferson's face, flexing subtly, creating that momentary purse of his lips. Like the best Renaissance figures, Borglum's Jefferson is both sensual and psychological, much more so than the other Rushmore faces. Of the four, his head seems to hold the most complex thought. Moreover, while Washington, Roosevelt, and Lincoln represent the static preponderance of their values, Jefferson, in his whimsical pose and comparative anonymity, seems still to be formulating his. Stare at Jefferson long enough and we might even change his mind. Stare again: The set of his mouth almost makes his eyes twinkle.

And when all was said and done, Jefferson did get the last laugh. In his new location—appropriately to the left of the more conservative Washington—he was still not quite comfortable. When Borglum set to work on Jefferson's nose, he encountered a troublesome crack running through the rock where the right nostril was supposed to go. Fearing that moisture would work its way into the fault, freeze, and eventually lop the nose from Jefferson's face, Borglum had no choice but to rotate the facial features five degrees to the north, set the head back another four feet, and tilt it upward about eighteen inches. "Finally the crack just escaped the right-hand nostril," he reported. "[I]t still cuts down across the right eye, past the nose and upper lip and through the middle of the chin. In that location, it is perfectly harmless because it is supported by all the mountain back of it." The ultimate effect of this change is that Jefferson's gaze is slightly higher than those of his brooding brethren. (Even then, Jefferson was still flawed; in 1939, workers had to patch a six-inch blemish of loose granite in his upper lip.)

In keeping with his character, Jefferson managed to bring out the best in his neighbors. In carving Washington, Borglum had removed twenty-five feet of granite before getting to rock he considered good enough. Then when he moved Jefferson to Washington's left, he found that he had to remove some sixty feet of flawed rock before he could begin actual sculpting. The unintended result was quite pleasing, even more so once the false-start Jefferson was dynamited away. Now Washington stood in sharp relief, his head "breaking out of his shell like a full-blown rose," Borglum exulted, and it was visible from three directions of the compass. What is more, the new orientation now allowed the afternoon sun to pass behind Washington's head and light the faces of Jefferson and, eventually, Lincoln.

A final bonus of the Jefferson shift was the decision, by necessity, to move the entablature from the front of the mountain to the narrow canyon behind the carving. The embarrassment of the Coolidge tiff had not dampened Borglum's enthusiasm to include an inscription, and he now contemplated a text in several languages: Latin or Greek, Chinese or Japanese, and possibly Sanskrit, as well as "Anglo-Saxon." But with the juggling of the lineup, there was no room for a grand entablature alongside the presidents. The only recourse was to move it to the rear, where it would eventually be integrated with Borglum's gestating, but yet to be announced, Hall of Records, similar to the one he had envisioned for Stone Mountain. "[I]nscriptions are harmful to sculpture pure and simple," noted the memorial commission's annual report for 1932, "and should be kept separate if possible." Borglum apparently had no remorse over the distancing of words and images, for in 1935, as Jefferson was nearing completion, he announced that "Jefferson is emerging as a splendid youthful figure.... As one looks upon [him], it is easy to understand how such a man could write the Declaration of Independence and the Bill of Rights. One need not resort to dusty tomes to appreciate [his] qualities."

The account of the carving of Jefferson is one of talent and persistence, of trial and triumph. But it did not tell the full story of Mount Rushmore. Quite frankly, there were few good years at Rushmore during which Borglum and his men labored diligently and productively without incident or interruption. Some years were simply worse than others. Correspondence from the 1930s is a saga of bitterness and backbiting. At times it seems almost a miracle that any work was accomplished at all, given the titanic feuding between Borglum and his workers, his commissioners, the state of South Dakota, the citizens of Rapid City and the Black Hills, various federal agencies, Peter Norbeck, and especially John Boland, the man with whom he was meant to work most closely. A lot of the clashes had to do with money—lack of it and control of it. But even more of the troubles at Mount Rushmore stemmed from Borglum's irascible temperament and uncontainable ego. He was a dedicated demon, a visionary bully, and he would allow nothing to get in his way, unless it was his own death, and even that was not a guaranteed deal-killer.

Yet not even Borglum could have managed Mount Rushmore all by himself. At the beginning of 1932, the memorial commission was broke again, and work on the mountain was called off for the summer. Only Peter Norbeck, the well-driller turned U.S. senator, saw green where others saw drought. Earlier in the year, Congress had authorized the Reconstruction Finance Corporation (RFC), Hoover's initiative to mitigate the Depression. South Dakota's piece of the federal pie amounted to $150,000. Even while public schools across the state were struggling to pay teachers' salaries and farmers were going bust—and despite the fact that three out of four South Dakotans lived east of the Missouri River—Norbeck managed to get $50,000 of the RFC allocation dedicated to Rushmore. And with that he turned around and persuaded Washington to regard the RFC money as a donation, which enabled him to appropriate an additional $50,000 in matching funds.

Throughout their years together, Borglum constantly criticized Norbeck as a "machine politician" who regarded Rushmore as "a vest pocket job ... to be farmed out as his private political perquisite." Meaner still, he looked down on Norbeck as a bumpkin—a "roughneck" with an "untrained mind." "He may wear garters in Washington," Borglum sneered, "but ... in South Dakota his socks are down over the tops of his boots."

Despite such relentless condescension, Norbeck still saved Borg-lum's bacon countless times, and he loved the Black Hills as dearly as Borglum did Mount Rushmore. He had a summer home in the hills, called Valhalla, and he had almost single-handedly created the vast, magnificent Custer State Park. While Borglum was busy chipping away on Rushmore in the early 1930s, Norbeck had won funding for another pet project, the Iron Mountain Road, a gem of highway engineering.

The seventeen-mile road commenced at the east entrance of the state park and wound westward through the hills, more like a garden path than a twentieth-century motorway. Norbeck mapped out the route himself, picking his way over, around, and through the jumbled mountain topography. When an especially attractive grove of trees or an appealing pile of boulders got in the way, Norbeck split his road into separate lanes, leaving nature undisturbed in the median. Rather than bulldoze invasive grades on the hillsides, he called for construction of wooden "pigtail" ramps and bridges that looped back on themselves like spiral staircases in their climbs and descents through tight canyons. And in anticipation of Mount Rushmore's completion, Norbeck carved snug tunnels through several ridgetops, aligned in such a way that when motorists entered the dark passages, Rushmore would be per-fectly framed in the distance, like a slide in a magic lantern.

By the end of the decade, Norbeck's Iron Mountain Road, along with another new road that approached more directly from Rapid City via Keystone, would deliver a half-million tourists a year to Rushmore and the interior of the Black Hills. Borglum could call Norbeck what he wished, but there was no doubting the senator's commitment to their shared pride and joy. Even as Norbeck battled with cancer of the mouth, he continued to go the extra mile for Rushmore and to run interference for its cantankerous sculptor.

Thanks to Norbeck's resourcefulness, Borglum was able to squeeze in two months of work in 1933, from October 1 to December 8. Carvers refined Washington's head, shaped the new Jefferson, and began clearing some of the rock for Lincoln. Still, Borglum was sore that the memorial could not afford to play a conspicuous role in the nation's grand celebration of George Washington's two-hundredth birthday. More and more, he blamed the general lack of progress and money and "every bit of trouble I have had" on Norbeck's "man Friday," John Boland.

Boland's task was difficult enough, handling payroll, invoices, and all the other niggling but essential administrative duties of Mount Rushmore. (Not to mention that he still had to look after his own business, the Rapid City Implement Company.) But nobody in the world, except someone dedicated to the health and wealth of his community, could have endured the additional discomfort inflicted by Borglum's ranting, ad hominem attacks.

Borglum's brief against Boland was as simple as it was severe. In his view, Boland was a corrupt apparatchik whose singular goal was to drag out the construction of Mount Rushmore for as long as possible in order to extend the rewards to local businesses whose pockets were being filled via a "pipe-line into the national treasury." In the years since Doane Robinson had first approached Borglum with the idea of carving something "massive" in the Black Hills, Borglum had chosen to look beyond the fundamental commercial motive that had sparked Robinson's brainstorm. He was building the new Acropolis, not a Coney Island spectacle. "I did not and don't intend that [Rushmore] shall be just a big thing, a three days' tourist wonder," he vowed. Yet with so many curiosity-seekers beginning to visit Mount Rushmore, a section of Borglum's studio had been turned into a lunch stand and souvenir shop. And while Borglum was toiling to complete "the greatest monument that civilization has ever undertaken," Boland and his fellow "nickel chasers" in Rapid City were conspiring, according to Borglum, to "degrade the standards of what I am doing . . . and cover [the hills] with hot dog stands." Boland, he alleged, did not look upon Rushmore as anything but "a lodestone to attract tourists long enough to be fleeced locally."

The other half of Borglum's case against Boland boiled down to pearls before swine. Borglum was building "a Memorial to the most vital characters in the history of the nation," and what did he get in return? "I am thoroughly disgusted with the way in which I have been taken advantage of right and left in Rapid City," he complained to Boland, "and [with] the total lack of gratitude, intelligent understanding or appreciation of the sacrifices [I have] made." To architect Frank Lloyd Wright, who had visited and admired Mount Rushmore, Borglum played less of the martyr and more of the patrician: "[E]ighty percent of the [Black Hills] population, including their best, belong to the unburied dead, and that part of them that is alive ... is concerned only with the most ordinary of material things.... My biggest fight in the Black Hills has not been with the granite, but [with] the stupid people." And to newly elected South Dakota governor Leslie Jensen he vaunted, "I hardly need to point out what I have done in bringing the name of South Dakota out of the swill barrel." In general, he added, South Dakotans were "oxen-minded."

Borglum's observations on the "burlesque" of tourism just beginning to overrun Rushmore were eerily clairvoyant, but his indictment of bland, bean-counting Boland as a conniving racketeer was off target, and cruel besides. When the ancient diesel power plant at Mount Rushmore sputtered and failed, obliging Boland to purchase power from a mining company in Keystone, Borglum accused Boland of outright sabotage, insisting that he had scuttled the plant in order to throw business to his cronies. In effect, he was making the same allegations of skullduggery, greed, and conspiracy that he had against Edward Deeds during the First World War. There was nothing to the charges this time, although Boland was not the sort to fight back. If he had a flaw, it was a tendency to drop quietly into a whiskey bottle for two or three days when the stress became unbearable. For the most part, though, he showed the forbearance of a saint, and like Norbeck, he bent over backward to accommodate Borglum's idiosyncrasies and offenses. Contrary to Borglum's characterization of Boland as a miscreant, it was Boland who faced down Borglum's creditors and kept the constable from his gate.

Beneath Borglum's exasperation over the finances of Rushmore was the even more pressing matter of his own poverty. When he began the carving, he had anticipated that his 25 percent honorarium would amount to at least $20,000 a year (with the total of $87,500 coming to him within five years). In addition, he had figured that with skilled, trustworthy lieutenants, he would have ample time to pursue other lucrative commissions. However, in most years, he made less than half the $20,000 expected, in the leanest years only a couple of thousand dollars. Yet regardless of his income, he continued to live like a prince. He owned a twelve-cylinder Cadillac coupe, driven by Charlie Johnson, a black chauffeur, masseur, and all-around factotum. He dressed dapperly in silk scarves, tailored suits and shirts, and fine felt Stetsons. ("With that scarf around your neck," one friend teased, "you look like a cross between an artist and a horse thief.") He built a new house and studio at his ranch in Hermosa; stocked it with cattle and blooded horses; and hired a foreman, housekeeper, cook, and tutors to look after his family. As a host, he was famously lavish, pouring the best liquor and wine. When he traveled, he insisted on top-of-the-line lodgings. In Washington, he kept up his membership at the posh Metropolitan Club, and during extended winter stays in San Antonio, he usually took a suite at the Menger Hotel, one of the city's finest. Nor had he sold Borgland in Connecticut, encumbered though it was by heavy taxes and notes to Eugene Meyer and others.

For Borglum, living beyond his means was the easiest thing in the world. All he had to do was ignore the bills. He bounced checks wherever he went. He overlooked the interest on bank loans. At one point, he was five years behind on his account at the Menger. In Rapid City, he considered it beneath him to buy a ticket before entering the movie theater, where he loved to take in double features. One time Borglum drove up to the gas station in Keystone and ordered owner Art Lyndoe, "Fill 'er up and put it on the books." When Lyndoe insisted on cash, Borglum growled, "Don't you know who I am?" To which Lyndoe replied: "Yes, sir, I do know who you are, and that's why I can't sell you anything on credit." John Boland's wife, Ethel, recalls hearing Charlie Johnson say of his service to Borglum: "I drive him around, and I rub him down. What I don't do as often as I should is get paid."

But the circle of creditors began to tighten in late 1933, and by the summer of 1934, Borglum's ranch was on the brink of foreclosure. He tried futilely to sell off several acres of Borgland, but Eugene Meyer stood in the way. Finally, Boland stepped in, and through his influence within the Black Hills business community, he was able to consolidate a number of Borglum's debts under an agreement that garnished a percentage of his future honorarium payments. But instead of expressing his gratitude to Boland for saving him from total financial ruin, Borglum accused Boland of treachery. "Foreclosure on my place was a frame-up" arranged by Boland, he complained to Fred Sargent, president of the Chicago and North Western Railway and newly elected chairman of the Rushmore National Memorial Commission. "You will appreciate," he had written to Sargent's predecessor, Joseph Cullinan, "how difficult it [is] for me to work with [Boland], who, in private and under cover, works against the man who is carrying the greatest burden of this work."

Borglum did not treat the men who worked for him nearly as badly, but he was still an extremely demanding boss, and he could be very imperious. Lack of money meant that he had to build "a monument with miners," he grumbled, half complaining, half boasting. "I have been given the scrapings ... left over in the mining camps. I have ... attempted to train them into drillers, engineers, blacksmiths—men who have worked a little at everything and not very much at anything."

He remained true to his Ruskin-infused notion of a hierarchy of talent: Only a few laborers were good enough to be artisans; only a few artisans had what it took to become artists. And, he stressed, the artist was the one who must always be in charge, the officer commanding the enlisted men. "Untrammeled leadership must exist . . . free and unrestricted in all finer work," he remarked to U.S. Senator Claude Pepper, comparing Rushmore to the myriad public works projects under way in America, most of which he considered crude and poorly managed. "[T]here is not a man on my job who . . . can do anything intelligently unless I stand over him."

Even his assistants, supposedly smarter than the "masses," disappointed him inevitably: "[T]hey take two steps forward[,] discover their rashness, [and] back they come. Like the Sioux Indian rabbit dance." With the departures of Tucker, Denison, Villa, and eventually Tallman, Borglum consolidated his authority even further and began signing his letters "Gutzon Borglum, Sculptor & Engineer." The workers called him simply "the Chief" or "the Old Man."

Most of the men readily recognized his brilliance as an artist and admired the zeal with which he attacked the mountain. Borglum did not hesitate to strap himself into a harness and swing over the side of the mountain. He was even known to grab a jackhammer from a driller to demonstrate just how and where he wanted a certain patch of granite shaped. Although now in his sixties, he would dash up and down the 500 vertical feet of stairs several times a day. The studio models served as excellent blueprints, and on occasion, Borglum actually suspended them from the side of the mountain so his carvers could refer to them directly as they drilled.

But the models were no more perfect than the granite of Rushmore, and to create art, even colossal art, still required intimate contact between artist and material. As he might have done with a smaller piece in his studio, Borglum would back off, sometimes to distances of several miles, to study the composition or the way light struck the faces at different times of day. Then he would rush back to the mountain, clamber onto the face, and indicate a change of mere inches to a chin or hairline. Once when carver Red Anderson was having trouble transferring the subtlety of the model to the mountain, Borglum directed him: "Don't look at the model. Turn your back on it and then reach behind you and feel it. The touch of your fingers will tell you more ... than looking at it will." This to a man whose callused hands were accustomed to the grip of a seventy-five-pound Ingersoll-Rand jackhammer. Yet Borglum was insistent, and Mount Rushmore was the better for it.

When workers did not do precisely as they were told or otherwise disappointed Borglum, he frequently blew up. If they were lucky, he simply chewed them out. But he also had the unpleasant habit of firing them on the spot. Usually he hired them back once he had cooled off, and after a while, the ritual became almost a joke among the men. Carver Merle Peterson calculated that Borglum sacked him eight times during his years at Rushmore—the record, he insisted.

Overall, the morale was quite good on Mount Rushmore, despite the intermittent shutdowns and Borglum's scrappy personality. With so many of the region's mines closed and the nation wracked by the Great Depression, most men were glad to have a job at all. Wages ranged from fifty cents an hour for unskilled labor to a dollar, then a dollar and a quarter, an hour for top carvers. During wintertime and other layoffs, men would eke out an existence as best they could, living on credit or traveling out of state to find jobs. Nearly always, though, they showed up back at Rushmore when work resumed.

Most of the men lived in the former houses of miners—shacks and cabins, in many cases—in or near Keystone. Keystone was a disheveled, false-fronted town of two or three hundred by the time that work on Rushmore commenced. It had a grocery store, a hardware store, a café, a blacksmith shop, a sawmill, a school, a hotel, several rooming houses, and not much else. The main gathering place was the pool hall, which for a while doubled as a drugstore. Eventually the Rushmore crew formed a baseball team and built their own diamond. Borglum loved the idea of his men wearing "Rushmore" on their uniforms. One of the stories most often told about Borglum has him showing up at games, striding onto the field, and stopping play to have words with one of his workers. Word got around that you had a better chance of getting hired at Mount Rushmore if you were good with a bat and glove.

Payday was Friday, and the men would "billy-goat" down the mountain, skipping a dozen steps at a time in their race to reach the bottom first. During Prohibition, the Black Hills were a bootlegger's paradise, and one of the local distillers was usually on hand to greet the Rushmore crew as it got off work at the end of the day. When the men discovered that tourists would pay money for the pieces of honeycombed rock broken from the mountain, they set a rate of two dollars a specimen, the same price as a pint of moonshine. Borglum, never a teetotaler himself, didn't object to workers drinking, but he had strict rules against drunkenness, or even bad hangovers, on the job. If a man showed up under the weather, Borglum sent him home to recuperate. Some Mondays, he had tomato juice delivered to the top of the mountain.

Working conditions improved over the years, but the work was always grueling. As the carving progressed, scaffolding was erected around the faces at eight-foot intervals and draped with tarpaulins so that men could continue to work in the rain and cold. Even then, men continued to drill from boatswain's chairs as well, and after a while the call boys were equipped with radios to communicate better with the winch men above the din of a half-dozen drills chattering away at once.

One of Borglum's ongoing frustrations was the effort and time it took to get up the mountain. He estimated that his men lost at least an hour out of every workday just getting to and from the job. The existing hoist was intended to carry only drill bits, dynamite, and other essential materiel. It also ferried water, coffee, and a hot midday meal, besides the occasional ration of tomato juice. In 1935, Borglum finally allowed his men to ride up in the hoist, five or six at a time, although Boland was quick to issue a memo clarifying that they did so entirely at their own risk. The crew's idea of safety was to outfit the "cage" with a primitive emergency brake and wooden sides that made it look like a flying outhouse.

Borglum ran a safe mountain for the most part. Still, accidents were inevitable, given the amount of exposure the men faced day in and day out. Blasting normally took place at noon and at the end of work, when the men were off the faces. But on a hot July afternoon in 1938, lightning struck the mountain, setting off charges while men were still at work. A carver who was swinging in his harness narrowly avoided obliteration. Instead the concussion merely blew him out of his shoes and left his ears ringing for weeks. He was the only man injured that day. On another occasion, a man was struck by a large scrap of granite pried loose by a coworker above him; fortunately, only his leg was broken. One day just after a group of workers had finished eating lunch on the base of the structure that secured the tram cable to the top of the mountain, the entire apparatus tore loose. Had they been seated there a minute or two earlier, they doubtless would have been flung into space. Yet another near-disaster occurred when a call boy failed to hear a driller's command to stop feeding cable. Assuming that his lifeline was taut, the driller backed blithely off the ledge below Washington's chin and freefell the length of the slack, some twenty-five feet. He was bruised from the abrupt stop and from slamming into the granite cliff, but otherwise no worse for wear.

The most spectacular calamity took place on June 2, 1940, as Rushmore was nearing completion. Five men were aboard the hoist, and just as it reached the steepest part of the cable in front of Lincoln's face, the drive wheel in the hoist house malfunctioned. With no warning, the cage began hurtling down the cable, picking up speed. A cool-headed Howdy Peterson waited until the cage reached the lower, more level stretch of the cable's span before applying the emergency brake. It worked at first, but when the brake started smoking, he had to release it for fear it would lose its bite altogether, and he did not dare reapply it for more than short intervals. Then, as the cage approached the hoist house, Gus Schramm, a burly two-hundred-pounder, reached over and yanked the brake so sharply that the lever snapped off in his hand, leaving them helpless to slow the final two hundred feet of their descent. The cage would have crashed into the hoist house much more violently if someone hadn't jammed a board or bar into the cable drum, slowing its revolution. Even so, the cage hit the hoist house hard and smashed to splinters.

Miraculously, no one was killed. Two of the men were shaken but not hurt at all. Schramm was knocked cold, and Howdy Peterson was cut, but not too badly. Hap Anderson was the least fortunate. No one seems to know whether he was thrown from the cage or jumped for his life. He was found lying on the ground nearby with a shattered arm and several broken ribs. Rushed to the hospital in Rapid City, he made a full recovery and later went back to work on the mountain.

Less sensational but no less dangerous was silicosis, the lung disease of miners, quarrymen, and masons. The Rushmore crew was issued masks to protect them from the fine granite dust, but they were not required to wear them, and most didn't because the masks were so hot and uncomfortable. The dust was particularly thick once the scaffolding was tented with tarpaulins and later during the work on the Hall of Records. Borglum was concerned enough about silicosis that in January 1941 he wrote to former congressman William Williamson, whom he now consulted on legal matters, inquiring about liability in the event that any of his men developed the disease. Williamson absolved Borglum, explaining that silicosis was "a risk assumed by the people working upon the mountain" and that it was "the duty of the workmen to use [masks] for their own potential protection." Borglum died unexpectedly three months later, believing that he had lost not a single worker at either Stone Mountain or Mount Rushmore. (By comparison, more than one hundred workers died building Hoover Dam, completed in 1936, and eleven on Golden Gate Bridge, completed in 1937.) He had no way of knowing that in 1948, mountain carver James Champion would succumb to silicosis. Seven years later, Alton "Hoot" Leach suffered the same slow death, Rushmore's second, albeit belated, fatality.

Borglum would have been heartbroken by the news, for he did care about the welfare of his men, even if he did not choose to mingle with them. He expected a hard day's work from them, no more, no less, although sometimes he was pleasantly surprised to learn that they were putting their hearts as well as their backs into the job. "You may say to one man, 'What are you doing?'" he wrote in one of his unfinished manuscripts on Rushmore, "and he will say, 'Getting this damn stone out of the way.' You may ask the same question of another, and he will say, 'I am getting five dollars a day.' But of the third you may ask the question, 'What are you doing?' and he will reply, 'I am building a monument to America.'"

The only other person on the mountain who grasped the full profundity of Borglum's endeavor was his son Lincoln. All his life, Lincoln had been his father's sidekick, tagging along on cross-country trips, treating Stone Mountain as his personal playground, and exploring the Black Hills. Lincoln and his sister Mary Ellis were educated by their mother and by tutors while living in Connecticut, Georgia, Texas, South Dakota, and sundry hotels in between. Both were extremely bright and devoted to their parents, but it was Lincoln, naturally, who walked more closely in his father's shadow. "I wish [that Lincoln] would bust into life, take it by the ears ... or if Life was a lady chuck her under the chin," Borglum had confided to a fellow father, and his wish soon came true. Lincoln chose not to attend college, opting to stay with his father and work at Mount Rushmore instead. He knew every inch of the mountain and was an expert on all aspects of mountain carving. Borglum trusted his son completely; what is more, Lincoln had a rapport with the men that his father lacked. When Borglum lost his head, Lincoln knew how to make things right.

When supervisor William Tallman injured his knee in August 1934, Borglum put twenty-two-year-old Lincoln in charge of all pointing on the mountain. The following year, Tallman resigned, and shortly thereafter, Borglum promoted Lincoln to "chief assistant" in charge of all pointing, drilling, and finishing. "Lincoln has become a remarkable executive," Borglum told Doane Robinson proudly. "He knows a hell of a lot ... and he takes all kinds of burdens away from me—and, I am just lazy enough to let him." Borglum was so confident in his son's ability that he allowed him to oversee the start of work in 1936 by himself, although Borglum, hardly lazy, did draft detailed written instructions in advance:

"On photograph No. 1 I have drawn a circle where you can locate [carver Jack 'Palooka'] Payne, to begin ... drilling under what will become Washington's ear and what will be the lefthand lapel of his coat. Put one or two men on the lapel, which I have marked No. 2.... You can put three men on the Roosevelt stone ... going back into the hole next to Jefferson's face as deep as you can.... I think that will keep you busy until I get there."

With his capable son on the mountain, Borglum once again felt comfortable being gone for extended periods of time. The place he believed he was needed most was Washington, D.C. In 1933, President Roosevelt had placed Mount Rushmore, its commission, and appropriations under the jurisdiction of the National Park Service, which in turn was under the Department of the Interior. Neither Park Service Director Arno Cammerer nor Interior Secretary Harold Ickes relished the new assignment. Cammerer was a nature lover who didn't like the idea of defiling a perfectly good mountain, and Ickes "groaned all night" when he learned that Rushmore was his responsibility. When dealing with

Borglum, Ickes confessed, "I always feel like equipping myself as a man does when he fusses with a beehive."

Borglum was not thrilled by the new arrangement, either. Roosevelt had assured him that the Park Service would function strictly as a bureaucratic channel for appropriations to the existing Memorial Commission, but Borglum sensed that tighter control was in the offing. He resented having to answer to a bunch of "clerks that democracy gathers out of the waste-basket of college men," and he especially hated the thought of having his shrine, his work of art, relegated to the status of just another national playground to be "invaded by the unwashed . . . and covered with peanuts and paper and concessions sold for the sake of a nickel. I don't like the disrespect the American public [is] permitted to show to their parks and monuments."

In light of this newest perceived threat, and with the need for more funding both chronic and acute, Borglum felt he had to launch his own assault on Congress and the administration. Meanwhile, Peter Norbeck, who was dividing his time between South Dakota, Washington, and cancer treatments at the Mayo Clinic, had his own idea of how to raise money, not to mention a proven track record at doing so. Without telling Norbeck, Borglum arrived in Washington in April 1934 and began knocking on doors. "I just ran into him at the Capitol as I stepped off the elevator," Norbeck told Boland. "He apologized for not having seen me." Norbeck soon learned that Borglum was proposing a plan that would abolish the memorial commission (which he regarded as ineffectual and a nuisance), transferring authority from Interior to the Treasury, and having Treasury either appropriate or borrow $355,000 for the completion of Rushmore. He boasted to Norbeck that he had "over 46 Senators who are friendly to me . . . and at least twice that many Congressmen. . . . I am also convinced that the Administration will support [me]."

Norbeck knew better. "[Borglum] wanted to see forty-five Senators," he confided to Boland. "After waiting a week . . . he had done nothing. . . .

He was to see the President also, but he has not been able to get into the White House . . . though previously he would run in at will." Norbeck was sure that Borglum's plan was futile; worse, he quickly realized that Borglum was aggressively impeding the senator's own efforts to win more aid for Rushmore. "As I have said before," Boland wrote Norbeck, "if we are to get any money, it will be through your efforts and not Borglum's, in fact, if we should fail to get money, I would be inclined to think it was on account of Borglum's actions and words."

Norbeck did have some success in 1935, although his request for $50,000 from the Public Works Administration was routinely denied. Congress had recently appropriated $500 million in an attempt to jumpstart the economy through federal spending, but most of that was earmarked for the Navy or nonfederal projects. (The distinction is important: Many people today assume that Rushmore had been bailed out by the Public Works Administration—subsumed by the Works Progress Administration in 1935—but while Rushmore was indeed a federal project, it was not per se one of the "make work" WPA projects of the 1930s.) Undeterred by the momentary setback, Norbeck drafted and secured passage of a bill that would release the remainder of the funds authorized under the original 1929 Rushmore legislation—money that previously had been held hostage by the insurmountable matching-funds clause. Norbeck got the matching-funds restriction dropped, freeing up $50,000 for use in 1935 and another $55,000 for 1936. For the first time in several years, Rushmore had breathing room.

But Norbeck was not done yet, even though his flagging health should have indicated otherwise. In 1935, he came back with a new bill that called for an additional $200,000 appropriation—nowhere near what he estimated it would take to complete Rushmore, but all he dared hope for from Congress. Borglum returned to Washington as well, promoting his same plan for $350,000 and a shift of authority from Interior to Treasury. Still unable to gain a presidential audience, he peppered Roosevelt with letters. Whereas a year earlier he had said only nice things about Norbeck to Roosevelt, now he took a nastier slant. In a letter to the president, dated March 15, 1935, Borglum ripped Norbeck as the mastermind of "a petty political racket." Also he insinuated that Norbeck, as a Republican, was not one of the president's men. (Borglum, the convert, was a different story.)

Norbeck never read Borglum's letter, but he sensed the sculptor's antagonism nonetheless. When Norbeck tried to arrange a meeting with Borglum to patch up their differences, Borglum canceled the appointment—twice. Finally, even the phlegmatic Norbeck had had enough. "It was really my hope that we could work together this year," he wrote to Borglum on June 6, "but since . . . you have decided the whole matter [of how to promote Rushmore], I can quite share your view that there is no need for a conference. . . . Personally, I wish you only well. I even wish you were more competent in business methods and had better understanding of our legislative trouble, and I wish so much you would be willing to accept help from those who could help you, but you will not,—so that settles that."

Norbeck may not have had Borglum's support, but he did win the favor of President Roosevelt, who apparently had shrugged off Borglum's mean-spirited correspondence. On June 28, Norbeck sat down with Roosevelt—a privilege still denied Borglum—and made the case for Rushmore. "[Y]our description of the progress of the work . . . and of its inspirational value to our people in the years to come," Roosevelt wrote Norbeck afterward, "convinces me of the need for legislation to authorize an additional appropriation of $200,000 for the completion of the project."

But even with Roosevelt's backing, Norbeck had trouble selling his bill. "You cannot eat art," one congressman sniped. Others wondered why a monument to Washington and Jefferson wasn't sufficient. In the end, the bill passed both houses, although, as Roosevelt had made clear, the appropriation was for strictly the "execution and *completion*" of the project. Norbeck took the money and ran. If the well ran dry again, he'd just have to drill another, provided he lived long enough.

News of the bill's approval reached Borglum in the Black Hills, where he and his crew were finishing up the head of Jefferson and making steady progress on the head of Lincoln. His time in Washington had not been wasted entirely, for among other things, he had lobbied vigorously to have Boland replaced by, or at least subordinated to, a government official who would take charge of orders and disbursements. Bookkeeping, Borglum grumbled, was "the milk in Mr. Boland's cocoanut [that] gives him the power to retard and block the work."

Borglum got what he asked for but not exactly what he expected. Julian Spotts was a National Park Service engineer who had supervised the construction of the Arlington Memorial Bridge in Washington, D.C. Spotts arrived in the Black Hills at the end of June 1936 and accomplished many things in his first weeks at Rushmore: He cleaned up the water supply, improved the air pressure and power to the mountain, and rehabilitated the rickety hoist. Yet Borglum resented Spotts for making technical decisions without consulting anyone and for meddling in the hiring and firing. Borglum's possessiveness was understandable. He had the most to gain and the most to lose. He was the one who cared the most about Rushmore, and he was its dynamo. When other people's confidence failed, it was his will and vigor that reinfected everyone involved, from call boys to congressmen. He had good reason to be severe toward interlopers, although the lanky, soft-spoken Spotts could not have been prepared for the rambling dressing-down he received from Borglum on August 20:

> [I]t's a little difficult for me, who created the great Federal memorial here at Rushmore—even determined three of the principle [*sic*] figures to be representative of our Federal history—raised most of the initial money, after the state of South Dakota had failed completely, secured the entire power plant as a gift to myself, presented

it to the work, interested the president, Mr. Coolidge sufficiently to come here and dedicate the rock I and my son Lincoln had selected—further Mr. Coolidge secured for me the law and quarter of a million going with it to carry on *my* plans and designs—it is a little difficult for me, under these circumstances, so built up into a solid background of service, to which I should add, although I do this reluctantly, lending the commission thousands of dollars, going without pay when the funds were low—it is difficult to find the unique work [has] become the victim of petty bureaucratic entanglements.

To others, Borglum was more succinct: Spotts was a "milk-fed capon," a "brainless jellybean."

Given Borglum's low regard for Spotts (an estimation confirmed when Spotts later ran off with the wife of one of the Rushmore workers), he was doubly reluctant to accept assistance from other federal agencies—even on projects that dearly needed a helping hand. Along with his decision to move the entablature to the backside of Mount Rushmore, Borglum envisioned embedding a room in the canyon wall there, similar to the one he had planned but never completed at Stone Mountain. Norbeck agreed that "a permanent fireproof room would make a wonderful Museum and Archive," and the Rushmore bill he had passed in 1935 had included a provision for "constructing a suitable museum." Soon Borglum began referring to the room as the Hall of Records and envisioned "a great room, at least 90 by 110 feet. . . . Into this room the records of what our people aspired to and what they accomplished should be collected and preserved[,] and on the walls of this room should be cut the literal record of conception of our republic; its successful creation; the record of its westward movement to the Pacific; its presidents; how the Memorial was built and, frankly, why." In concept at least, it shaped up to be a cross between the painted caves of Lascaux, an Egyptian mortuary temple, and a Cold War fallout shelter.

The entablature was very much alive, too. After the death of Calvin

Coolidge in 1933, Borglum had come up with the idea of holding a national competition to select the best text for the inscription, and in 1935 he enlisted the Hearst newspapers, whose owner, William Randolph Hearst, had a proven nose for patriotic publicity stunts. Hearst also had a soft spot for the Black Hills because a great deal of his inherited wealth derived from the Homestake mine. The Hearst papers reached five million readers, thousands of whom, from grade-schoolers to grownups, submitted essays of six hundred words or less. The winner, John Edward Bradley, received $1,000 and a promise from Borglum that his essay on the creation and expansion of America would be inscribed on the canyon wall behind Mount Rushmore.

Borglum pictured a grand stairway leading up to the Hall of Records and the entablature. How it would be built soon became a sore point. Both Norbeck and Boland suggested that the stairway be built using the free labor of the Civilian Conservation Corps. Borglum would have none of it. Since the inception of the federal work program in 1933, the CCC had established more than twenty camps in the Black Hills, at times employing nearly a thousand men. CCC crews fought forest fires and built dams, trails, and many of the facilities in Custer State Park, Wind Cave National Park, Jewel Cave, and Badlands. In 1935, John Boland had used CCC workers to erect a new restroom at Rushmore, which gave Borglum a chance to observe their workmanship firsthand. The CCC, he concluded, was a pack of "non-productive, incompetent, no-accounts"—a prejudice shared by his Rushmore crew, whose second favorite recreation, after baseball, was brawling with "Cee Cees" at Saturday night dances in Keystone and nearby Rockerville.

Borglum refused to submit drawings of the stairway for consideration as a CCC project, thereby provoking the ire of Senator Norbeck, who pointed out that the cost of the stairway was not covered by the recent congressional appropriation. "We were all set to go when you vetoed my effort," Norbeck chided. "We would have been $50,000.00

ahead but I guess I was foolish for expecting your cooperation." He scoffed at Borglum's pledge to fund the stairway with private donations. "You might as well say 'I am determined to finish Stone Mountain,' or 'I am determined to change the magnetic center of the earth.' . . . Your ability as an artist and even greater ability as an advertiser is marvelous. But your helplessness in getting funds was fully proven when we shut down in '32."

Norbeck was showing extraordinary spunk for a man on his deathbed. Treatments at the Mayo Clinic had not slaked his cancer. He could still write, but he could hardly talk anymore. And there was some question whether he would have the strength to attend the most important public event held at Mount Rushmore thus far: a visit by Franklin Roosevelt scheduled for August 1936.

Roosevelt was up for reelection that fall, and to burnish his standing among the traditionally non-Democratic voters of the Midwest and West (who had made an exception for him in 1932), he planned a tour of the drought-ravaged region and a series of conferences to address the dire agricultural crisis. Although the Dust Bowl of Oklahoma, Kansas, and Nebraska received the most attention during the "dirty thirties," in fact the northern plains—the Dakotas, Wyoming, and eastern Montana—were much more severely stricken. On a trip across the South Dakota prairie in 1933, Lorena Hickok, an observer for the Federal Emergency Relief Administration (and First Lady Eleanor Roosevelt's rumored lover), had seen farms "that looked as though there'd never been even a spear of grass there."

As bad as conditions were in 1933, they were even worse by 1936, indisputably the bleakest year of the Depression. Grasshoppers ate crops down to their roots and even the laundry on the line. Dust storms blotted out the midday sun. South Dakota counties west of the Missouri River that normally could count on a modest seventeen or eighteen inches of rain a year received as few as five or six. For most farm families the choice was go on relief or go down the road. Those who stuck it out bravely took to calling western South Dakota "Next Year Country," as in "Since I came to this goddamn country in 1880, there's only been two good years—1916 and Next Year."

Newspapers dubbed Roosevelt's trip "the Drought Tour." When Borglum got word that Roosevelt might pause in his inspection of the plains in order to visit Mount Rushmore, he sprang into action. Times were tough for farmers, but he had his own drought that needed addressing. Calvin Coolidge's visit in 1927 had been a godsend for Rushmore, generating enormous publicity and helping to ensure the essential support of the federal government. A Roosevelt visit, however brief, might be just the cloudburst needed for final fruition. Toward this end, Borglum orchestrated a dedication ceremony for Thomas Jefferson, whom Roosevelt admired so ardently. He would raise and lower a series of flags, invite Indians to dance, have Roosevelt named an honorary chief, and then set off a few sticks of dynamite, much as he had done at earlier dedications. Also he envisioned a series of eloquent speeches, by himself and the president.

Rain accompanied Roosevelt's train across the parched plains, but fortune was somewhat less generous toward Borglum. Roosevelt had decided to spend the night of Saturday, August 29, at the Alex Johnson Hotel in Rapid City, attend church the following morning, and then motor to Mount Rushmore. His staff informed Borglum that the president would stay at the mountain for only twenty minutes and would not make a speech. That of course meant that Borglum had to abbreviate his own remarks, in which he had intended to compare Rushmore to the Parthenon and himself to Phidias. "Mr. President," Borglum had written in his now unusable draft, "it is worthy to note that through the hours of national distress ... this symbol of faith has grown in the very heart of our promised and distressed land. Need we any greater surety that the soul, the courage, conscience and confidence still live, that the dreams of our great shall not perish from the earth." Borglum then figured to close with an appeal on behalf of the entablature, the Hall of Records, and the grand stairway.

But he never got his chance. He had tried to impress on the president's handlers the importance of arriving at Rushmore by noon, when the sunlight still brightened the faces. Instead Roosevelt enjoyed a leisurely lunch at the Alex Johnson (which had quietly installed ramps for the president's wheelchair) and then pulled into Rushmore at 2:30. Borglum was beside himself. "He even threatened to go ahead with the dedication and let the president go to—," William Williamson recalled, "and had he not been the President of these United States, I suppose he would have done just that."

Roosevelt remained seated in his open car for the entire ceremony, surrounded by a crowd of three thousand. On the reviewing stand sat Doane Robinson, South Dakota governor Tom Berry, Representative William Williamson, and Senator Norbeck, his ruined throat swathed in a towel. While all the dignitaries were dressed in Sunday suits, Borglum wore white flannel trousers, a white shirt with the sleeves rolled up, and his signature scarf and Stetson. Twenty-year-old Mary Ellis Borglum pushed a button to signal her brother Lincoln at the top of the mountain, who in turn detonated three charges that sent boulders crashing down the now shaded slope of Mount Rushmore. Workers wrestled the cumbersome, seventy-foot American flag—the same one used in the Washington dedication—from the face of Jefferson while an airplane dropped dozens of miniature parachutes carrying chips of granite and still more flags.

Although Roosevelt had vowed not to give a speech, Borglum prodded him anyway: "I want you, Mr. President, to dedicate this memorial as a shrine to democracy; to call upon the people of this earth for one hundred thousand years to come ... to see what manner of men struggled here to establish self-determining government in the western world."

On the spot, Roosevelt responded graciously. "I am very glad to have come here today informally ... because we do not want formalities where nature is concerned. What we have done so far [at Rushmore] exemplifies what I have been talking about in the last few days [of the Drought Tour]—cooperation with nature and not fighting with nature." Roosevelt celebrated Rushmore as a "great work" of "permanent beauty" and "permanent importance":

> I think that we can perhaps meditate on those Americans ten thousand years from now when the weathering on the faces of Washington and Jefferson and Lincoln shall have proceeded to perhaps the depth of a tenth of an inch—meditate and wonder what our descendants ... will think about us. Let us hope that they at least give us the benefit of the doubt—that they will believe we have honestly striven every day and generation to preserve for our descendants a decent land to live in and a decent form of government to operate under.

After the speech, Borglum invited the president to his studio to show him the model and the location where he intended to carve Roosevelt's cousin Teddy. But Roosevelt was out of time. The real-world concerns of democracy were pressing on him even as he was delivering his lofty remarks on the mountain. Nine years earlier, Calvin Coolidge had departed Rushmore to seal the fate of Sacco and Vanzetti. Now Roosevelt returned to the presidential train in Rapid City to deal with his own crisis. Earlier that day, the American destroyer USS *Kane* had been bombed while evacuating American citizens from the war then raging between fascists and republicans in Spain—a sober foreshadowing of the global storm to come. "[Rushmore] can be a monument and an inspiration for the continuance of the democratic republican form of government," Roosevelt had told his audience that afternoon, "not only in our own beloved country, but, we hope, throughout the world." Current and imminent challenges to that hope would prevent the president from fulfilling his promise to see Rushmore when it was complete. Nor would Peter Norbeck, who lost his fight with cancer three months later.

Compared to the Roosevelt event of 1936, the dedication of Abraham Lincoln the following September was almost anticlimactic, although the popularity of the honoree and the quality of the carving were not at all to blame. Over the previous twenty-seven years, since Borglum had installed the *Seated Lincoln* in Newark, Abraham Lincoln had become an even more revered icon. His face had appeared on postage stamps, the penny, and the five-dollar bill. In 1930, D. W. Griffith had released his first sound film, *Abraham Lincoln*, starring Walter Huston (who would reign as Hollywood's Lincoln until 1939, when Henry Fonda upstaged him in John Ford's *Young Mr. Lincoln*).

Nor could the public seem to read enough about Lincoln. Carl Sandburg's folksy 1926 biography, *Abraham Lincoln: The Prairie Years*, had been reprinted almost as many times as Parson Weems's *Life of George Washington*, and the world now awaited Sandburg's four-volume sequel, *The War Years*. All the while, other authors had been adding to the groaning shelf of Lincoln literature. Notable examples included Albert Beveridge's academic *Abraham Lincoln* (1928), Edgar Lee Masters's carnal *Lincoln the Man* (1931), Dale Carnegie's motivational *Lincoln the Unknown* (1932), and L. Pierce Clark's Freudian *Lincoln, A Psychobiography* (1933). Like Washington, Lincoln had undergone a rigorous debunking—with fingers pointed at his mother's possible illegitimacy, his ambivalence toward organized religion, and, according to Masters, his "lazy mind." Nevertheless, Lincoln had endured as America's favorite son, equal to and even surpassing Washington. And if Jefferson was the Democrats' darling, Lincoln was very much the Republican MVP. He too was trotted out to personify this or that American virtue. During Prohibition, for example, his life was offered up as evidence of just how far a man could go in this world if he didn't drink.

Since 1910, more than three dozen major Lincoln statues had been erected in the United States and Europe, depicting him variously as rail-splitter, militiaman, lawyer, candidate, congressman, debater, president, and emancipator. In 1932, Paul Manship (who would soon sculpt the gilded Prometheus at Rockefeller Center) had carved an oversized Lincoln, *The Hoosier Youth*, in Fort Wayne, Indiana. By far the most conspicuous Lincoln sculpture was Daniel Chester French's seated figure in the Lincoln Memorial. In April 1937, as Borglum was finishing up the Rushmore Lincoln, he again lashed out at French's monument, calling it "one of the great failures in American architecture."

Despite the wealth of recognition paid to Lincoln in recent years, Borglum still regarded this president, above all others, as his personal franchise. As always, he admired Lincoln's "iron purpose" in preserving the Union. More than ever, though, he stressed Lincoln's timelessness. "Each hundred years," Borglum wrote to President Roosevelt, "it will be said: '[Lincoln] grows ... more securely into his place with the gods of order, peace and good will.... [H]e looks with purest human understanding into the tragedy, the mystery, the preciousness of existence.'"

Lincoln on Rushmore was meant to be no less eternal, and after Borglum had decided to move the entablature, Lincoln's location was fixed. He and Washington, as Christ and Moses, would enfold Jefferson and Roosevelt, immortal apostles. The plan was to carve Washington, Lincoln, and Jefferson all the way to their waists. Washington's left hand would grip the hilt of his sword, Jefferson's left hand would rest on Washington's left arm, and Lincoln's left hand would clutch the left lapel of his own coat. Regrettably, Borglum was not allowed adequate time, money, or rock to flesh out these three figures (today one can barely discern the outline of Lincoln's fingers), but he did do some of his best work on Lincoln's face. As with Washington, the blasting crew had to remove eighty feet of granite before carving could begin. Even then, they encountered a band of pegmatite running across Lincoln's left cheek and nose. Some see it as a birthmark—or is it a smudge from the president's inky finger? Either way, it is nowhere near as grave as the imperfection that had threatened Jefferson's nose or the blemish on his lip that required plastic surgery.

The big debate with Lincoln was whether he should be bearded or clean-shaven, a difficult decision for Lincoln himself during his lifetime. Peter Norbeck, who had admired Borglum's Lincoln in the Capitol, had lobbied for a smooth chin. But Norbeck was no longer living, and Borglum, intrigued by the sculptural possibilities of carving whiskers from granite, deferred to his own impulse. While acknowledging that Lincoln was more "spiritual" without a beard, he preferred "the strength the beard adds." Lincoln's features took shape fairly quickly in 1936 and 1937. After all, Borglum knew the Lincoln face by heart, and by now his men had nearly a decade of carving experience.

It was on Lincoln that Borglum perfected the trick with the eyes. There is no definitive evidence to prove that Borglum copied the eyes of Daniel Chester French's *Lincoln*, but regardless of who taught whom, effecting the feat on such a colossal scale presented its own distinct challenge, and Borglum's men did a superb job. Unlike the convex iris in a normal eye, the irises of Lincoln and his Rushmore companions are concave bowls cut deep enough into the granite to create shadows—the "color" of the eyes. The one break in each shadow is at the very center of each pupil. Here Borglum left a rectangular shaft about eight inches across, the length varying from president to president. On Lincoln, the shafts are two feet long—baguettes of protruding rock.

This was one of the few moves that the masters of Greece and the Renaissance had never discovered. Michelangelo's *David* is an indisputably exquisite example of stone brought to life. Yet his eyes are blind, whereas those of the Rushmore presidents reveal clear sparks of life. Borglum had found a way to penetrate the skulls of his subjects as surely as if he had struck their optic nerves.

The Lincoln face was dedicated on September 17, 1937, the sesquicentennial of the ratification of the Constitution, with five thousand in attendance, nearly twice the number that had been present for Franklin Roosevelt's appearance. (Police had sealed off FDR's route to Rushmore early in the day, and many had watched the presidential motorcade from Rapid City sidewalks.) This time, Borglum was the center of attention and gave the address he wished he could have delivered a year earlier. "It is my . . . bounden duty as the creator of this memorial," he declared, "to emphasize the cultural necessity to make of this colossal undertaking something more than the 'biggest' in the world, that is, to make it a great work of art—a work of art as great for us and our time as the subject merits, and our ability permits, determined . . . that it shall rank with the great records of awakened Egypt, Greece and Rome."

Borglum was an expert at tooting his horn and grinding his axe simultaneously, and he finished his speech with characteristic virtuosity: "We have literally driven a super-clipper into the stratosphere of noblest human aspirations, on a crust and a gallon of gas and . . . in spite of a resisting, unbelieving world." His remarks were capped by a crescendo of dynamite. Next the flag was pulled away from Lincoln's universally worshiped visage, and the crowd drove home over the Black Hills' ever-improving roads, proud and replete.

The day had indeed gone well, but Borglum still was not satisfied. Of the fifty or so men who had worked on Rushmore in 1937, he was the only one who had not been paid. His contract, which he had signed in 1927, had expired in May. Throughout the summer and fall, he fought tooth and nail for a more lucrative deal. His two principal demands were that his commission be upped from 25 percent to 30 percent and that he be repaid the $100,000 that he claimed he had already spent on Rushmore out of his own pocket. The contract he begrudgingly signed in November stipulated none of the above—not the boost in honorarium, nor the $100,000. All he got was the same old terms as before, plus the final $1,700 he had coming from the old contract.

Borglum was incensed, and he came away from the negotiations determined to get even with the insulting, unappreciative, and meddlesome "cabal" that he felt was endangering his dream. The following winter and spring, he went on the warpath, a rampage as fierce as any he had ever staged in the past.

In the spring of 1938, Borglum left his son to supervise Mount Rushmore (along with Julian Spotts) and took up quarters at the Metropolitan Club in Washington. He had turned seventy the year before. He had been carving mountains for more than twenty years, but he still had plenty of fuel for one final assault on the powers that be. "We must not let him get away from us," Senator Norbeck had confided to Boland several years earlier, "or we will have a Stone Mountain deal." But now there was no Norbeck to ride herd on Borglum or to mend fences. Borglum would be Borglum, unfiltered. He knew how to be cordial and courtly at just the right moments, vengeful and unvarnished when the situation demanded. And he played his old game of brinksmanship with consummate cunning, daring those who remembered Stone Mountain to call his bluff. "I tell you I am not going [back] to Rushmore until [the situation] is corrected," he swore. Whatever his audience thought of Gutzon Borglum—as an artist, as a politician, as a member of the human race—he had a way of commanding their full attention.

The primary objective, as always, was to raise more money. Although Congress had made clear in 1935 that it had given Rushmore its last dollar, Borglum had never taken the provision seriously. Now, only three years later, he was back, pushing for an additional $600,000 to complete the faces, Hall of Records, entablature, stairway, entrance, and landscaping. In addition to the money—$150,000 more than had been appropriated over the previous nine years—Borglum wanted to dissolve the existing memorial commission and replace it with a smaller, ten-man commission, which this time would include him and be legally bound to carry out his designs. The new commission would answer nominally to the Treasury Department—thereby banishing Interior and the bothersome National Park Service. And although Borglum never said so outright, not to Congress anyway, his underlying goal was to stack the commission with his allies and then remove Boland as the chairman of the executive committee. In short, he wanted as near to total control as one could have over a publicly funded project.

He still had plenty of friends in Washington. The president, it is true, remained standoffish toward Borglum, but he was by now an avowed fan of Mount Rushmore. Until Borglum could meet with Roosevelt in person, he pelted him with more letters, spelling out his concerns. "Mount Rushmore has been bullied, starved, victimized from the beginning by local, cheap ward politicians [and] a man from the Park Department," Borglum complained on May 9, 1938, "so far interfering with the proper course of that work that I must now request that this interference must all stop, and stop at once." Once again he drew a line in the dirt, this time right at Roosevelt's feet: "I shall not return to the work until these matters are corrected."

Borglum had not been so forward with a president since he had tried to put words in the mouth of Calvin Coolidge. He had been only slightly less brazen before the House Committee on the Library four days earlier. On April 28, Representative Kent Keller, a Democrat from Illinois and longtime Borglum ally, had introduced a bill that included most of the items on Borglum's wish list. Instead of going for $600,000, Keller had cut the number in half, knowing it wasn't enough, but advising Borglum that it was all they could hope to get. The hearing on May 5 was less a debate over the merits of the bill than it was a chance for Borglum to tell of his own version of the Rushmore story. He talked about how he had carved the greatest of memorials, using "forgotten men" from the mining camps, and how he had cut his own salary in order to employ Jesse Tucker, only to have Tucker badgered by "a local political leader" until he resigned. He described the shortage of power,

the ineffectiveness and absenteeism of the existing Rushmore commission, the parsimony of the state of South Dakota, and the interference
of the Park Service. He waxed eloquent on the concept and contents of
the Hall of Records. And to hear Borglum tell it, he was the one who
had raised all the money up till now. He hardly mentioned Norbeck's
name at all.

With Keller chairing the meeting, Borglum was received as a distinguished diplomat. The only sticky spot came when Representative Allen
Treadway of Massachusetts inquired, "I wonder if there is not some reason—not criticizing, of course—in connection with your desire to control
the whole proposition [of Rushmore]?" To which Borglum countered
humbly: "I would not want to control it." Finally, South Dakota congressman Francis Case entered into the record a statement by John
Boland, which, in light of all the dastardly things Borglum had said and
done to Boland over the years, could easily have been a bombshell, but
instead revealed only the very best of Boland's character. "Mr. Borglum
is an artist, and I am a businessman," Boland reasoned, "therefore it is
only natural that we should at times disagree regarding the business
functions of the Commission. Such differences, however, have never
been serious and an amicable understanding has always been reached....
My only desire is to have the Mount Rushmore project completed in the
best possible manner and to have Mr. Borglum carry on his great work."

The library committee reviewed the Rushmore bill favorably,
although amendments kept the commission size at twelve and saw the
wisdom of excluding Borglum from its membership. The bill also
carved 1,500 acres from the Harney National Forest and gave them to
Mount Rushmore National Memorial and specified that admission to
Rushmore be free. Considering the hard times of the Depression and
the failure of several other national memorials to win funding, no one
expected the Rushmore bill to pass either the House or the Senate,
where it was sponsored by Key Pittman, a Nevada Democrat and one
of Borglum's Black Hills fishing companions. When the bill came

before the House on June 6, Borglum couldn't bear to listen to the debate and retreated to the Metropolitan Club. The Speaker of the House apparently misheard a request for postponement by a still-skeptical Treadway, and the bill abruptly came up for a vote—and passed almost as suddenly. Much of the credit for shepherding the legislation through an unusually stingy Congress belonged to Francis Case. Nevertheless, columnist Drew Pearson opined, "[T]he most amazing piece of lobbying of the entire ... session was put across by turbulent Gutzon Borglum."

Borglum was ecstatic. He was vindicated. And his pledge to Congress notwithstanding, he was in command. With the passage of the bill, the old Rushmore commission was automatically disbanded. Of the twelve names Borglum submitted to the president for appointment on the new commission, ten were selected—including Keller and Pittman, the latter becoming chairman. (One of the two nominees not chosen was First Lady Eleanor Roosevelt.)

Boland knew full well that his defenestration was near, but he was determined to leave his desk in order. He prepared a detailed inventory of Rushmore's fixed assets and kept up with the day-to-day duties of bills and disbursements. Neither publicly nor in his correspondence did he utter a harsh word against his nemesis; until the bitter end, his loyalty was to Rushmore. Borglum, on the other hand, saw only craven deception behind Boland's cooperation. "Boland is bucking like the unmanly thing he is, carrying on clandestine relations with the men [and] willing to take any kind of job that he might escape the humiliation of dismissal." He allowed Boland to linger until August—"to gasp ... like a trout in the sun"—before finally accepting his resignation, effective the eleventh. Even then, Boland remained a team player, and in 1941, after Borglum's death, he enthusiastically accepted the position of president of the Mount Rushmore Memorial Society. In a sense, Borglum's prediction had come true: Mount Rushmore did enrich the life of John Boland, although never in the way Borglum imagined.

On August 4, Borglum's handpicked commission convened at Mount Rushmore and designated Borglum as "general manager of the Mount Rushmore National Memorial" and vested him with "full power and responsibility for carrying out the work ... and full authority to employ such artists, sculptors, architects and other employees, and to make such expenditures as he may determine necessary for the completion of the memorial."

"Prometheus is unbound," New Jersey friend William Mill Butler cheered when he got word of Borglum's exalted status. William Randolph Hearst, whom Borglum had visited the previous year in California and who had been such a help with the inscription contest, likewise couched his congratulations in mythological metaphor: "How you escaped the Scylla and Charybdis of the New Deal I do not know. . . . Very few succeed in avoiding the awful [Interior Secretary] Ickes—a modern Cyclops—if not with one eye, at least with a one track mind. You are as wise as Ulysses." Borglum thanked Hearst by promising to include his bust in the Hall of Records alongside those of Benjamin Franklin, Thomas Paine, and Andrew Jackson.

The end was in sight. "I am not out of the woods yet," Borglum had written to son Lincoln before leaving Washington, "but I am so darned near it that I can see daylight."

Under Lincoln's guidance, work on Rushmore had made great progress that summer, particularly on the figure of Roosevelt, which had proved troublesome. The modeling phase of Roosevelt had been relatively easy. Borglum had simply adapted the bust he had done of Roosevelt shortly after his death. Actual mountain carving was not so straightforward. Over two seasons of work, Roosevelt had given the crew fits. They blasted away forty, sixty, eighty feet of rock, and still they couldn't find what they wanted. At last, after peeling one hundred and twenty feet of material, the men struck workable stone just in the nick of time—for what most viewers of Mount Rushmore do not realize is that only thirty feet of granite separate Roosevelt's parted forelock from the canyon behind his head, and the ridge of rock that connects Roosevelt to Jefferson is a dike of pegmatite barely three feet thick. Any further blasting, any less granite, and Roosevelt might not have made the cut at all.

Despite these difficulties, Roosevelt's position on the mountain seems to suit him perfectly. Carved so deeply in the mountainside, he is the bully president too tough to tumble. He turns his head toward Lincoln, a president he admired, and shrinks from Jefferson, whom he did not admire. Then, too, it is only poetic justice that Roosevelt, the lone twentieth-century president, should take a backseat to his more venerable seniors.

With Roosevelt roughed in at last in 1938, the crew continued to refine the other three faces and began to excavate the Hall of Records. During the tenure of the National Park Service, Borglum had been pressured to concentrate on the faces exclusively. Now he was his own boss, and by the end of the year, the doorway of the hall was framed and the chamber opened up to a depth of ten feet. And for the first time, Borglum had the money and initiative to keep a crew on through the winter. He talked optimistically about finishing all four faces and most of the hall by the end of 1939, the fiftieth anniversary of South Dakota's statehood.

What he did not count on was that the following spring, President Roosevelt would put Rushmore back under the strict supervision of the National Park Service. More distressing, Borglum's health began to fail. Prometheus, it seemed, would never be free of the rock. Ulysses would never get home.

chapter 11

SORRY OLD WARRIOR

THE YEAR OF 1939, which should have been one of the best in Borglum's life, was instead full of more turmoil. With work on Rushmore continuing throughout the winter, the Borglums had stayed on at the ranch in Hermosa. In March, Mary came down with the flu and nearly died. Borglum scarcely left her bedside, which in turn eroded his own health. "I have been in a low, dull degree [of] ill," he alerted his doctor, "brought about, I am certain, by my anxiety and watchfulness over her. I have not slept two consecutive hours for over ten days.... I have a dull headache that came about the third or fourth day after her illness had struck." In addition, he reported that he was experiencing shortness of breath and that his prostate had been bothering him on and off for the past four years. Mary Borglum was convinced that hard work and worry were taking years from his life.

If March and April were cruel, May brought its own unpleasantness. At the first of the month, President Roosevelt, in an effort to streamline the mushrooming federal bureaucracy, had put Mount

Rushmore back under the supervision of the National Park Service. Although Borglum was not in the best of shape to lodge a protest, he nevertheless gave it all he had. "It is worse than ominous; it is sinister," he wrote to Key Pittman, chairman of the memorial commission, upon learning of Roosevelt's decision. "I will have nothing whatever to do with that [Park Service] group." To Arizona congresswoman Isabella Greenway, another of the handpicked Rushmore commissioners, he delivered an even blunter ultimatum: "If the work . . . is turned over to the Park Service as the Park Service is now organized, I shall abandon the work."

Early in June, he took a train to Washington, where once again he hoped his presence could bend the will of the government. And at last he was granted an interview with Roosevelt. "No time in the history of my work have I [been in greater need of] friendly, disinterested, scholarly support as at this moment," Borglum wrote to the president upon arrival in the capital. "I beg of you . . . to give it to me." At a brief meeting at the White House on June 5, it was Roosevelt's charm that melted Borglum, not the other way around. The president emphasized that he would not change his mind about the Park Service, but he reassured Borglum that the Park Service's involvement would be "the least possible." Borglum was assuaged and not just a little bit starstruck. "It was a great pleasure to see and note that you are as well as you are," he wrote Roosevelt before leaving town. "I am heading back to the great Memorial with renewed heart." Then, contritely, he allowed, "I am no easy burden."

But once Borglum returned to Mount Rushmore, he quickly realized that his carte blanche had been revoked. This time it was the Memorial Commission, previously in his corner, that reined him in. In the interest of financial prudence, the commissioners directed him to curtail work on the Hall of Records until the four faces were complete. Borglum, sensing for once that discretion was the better part of valor, reassigned the men who had been drilling in the canyon.

Yet he never quit dreaming. "[T]he four figures, the Hall of Records and the sculptured stairway that will lead to this work [are] all one item," he insisted. Rushmore would never be done until all of its components were done. Except with Borglum, the components kept evolving. "Mr. Borglum has in mind other projects going into infinity," Key Pittman had told Congress.

To read Borglum's description of the Hall of Records and stairway makes clear why the commission, the Park Service, and Congress were united in their skepticism. Borglum had borrowed a phantasm straight out of Hollywood. In 1935, he had seen *She*, the film adaptation of H. Rider Haggard's tale of an African queen who lives without aging in an underground temple. Randolph Scott plays a white explorer, and Helen Gahagan is Queen Ayesha—"*She who must be obeyed.*" In adapting the story for the screen, producer Merian C. Cooper had exchanged Africa for the Arctic and had borrowed sets from his 1933 epic *King Kong*, most notably the massive portal and stairway, which he now placed before Ayesha's Temple of Kor. Beguiled by *She*, and obedient after a fashion, Borglum conceived his own stairway to eternity, 800 feet long and 15 to 30 feet wide, to be built out of the granite blocks excavated from Mount Rushmore. "There [will be] nothing like it in history but the steps leading ... to the Parthenon from the Acropolis," he vowed to Franklin Roosevelt (which explains in part his reluctance to use CCC labor).

The stairway would flank Abraham Lincoln's left side, climbing to a small canyon, roughly a quarter of an acre, tucked behind the presidents. Rather than burrow into the back (west) side of Mount Rushmore, Borglum had located the opening to the hall on the opposite (east) wall of the little canyon. In his mind's eye, he pictured the hall's entrance as "a perpendicular rise of 60 feet from the ... granite floor ... with great cast glass doors ... surmounted by an eagle with a wing span of 38 feet. Pylons on each side of the panel ... rise like great protecting barriers; upon these are carved two colonial torches, the flames from which are more than thirty feet in length in full relief. . . . I want to finish the inner entrance wall in mosaic of blue and gold lapis. . . . Cut into the panel under the edge [of the entrance] are the words: 'America's Onward March,' and below, 'The Hall of Records.'"

Initially the interior of the hall was to be a single room, 100 feet by eighty feet, with a thirty-two-foot vaulted ceiling, like a Gothic cathedral, on which would be placed a cross pointing to the North Star. "We all know this world is changing," Borglum explained, "and in the course of time we will be rolled over, and we are trying to tell our children's children where we are today." On the walls would be a historic frieze "showing the adventure of humanity discovering and occupying the West World" and the long-awaited inscription, authored by John Edward Bradley, chronicling "the nine great steps the Anglo-Saxon has made pursuing the star of empire"—beginning with the Declaration of Independence and Constitution and wending through the Louisiana Purchase and the acquisitions of Florida, Texas, California, Alaska, and finally the Panama Canal.

The hall would also accommodate a series of carved recesses holding cabinets of bronze and glass. The cabinets would contain more records, stamped on aluminum sheets and sealed in watertight tubes. Borglum belittled the seven-foot-long time capsule interred during the 1939 New York World's Fair as "a trivial performance [that] shows a complete lack of appreciation of our civilization." By contrast, his voluminous cabinets would carry, among other things, comprehensive archives of travel, immigration, religion, and literature, with emphasis on the American Revolution and "the founding of a new, free, self-determining nation in a virgin world, resulting in . . . amazing inventions." Borglum's list of inventions, which he jotted in notebooks and letters over the years, included electricity, photography, radio, motion pictures, aviation, and the submarine—a virtual manual for modern living. He stipulated that the cabinets in the Hall of Records could be opened only by an act of Congress, though copies of the archives would be available in the libraries of Congress and several American universities.

Last but not least came the busts. Over the years, Borglum's list grew from a half-dozen to well over twenty, depending on whom he had made promises to most recently. The assembly of American demigods included Benjamin Franklin, John Hancock, Patrick Henry, Thomas Paine, John Marshall, Alexander Hamilton, Andrew Jackson, Daniel Webster, William Travis, and James Knox Polk—to which sometimes were added Robert Fulton, Oliver Wendell Holmes, Alexander Graham Bell, the Wright brothers, John Pershing, Elihu Root, Calvin Coolidge, and Franklin Roosevelt. Finally came the mortal stalwarts who had helped to make Rushmore possible: Doane Robinson, Peter Norbeck, William Williamson, Kent Keller, Key Pittman, and even John Boland.

When Borglum added up all the items he wanted to warehouse in the hall, he realized that one room would not be enough, and he allowed himself to imagine as many as six. "My plans are to make the Shrine of Democracy one of the *truest* most complete Memorials ever built," he enthused. Unfortunately, nobody saw the big picture quite the way Borglum did. When he pulled his drillers from the hall in July 1939, they had spent $16,000 cutting a hole fourteen feet wide, twenty feet tall, and seventy-five feet deep—a shelter big enough for mountain goats, but hardly the Temple of Kor.

The summer was not without its bright notes, however. On July 2, twelve thousand people gathered at Mount Rushmore for the dedication of Theodore Roosevelt. As Borglum had promised, the unveiling coincided with the fiftieth anniversary of South Dakota statehood. No living presidents were on hand this time; the senior elected official was Governor Harlan Bushfield, a Republican, who had the poor taste to poke at the federal government's recent orgy of spending.

The rest of the "Golden Jubilee" went much better. Highlights included an appearance by western film star William S. Hart, whose fame had faded somewhat since the silent era, but whom Borglum for some reason dubbed the "heir to ... Crazy Horse." Hart spoke in both

English and Lakota, the latter for the benefit of Chiefs Red Cloud, Henry Standing Bear, and a gathering of Indians, whose own portion of the pageant was directed by Francis "Bud" Duhamel, owner of Rapid City's biggest department store, an adjoining trading post, plus Sitting Bull Crystal Caverns, one of the first tourist attractions to spring up alongside the road to Rushmore. The wife of Rapid City attorney George Phillip, dressed as Sacagawea, sang a tune called "The Indian's Lament," and then everyone sang "God Bless America."

The festivities carried over into the evening, climaxing with a stirring display of fireworks. Sparkling shapes of an Indian, a steamboat, a locomotive, a map of South Dakota, and another of Old Glory symbolized key elements in the state's history. Finally, after the glare of rockets had faded, twelve enormous spotlights were turned upon the faces of Rushmore—the first time the mountain had been lit in its entirety. "[M]y service to my time," Borglum orated, "is to ... divine accurately what lies at the heart and soul of my race and record as nearly as possible ... the truth of our race's ... secret dreaming. We are at the spearhead of a mighty world movement—an awakened force—in rebellion against the worn and useless thought of yesterday." Behind him shone the illuminated faces of Washington, Jefferson, Lincoln—and now Teddy Roosevelt.

Roosevelt, although set back almost in an alcove, was conspicuous and commanding, his moustache as coarse as the sculptor's. Borglum had also done a fine job capturing Roosevelt's distinctive cheeks and jowls and the subtle dent of his chin. The biggest challenge of all, however, other than finding suitable rock, had been Roosevelt's eyeglasses, an essential component of any accurate portrait of the astigmatic Rough Rider. Fortunately, Borglum had already solved this problem in the statue he had done of Woodrow Wilson for Poland. On the bridge of Wilson's nose, he had shaped the band that pinches the spectacles to the president's face; underneath the eyes, he had carved slight ridges to indicate where the glasses touch the upper cheeks. But the actual lenses he left to the imagination: Knowing that Wilson wore spectacles, the viewer elects to *see* Wilson wearing spectacles. With Roosevelt, this sculptural sleight of hand works even better, first because Roosevelt's eyes are famously squinty, and second because the viewer is obliged to stand so far away. Roosevelt's eyewear is as convincing, and as playful, as the emperor's new clothes. Borglum had saved one of his best stunts for last.

A great deal of work still lay ahead, but finally Mount Rushmore was in focus. "The [faces] are so near done," Borglum announced, "I have only to press that cheek in a little, shape that lip a little better ... and open an eye, have it look that way or this way." And it was clear that he was extremely proud of his accomplishment. "My very dear wish," he wrote to one of Franklin Roosevelt's aides, "is that you could come here and see just what a ... real sculptor can do to a rotten old rock that has been making faces at the moon for millions and millions of years; wrinkled, worn, torn—scarred by ice and snow and wind from the northwest. I have rubbed it all out. Talk about a beauty parlor, I've got the biggest one in the world!" He figured that in one more year he'd be finished with the faces altogether. And then perhaps he could turn his attention back to the Hall of Records.

But unexpectedly more obstacles fell into his path. In February 1940, he could not ignore his prostate problem any longer and underwent surgery, choosing a doctor in Colorado to avoid having his name appear on the well-publicized patient list of the Mayo Clinic in Minnesota. Assuring friends that he was still "a strong cuss," he was nonetheless confined to hospital and home for six weeks.

Insult was soon added to injury when the high-minded journal *Scribner's Commentator*—to which Borglum himself had contributed articles—chose the month of March to inflict its own form of public humiliation. Borglum is caricatured on the magazine's cover as a pudgy mountaineer with a Hitler moustache. The blurb underneath reads simply and caustically, "Million-Dollar Chisel." The story within, by Samuel Lubell and Walter Everett, begins: "Gutzon Borglum is living proof of the fact that a man need not necessarily be a prospector to extract gold from a mountain." The authors go on to describe Borglum as a "virtual dictator" whose success as a sculptor of patriotic subjects is attributed to "the fact that he accepts myths as legends." And the reason Rushmore had taken so long is made plain: "Borglum doesn't want to finish the project because then, having created his greatest work, he'll have nothing further to occupy his mind. Having definitely established his immortality, he's now worrying apparently about his remaining years." Making matters worse, the article was then reprinted by the much more widely circulated *Reader's Digest*.

Borglum's fury was uncontainable. Coauthor Lubell received the brunt of his wrath, because it was he who had come to South Dakota and done the interviewing—and because, in Borglum's words, he was "a Jewish scavenger." When Lubell visited Mount Rushmore, "[H]e sought me out in the manner the Jew generally seeks one—breaks in on you . . . asks insolent questions and sticks his nose into everything he should not," Borglum snorted. "I don't know Everett but Lubell is a scurrilous little skunk who left his deodorized trail about the country. He better not come here again."

The timing could not have been more unfortunate, for just as the *Commentator* and *Reader's Digest* articles were appearing, not only was Borglum in poor health, but he was also endeavoring yet again to extract money from Congress. As far-fetched as it seemed, he was requesting the largest appropriation ever—$600,000, enough to complete the Hall of Records, the stairway, the landscaping, and all the final filigree of the memorial. As usual, he tried every ploy he could think of, including the perennial reminder that he was building a "memorial to the philosophy of [our] government." Mostly, though, his rationale was purely pragmatic. Rushmore deserved the money because it was earning money. The logic went as follows:

Every year, more and more tourists visited Mount Rushmore; in 1939, the number had reached 300,000—seventeen hundred cars a day in the summer months. The Black Hills, and South Dakota as a whole, had likewise enjoyed a steady rise in tourism over the previous decade. Citing chamber of commerce sources, Borglum claimed that 80 percent of the overall increase in regional tourism was directly attributable to the public's interest in Mount Rushmore. (He chose to downplay factors such as construction and improvement of roads, new bridges across the rivers of the Midwest and West, and increased ownership, reliability, and comfort of the family automobile.)

In addition to the enormous sums of money that tourists poured into hotels, restaurants, and other retail amenities—$25 million annually, Borglum reported—they purchased millions of gallons of gas. The federal tax on gasoline was one cent a gallon. Since 1928, the increase in total gallons of gas sold in South Dakota "above normal consumption"— "normal" being Borglum's estimate of how much gas the state would have sold *without* tourists—came to 415 million gallons.

From here, the math, the deduction, and the injustice were patently clear, or so Borglum contended. In eleven years, Mount Rushmore had earned $4.1 million in gasoline taxes for the federal government. In return, Rushmore had received less than one-fourth of that amount in federal funding. "No monument ... can show a monetary value comparable to this," Borglum declared. "[I]n all of [Roosevelt's] labors and the billions he has spent to sweeten the life of the American people, Mount Rushmore [is] the only investment ... yielding him four hundred percent." In light of such big dividends, a $600,000 appropriation was "paltry." By the same token, Borglum wrote South Dakota governor Bushfield, the state should give Rushmore $25,000 a year for promotion of the memorial. After all, South Dakota and Rushmore were now synonymous, a fact made manifest with the addition of the words "Rushmore Memorial" to the state's license plates in 1939.

Despite his ordered and ardent pleadings, Borglum didn't get a dime from the state, and Congress approved only $86,000, dashing his hope of resuming work on the Hall of Records and the stairway. "I have the money in my eye, but that is not enough," he had written to Frank Lloyd Wright in April, soliciting the renowned architect's input in the design of the stairs. Now that these new projects were beyond reach, Wright could offer only commiseration. "You are a sorry old warrior," he responded, "all scarred up and bleeding grandly."

Wright was right. Borglum had indeed been knocked about. Another reason he and Mary had spent the winter of 1939–1940 in South Dakota—besides overseeing the work on Rushmore—was that they had abandoned Texas. When Borglum had moved his family to San Antonio in 1925, having departed Georgia so abruptly, he had sized up Texas as the next great forum for his talent. "There is a great big story of civilization lying about there," he told oilman Joseph Cullinan, "for after all, when Texas came into the realm of Anglo-Saxon thought, America became a continental empire."

But nearly all of Borglum's ambitions in Texas had come to naught. At one point he had contemplated buying a large tract of ranchland in the Rio Grande Valley, but he could not find a backer. The Texas Trail Drivers managed to fund the model of their memorial but ran out of money before the colossal enlargement could be carved and cast. The Civil War monument for Fort Worth never caught on, either, and the same was true for so many other Texas projects between 1925 and 1937.

Despite hundreds of hours sketching and cajoling, Borglum was unable to carry out his scheme to revamp the Corpus Christi waterfront (although the improvements done after World War II bear a striking resemblance to Borglum's original scheme, including a sculpture of Christ calming the waters installed in front of the First United Methodist Church on Shoreline Boulevard). His interest in highways prompted him to propose a lushly landscaped road from the Oklahoma border to Mexico. It too went nowhere. He designed a Greek amphitheater for Brackenridge Park in San Antonio. He proposed carvings for the cliffs of Hueco Tanks and Santa Elena Canyon, both in West Texas, and another at Enchanted Rock, a Stone Mountain–like formation in the Hill Country northwest of San Antonio. Again nothing.

The ultimate frustration, however, was the centennial of Texas independence, celebrated in 1936. Scores of commissions were up for grabs, including monuments to the heroes of the Alamo and the battle of San Jacinto. But even though Borglum had made numerous friends in high places throughout the state, he still could not get past the "pasture-bred mavericks" who called the shots. "There is well over a quarter of a million in sculpture work in Texas being turned over into the garbage heap of poor incompetent ne'er do wells who flatter [the] local and corrupt political gang," he complained. Texas was Rapid City or Georgia all over again. And as he had done in Georgia and threatened to do so many times in South Dakota, he cut his losses and pulled up stakes. *Time* magazine for August 9, 1937, reported:

> Out of San Antonio, Tex., last week rumbled one of the last vans full of plaster and clay models of sculpture by Mountain-Carver Gutzon Borglum, who closed up his studio and left for good after the contract for San Antonio's greatest memorial, the Alamo Cenotaph, was awarded not to him, but to pudgy Sculptor Pompeo Coppini. During the twelve years he called San Antonio his home, big-eared irascible Sculptor Borglum never finished a Texas job.... Wrote he from Mount Rushmore, S.D., where he is finishing his colossal head of Lincoln: "What is it in Texas that fights and resists any plan to deal with her history ... with the nobility, honesty and dignity that befit a great people?"

In rebutting *Time*, Borglum did not attempt to smooth any feathers that the article may have ruffled: "My leaving Texas had nothing to do with the worthless monumental development ... there," he wrote to the editor. He insisted that the real reason he had departed was to return to California. He and Mary had traveled to Santa Barbara earlier that spring and had picked out a piece of property in nearby Montecito. They had even talked to Frank Lloyd Wright about helping with the design of a house and studio. But that deal had collapsed as well, and the Borglums fell back to the Black Hills. For some reason, they never considered Borgland as an alternative, and the Connecticut estate continued to languish—unvisited, indebted, unkempt.

And still he had Rushmore to finish. "I am mad about California, but I am doing something here that belongs to all the people of the United States," he told a gathering of South Dakota newspapermen in June 1940. "I will probably be here until I die." In truth, his presence at the mountain had decreased markedly after his surgery that winter. Lincoln Borglum had held the title of supervisor since 1938, and his father had relinquished the day-to-day management almost entirely. After the near-disastrous crash of the hoist that June, he had demanded that the National Park Service purchase a new, safer tram. But the budget wouldn't allow such an expense, and thereafter he cut back on his trips up and down the mountain.

Borglum had promised that the figures of Washington, Jefferson, Roosevelt, and Lincoln would be completed by July 1, and his seasoned crew came close to fulfilling his prediction. When work shut down for the winter, the task remaining was mostly one of cleanup—final touchup of hair, collars, Lincoln's hand. Borglum had always intended to remove the rubble at the base of Mount Rushmore. Now the likelihood of getting it done was as remote as that of shaping the presidents to their waists. And Congress would have to undergo a dramatic change of heart if the Hall of Records and stairway were ever to be resumed.

At the beginning of 1941, America had its eyes turned elsewhere. Europe had been at war for a year and a half; the Germans were stepping up their harassment of American ships in the Atlantic. Borglum, like millions of his fellow countrymen, had been slow to come to terms with the situation abroad. He had applauded the Neutrality Act of 1939, which had repealed the arms embargo and allowed the United States to sell munitions to belligerent powers. But at the same time, he didn't want America in the fight. "There is only one service that you can render greater than [the Neutrality Act]," he wrote to President Roosevelt in October 1939, when the war in Europe was barely a month old, "and that is, stand like a mountain against sending our boys into foreign lands to die in foreign wars!"

Inevitably, though, the "complete breakdown" of Europe got his dander up. He bore a very personal grudge against Adolf Hitler, who had torn down his statue of Woodrow Wilson when the Nazis invaded Poland. But his enmity ran much deeper than that. Throughout his life, Borglum had never hesitated to frame an issue in the broadest context possible, and so it was with the latest war overseas. The Third Reich threatened not just one segment of people or one continent, but the very foundation of humanity. "It is only because of the Atlantic Ocean . . . that we have escaped Hitler's heel," he told a friend. And despite having recently labeled Samuel Lubell a "Jewish scavenger" and Eugene Meyer an "ultra-Jew," he apparently chose not to connect his own personal anti-Semitism with the wholesale "murder lust" he saw rampant in Europe. To Senator Burton Wheeler of Montana he exhorted: "There is one single human obligation now before all decent fathers, mothers, governments—stop Hitler and his cut-throats."

Once again, Borglum was too old to don a uniform, but that did not keep him from dusting off his old war stories. "I was brought up on scalps, disemboweled pioneers, Indian atrocities of every sort," he told Senator Wheeler. "That is all baby work compared with these [Nazi] masters of crime, that have raped, wrecked, burned everything in their way." And in a four-page letter to Roosevelt, he recapped the saga of the aircraft scandal and recited his credentials as an aviation expert: the "extraordinary commission" given him by President Wilson, the "sabotage" and "looting" by Deeds (spelling his name "Dietz"), and his own expertise in all matters relating to aircraft and their operation. "I had been one of three men appointed to witness ... Orvil [sic] Wright's first flight ... at Fort Myer in 1909," he vaunted. "I flew solo in Texas the second time I was in a plane—my pilot worn out and sound asleep in the pit. I flew the plane two hundred miles, in a storm." Finally, he revealed the real purpose of the letter: He wished to warn Roosevelt "against any organization that will [attempt to repeat] the colossal miscarriage of 1917–18.... [T]he most sinister interests in America have awakened and are planning now this instant [to] control the vast sums that will be necessary to carry out your plans."

As a reawakened champion of fiscal patriotism, Borglum allowed a measure of chagrin for having demanded so much money for Rushmore the year before, at a time when Roosevelt was striving to boost the defense budget. In a letter to Memorial Commissioner William McReynolds, who worked in the Treasury Department, he grumbled about the "niggardly appropriations," but then declared that he would revert to seeking private funding for Mount Rushmore "rather than have a word said in slight ... to this undertaking." Down deep, however, he had to know that, given the nation's current jitters, private funding was that much farther out of reach.

So many other things were beyond his reach as well. Like most men his age, he resented the idea that a new world was replacing his own. He had always relished playing the contrarian, but lately his disparagements of this or that trend in art and society had begun to smack of fogyism. The "flare and glare of confused light" had turned Broadway into "a house of ill fame on fire," he lamented to New York mayor Fiorello LaGuardia. The new wave of architecture was no better. Skyscrapers such as the Empire State Building, completed in 1931, were "ghostly" and "cold." Rockefeller Center, completed in 1940, was a bundle of "lifeless chimneys, leaning like naked, unfinished grotesques against the sky." And of modern art: "[I]t is the reign of jazz, it is the reign of the negroid, it is the reign of barbarism, it is the reign of the

neurotic." Gazing ahead, Borglum could glimpse no promise more iri-
descent than Mount Rushmore. Now more than ever, he postured, the
Shrine of Democracy should serve as a beacon for "that great body of
civilization that ran away from the holocaust ... in Europe."

For once, the Interior Department agreed with him and tentatively
wrote $278,000 into its budget for 1942. Somewhat reinvigorated, Borg-
lum saddled up and rode east to fight the good fight one more time.
But in Chicago his prostate acted up, and doctors urged more surgery.
He came through the operation on February 17 in good shape. But then
bad luck, which is said to come in threes, caught up with him. First,
Mary Borglum, who had accompanied him to Chicago, fell on the ice
and broke her wrist. Next, while Borglum was still convalescing in hospital, he received word that Roosevelt had slashed the Rushmore appropriation from the Interior budget. Two days later, a blood clot worked
its way into his pulmonary artery and nearly killed him. Mary Borglum, her arm in a sling, summoned Lincoln from South Dakota and
daughter Mary Ellis, who was married and living in Reno, Nevada.
They rushed to Chicago, cautiously optimistic that the stubborn Viking
had survived the worst.

But on March 6, another embolism clogged Borglum's heart and
killed him within minutes. He was eleven days shy of his seventy-
fourth birthday—although when he had entered the hospital, he had
given his age as only sixty-nine.

Was he vain, or had he simply forgotten his date of birth? Then
again, what did four years matter to a man who had measured time in
millennia, who had packed a millennium of creativity and controversy
into his own flamboyant career? "If you really want fun out of life,"
Borglum had written in a 1935 essay, "The World as I Want It," "tackle
something that's bigger and abler than yourself—tackle the gods—that
will test the best in you and possibly defeat you—and that too is sometimes better than success. Then tackle them again and again. You learn
only from the gods!"

In July 1941, President Roosevelt signed a resolution, written by South Dakota congressman Francis Case, permitting Borglum to be buried at Mount Rushmore. Sensing perhaps that Borglum would never rest if he were interred so near his unfinished masterpiece, his family politely declined Congress's offer. Borglum had lived so many places in his life—Idaho, Nebraska, England, Spain, France, New York, Connecticut, Georgia, Texas, South Dakota—but California was the one place he yearned to live again. "I am planning to return to my old home in California, where I was brought up and which I love very much," he had remarked in 1936, when he was first thinking about leaving San Antonio. And so he finally got his wish. His remains were placed in a mausoleum in a "court of honor" at Forest Lawn Cemetery, Southern California's answer to the ancient tombs of the upper Nile.

And even though Mount Rushmore never got the entablature Borglum had envisioned, his own memorial was marked by an inscription, this one composed by author and friend Rupert Hughes: "As a patriot he stripped corruption bare," the bronze tablet reads. "As a statesman he toiled for equality in the rights of man. At last he carved a mountain for a monument. He made the mountain chant: 'Remember! These giant souls set America free and kept her free. Hold fast your sacred heritage, Americans! Remember! Remember!'"

With Borglum's death, Congress declared Mount Rushmore a fait accompli. Fifty thousand dollars still remained from the last appropriation, and Lincoln Borglum, twenty-nine and now in full charge of the memorial, used it to clean up as best he could. Rushmore would never be finished, he acknowledged, but it did achieve a sort of resolution. In its interrupted state, it has come to exemplify what art scholars now call the "process aesthetic"—work that is still emerging from its raw material. Michelangelo and Rodin had done much the same with their sculpture, although in their instances the effect was intentional.

At the end of the summer, the crew began dismantling the cables, booms, scaffolding, sheds, and the hoist that had dangled from Rushmore for the past fourteen years. The last day of work was October 31. The granite skin of the four faces had been made smooth by thousands of hours of patient "bumping." The eyes were sharp. Teddy's glasses were on straight, his hair parted and groomed. For better or worse, Mount Rushmore was ready for its close-up.

And just in the nick of time. The same day that work on Rushmore shut down, a German submarine sank the American destroyer *Reuben James*; five weeks later Japanese planes surprised the Pacific fleet at Pearl Harbor. Several months before his death, Borglum had lauded his creation as a record of "how a little handful of men came over to this Western hemisphere . . . strong enough to start something. They came here for freedom. . . . I do not believe anything on earth can destroy that spirit—and I believe one other thing, that we will have to start in and start right now to protect that spirit. . . . Here in the middle of the Western world . . . we are cutting deep into the granite a promise to ourselves, our children and our children's children that we will carry on—if, as Lincoln said, 'we stand together and believe.'"

In December 1941, at the beginning of a bloody war, seeing Mount Rushmore was believing.

As historian Rex Alan Smith has noted, Mount Rushmore was begun at a time when it could not be finished and finished at a time when it could never have been begun. Of the total expenditure of $989,000, the federal government had contributed $836,000. Borglum received approximately $170,000, or an average of ten thousand a year, dating back to 1924, when he got his first letter from Doane Robinson. In hindsight, the cost seems a bargain, considering the size of other federal projects during the 1930s and war years—even more of a bargain when one appreciates what it contributed to the morale of the nation and the economy of South Dakota.

Borglum and Robinson had been correct: Rushmore was a "fulcrum" for tourism. After a wartime dip in visitation—as low as thirty thousand in 1944—the crowds began to flock to the memorial once gas rationing was lifted. Americans, their patriotism and prosperity rekindled, were pouring onto the open road—the old Lincoln Highway and Black and Yellow Trail now braided into an asphalted interstate highway system—driving sumptuous new cars, giddy to take in everything that the U.S. of A. had to offer. For those traveling from the East, Rushmore was the first major oasis, the first taste of the true West after crossing the Mississippi. Today, an extraordinary percentage of the two and a half million people who visit Mount Rushmore each year do so out of nostalgia for that family trip they made in the back of a station wagon in the 1950s. Rushmore may have been a child of the Depression, but it quickly became a touchstone of the Baby Boom.

Borglum had always worried about Rushmore's future as a tourist destination—not whether people would come, but whether they would regard it as more than just another roadside attraction. The problem lay not with the intrinsic character of the monument, he realized, but with the surrounding community. In 1927, on the same day he had signed his contract to carve Rushmore, he had written to Doane Robinson: "Of course this is going to make Keystone boom and hell will be popping in that whole neighborhood, which means only one thing: that we ought to be awfully careful and guide wherever we can and whenever we can the local inhabitants and protect the tourists.... [Y]ou know it is much easier to get people to agree to do things beforehand than when they get right into the swim of it and are beginning to make money."

So much for wishful thinking. Federal legislation ensured that the memorial would be protected by a 1,500-acre buffer of relatively undisturbed landscape (reduced in 1948 to 1,270 acres), but that had not stopped "nickel-chasers" from pressing up to the very borders. In the summer of 1939, Borglum groused that a group of local business owners had employed "a fat boy in the neighborhood," dressed him in "drug-store cowboy costume," and planted him a mile and a half below Rushmore, at the Y where the Rapid City and Iron Mountain roads join, ostensibly to give directions to travelers, but really to steer them to trinket shops, eateries, and tourist camps. "It all amounts to an intolerable nuisance," Borglum wrote to Governor Bushfield. Given the gauntlet that visitors now had to run through "'Rushmore this' and 'Rushmore that,'" he was doubly glad that he had carved the actual monument "against the Heavens," where it was "out of the mob's reach."

Inevitably commerce did creep into the memorial grounds, although Borglum tried his best to control it. Begrudgingly he had permitted postcards and a few other souvenirs to be sold at a small counter in his studio, though he insisted on choosing the photos and the printing himself. He eventually authorized manufacture of miniature reproductions of the Rushmore faces, but again he oversaw the design and workmanship. The one thing he would never condone while work was still under way was expansion of concession stands. "I told [Norbeck] that no hot dogs nor ... notion counters would be permitted," he wrote George Phillip, "[and] that if he should only be patient until I got through with the work, he could turn my studio into a house of ill fame if he wanted, but while I was still there, he could not."

Not until after Borglum's death did Rushmore begin to cater to tourists in a much bigger, unabashed way. Borglum's original studio was turned into a full-blown restaurant and gift shop. Then in 1958, the National Park Service opened an even more elaborate concession building directly in front of the four faces. Visitors could sit at tables in the capacious Buffalo Dining Room (named for its large buffalo-hunt mural), eat a hot meal (or hot dog), and gaze through immense plateglass windows at Mount Rushmore. Some insisted that the view was even better from the adjoining gift shop, which sold everything from Native American crafts to Black Hills gold jewelry and miniature ceramic replicas of the memorial. "Gifts are chosen to represent the arts and crafts of the area from which they come," explained one guidebook, "so they are not just copies of the cultures of others. For example, an Oriental vase will be *Oriental* and not imitation." The concession building opened onto a large viewing terrace for those who preferred an unadulterated glimpse of the presidential faces, a thousand feet away. One can only surmise how Borglum would have felt about such heresy. Lincoln Borglum could do little to stop it himself; he had resigned as superintendent in 1943 and settled in his adopted state of Texas. Mount Rushmore National Memorial was now entirely in the hands of the National Park Service, an agency that, for reasons already obvious, held no special fondness for the sculptor.

One battle in which Borglum did prevail, however, was over the addition of more faces to Rushmore. It was not a close fight, but it was not an easy one either—and to some extent it has never really ended. Over the years, various groups have come forward with proposals to add another great man to the Rushmore four—Woodrow Wilson, Franklin Roosevelt, Dwight Eisenhower, John F. Kennedy, Ronald Reagan, John Wayne, Elvis Presley—and each time the Park Service has had to hold its ground. Of all the campaigns to turn four faces into five, by far the most fascinating and formidable was the one to initiate a woman into the men's club.

Rose Arnold Powell bore a striking resemblance to Carol Kennicott, the plucky heroine of Sinclair Lewis's 1920 novel, *Main Street*. Both grew up in Minnesota. Both eventually chafed at the conventions of small-town, middle-class, married life at the turn of the century. And both eventually broke with their husbands and moved to Washington to join the burgeoning women's movement—or "woman movement," as it was known then. In Powell's case, she had been a schoolteacher, dictionary salesperson, and administrator for the Internal Revenue Service. She was already in her mid-forties when she read a biography of Susan B. Anthony, the nation's most prominent suffragist.

Suddenly Powell had a vision. She let go of her old life, moved to Washington, and became the founding secretary-treasurer of the Susan B. Anthony Forum, the primary goal of which was to heighten recognition of Anthony and the woman movement. In 1927, when she discovered that President Coolidge had attended the dedication of Mount Rushmore and had agreed to write the inscription for the memorial, she dashed off a letter urging him to use his influence to add Anthony to the mountain. "Somehow," she implored, "I can not help but feel that this admirable piece of work which will last throughout the centuries will not tell the whole truth unless some reference is made to the part women played in the development of our country." Coolidge was predictably silent, but Powell now saw her mission laid out before her "like a white streak." She would put Susan B. Anthony on Mount Rushmore or die trying.

Her next opening did not come for another six years, when she got wind that Borglum was in Washington, ginning up support for Rushmore. Borglum, keen for help from any and all quarters, agreed to meet with Powell at the Willard Hotel. He was moderately gracious and entirely noncommittal. "I showed him a picture of her which he did not like and I told him I would send him another," Powell recalled. She sent the picture, but Borglum did not write back, at least not for some time. "I think I understand how a man might feel taking up the cudgels for a woman," Powell wrote after not hearing from him for three months, "though [Anthony] is second to none in the group of men who will be honored.... [She] suffers the disadvantage of not having her marvelous life known by men.... Now is the time to remedy the situation before it is too late. I *know*, Mr. Borglum, that what I ask is *right*."

Borglum, who in fact was attracted to strong women, and they to him, remained unmoved. "Women are wonderful things," he confided to a male friend, "but most of them are still hovering and it is going to be a little difficult to guess or determine just how they will settle into the picture. I do not forget that my mother was a woman and that man owes more to them than to any expression of nature. [But] they form no part of the group of four who built and preserved our territory. That was a man's job—don't forget that."

Despite Borglum's impassivity, Powell continued to pound away. What she did best was write letters, and over the next two years she wrote scores, perhaps hundreds, to everyone she could think of: the Rushmore commissioners, President Roosevelt, the Interior Department, the National Park Service, women's organizations, and every month or so another to Borglum. "My decision to write you again reminded me of the Bible story of Jacob wrestling with the angel and his determination to hang on to him in the words, 'I will not let thee go until thou bless me.'" Still Borglum did not answer her, although to those who had been prodded by Powell and who now prodded him, he reminded a) that Rushmore was a memorial to presidents only, and b) that there was no more room on the mountain for another figure, regardless of stature or gender.

Powell was particularly annoyed by the so-called empire-builder criterion for selecting the four presidents. "What did territorial expansion mean apart from the energy, the courage, the vision to make mere acres of ground a means to the attainment of higher values, the right to a more abundant life, increased liberty, and the pursuit of happiness[?]" she implored.

> I make this last point because the 'territorial' motive ... [has been] overemphasized. ... Immortalizing dust is a strange conception on which to base [Rushmore's] outward expression. The immortal thing about the memorial will be the personalities and their great contributions to human welfare. ... [If Susan B. Anthony were included], it will proclaim to all succeeding generations that *men and women* built this republic; that in the twentieth century women were brave enough to fight for a woman's *right* to be included and won their fight. It will be a disgrace to both men and women in this enlightened day if they allow this narrow-gauge memorial to be completed according to the present plan. ... There will undoubtedly never be another memorial of this character com-

memorating this particular period in history. It will not tell the truth without a woman in it.

Finally Powell found the ally she was looking for. Eleanor Roosevelt was a feminist of unimpeachable credentials and the first truly activist first lady. It was said that when women voted for Franklin Roosevelt, as the majority of women did, they were actually casting a vote for his wife. In the election year of 1936, the Democratic Party looked for ways to solidify further the support of women. One gesture was to push through approval of a Susan B. Anthony commemorative stamp (three cents), the first U.S. stamp or coin to bear the image of a flesh-and-blood woman (as opposed to the Liberty goddess or a generic Indian woman in headdress). Eleanor Roosevelt had encouraged the stamp, which was issued in August, three months before the election, and she likewise had been receptive to the notion of Anthony on Rushmore. In April 1936, she wrote to Borglum, exhorting him to do the right thing.

Borglum, needless to say, did not want to irk either the first lady or her husband—he was angling to have FDR visit Rushmore that summer. And so he parried very carefully. "No man living ... places woman in a more lofty position in civilization than I do," he assured Mrs. Roosevelt. "I have resented all my life any and all forms of dependence or second place forced upon our mothers"—a poignant comment when one recalls that his own mother was a "second place" wife. "But," he continued, "I feel in this proposal that it is a very definite intrusion that will injure the specific purpose of the memorial."

His diplomatic deflections had little effect, however, and Powell, with Eleanor Roosevelt's endorsement, succeeded in getting legislation introduced in both the House and the Senate that would add Susan B. Anthony to Mount Rushmore. The bills were hollow political ploys at best, and they fell flat, but they nettled Borglum just the same.

The aggravation might have been more prolonged if Powell's life had not taken an abrupt turn. In October 1936, while hurrying to yet another meeting on behalf of Susan B. Anthony, she was struck by a taxi on Sixteenth Street in Washington. Unconscious and severely bruised, she spent several weeks in the hospital. Her recovery was slow and halting, and after several months, she returned to Minnesota and the care of relatives. But those who assumed that Rose Powell was hors de combat had underestimated her mettle. In 1939, although permanently handicapped, she was ready to wave the Anthony banner once again.

This time Borglum did not ignore her letters, for he now grasped that, if he played his cards right, Powell and Anthony could figure nicely into his plans. That fall, Borglum was preparing to return to Washington to ask for another $300,000 to fund the Hall of Records and grand stairway. He had iterated endlessly that there was no space on the front side of Rushmore for any more faces. But the back, or west, side was still up for grabs. Shrewdly he wrote to Powell and her compatriots in the woman movement that, if they would support legislation for the hall, he would find a spot for Susan B. Anthony on the west side of Mount Rushmore.

What Borglum had in mind of course was including a bust of Anthony in the group of twenty or so others *inside* the Hall of Records. "I would rather have my [own] bust in that hall than my head on the Mountain," he asserted. Powell, who had never been to Mount Rushmore, recognized sweet talk when she heard it and kept urging him to place Anthony's face either on the cliff *beside* the entrance to the Hall of Records or, better yet, on the canyon wall *facing* it. "The inside location," she reasoned with her usual iron courtesy, "will always suggest that women are of secondary importance. It will be the outside pictures of the Memorial that will always have greater educational value. ... No woman should have the desire that the feminine symbol should outlast the masculine and for that reason [be] placed inside. Let these honored heads wear away together." She also urged that the Anthony image be of the same scale as that of the four presidents. And one more thing: How about adding another woman of distinction—say, Elizabeth Cady Stanton?

With time running out on his chance to finagle a further appropriation from Congress, Borglum finally assented. "I have just received your letter," he wrote to Powell on January 3, 1940, "and there is nothing in it that I am in variance with. If we decide that the West side of the mountain is suitable, I am for it. We must work out a design that is fitting and in no sense harmful in the manner of lighting or location ... and I am entirely for giving Miss Anthony one or two companions." But in a telegram to Powell sent later that day he was much less specific: "Suggest the following be given to AP [Associated Press] and United Press tonight so as to reach Congress tomorrow. Quote: 'Mr. Borglum ... has given his word that adequate and noble recognition of woman's part in the development of American freedom and culture will be incorporated in his designs and become part of the completed Memorial.'"

This time Powell took the bait. "Now that we see eye to eye with regard to the manner in which WOMAN is to be honored at Mount Rushmore," she responded ebulliently, "I want to be of all possible help to you in securing the funds you need; and realizing that in [an] election year men are disposed to give women more consideration than in other years, ... I am eager to see the [appropriation] bill introduced and passed at this session." She suggested that he increase his request to a million dollars and commenced her usual salvo of letters to people in high places.

The outcome was not what either had hoped. This time it was Borglum who entered the hospital—his first prostate surgery—and Congress, despite the epistolary efforts of Powell, gave Rushmore its "niggardly" $86,000. With that, the Hall of Records—and Susan B. Anthony—were put on indefinite hold.

Even then Powell would not admit defeat. After Borglum's unexpected death in March 1941, she wrote to Mary Borglum: "When I read of his passing I devoutly hoped that he left definite instructions to carry out that marvellously complete vision [of adding Anthony and finishing the Hall of Records]. I have no doubt that adequate funds, which Congress would not give him in life, it will now give him in memoriam. . . . And now I am going to appeal to you and your son to carry out your husband's vision . . . in which he recognized the importance of the Woman and the Woman Movement ADEQUATELY. . . . I will deeply appreciate the assurance that she would be established on a level with her peers."

Both Mary and Lincoln Borglum wrote Powell over the ensuing months, gently trying to persuade her that the hall and the inclusion of Susan B. Anthony were now permanently out of reach. But still Powell persisted. She pecked away at Lincoln throughout the war and well into the 1950s, urging him to use his influence, even after he resigned as superintendent, to keep the Anthony idea alive. Well into her eighties, she petitioned Vice President Richard Nixon to help in a cause born during the Coolidge Administration. Powell finally died in 1961, less well-known than Susan B. Anthony, to be sure, but no less indefatigable.

In the second half of the twentieth century, after Powell's death, the clamor for Susan B. Anthony on Mount Rushmore subsided, as women found other forums in which to make the case for equal rights and recognition. Still, the issue of whom Rushmore did and did not represent would not go away. Nobody had a greater vested interest in this debate than the Native Americans of South Dakota.

chapter 12

EXPEDIENT EXAGGERATION

FOR HIS GENERATION, Borglum had a rather enlightened view of Native Americans. "You ask me why I am interested in the American Indian," he had told a Washington audience in 1934. "Perhaps my first reason is that I have known him all my life." Some of Borglum's most cherished, if apocryphal, recollections of childhood on the Nebraska prairie were of racing his pony against Indian boys, of meeting Lakota chiefs on trips with his father, and of "the Indian . . . who wrapped me in his blanket while he shivered half naked in a blizzard." Nostalgic embroidery aside, the underlying sentiment was heartfelt. "I believed in the Indian," Borglum said. "I still believe in him."

He had particular admiration for the Lakota Sioux. They were "the Romans among the red men . . . that great war-like race." And among the Lakota, he especially favored the Oglala—"the Aristocrats." To be sure, Borglum's categorical appreciation of Indians exuded a certain "noble savage" unctuousness, but his record of aid and loyalty to the Lakota during his years in South Dakota set him apart from most of the other armchair humanitarians of the day. Had he more time and wherewithal, he might even have gotten around to sculpting a major monument to the Lakota—not on Mount Rushmore or in the Hall of Records but somewhere not too far away. The figure mentioned most often was Crazy Horse.

In the thirty-seven years between the massacre at Wounded Knee and the driving of the first drill at Mount Rushmore, the Lakota had endured great hardship. The federal government had continued to use the tribe for target practice, throwing one program after another at it, ostensibly aiming to improve the quality of life on the reservation but ultimately managing only to rend the fabric of Lakota culture even further. Indian religion was outlawed, including the fundamental ritual of the sweat lodge and the most sacred of ceremonies, the sun dance. At reservation schools, children had their braids chopped off and were punished for speaking their native language. In early negotiations with the U.S. government, Oglala Chief Red Cloud had demanded that the government provide care and sustenance to the Indians until the "seventh generation." Inept bureaucracy and outright corruption now had many people wondering if there ever would be a seventh generation, or even a third or fourth. What had begun as a policy of "assimilation" had evolved into a policy of oppression, and, inadvertently perhaps, also one of extinction.

Borglum's initial exposure to South Dakota's Indians had been cursory. He invited a group of Pine Ridge Oglala to participate in the first Rushmore dedication ceremony in 1925. But it was not until 1931 that he fully appreciated just how drastically the Lakota had deteriorated since his childhood encounters, halcyon by comparison. That October he had come away from a trip to Pine Ridge appalled by the conditions there. "The drought has killed their food crops and seventy five percent of the tribe is starving," he alerted President Hoover. "They are marooned, so to speak, on a vast barren area, timberless and practically gameless, . . . [and] even their streams have dried up. . . . In my youth I knew these same people, bought buffalo hides and ponies from them, now they have no skins and few have more than a pony for transportation to town. In all my forty years of travel, I have never seen a picture more forbidding, more hopeless ... than I saw at Pine Ridge, where [the people are] so completely trapped by an alien imposed civilization, and by that civilization corrupted, beggared, and crushed."

Seizing the initiative, Borglum organized a campaign to deliver food, blankets, and clothing to Pine Ridge before the onset of winter. In a matter of weeks, he was able to commandeer sixty-five head of cattle (five from his own herd), one hundred sheep, two railroad cars of clothing, and five thousand army blankets. To show their gratitude, the Oglala invited Borglum to become an honorary member of the tribe at a ceremony at Pine Ridge. For the occasion, Borglum offered to provide a feast of buffalo meat, traditional food that most Indians had not tasted in decades, some never at all. On the day of the ceremony, he and Lincoln attempted to shoot a buffalo bull on a (white man's) ranch south of Pierre. Firing from the car window, Lincoln wounded the animal but did not kill it. Mounted ranch hands eventually chased the buffalo down and finished it off, although not in time for that night's dinner at Pine Ridge. The papers had fun with the story, but the Indians seemed genuinely touched by Borglum's gesture. Wearing a full-length feather headdress (and looking a bit like Calvin Coolidge), he was welcomed into the tribe and given the honorific *Inyan Wanblee*—"Stone Eagle."

Less vital than the relief effort and not as conspicuous as the induction ceremony, but in some ways just as remarkable, was a letter written to Borglum the following day by Lakota Chief Luther Standing Bear, the Carlisle-educated author of *My People the Sioux*, one of the first, and certainly one of the most acclaimed, autobiographies ever written by a Plains Indian. "Let me thank you for your great spirit of humanitarianism," Standing Bear wrote from California, where he had found work as an actor in Hollywood westerns. His real reason for writing, however, was to "suggest to you now what I suggested to some of the chiefs . . . last summer regarding the face you are carving on Rushmore Mt? I think it would be most fitting to have the face of Crazy Horse sculp[t]ed there. . . . True other Indians have received more attention in the white man's history but nevertheless Crazy Horse is the real patriot of the Sioux tribe and the only one worthy to place by the side of Washington and Lincoln." Standing Bear did not mention that his sister, Black Shawl, had been Crazy Horse's wife.

Borglum did not respond to Standing Bear—just as he would turn aside Rose Arnold Powell's first letters. However, he did continue to campaign for better conditions on Pine Ridge. In 1934, the Roosevelt Administration proposed a series of reforms to Indian policy. The thrust of the Indian Reorganization Act—or "Indian New Deal," as the legislation was soon called—was self-determination and a general restoration of native language, craft, religion, and council form of tribal government. For Commissioner of Indian Affairs John Collier, a top priority was overhauling the old system of individual land allotments, thereby allowing tribes to live more communally. Critics condemned the plan as yet another outbreak of Roosevelt socialism, but Borglum was not one of them. In a speech broadcast by NBC radio in February, he urged that Indians be permitted to live "without interference by the white man." Addressing the Indians directly, he exhorted, "[Y]ou now have for the first time in eighty-six years a chance to return to some of the freedom and rights of your fathers."

In the same speech, Borglum also inserted a startling declaration: "I am making images of the Great White Chiefs who built the White Man's Government. I am making these in the . . . Hunting Ground of your Great Spirit. I know you are glad of this for *I shall make for you if the Great Spirit gives me life one of your great chiefs to be there in the mountains forever with the great White Chiefs.* . . . I have promised you in Council on the Great Pine Ridge Reservation that if you will choose from among your fathers one of the Great Plains Chiefs, I will carve his face in the stone where the Eagle rests.... You know that I have never spoken to you with a split tongue." (Emphasis added.)

What exactly did he mean by "where the Eagle rests"? Borglum had made his radio address in 1934, before the Hall of Records had taken shape. Surely he was not promising to add the face of an Indian chief to the front side of Mount Rushmore. If he had another location in mind, he did not disclose it.

Meanwhile, there was more big news in Lakota country besides the Indian New Deal and Borglum's strange proposal. Eleven years earlier, the Sioux Nation had filed a claim against the federal government. Their attorney, Ralph Case, a white man who had grown up among South Dakota's Indians, had advised his clients that they could not expect to get the hills back outright, but the government could be forced to pay for what it had taken. Case had estimated the worth of the Black Hills in 1877 at $156 million; with interest, the total in 1923 came to $600 million. The government tried to whittle down the size of Case's appraisal, even while many Sioux contended that the number should have been much higher; after all, a single mine, the Homestake, had been extracting millions of dollars in gold from the Black Hills annually. And so, on May 7, 1934, while Standing Bear was lobbying Borglum to carve Crazy Horse into the Black Hills, Ralph Case filed a series of petitions expanding the Sioux Nation's claim, upping the demand to nearly one billion dollars. At a glance, these tandem efforts might have seemed incompatible with each other. But in fact both reflected the Sioux Nation's undying ambition to take hold of something that they believed was rightfully theirs.

The Black Hills land claim would drag on for another fifty years, and indeed it still continues today. Borglum, for his part, was just as slow to follow through on his commitment to carve an Indian head *somewhere* in the hills. All the while, however, he continued to welcome Indians to Mount Rushmore, most notably the Oglala holy man Black Elk. In 1932 the poet John Neihardt had published an extraordinary book, *Black Elk Speaks: Being the Life Story of a Holy Man of the Oglala Sioux*, in which Black Elk, via Neihardt's King Jamesian prose, recounts the highs and lows of his momentous life. As a young boy, Black Elk, who was Crazy Horse's cousin, had taken part in the battle of the Little Bighorn. Later, he had traveled to Europe with Buffalo Bill's Wild West show, returning home to join the Ghost Dance movement and narrowly escaping death at Wounded Knee.

For all the sweep of Black Elk's saga, the most riveting and enduring aspect of his narrative is his description of a vision that had come to him in 1871, at the age of nine. Young Black Elk had become deathly ill and had fallen into a trance. As his fevered vision progresses, he is handed a stick from which sprout branches bearing many leaves. "Behold, the living center of a nation," he is told, "and with it many you shall save." Soon he is transported to the top of a mountain—reckoned by Black Elk to be Harney Peak in the Black Hills—from which he can see "the hoop of the world. . . . And I saw that the sacred hoop of my people was one of many hoops that made one circle, wide as daylight and as starlight, and in the center grew one mighty flowering tree to shelter all the children of one mother and one father. And I saw that it was holy."

Black Elk carried the memory of his vision with him all his life—to Little Bighorn, Europe, and back again—and even more privately through his years as a practicing Roman Catholic on Pine Ridge. Not until he was sixty-eight, when Neihardt came to the reservation to research the Ghost Dance, did Black Elk finally divulge his great vision. One of the reasons he had kept it to himself for so long is made clear in the final chapter, in which Black Elk considers the lesson of Wounded Knee: "I did not know then how much was ended. When I look back now from this high hill of my old age, I can still see the butchered women and children lying heaped and scattered all along the crooked gulch. . . . And I can see that something else died there in that bloody mud, and was buried in the blizzard. A people's dream died there. . . . And I, to whom so great a vision was given in my youth,—you see me now a pitiful old man who has done nothing, for the nation's hoop is broken and scattered. There is no center any longer, and the sacred tree is dead." Because of its compelling vision of genesis and apocalypse, *Black Elk Speaks* has been called "the Indian Bible" and continues to be one of the most widely studied and respected Indian writings.

In 1936, four years after the book's publication, Borglum invited Black Elk to Mount Rushmore. The previous two summers, Black Elk, his family, and a number of other Oglala had pitched their tepees on the property of Sitting Bull Crystal Caverns as guests of the Duhamel family. The caverns, said to have been a favorite camping spot of Sitting Bull, contained a colorful array of stalactites, stalagmites, and "dog-tooth" crystals. In exchange for food, fuel, water, and a percentage of the gate, Black Elk and his group performed twice-daily "pageants," a diversion far more fascinating than underground geology. Typical programs included sign language, flute playing, smoking of the sacred pipe, and various dances—grass, kettle, hoop, eagle, rabbit, buffalo, and even an abbreviated version of the sun dance. In one of the pageant's highlights, Black Elk would appear in traditional breechcloth, buffalo-horn headdress, and face paint and cure a "sick" child through prayer and the magical shake of a Lakota rattle. The entire affair was intended to be educational, and doubtless it was, yet one cannot imagine Mohammed or Saint Paul having to sing for their suppers on the lot of a glorified rock shop.

When word got out that Franklin Roosevelt might visit the Black Hills in August, Borglum immediately thought of asking Black Elk's contingent to perform for the president, as Indians had done at previous Rushmore events. But when it was announced that Roosevelt's stay would be short, the Indians were cut from the program. Black Elk was disappointed, and as consolation, Borglum invited him to visit Rushmore on his own, several days ahead of the president. Escorted by Borglum to the top of the carving, Black Elk offered a half-hour-long prayer to the Great Mystery. In a translation provided by his son Ben and printed in the *Rapid City Journal*, Black Elk asked that the greatness of the men on the mountain be "carried on through changes of nations and of races"—whatever that meant. In fact, no one knows exactly what Black Elk did say atop Mount Rushmore, least of all Borglum, who in a letter to President Roosevelt a day or two later referred to the world-renowned Lakota holy man as "Black Bear." (In light of this gaffe, one now wonders if the Lakota Black *Horse*, who had appeared at the top of Rushmore during the 1925 dedication, was not misidentified as well.)

In a nutshell, this was Borglum's posture toward the Lakota throughout the 1930s: indulgent, yet not as intimate as he professed. "I would trust an Indian, off-hand, 9 out of 10, where I would not trust a white man 1 out of ten," he wrote in January 1937, but still he was no closer to giving the Indians the memorial he had promised. Finally, in 1938, he settled on a plan. He had dealt with the demands of Rose Arnold Powell by promising Susan B. Anthony a spot on the rear of Rushmore. With the Lakota, he offered a memorial in an entirely different state.

A group of prominent Nebraskans, led by Everett P. Wilson, history professor at the State Teacher's College at Chadron, had formed a committee to erect a series of monuments to Lakota chiefs—Red Cloud, Spotted Tail, Sitting Bull, Crazy Horse, and others—in Chadron State Park, southwest of Pine Ridge and southeast of the Black Hills. Borglum, grabbing the chance to solve two problems with one stone, agreed to cooperate. "I'm not as young as I was, and I don't like to take on new fights," he told the *Nebraska State Journal* in November 1938. "But now I want to build a monument, not from cement and sand [as Lorado Taft had done with *Black Hawk* in Illinois], but from granite boulders. We'll [m]ake this monument out of Rushmore granite, hauled down here in pieces of thirty, sixty and eighty tons. We'll make a whole tribe of Indians. We'll make them fourteen to sixteen feet tall and reproduce them as our forefathers first knew and saw them—wild and carefree."

Borglum died before the Nebraska scheme took shape, and the envisioned memorial was never built. (Today the most significant sculpture in that corner of Nebraska is *Carhenge*, a circle of old automobiles, embedded nose-first in a field beside Highway 385, south of Chadron.) If the Lakota were ever going to get their Crazy Horse memorial, they would have to look elsewhere. And as chance would have it, a brash young sculptor had just arrived on the scene, looking for something enormous to carve. His name was Korczak Ziolkowski.

In some ways, Ziolkowski had a great deal in common with Gutzon Borglum. In others, they were exact opposites. Ziolkowski was born in Boston in 1908 to second-generation Polish-Americans. He was orphaned at the age of one, and by age eighteen, tall and strapping, he had left his guardian and taken up the woodcarver's craft. In the 1930s, he expanded his sculptural repertoire to include marble portraits. Ziolkowski's family and biographer imply that when Ziolkowski and Borglum came together in 1939, they were already peers—that they had first made each other's acquaintance as fellow members of the National Sculpture Society and the Players Club in New York, and that Borglum had admired Ziolkowski's bigger-than-life bust of Ignacy Paderewski, which had won an award at the 1939 New York World's Fair.

More accurately, by 1939 Borglum had long since distanced himself from the Sculpture Society and was not active at the Players. And while he had known Paderewski, he loathed everything about the world's fair and wouldn't go near it. Moreover, he denied ever having invited Ziolkowski to work with him on Mount Rushmore. "This pseudo-sculptor," Borglum explained in 1940, "drifted into my place [in the Black Hills] unasked as any passerby might. He and his wife [Dorothy] slept in their car, or insisted upon it. I gave them a cabin. He explained who he was, with great importance. I took him to the mountain and gave him work. . . . He assured me he was one of the great artists of America—and in his own mind and in his wife's mind he was the only great artist in America. He had no work to show me except a photo-

graph of a piece . . . which he claimed to be the Governor of Connecticut, as work [it was] no good. . . . [On the mountain] I gave him specific
work to do. Paid him $1.25 an hour. . . . He was there for, I think, three
weeks altogether, and there is not a day's work [that he did] on the
mountain of any value."

Other accounts describe a more classic clash of egos: Borglum and
Ziolkowski liking each other at first, taking each other's measure over
multiple rounds of cocktails—they both loved their Manhattans—and
finally concluding that Mount Rushmore wasn't big enough for the two
of them. More sensational stories describe an altercation, possibly
fisticuffs, between Lincoln Borglum and Ziolkowski over chain of command on the mountain. The upshot, regardless, was that Borglum fired
Ziolkowski after only nineteen days on the payroll, advising that he
pursue his own career in the East. Ziolkowski stuck around long
enough for his wife to help direct the South Dakota fiftieth-anniversary
jubilee at Rushmore on July 2. On his way home later that summer, he
apparently detoured through Georgia, where, according to Borglum
family correspondence, he attempted to pass himself off as Borglum's
right-hand assistant in order to win the job of completing Stone Mountain. Spurned again, he finally returned to West Hartford, Connecticut,
where he most likely would have remained forever, an ambitious, if
middling, sculptor of the East Coast's who's who. But then, serendipitously, came a letter from Pine Ridge.

Luther Standing Bear had died earlier that year while working on,
of all poignancies, *Union Pacific*, Hollywood's epic of western expansion. The Crazy Horse cause now fell to his brother Henry. Whether
Henry Standing Bear had met Ziolkowski during his brief time in
South Dakota is not known. Either way, Standing Bear saw a notice
and/or photo of Ziolkowski's Paderewski, and, having finally
despaired of getting Crazy Horse on Rushmore, he wrote to the only
other sculptor of big heads he knew of. "A number of my fellow chiefs
and I are interested in finding some sculptor who can carve a head of

an Indian chief who was killed many years ago," Standing Bear inquired. "This is a matter of longstanding in my mind which must be brought before the public soon. The main thing now is to know if some one can do the work when money raised." (The Ziolkowski family says that Standing Bear explained his motive even more clearly in a second letter: "My fellow Chiefs and I would like the White Man to know the Red Man had great heroes, too." Regrettably, this letter is now "lost," according to a Crazy Horse Memorial spokesman.)

Even then, Ziolkowski did not return to South Dakota for another seven years. He devoted the next three to carving a thirteen-foot-tall statue of Noah Webster in West Hartford, again using his purported link to Borglum to garner community support. Finally, after several years in the Army, he again turned his attention to Standing Bear and Crazy Horse. Ziolkowski's biography stresses that initially he did not want to carve a colossal statue of Crazy Horse in the Black Hills, so near Mount Rushmore, but agreed to do so only at Standing Bear's insistence. In 1946, Ziolkowski filed a mining patent on a mountain ten miles southwest of Mount Rushmore and five miles from the town named for Crazy Horse's arch-enemy, Custer. (He was eventually able to purchase the mountain outright, and he named it Thunderhead.) Using a piece of marble left over from the Webster statue, he carved a model of an Indian riding a horse. The Indian is bare-chested, his long, unbraided locks streaming behind him, with a single feather sticking straight up from the top of his head. His left hand points forward, between the horse's ears. Both Indian and horse are unfinished—the former from the waist down, the latter from the shoulders back.

In the half-century since Ziolkowski carved the original model for the Crazy Horse memorial, opinions of its aesthetic merits have been divided. Some people, including many Indians, fairly weep when they first glimpse the noble profile. Others gag. "Crazy Horse doesn't look very Indian and neither does his pony," the Lakota author John Lame Deer gibed in 1972. "[T]he feather coming out of his hair looks like an air valve sticking out of a tire. The chief's arm is pointing ahead like 'this way to the men's room.'"

One thing on which all agree is that Ziolkowski's rendering is not a likeness of Crazy Horse. On June 4, 1948, a crowd of dignitaries attended a ceremony marking the official commencement of what the *Rapid City Journal* figured to be "the greatest sculptural effort ever attempted by man." Among those present were two survivors of Little Bighorn, High Eagle and Comes Again. "Both Indians, aged and stoic, said they remember Crazy Horse well," the *Journal* reported, "and High Eagle took exception to Ziolkowski's model....He said the nose of Crazy Horse was thin and straight, while the nose of the model was wide and pugged." Ziolkowski was quick to explain that he intended his Crazy Horse to represent all Indians. So much so, apparently, that he had never bothered to ask eyewitnesses what the Oglala had actually looked like. He simply imagined an Indian in his head and carved it.

But what Ziolkowski's scheme lacked in elegance and authenticity, it made up for in scale. Ziolkowski had in mind a monument 500 feet tall, 600 feet wide—a carving ten times the volume of Mount Rushmore. He offered no prediction when he would complete the colossal Crazy Horse, but the intensity of his conviction won over Standing Bear. After 1939, no further pressure was put on Borglum to make room for an Indian on Rushmore.

Still, the urge to tinker with the memorial was unceasing. No amount of speechifying by Borglum during his lifetime could have prevented the public from reinterpreting Rushmore, from casting the faces in fresh light—the spectrum ranging from the comical to the commercial to the profoundly political. Far and away the most famous appropriation of the Rushmore image came in 1958. The unlikely usurper was a portly English movie director by the name of Alfred Hitchcock.

Hitchcock loved using famous locations to pique excitement in his movies. In 1929, while still working in England, he had sent police scrambling across the roof of the British Museum in *Blackmail*. In *The 39 Steps* (1935), sometimes called "the British *North by Northwest*," an accused murderer/spy is chased across the breathtaking Scottish heath and highlands. And in *Saboteur* (1942), another prequel to *North by Northwest*, an accused murderer/foreign agent flees across the American continent; the gripping climax takes place atop the torch of the Statue of Liberty. *Vertigo* (1958), the movie Hitchcock made immediately before *North by Northwest*, has its finale at one of California's picturesque missions. If Hitchcock was ever going to top his previous cliffhangers, he would have to film an honest-to-goodness cliffhanger from a very conspicuous cliff.

North by Northwest is yet another Hitchcock tale of mistaken identities, in which foreign spies (presumably Soviet, although the script is not specific) confuse Roger Thornhill, a glib Madison Avenue smoothie (played by the ultimate smoothie, Cary Grant), for American agent George Kaplan. In fact, there is no George Kaplan; he is simply a fictional figure created by the Americans to lure the bad guys from the shadows. ("In the world of advertising there is no such thing as a lie," Thornhill quips to his secretary in an early scene. "There is only the expedient exaggeration.") Turning the tables, the Soviets frame Thornhill, believing he's Kaplan, for a murder in the lobby of the United Nations building. To save his skin, Thornhill elects to become the nonexistent Kaplan and flees New York aboard the westbound *Twentieth Century Limited*. On the train, he hooks up with Eve Kendall (a cool but come-hither Eva Marie Saint), who, it turns out, is a flesh-and-blood American undercover agent who has aligned herself coquettishly with the foreign spies (James Mason and Martin Landau) in order to win their confidence and stop them from spiriting government secrets out of the country. Along the way, Thornhill is lured onto the Indiana prairie (California's Central Valley, actually), where he is buzzed famously by a crop duster—the only time in the entire adventure that

Thornhill's celestially pressed suit and lily-white shirt are compromised. The whole web of misperception and misdirection is baffling to Thornhill, although from Hitchcock's perspective, the final destination is never in doubt. An early working title to the script had been *The Man on Lincoln's Nose.*

On July 28, 1958, Metro-Goldwyn-Mayer location manager Charles Coleman arrived in Rapid City to scout Mount Rushmore. The National Park Service, which had just opened its new gift shop and restaurant earlier that year, was only too pleased to show off the memorial to Hollywood. But knowing Hitchcock's reputation, the Park Service was careful to set very clear ground rules. In granting MGM a permit to shoot at the memorial, the Park Service stipulated: "No scenes of violence will be filmed near the sculpture, on the talus slopes below the sculpture, or any simulation or mock-up of the sculpture.... Scenes of violence may be filmed in other parts of the Memorial area, but film editing or otherwise may not lead viewers of the finished and released motion picture to believe that violence occurred on or near the sculpture."

Hitchcock would see about that. He had hit a similar impasse with the United Nations, which had refused to let him film any scenes at its New York headquarters. Hitchcock had solved the problem by building a replica of the Delegates Lounge and then had sneakily shot footage of Grant striding from the famous building. As for Rushmore, his location man had undoubtedly warned him of the extreme difficulty, if not impossibility, of filming on the faces. At one point, Hitchcock and screenwriter Ernest Lehman had discussed a scene in which Grant, hiding beneath Lincoln's nose, gives himself away by sneezing. But by the time the cast and crew arrived in Rapid City on September 15, Hitchcock had already abandoned the nose scene (along with the *Nose* title) and made up his mind to shoot the remaining face scenes using studio mock-ups. He would capture whatever other atmosphere he could as opportunity and the National Park Service allowed.

Gutzon Borglum with his son Lincoln in his studio. Atlas *and a model of* Seated Lincoln *are behind them.*

Wars of America, *Newark, N.J.*

Photo mock-up of Borglum's scheme for Stone Mountain

Gutzon Borglum with bust of Lincoln

Mount Rushmore model with Louella Borglum

*Doane Robinson, who first
conceived Mount Rushmore*

*U.S. Senator Peter Norbeck
with Gutzon Borglum*

Mount Rushmore before carving commenced

Mount Rushmore showing original location of Thomas Jefferson to George Washington's right

Mount Rushmore nearly complete, circa 1939–40

*George Washington profile
with pointing mechanism*

*Carver Merle Peterson
"honeycombing"*

Close-up of Roosevelt eyeglasses, with flag

Borglum supervising carving of eyeball

North by Northwest

Ben Black Elk with tourists

Crazy Horse Memorial

The apparent priggishness of the Park Service did not reflect a larger societal aversion to violence; after all, Hollywood had been exterminating villains—gangsters, Martians, Indians, Germans, and Japanese—by the screen-full for years, and audiences rarely blanched anymore. Even so, in a decade that had already witnessed Senator Joseph McCarthy's pogrom against "Un-Americanism" and condoned the execution of convicted spies Ethel and Julius Rosenberg, the subject of democracy was as serious as cancer, and one dared not take it lightly. Under the circumstances, the Park Service was right to be wary of Hitchcock. To him, "art came before democracy," or so he had told the French film journal *Cahiers du Cinéma*, and as a fresh and not always reverent observer of American manners and scenery, he knew just how to jangle the native nerve—for the sake of suspense and ultimately for the sake of cathartic diversion. "How can you tell who a spy is these days?" Hitchcock had asked a Hollywood columnist. "They no longer sport cloaks and daggers. They might be the nuclear physicists or the wives of millionaires." Audiences, he knew, would always be afraid of the dark, of heights, of strangers. To which he now added a whole new case of shivers: the Cold War.

The MGM crew was in South Dakota for only three nights and two days. The evening of their arrival, Grant and Saint strolled down the block near the Alex Johnson Hotel, window-shopping. Grant bought a black western tie for seventy-nine cents. Hitchcock posed before a photo of Mount Rushmore, drolly lending his doughy profile as a fifth face. At the memorial the following day, Grant, Saint, and James Mason were presented Lakota war bonnets by Black Elk's son Ben, who in recent years had become the memorial's unofficial greeter. Indeed, he was such a conspicuous presence at Rushmore that he was now called *the* "Fifth Face."

Hitchcock wound up shooting only a handful of scenes at Rushmore. In the first, Grant is studying the Rushmore faces through a coin-operated telescope on the observation deck. "I don't like the way

Teddy Roosevelt is looking at me," he says to the American agent who has secretly accompanied him to the mountain. "Perhaps he's trying to give you one last word of caution," the agent replies, applying an especially macabre twist to American diplomatic history. "Speak softly and carry a long stick."

In another scene, Saint's character is called on to prove her allegiance to the spy leader by pretending to shoot Grant with a gun in the Rushmore cafeteria—a moment eternally cherished by film buffs, for even before the gun fires its blank, a young boy in the crowd can be seen with his hands over his ears. As Grant falls to the polished floor, feigning death, Hitchcock makes sure that the four faces of Rushmore gawk over the shoulders of the other aghast witnesses.

Nor did Hitchcock spare violence in the final chase, none of which was shot at Rushmore. In fact, he didn't even bother to send his cast up the mountain. Instead he built a model and backdrops of Rushmore in an MGM studio in Culver City, California. Art director Robert Boyle had based his set designs on photos he had taken while lowered over the faces of Rushmore earlier that summer. Perhaps his model was not quite to scale, but it didn't really matter. The audience had never been that close to Mount Rushmore and had no way of knowing just how preposterous it was for Grant and Saint to descend between the faces of Washington and Lincoln—she barefoot, he in loafers. Besides, the chase was on, and suspense quickly banished any shreds of disbelief.

Hitchcock knew precisely what he was doing and what he could get away with, and he shrewdly cast the Rushmore presidents in their own double roles. First, by their sheer scale they stack the odds against Grant and Saint as they struggle to safety. Second, Lincoln and Roosevelt play the part of oversized bystanders, underscoring the audience's own rapt helplessness as Grant and Saint cling, white-knuckled, from the absolutely convincing cliff of Rushmore.

MGM gave the National Park Service an advanced screening of *North by Northwest* in early July 1959. The feds were stunned. In the climax, Mason attacks Grant with a knife on top of Rushmore, they tussle, and Grant finally pitches Mason over the side. And then, as Martin Landau tries to loosen Grant and Saint's grip on the cliff, he is shot by a deputy, and he too plummets to his just demise. While most viewers gasped in relief and triumph, the government howled in protest. "The movie is a per se violation of the [no violence] agreement," the Park Service told *Variety*. "[I]t is an act of deliberate desecration of a great National Memorial," Secretary of the Interior Conrad Wirth asserted, "to even imply that a game of cops and robbers . . . has been played over the sculptured faces of our most honored Presidents." The Park Service demanded that its name be removed from the final credits.

The Park Service's cries of foul play found a sympathetic ear in South Dakota's newly elected senator Karl Mundt. As a congressman twenty years earlier, Mundt had taken offense at another film, *The Plow That Broke the Plains*, a government-produced documentary illustrating the poor agricultural practices that had contributed to the Dust Bowl. The film portrayed South Dakota as a virtual wasteland, as it quite nearly was in the mid-1930s. Mundt chose to see *The Plow* not as a cautionary tale, but rather as a "libel on the Dakotas" perpetrated by "hellhounds of publicity in search of some freakish, desolate, weird effect of the drouth." Mundt fought the film for three years and finally succeeded in having it pulled from distribution in 1939. He hoped to do the same with *North by Northwest*.

Besides being a film censor, Mundt had been acting chairman of the witch-hunting House Un-American Activities Committee and an ally of reactionary senator Joseph McCarthy and then-congressman Richard Nixon. In 1951, Mundt had told McCarthy: "[I]t is no longer necessary to catch a man with a bomb in his hand or with a Communist membership card in his pocket. . . . [W]henever there is a reasonable doubt about a man's character, and [we are] unable to determine whether he is a loyal American or a Communist spy, [we must] give the benefit of the doubt to the government and to the 130,000,000 Americans, whose life and future are entirely in the hands of any disloyal elements." To Mundt, anyone who did not display national loyalty was a communist, and it went without saying that all communists were traitors.

By 1959, McCarthy was in disgrace, Nixon was tamed somewhat by the vice presidency, but the Cold War persisted, and Senator Mundt was the patriot he had always been. He was too late to prevent the release of *North by Northwest*, which opened in New York on August 6, but he vowed that the effrontery would not be repeated. While most reviewers praised the movie as "hypnotizing" and "nightmare-real, " Mundt's sympathies lay resolutely with the citizen who had written, "What has become of our sense of pride in our country and our morals? . . . The Russians will probably say, 'See what the Americans think of their great forefathers! They step on their faces!'" Mundt read this and similar letters into the *Congressional Record* and suggested legislation "to deny any such commercial use of our national park areas as that which was extended . . . to MGM."

Nothing ever came of Mundt's threat, and, if anything, the controversy fomented by the senator and the National Park Service worked in Hitchcock's favor. The only apparent inconvenience to Mount Rushmore was an abrupt increase in unauthorized climbing. In the weeks following the release of *North by Northwest*, more than three dozen people were apprehended while trying to reenact, or at least revisit, scenes that—according to erroneous press reports never corrected by Hitchcock or MGM—had been filmed on the actual faces of Mount Rushmore.

While the Park Service may have felt legitimately duped by the studio, in retrospect, its charge that *North by Northwest* was somehow unpatriotic hardly seems justified. On the contrary, the movie has come to be seen as a paean to the American way of life: Cary Grant sits down to a martini lunch at the Plaza, a man of means so well nourished that he can afford to "think thin." Later, Grant whisks through the well-heeled crowd of Grand Central Station to board the sleek *Twentieth*

Century Limited, whose dining car is appointed in white linen and whose passengers are gorgeous blondes with darling little safety razors in their overnight kits. Next, Hitchcock unfolds the American heartland and the chiseled achievement of Mount Rushmore. "Gay surroundings," Soviet agent James Mason says of the glorious South Dakota setting, his voice edged with equal parts disdain and jealousy.

In the end, Hitchcock pays Mount Rushmore the supreme compliment, for at no point during the film does he actually call it by name. He assumes that his audience knows exactly what Rushmore is, where it is, and what it means. Two decades earlier, Borglum had worried that, without a proper inscription, no one would remember what his monument stood for. Alfred Hitchcock harbored no such doubts.

And if democracy was hanging in the balance—as many believed it was in 1959—what better place for it to teeter than on the brow of its most recognizable monument? In *North by Northwest*, the primary goal of the Americans is to keep James Mason from sneaking out of the country with a spool of microfilmed secrets. Yet metaphorically, the more important tug-of-war is over Eva Marie Saint. On the ramparts of Rushmore, it is Cary Grant, not the commie creep, who gets the girl. In short, democracy wins. (Okay, Grant is British and bisexual, but his character is straight American.) What is more, despite numerous racy flirtations throughout the movie, neither Grant nor Saint ever breaches the bounds of Main Street propriety. Hanging from the cliff, about to fall, he suggests to her, "If we ever get out of this alive, let's go back to New York on the train together."

With her life now at exponentially greater risk than her reputation, Saint asks, "Is that a proposition?"

Grant, expending his last ounce of gentlemanly aplomb, replies, "It's a proposal." At which point they tumble not from the face of Rushmore but, by way of Hitchcock's winking montage, into a Pullman berth just as the train, a Freudian express this time, enters a tunnel—leaving Grant just enough time to address her quite properly as

"Mrs. Thornhill." Finally, nobody's identity is ambiguous. All is as it should be in America. The expedient exaggeration has paid off.

The expedient exaggeration was not done with Mount Rushmore, however. In the forty-plus years since the release of *North by Northwest*, the image of Rushmore has been borrowed, bent, reconfigured, and reproduced thousands of times, and not always for purposes as aesthetically or allegorically honorable as Alfred Hitchcock's. In today's world—in which the American flag sometimes stands for Old Glory and at other times for Old Navy or Ralph Lauren—patriotism is fair fodder for free enterprise. The gift concession at Mount Rushmore, not to mention scores of emporia for miles around, have plastered the Rushmore profile on mugs, Christmas ornaments, refrigerator magnets, golf balls, shot glasses, key chains, playing cards, flashlights, socks, puzzles, spoons, thimbles, snow domes, and computer mouse pads.

In the interest of advertising, the Rushmore four have been married to the Quaker Oats man, commentator Rush ("Listen to RUSH more") Limbaugh, a Dodge *Dakota* truck, and the deadpan yokels who promote Bartles and James wine coolers. Through the miracle of airbrush, the presidents have been given arms and hands to better promote Coke, beer, and cell phones. They've worn sunglasses, neckties, bicycle helmets, and Sony headphones. The front cover of *America's Most Difficult Golf Holes* places a tee to the left of Washington and a green on Lincoln's head. An ad for nasal spray presents the four faces with Rudolph-red noses; the adjacent text reads: "Block Allergy Symptoms Before They Become Monumental."

Illustrators and cartoonists have found room on Rushmore for Mickey Mouse, Buddha, Bozo the Clown, Casper the Friendly Ghost, the Three Stooges, Alfred E. Neuman, Bart Simpson, the Happy Face, the Beatles, Elvis Presley, and various space aliens. Li'l Abner, Joe Palooka, Pogo, "Peanuts," Beetle Bailey, Broom Hilda, "Tumbleweeds,"

Shoe, the Wizard of Id, and Curious George have all visited Mount Rushmore over the years. *Mad* magazine cartoonist Don Martin, perhaps Rushmore's most devoted lampooner, has variously dispatched his crew of black-and-white buffoons to shine the presidents' shoes, snip shrubs from their noses, and swab their ears with tree-sized Q-tips. When *Playboy*'s cartoonists come calling, Rushmore usually sprouts breasts, or the presidents become dirty old men peeping on lover's lane or ogling short-shorted female alpinists. A more recent epidemic of greeting cards and T-shirts focuses on the bare bottoms of the presidents—the seldom-seen backside of Rushmore. And not surprisingly, the supermarket tabloids have also found a way to ridicule the sublime. "Mount Rushmore Presidents Are Crying," blared the *Weekly World News* in 1992. "Experts confirm: *Human tears* flowing from stone faces!"

Rushmore has had gigantic pies flung in its face, Rogaine and hair curlers applied to its locks, an immense "Keys While You Wait" sign planted in its granite brow. Perhaps the most overworked veins of humor are Rushmore-as-falling-rock and Rushmore-as-misguided-obsession. The former is self-explanatory: Teddy's or George's severed head stops traffic on a mountain road—oops! The latter category features husbands carving backyard Rushmores, highways drilled through the middle of the Rushmore heads ("I'm sorry, Payson, but we can't stop progress"), third eyes added, and the tops of the heads bulldozed away.

For cartoonists with appetites more political, Rushmore is like a frozen TV dinner. When inspiration runs low, pen-and-ink pundits simply reach into the icebox of ideas and thaw out a Rushmore hunger-buster. During World War II, they drew Hitler flinging mud at the four presidents. More recently, to float an environmental message, they have shrouded the faces in a cloud of acid rain or mined gold from the presidential teeth. When portions of the federal government, including the National Park Service, were forced to shut down briefly in 1995, cartoonists drew Washington, Jefferson, Roosevelt, and Lincoln lounging about in casual clothes, drinking coffee, and watching television. And during the 1997 sex scandal of President Bill Clinton, two little boys were shown in front of Rushmore, one explaining to the other: "I think they're up there because none of them ever got caught with a babe in the White House."

Sooner or later every president worth his salt has his profile spoofed on Rushmore—usually as a way to highlight his vaulting ambition and gross shortage of qualifications for such exclusive ascension. Likewise, Rushmore is the ideal medium for exaggerating physical features. And so Lyndon Johnson appears on Rushmore with Dumbo ears, Richard Nixon with the Matterhorn for a nose, Jimmy Carter with teeth the size of glaciers, Ronald Reagan with a Gibraltaresque pompadour. In one cartoon of Bill Clinton, all we see is his back as he embraces paramour Monica Lewinsky, whose mountainous, universally recognized visage peeks over the president's shoulder.

Alfred Hitchcock may have been the first to build a large model of Rushmore, but by no means was he the last. Borglum's ancestral home, Denmark, owns one of the most impressive copies—constructed out of a million and a half plastic Lego pieces. Gorky Park in Moscow installed a Rushmore look-alike, as did Mini World Park in Thailand. By far the biggest, most expensive Rushmore reproduction can be found in Imaichi, Japan. In 1995, Japanese businessman Kenichi Ominami shelled out $27 million (including a generous contribution to the Mount Rushmore Memorial Society) to erect a one-third-scale Rushmore in his Western Village, a theme park that already boasted a steam train, a Mexican village, a theater for cowboy-and-Indian stunts, and a robotic Marilyn Monroe. As one observer noted, not since the London Bridge was transplanted to Arizona "has a cultural icon been so bizarrely mismatched with a new surrounding." But that was before Parker Brothers issued its National Parks version of Monopoly, assigning Rushmore to the low-rent district formerly occupied by Baltic Avenue—and pairing it with the Washington Monument, a building that Gutzon Borglum despised so intensely.

For every person who has dared to copy Mount Rushmore, a dozen more have selected the genuine article as a backdrop for their "special event." On July 23, 1962, the United States and Europe exchanged live television images, the first intercontinental broadcast via America's brand new satellite, Telstar. For its contribution, Europe beamed footage of the Champs Élysées, the Sistine Chapel, London's tower of Big Ben, and an Italian performance of *Tosca*. The United States reciprocated with live shots of hula dancers, a crowded Detroit expressway, a Cubs-Phillies baseball game, and a press conference at which President John F. Kennedy discussed German-Soviet tensions and nuclear testing. American landmarks beamed by Telstar included the Statue of Liberty, the Golden Gate Bridge, Niagara Falls—and Mount Rushmore. The three-hundred-voice Mormon Tabernacle Choir had been bused from Salt Lake City to Rushmore for the occasion and offered inspiring renditions of "A Mighty Fortress Is Our God" and "The Battle Hymn of the Republic," the faces of the presidents hovering proudly above. The Telstar transmission also featured scenes from a buffalo stampede in Custer State Park and a close-up of America's own Big Ben—Ben Black Elk, surely the first Indian to have his image bounced off the stratosphere.

As caretakers of the Shrine of Democracy, the National Park Service is duty-bound to entertain all reasonable solicitations for use of the memorial (Senator Mundt notwithstanding). That, after all, is what democracy is supposed to be about: freedom of expression, within reason, of course. Even so, democracy can sometimes be fickle. The Park Service refused to let millionaire publisher Malcolm Forbes pose for photos on his Harley-Davidson on the viewing terrace but then allowed comedian Jerry Seinfeld to shoot an American Express commercial at the memorial. The Seattle-based band the Presidents of the United States of America, sporting nose rings and green, yellow, and orange hair, was permitted to perform in the parking lot outside Borglum's studio.

In 1987, the Park Service turned down a request by the producers of the top-rated soap opera *General Hospital* to tape atop the faces but allowed some scenes to be shot in the memorial's amphitheater. As with *North by Northwest*, the *General Hospital* plot, such as it was, pitted good agents against bad, with the fate of the Earth hanging in the balance. Somehow, Rushmore came through with its dignity intact—and lived to witness forty-three-year-old Ashrita Furman break the Guinness ten-kilometer gunny-sack record (one hour, twenty-four minutes), hopping back and forth in the flats across from the memorial's main entrance.

Surely the most dazzling couple to appear in the Black Hills since Cary Grant and Eva Marie Saint was Regis Philbin and Kathie Lee Gifford, who in 1998 shot two segments of their morning variety show *Live with Regis and Kathie Lee* at Mount Rushmore. This time the National Park Service and the state of South Dakota rolled out the red carpet. Governor William Janklow declared September 14 "Regis and Kathie Lee Day" and dubbed the two hosts "Rowdy Regis" and "Cowgirl Kathie Lee." Janklow, a notorious sourpuss, was later favored with a warm on-air embrace by exercise sweetheart Richard Simmons, who, ignoring the mountain chill, appeared heroically in a rhinestone tank top and satin candy-striped gym shorts. "I think I'm in love," Simmons cooed after his gubernatorial hug. When a B-1 bomber from nearby Ellsworth Air Force Base swooped low over the memorial, Kathie Lee dripped genuine tears on her genuine Lakota buckskin dress. "Does that make you proud to be an American *or what?*" she asked the adoring audience. Everyone agreed that the shows were some of the best advertising Mount Rushmore had ever received.

In the sixty-five years that followed Franklin Roosevelt's brief stopover in 1936, only three other presidents visited Mount Rushmore. Dwight Eisenhower came in 1953. George Bush made a much bigger splash in 1991, when he and his wife appeared at Rushmore's fiftieth-anniversary celebration. The July 3 extravaganza was produced by Radio City Music Hall and featured James Stewart and native South Dakotans Tom Brokaw and Mary Hart, among others. Hart praised Gutzon Borglum as a "consummate sculptor," "brilliant engineer," and "eternal romantic." Brokaw saluted the "drill-dusty" call boys, powder men, winch operators, drillers, pointers, mud mixers, steel nippers, and roustabouts—twenty of whom were in the audience—who had "put the curl in Lincoln's beard, the part in Teddy's hair, and the twinkle in Washington's eye."

It was left to Bush to eulogize the four presidents of Mount Rushmore. Washington, he said, "sought not the security of power, but the power to secure America's independence." Jefferson demonstrated "the majesty of individual determination and imagination." Lincoln showed that "'the better angels of nature' can banish darkness that threatens us all." And Roosevelt "won renown as a warrior, but also received the Nobel Prize for Peace. He helped hack the Panama Canal out of wilderness, but also led the battle to preserve our nation's natural beauty." Together, they were all "fighters, as Americans have always been. Fighters for independence. For freedom. . . . For the values and lands we revere."

The program also included a token Lakota, White Eagle, who told the mostly white crowd, "I can feel the dignity and the pain of my fathers as we stand together on this sacred land we call *Paha Sapa*." Then in a fine, operatic voice, he sang "So Many Voices Sing American Songs." He was followed by Rosemary Clooney, who performed "America the Beautiful." Finally, at the end of the show, a chorus of children and grown-ups joined in Woody Guthrie's populist anthem, "This Land Is Your Land," naturally leaving out the verse:

> Was a big high wall there that tried to stop me
> A sign was painted said: Private Property
> But on the back side it didn't say nothing—
> God blessed America for me.

The chorus then finished with a rousing version of "The Air Force Song":

Off we go into the wild blue yonder
Climbing high into the sun
Here they come
Zooming to meet our thunder
At 'em, boys, give 'er the gun
    Give 'er the gun.

With that, another B-1 bomber roared reliably overhead. Afterward, the president went fishing in Horsethief Lake—expressly stocked with rainbow trout in the tradition of Calvin Coolidge—and later he attended a picnic, at which First Lady Barbara Bush wore one red tennis shoe and one blue.

Bill Clinton's visit to Rushmore eight years later could not have been more different. He arrived on July 6, 1999, with only a few hours' warning and appeared just in time to catch the evening lighting ceremony. Tourists who happened to be on the observation terrace were surprised to have the president standing among them in jeans, cowboy boots, and leather jacket. He stayed about an hour, gave no speech, then drove on to Crazy Horse Memorial, where, much to the glee of the Ziolkowski family, he lingered for nearly twice as long. His ultimate destination, however, was Pine Ridge Reservation, where he spent most of the following day touring tribal housing projects and stressing the need for economic development in America's depressed communities. At the time, Shannon County, which is totally absorbed by Pine Ridge, was the poorest county in the United States. "We have to find a way to fix this," Clinton declared. "We cannot rest until we do better, and trying is not enough." Nearby a protester held a sign, "Stop Lakota Ethnic Cleansing." In another speech before departing from Rapid City aboard Air Force One, Clinton referred to Mount Rushmore and Crazy Horse Memorial as "two of the proudest monuments in all America."

The nearness of America's poorest community to two of its proudest monuments is more than ironic. Over the past thirty years, Rushmore has continued to be a major sore point among many Native Americans—because it is built on land that Indians claim still belongs to them and because the Great White Fathers who watch over the Black Hills personify a government that has betrayed and injured Indian people repeatedly. As Indian indignation increased in the 1960s and 1970s, it was only a matter of time before a tremendous insult became a tremendous target.

chapter 13

DOKSA BLACK HILLS

Leo Zwetzig was born in Rapid City in 1941, the year that carving on Mount Rushmore ceased, and he has lived most of his life in Keystone. His father and brothers took jobs as loggers and miners, while the tourist industry boomed around them. Finally, in 1967, he got a summer job at Mount Rushmore, clearing dead timber for fire prevention. By 1970 he had worked his way up to the position of chief ranger in charge of law enforcement, even though he had no formal police training. "Back then," he recalls with a quick smile, "our job was to welcome visitors and pat them on the back. We treated them as great people. After all, they were the ones keeping us in business. The National Park Service didn't believe that bad people ever came to their parks, especially Mount Rushmore."

The worst that ever happened at the memorial was that occasionally someone had a purse stolen, or people locked their keys and/or pets in the car. Rangers like to tell of the exasperated parents who abandoned their sullen teenager at the memorial and got most of the way across Wyoming before reconsidering. And then there was the preacher from Montana who thought he was Jesus Christ and sneaked onto the mountain with the intention of saving the world by jumping off it. Zwetzig discovered him clinging to the cliff near the Hall of Records. The man had removed his shirt and shoes, and his feet were so cut up that rangers had to piggyback him down the mountain. At the bottom, they met his wife and daughter, who agreed to take him to the hospital in Rapid City. As their car pulled away, the daughter was heard whining, "Mommy, is it too late to go to Reptile Gardens?"

Rushmore, though, was largely a place of innocence—until the summer of 1970. That August was shaping up to be the busiest month in Rushmore's history so far, with more than half a million visitors expected. Over the previous decade, annual visitation had more than doubled, from one million a year to two. Crowds at the visitor center had become so great during the busy days of summer that the Park Service gave up giving interpretive talks and began blaring prerecorded announcements over the public address system.

The twenty or so Indians who gathered in the Rushmore amphitheater on the morning of August 24 were hardly tourists, however. For several weeks, the Lakota had been demanding the return of one hundred thousand acres of the Badlands Aerial Gunnery Range, which had been sliced off from Pine Ridge Reservation for military use during World War II; instead of giving this spectacularly rugged real estate back to the Lakota, the government had announced its intention to add it to Badlands National Monument, located east of the Black Hills and just north of the reservation. On the 24th, the Gunnery Range protest shifted from remote Sheep Mountain in the Badlands to Rushmore, a locale with a decidedly higher profile.

The demonstrations began peaceably enough. With the Park Service's permission, Indians beat drums, sang traditional songs, and danced. Tourists regarded them as a curious sideshow—a provocative complement to Ben Black Elk, who at seventy-one was still dressing in traditional garb and posing for photographs by the hundreds every day. Speeches and handbills issued by the protesters called for not only the return of Gunnery Range land but also the Black Hills. "Our movement protests the many, many broken treaties ... written with pens that do not always follow a straight line," Leo Wilcox, a Pine Ridge Oglala, stated. He dubbed Mount Rushmore "a hoax to democracy."

Throughout the week, the Indian numbers increased, and by Saturday, 150 had gathered, including leaders of the American Indian Movement. AIM had been founded in Minneapolis two years earlier. The federal government's so-called "termination" and relocation policies of the 1950s had dispersed thousands of Indians from reservations to urban centers halfway across the continent. By the mid-1960s, nearly half of all Native Americans lived in cities, where some found jobs and nearly all endured a brand of bigotry previously reserved for blacks and immigrants. And it was in the cities—and in the jails, where too many wound up—that Indians received their first exposure to the politics and tactics of the New Left. If there could be Black Power, they realized, then there could also be Red Power. In July 1968, three Minnesota Chippewa, Clyde Bellecourt, Dennis Banks, and George Mitchell, created AIM to fight injustice in all its forms and to promote solidarity not just within tribes but also among all tribes. AIM organized night patrols to monitor abuse of Indians by Minneapolis police and later established "survival schools" to teach Indians how to negotiate the labyrinth of urban blight, bewildering entitlement programs, and a legal system that they perceived was tilted against them.

Unlike previous Indian organizations, AIM employed an array of tactics that included demonstrations, occupations, and if need be even armed resistance. AIM Indians rarely flashed the "peace" sign. Instead their motto was "United We Are One Powerful Fist." Indians who had given up their braids and abandoned the old customs to avoid harassment and ridicule now grew their hair long and began wearing beads and feathers. Indians who continued to behave like whites were branded "apples"—red on the outside, white on the inside, a slur the equivalent of "Oreos" among blacks. The descendants of warriors were called on to become warriors again. Soon AIM was a national organization, spreading from the cities back to the reservations.

In November 1969, a group of Indians representing many different tribes landed on Alcatraz Island in San Francisco Bay and claimed it as Indian property. Nine months later, as another group of Indians gathered at Mount Rushmore, the Alcatraz occupation was still ongoing and very much on the minds of the Black Hills protesters. With the arrival of AIM leaders Bellecourt, Banks, and up-and-coming firebrand Russell Means—a Pine Ridge–born Oglala who had grown up in Oakland and directed an Indian aid office in Cleveland—the rhetoric at Rushmore sharpened dramatically. One of the demonstrators had discovered that among the many "authentic" souvenirs for sale at the Rushmore gift shop were postcards of the 1890 massacre at Wounded Knee—ghoulish photos of stacked corpses and the twisted dead form of Chief Big Foot. "Look! Look at these!" Russell Means recalls exclaiming to the Park Service officials. "Think of the Jews at Dachau and Auschwitz. If the park sold pictures of their remains, would you buy them?" The Indians met with Rushmore superintendent Wallace McCaw and demanded not only that the postcards be removed but also that Indians be authorized to run (and profit from) the Rushmore concessions.

By Saturday night, the Indians made their move. A group of twenty or thirty, including Means and John Trudell, a Santee Sioux who had just come from Alcatraz, decided to storm the mountain. As a precaution, Leo Zwetzig and several uniformed rangers had already taken up positions on the summit. None in the group had any more police training than Zwetzig; their abilities lay in traffic control and tour guiding. Zwetzig, in fact, was the only Rushmore ranger authorized to carry a gun, a .38 Special, although one other ranger, Claire Patterson, had brought his own shotgun from home.

"Evening came," Zwetzig remembers, "and it started to get dark and cool. We went down inside the Hall of Records. We heard some whispering and I told Claire, 'They're right across from us.' Claire jumped out and said, 'First guy who moves gets blasted.' It was really an Old West kind of deal," admits Zwetzig, who still favors pearl-button shirts, bandannas, and the broad moustache of a cowboy. Zwetzig and Peterson escorted a handful of invaders off the mountain, but twenty more slipped by them and gathered in a small, wooded grotto a hundred yards or so back of Mount Rushmore—today known officially as "the Indian camp."

The occupation of Mount Rushmore had begun. A typed press release distributed by the invaders declared:

> The Sioux Indian people of South Dakota ... are protesting the violation of the Fort Laramie Treaty of 1868, in which the U.S. Government agreed the Sioux could retain the Black Hills and their Reservation lands as long as the grass grows and the water flow[s]. When the government sent General Custer into this area with an expedition which found gold, [it] then responded by taking the Black Hills by a fraudulent treaty.... The Government further desecrated the Black Hills which [are] sacred to the Sioux people by erecting the faces ... of (4) white men on our land. The next illegal step by the government was to make the area into a National Park for the "white people." The Sioux people have not been paid for their land, nor shared in the billions of dollars in revenues taken through timber, tourist trade, and the mining of gold and other minerals.... This is a non-violent protest and we do not plan to destroy the monument or any other property, all we want is equal and fair treatment and our land back.

Not only were the Indians well versed in the history of broken treaties; they also had compiled rap sheets on the four presidents who trespassed on their sacred hills. As a young officer, George Washington was said to have fought and killed numerous Indians, including women and children, during the French and Indian War. Indians also allege that Washington initiated the practice of "skin scalping." The Indian tradition was to remove the hair of dead or wounded enemies, but they universally abstained from slicing into the flesh of the skull—that is, not until a bloodthirsty Washington raised the ante. "It [took] dozens of ... My Lai massacres for George Washington to become a hero," Russell Means explained, although history has yet to uphold the skin-scalping charge.

Thomas Jefferson's record of callousness toward Indians is much easier to trace, beginning with his description of Native Americans in the Declaration of Independence as "merciless Indian Savages." As an intellectual shaped by the Enlightenment, Jefferson saw no future in the "hunter state" of the Indians. It was Jefferson who first codified the government policy of Indian "removal," in which tens of thousands of Indians were ousted from their traditional homelands. And even though Jefferson was careful to advise Meriwether Lewis and William Clark to treat peaceably with the Indians whom they encountered in their exploration of the Louisiana Purchase, the 1803 acquisition nonetheless led to the seizure of more than 800,000 square miles of Indian lands in the West—this after Jefferson had already "obtained" another 200,000 square miles of Indian land in present-day Indiana, Illinois, Tennessee, Georgia, Alabama, Mississippi, Arkansas, and Missouri. Finally, Jefferson made clear that those Indians who resisted "civilization" would inevitably face "extermination."

Abraham Lincoln's record was hardly any better, by Indian reckoning anyway. In 1832, Lincoln had served as a militia captain in the Black Hawk War, named for the Sac and Fox chief who had endeavored unsuccessfully to reclaim Indian land on the Illinois side of the Mississippi River. Lincoln encountered no Indians during his brief campaign but later admitted that he had endured "a good many bloody struggles with the mosquetoes."

He could not joke away his role in the Great Sioux Uprising of 1862, however. After years of confinement on a Minnesota reservation and consistent mistreatment by government agents, the Santee Sioux had exploded in a fit of violence. By the time their rampage was quelled two months later, more than 350 whites were dead, the largest massacre of whites by Indians in U.S. history. Even so, the losses in Minnesota, horrific and tragic to be sure, were small compared to the carnage under way in the East. In the battle of Antietam on September 17, the bloodiest day of the Civil War (and the bloodiest day in American history, including September 11, 2001), nearly 5,000 Union and Confederate soldiers died and more than 18,000 fell wounded.

Despite his preoccupation with the war, Lincoln still found time to look over the list of condemned Santee. Painstakingly, he winnowed the number down to thirty-nine—accepting the advice of his military men that unless some were made to pay for the massacre with their lives, the white citizenry would exact wholesale revenge on the entire Santee population. In Mankato, Minnesota, on December 26, with approval of the White House, thirty-eight trap doors were sprung on an immense gallows, and the necks of thirty-eight Santee (one had been spared at the last minute) snapped simultaneously, breaking yet another record: the largest public execution in American history, ever. Shortly after the Indians were buried in a mass grave, doctors exhumed the bodies and appropriated the skeletons for educational use. Dr. William A. Mayo, father of William and Charles Mayo, the eventual founders of the Mayo Clinic, became the proud owner of the Santee warrior Cut Nose.

As a final twist of the knife, six days after the Mankato executions, Lincoln issued his Emancipation Proclamation, declaring that all slaves in regions of the country still in rebellion were "then, thenceforward, and forever free." The juxtaposition of these two events—one a sweeping condemnation, the other a categorical reprieve—was particularly galling to Indians and further fueled their enmity toward Lincoln. One hundred and forty years after Mankato, Gregg Bourland, chairman of the Cheyenne River Sioux Tribe, still curses Lincoln's name. "Lincoln has Indian blood on his hands," Bourland lectures. "To us, he was Hitler."

Theodore Roosevelt gets off the easiest in the Rushmore rogue's gallery, although he is far from exempt. Russell Means, in his autobiography *Where White Men Fear to Tread*, calls Roosevelt "the biggest thief ever to occupy the White House." He accuses Roosevelt of violating "scores of treaties, and illegally nationalizing more Indian land than any president, before or since. He called his booty 'national parks' and 'national forests' to cement the thefts into law." Particularly upsetting to the Oglala is Roosevelt's executive order of January 25, 1904, which turned over fifty square miles of Pine Ridge Reservation to white homesteaders. "One can readily see why the head of Roosevelt is carved forever into the mountains of the Sioux homelands," asserts Lakota attorney Mario Gonzalez, "for he gives rationale to stealing Indian lands under the guise of democratic virtues."

The 1970 siege of Mount Rushmore was not as determined as the Alcatraz takeover and was far less dangerous than AIM's subsequent occupation of the Bureau of Indian Affairs building in Washington in 1972 or its theatrical, two-month showdown with federal officers at Wounded Knee on the Pine Ridge Reservation in 1973. Yet from the standpoint of Mount Rushmore National Memorial, and the entire National Park Service, the 1970 protest marked a coming-of-age, a point of no return.

After hasty conversations with higher-ups in the Park Service and the Department of the Interior, Superintendent McCaw decided that the best response was to avoid further confrontation and to wait the Indians out—so long as they stayed off the faces. "We were told to take good care of them," Zwetzig says, shaking his head wryly. "And so we did." Indians were allowed to come and go freely, and soon the Indian camp was well supplied with food, water, and shelter. "Indians went by at all hours of the night," remembers Gene Koevenig, a maintenance employee who was then living in a Park Service house at the foot of the mountain next to Borglum's old studio. "We gave them water. We delivered their mail. They borrowed axes from us to cut down our trees, then they borrowed files to keep the axes sharp. Rangers even helped an old woman, Lizzie Fast Horse, get up to the camp." On August 30, Superintendent McCaw confessed to the *Rapid City Journal*, "Actually, we've more or less been operating a catering service."

The Park Service's worst fear was that Indians would pour gallons of red paint over the faces of the presidents. Twenty-four-hour vigilance kept this vandalism from happening, and the closest the Indians came to painting the memorial was several bed sheets strung a hundred yards to the north, proclaiming "Sioux Indian Power." But after the occupation had ended, when rangers were finally able to enter the Indian camp, they did discover several cans of red paint. On several rocks, not visible to the general public, someone had scrawled "Indian Land." Nearby was a large red silhouette of a hand, its middle finger extended in sign language that whites had little trouble translating.

Although the faces of Rushmore may not have turned red, the memorial was embarrassed in other ways. "One afternoon," Russell Means asserts in his autobiography, "I climbed over to the top of George Washington's head, opened my fly, and peed on him. I had hoped he would have permanent, yellow-stained tears, but the park staff whitewashes those heads every year." Asked to confirm Means's story, a Rushmore ranger scoffs at the whitewash portion of Means's remark, but then adds wryly: "In Yellowstone National Park, there was supposed to have been a bunch who called themselves IPOF—'I Pissed in Old Faithful.'" Perhaps, he shrugs, "There could be a Rushmore equivalent called 'I Pissed Off George.'"

In the first days of the occupation, one of the Indians had declared to the press, "They'd have to kill me to get me off." But eventually the Park Service strategy of watching and waiting paid off. After ten uneventful days, most of the AIM leaders had departed from the mountain, and by mid-September, as temperatures began to dip below freezing, the resolve of those remaining began to erode. On many nights, the camp was occupied by as few as two people, with others paying only intermittent visits, never lingering for very long and rarely overnight. By the end of October, the final two hangers-on had tired of the chilly vigil, and they slipped quietly from the mountain of their own volition. Very few of the tourists at Rushmore that fall had ever known the Indians were there. Even fewer knew they were gone.

The Park Service had all winter to rethink its policy on demonstrations. "That old ball game of patting them on the back and saying they're all nice people didn't work anymore," Zwetzig acknowledges. "I was sent back to Washington to train with the U.S. Capitol park police. I learned that the Washington Monument had twenty-four-hour protection—but at Mount Rushmore, out here in the middle of the prairie, we didn't have anything. So they gave me five positions, and we had meetings with local and federal law-enforcement people. Come spring, we were ready for them."

The Indians reappeared at Mount Rushmore on June 4. In addition to food, camping gear, and cans of red paint, they now carried baseball bats and ax handles. Again they were led by Russell Means and Clyde Bellecourt, along with Means's brother Ted and Bellecourt's brother Charles. The Indians' press release repeated the demands of the previous year: return of the Gunnery Range, return of Indian lands as spelled out in the Treaty of 1868, and Indian control of all concessions throughout the national park system. "Talk about a naïve demand!" Means admits. "Sure, all those white ranchers, miners, real-estate speculators, land developers, and owners of souvenir stands, restaurants, gift shops, and motels ... were going to leave the Black Hills just so we could come down off Mount Rushmore! But we had come to make a point. That was *our* mountain."

At dawn two days later, forty Indians made a run for the faces. Once again, rangers let them pass, but this time they didn't let them stay. "I had fifty South Dakota National Guardsmen, twenty-four United States park police out of Washington, and a dozen law-enforcement rangers from other parks ready to go," Zwetzig iterates. "We had Rapid City police, Pennington County sheriff's deputies, federal marshals, FBI." All were armed to the teeth. "We powwowed with the Indians for a while, and when they refused to come down, we went up and got 'em." At the Indian camp, they came upon twenty-one protesters, nine men and twelve women, sitting on the ground passively, silently. (The other twenty Indians were thought to have escaped through the perimeter established by the National Guard.) "They just sat there while we handcuffed 'em," Zwetzig continues. "We started to drag 'em off and it hurt pretty good on that granite. Once they got a little hide taken off 'em, they decided it was better to walk."

All were charged with trespassing, a misdemeanor with a maximum fine of $500. Perhaps the most noteworthy aspect of the day's drama was that the Park Service never closed Rushmore to tourists, even for an hour. Visitors watched from the observation terrace as the day's drama unfolded in front of them—an updated *North by Northwest*, this time with a cast of several hundred. By five o'clock, everybody was off the mountain, and Superintendent McCaw told reporters, making a lame stab at Hitchcockian understatement, that it had been just another day at Mount Rushmore.

In a way, he gave a straight answer. Although arguably there has never been a day so adrenaline-filled at Rushmore, before or since, this was the new norm that the Park Service had now trained itself to expect. In the course of a single year, Rushmore had evolved from a shrine to a citadel. Thenceforth it never dared let down its guard.

The following year, the assault came not from below but from above. Late in the afternoon of June 9, 1972, the heavens began to spew, and by midnight ten to fifteen inches of rain had fallen on the Black Hills. "Each rain drop was like an entire glass of water," one resident recalled. Every creek and ravine leapt its banks. Thousands of houses, businesses, mobile homes, vehicles, bridges, and roads were swept away. By dawn, 238 people had drowned. Rapid City was ravaged the worst, but Keystone, situated in a tight canyon at the confluence of

Grizzly and Battle Creeks, took its own wicked hit. The Four Presidents Motel broke in two under the force of the flume. Eleven campers who had pitched tents beside Grizzly Creek never made it to high ground.

Rushmore was one of the few safe spots, and for the next few days it became Mount Ararat, the visitor center a temporary Ark. Park employees offered shelter and first aid to hundreds of stranded locals and visitors. Not surprisingly, tourism for the month dropped off drastically, half that of the previous June. But still the travelers persevered, a quarter-million braving washed-out roads and moldy motel rooms to see the great carving. A month later, Rushmore welcomed its third-biggest crowd.

The more tourism flourished in the Black Hills, the more it rankled many Native Americans. To counter the bad publicity engendered by the flood and the recent spate of Indian disturbances, and to capitalize on the overall libertinism of the early 1970s—in other words, to show that South Dakota was hip, not hostile—the state Department of Tourism had launched a new advertising campaign under the slogan "Roam Free in South Dakota." In rebuttal, the American Indian Movement borrowed a page from the United Farm Workers' playbook, calling for a general economic boycott of the state. Its slogan, disseminated through handbills and speeches, urged Americans to "See South Dakota Last." AIM also vowed to "blow out the birthday candle" of the upcoming national bicentennial through acts of civil disobedience and perhaps violence. The whole affair was supposed to kick off at a rally at Mount Rushmore on July 4, 1975.

Tensions had been running high for some time in Indian Country. On February 6, 1973, two hundred Indians had converged on the county courthouse in Custer to protest what they perceived to be lax prosecution of a white man who had murdered a Pine Ridge Indian outside a bar in nearby Buffalo Gap. A riot erupted in which a number of Indians were beaten, two police cars were overturned, and a chamber of commerce building was torched. Later that month, AIM's opposition to a corrupt tribal government of Pine Ridge led to a takeover of a Catholic church and trading post near the historic massacre site of Wounded Knee. AIM and its adherents were soon surrounded by U.S. marshals and FBI, and for ten weeks, their war of words and gunfire drew the attention of the entire world.

Ever since the occupations of Mount Rushmore in 1971 and 1972, the Park Service had received intermittent bomb threats—so many that the memorial had decided to add a retired "military master bomb disposal expert" to its payroll, under the benign title of "park technician." One such threat in 1972 was described in a confidential Park Service memo as a plan "to blow the Mount Rushmore Sculpture off the mountainside" over the weekend of August 5 and 6. The report said that the bombers intended to use "a trenching machine to dig a trench behind the sculpture, into which was to be placed 300 cases of dynamite." Nothing ever came of it, but even far-fetched rumors were taken seriously.

In the middle of June 1975, Rushmore superintendent Harvey Wickware (successor to Wallace McCaw) received a tip from the FBI that AIM was planning a "Bicentennial Campout at Mount Rushmore" on July 4, the first of what was presumed to be a series of Indian anti-celebrations leading up to the real bicentennial a year later. Wickware tried to keep an open mind, figuring that if he refused permission for the rally, the alternative might be another violent confrontation. But before he could sit down with AIM leaders to discuss the conditions for assembly at Mount Rushmore, two events took place in rapid succession that raised the level of anxiety exponentially.

The first occurred on Pine Ridge. On June 26, Indians and FBI agents opened fire on one another at an Indian encampment along White Clay Creek near the village of Oglala. Two FBI agents and one Indian were killed. Within hours of the shoot-out, hundreds of federal agents were en route to Pine Ridge from all over the country. Suddenly every Indian was a suspect, or so it seemed from the extraordinary number interrogated, and all of South Dakota was on pins and needles.

Throughout the day of the shootings, Leo Zwetzig had monitored radio reports emanating from Pine Ridge, and that night before going off duty, he had doubled the Rushmore security detail from one police-man to two. The following morning at five minutes to four, one of the officers, accompanied by the night maintenance man, happened upon a civilian with long brown hair and beard whose red Ford pickup was stopped at the lower entrance to the memorial. (An official incident record, filed later that day, did not specify the man's race, although he was presumed to be Caucasian.) He explained that he was having "choke problems," but then had no difficulty driving off. Five minutes later, a bomb exploded on the viewing terrace. At such an early hour, there were no injuries and no eyewitnesses. Zwetzig, who lived in Park Service housing a mile away, was shaken awake by the noise. "My first thought was that it was AIM or someone associated with them. I mean, those murdered FBI agents hadn't even been evacuated from Pine Ridge yet. What else would I have thought? We had heard that a National Guard Armory had been robbed and that explosives and grenade launchers had been taken." As Zwetzig threw on his clothes and raced up the hill to the memorial, he figured that someone had "done a nose job on George."

The damage could have been much worse. The bomber had ven-tured nowhere near the faces. Instead, eleven of the four-by-eight-foot panes of glass at the front of the visitor center were shattered; the pub-lic-address speakers were ruined; and a small hole, a foot wide and only a couple of inches deep, was gouged in the patio. That was all. A main-tenance crew had the mess cleaned up and the windows covered by the time tourists arrived later in the morning, and a robust crowd of four-teen thousand enjoyed the memorial that day, unaware, unalarmed. The Fourth of July was a week away.

Red paint was now the least of the Park Service's worries. Clyde Bellecourt's repeated threat to "blow out the birthday candle in places like Mount Rushmore" was beginning to seem more than metaphoric. Concerned that the June 27 intruder (or intruders) had placed additional explosives on or near the faces, a bomb squad from Ellsworth Air Force Base combed the area, and a ranger was lowered over the faces to inspect every nook and nostril. The only thing the Air Force's dog turned up was a stash of marijuana near the employees' dormitory.

As July 4 neared, rumors continued to pour in from every source and direction. Three "known demolition experts with AIM affiliation" were said to have been spotted in Rapid City, and one of them reportedly had made two different trips to Mount Rushmore to case the grounds. Four carloads of "known AIM members" toting shotguns had checked into a Rapid City motel. By the time Ted Means appeared at Superintendent Wickware's office on July 3 to request a demonstration permit for the following day, the Park Service had already established an emergency command post to deal with whatever he had in mind. Unbeknownst to Means, Rushmore's holiday manpower now included forty-seven park rangers, twenty-two park police officers (including a National Park Service SWAT team), sixteen South Dakota highway patrolmen, sixteen county sheriff's deputies, and fifteen FBI agents. "Our plans were based on only ranger personnel being visible to the public," noted a Park Service memo written later in the summer. But in fact, they were braced for the Alamo. The gift shop and food concession were ordered closed for the day, and buses were parked nearby in the event that park employees needed to be evacuated.

Much to Wickware's surprise (and suspicion), Means was quite civil and agreed to all of the Park Service's terms regarding the size of the rally (no more than one thousand participants), time (12:30 to 4:00 P.M.), location (one of the parking lots), and decorum (only one bullhorn allowed and no fires, no blocking of roads or paths, and no endangerment of "public safety, good order or health").

The Fourth arrived clear and very hot. Instead of the thousand demonstrators expected, only three hundred Indians marched three miles uphill from Keystone to Mount Rushmore. The ceremony at the memorial began with a prayer service honoring Indians killed at the hands of the federal government—in the past as well as more recently. Dennis Banks, who was on trial for charges stemming from the Custer courthouse riot, endeavored to put his own circumstances into a broader, more ominous bicentennial context. "For one hundred and ninety-nine years we've been on trial, and for one hundred and ninety-nine years we've been found guilty," he told his sweating audience, which was supplemented by a sprinkling of curious tourists. "The next two hundred years will not be like the last. All this year the United States of America will be on trial by Indian people. How white America handles the next year will determine its punishment." Next Clyde Belle-court called on the United States to honor its treaties and once again repeated his threat "to blow out the candles on the birthday cake." Finally Ted Means pointed to the presidents on the mountain. "Those four faces are an example of the hypocrisy that exists in this country today," he railed. "But the day is coming for the white man."

The day, however, was not July 4, 1975. After four hours of speeches and some milling about, the Indians backtracked peacefully down the hill to their caravan of vehicles in Keystone. Most of the police on hand never had to leave their hiding place in the basement of the visitor center. "The park had over 22,000 visitors on the day of the demonstration," Wickware wrote to South Dakota senator George McGovern, "most not even realizing the degree of security provided them." Still, he warned, "it is doubtful that a similar situation will not occur in the future, especially through the Bicentennial year." Accordingly, he made a request for more security personnel and training.

Despite AIM's portents of a great reckoning during the year leading up to the bicentennial, nothing untoward occurred at Mount Rushmore or, for that matter, in the rest of the Black Hills. "We heard continuous rumblings that Rushmore was to be the focal point for some sort of action," recalls Tom Greene, a member of the first FBI SWAT team to arrive on the scene after the 1973 killings at Pine Ridge. If anything, it was the Indians who were now in the crosshairs. At the height of the Pine Ridge murder investigation, the FBI had more than three hundred agents deployed in western South Dakota. Indian agitators not already in jail or under indictment were either in hiding or under intense surveillance.

During the summer of the bicentennial, Mount Rushmore was one of the safest places on earth, although, to be on the cautious side, the FBI's SWAT team rappelled out of a helicopter on the morning of July 3, landing on George Washington's head in full view of the public below—"just to make sure everybody knew we were there," Greene explains. Armed with M-16 rifles, .357 Magnum sidearms, flak vests, walkie-talkies, binoculars, and C rations, five agents camped for two days, guarding the shrine against the remote possibility of invasion. Again, nothing happened. "We felt that it would be creating a situation where Indian people would be forced to react to . . . racist tactics [by white law enforcement]," Russell Means told the *Rapid City Journal*, explaining why protests had been called off. There were just too many cops.

In fact, the only Indians to act on the candle-blowing ultimatums did so within the comparatively benign covers of popular novels. In Dan O'Brien's *Spirit of the Hills* (1988), two Indian activists, one more militant than the other, argue over whether to blow up Mount Rushmore. "'Don't do it,'" the more moderate of the two says. "'First, you'll never get away with it, and second, if there is still a [AIM-like Indian] movement, it will put it back a hundred years.'"

The more truculent Indian responds: "'What's the difference? . . . A hundred years ago that mountain didn't have a name. It was just a mountain, without those fucking heads on it. . . . [W]hen we get done, it will be just a mountain again. . . . I hope after we're through that not one single white man comes to see it again. I hope it is a wasteland for them.'" In the end, the bombers are interrupted and the mountain is spared defacement—although the surrounding forest is engulfed in fire, creating a wasteland of a different sort.

In David London's *Sun Dancer* (1996), instead of blowing up Rushmore, one of the heroes, aptly named Clem Blue Chest, skewers his pectoral muscles with steel spikes from the Union Pacific and Northern Pacific—the two railroads that hem in the original Great Sioux Reservation—and in an extreme interpretation of a traditional sun dance, he dangles himself most tortuously from the face of Abraham Lincoln. His half-brother Joey Moves Camp tries to save him by rappelling from the top of the mountain and cradling Clem in the carved cup of Lincoln's eye—only to discover that "the haven of Lincoln's eye was out of reach and always would be." All the while, the pain-wracked sun dancer whispers phrases worthy of Black Elk: "'*Mitakuye iyasin.* All my relations. All my relations. The embrace of everything . . . the whole balance." In the gruesome, if uplifting, finale, Mount Rushmore is again spared demolition, and Clem dies a martyr, jerked off the mountain by a military helicopter, ascending "over the gutted Black Hills, over mines, power plants, and poisoned rivers"—toward the sun, toward heaven, Christ-like.

The fate of the real Indian trespassers is far less melodramatic. Charges against the 1971 climbers were eventually dropped. The driver of the red pickup that had "stalled" at Mount Rushmore on June 27, 1975, was eventually tracked down and questioned, but authorities could not produce sufficient evidence to link him to the visitor-center bombing. (At best, they surmised that he had been an unwitting chauffeur for the actual bomber, who got away through the woods.) As for the murder of the FBI agents at Pine Ridge, only one Indian was convicted: Leonard Peltier, who remains in federal prison to this day, the most controversial Indian celebrity since Crazy Horse.

★

But even as the threats of civil disobedience against Mount Rushmore subsided, other critical events unfolded. The first occurred in June 1980 with a seismic thump, carrying the full weight of the U.S. Supreme Court. The Sioux Nation case concerning the government's violation of the 1868 Black Hills treaty had been stumbling through the court system since the 1920s. In 1956, the eight Sioux tribes involved in the case replaced their longtime attorney, the well-meaning but rather lap-doggish Ralph Case, with a pair of Washington pitbulls, Arthur Lazarus Jr. and Marvin Sonosky. In 1979, after more than two decades of legal thrusts by Lazarus and Sonosky, the U.S. Court of Claims had awarded the Sioux Nation $17.5 million, plus interest, for land and resources taken from the Indians between 1868, the date the treaty was signed at Fort Laramie, and 1877, the date the treaty was officially broken and the Black Hills were taken from the Sioux. The court stated that the government, in its 1877 negotiations with the Indians, had given the Sioux the unpleasant choice of "ceding the Black Hills or starving." Never in American history, the court concluded, had there been "[a] more ripe and rank case of dishonorable dealing."

On June 30, 1980, the Supreme Court concurred. Writing for the 8–1 majority, Justice Harry Blackmun determined that Congress had failed to make a "good faith effort" to pay the Sioux for the lands it took from them—a violation of the Fifth Amendment, which stipulates "nor shall private property be taken for public use, without just compensation." After reviewing the long history of white-Sioux relations—an expository jaunt that cited Doane Robinson's *History of the Dakota or Sioux Indians*, among other sources—Blackmun painstakingly called attention to not only a glaring breech of law, but also a source of profound national shame. And on that stern note, the country's longest-running and largest Indian claim seemingly came to a close. Figuring up the interest, the total due the Sioux was $106 million.

Most Sioux had difficulty believing that the 123-year-old injustice had finally been resolved. The running joke in Indian Country whenever someone asked an Indian for money was "*Doksa* Black Hills," shorthand for "I'll pay you when I get my Black Hills settlement"— meaning never. Nobody ever imagined a day when money would change hands. And even if the money *was* real, when divided it might amount to as little as fifteen hundred dollars per person. "With the distribution of funds," observed Vine Deloria Jr., Lakota author of *Custer Died for Your Sins*, "will come the drug dealers, bootleggers, used-car dealers and appliance salesmen who would normally cross the street to avoid saying hello to an Indian. One great spasm of spending will occur and the people, as poor as ever, will return to normal lives. . . . The final disruption of community life may be as great as the original taking of the Black Hills."

Within days of the Supreme Court decision, Oglala tribal attorney Mario Gonzalez, a Lakota raised on the reservation, filed the first in a series of lawsuits aimed at halting the process that would determine precisely which Indians were qualified to receive the $106 million, and in what portions. First he argued that Lazarus and Sonosky's contracts with the Oglala had expired before the case had come before the Supreme Court, and therefore they did not represent the tribe. Second, and more fundamentally, Gonzalez urged a closer reading of the Fifth Amendment, which, he pointed out, allows the government to take private land for *public* use. In the case of the Black Hills, he submitted, the government had taken Indian land in order to turn it over to *private* users—miners, loggers, ranchers, homesteaders. Under this interpretation, such a taking should not be judged as strictly an issue of compensation. More accurately, the Black Hills still belonged to the Sioux Nation and should be returned immediately, with a stiff penalty paid to the Sioux as well. He set the price at $11 billion—$1 billion for a century and a quarter of "hunger, malnutrition, disease and death" and $10 billion for the resources that whites had extracted from the hills over the years. Later on, he would single out the Homestake Mining Company in a suit, demanding $6 billion, plus title to its property.

Neither of Gonzalez's suits succeeded as such, but he did accomplish one important objective: He stopped the Secretary of the Interior from paying out the $106 million. Today, the entire sum—minus $10 million paid to Lazarus and Sonosky—sits in a government account steadily gathering interest. In twenty years, the balance has swollen to nearly $600 million. And still the Sioux decline to touch it. "I look at what I did as damage control," Gonzalez reflects today. "If we had taken the money, we would have lost our pride. Now we still have hope that someday we will get the Black Hills."

Russell Means frames the matter more bluntly: "The white man is crazy. He believes he owns the Black Hills, but he never will. The hills belong to the Sioux people . . . and they are *not for sale.*"

In 1981, a year after the Supreme Court decision, Means, his brother Bill, and a number of other Indians decided to back up their words with more action. In April, an AIM group led by Means occupied federal land at Victoria Lake, twelve miles southwest of Rapid City and less than ten miles from Mount Rushmore, where they declared their intent to build a permanent, 800-acre "spiritually governed self-sufficient community." "I'm home and I intend to live out my life here," Means postured to the press. The group made it through the first winter without serious disturbance, living in tepees and makeshift shelters. But in July 1982, the spiritual atmosphere at the camp was shattered when one of the residents shot a white intruder in the back of the head with a sawed-off .22 rifle. Initially, Indians at the camp insisted that the man had killed himself accidentally, but then other witnesses came forward with a more grisly tale of point-blank murder. Afterward, Russell Means, who was nearby but not present at the actual killing, was alleged to have asked, "Who's gonna get the white man's scalp?" Once again, the American Indian Movement had become its own nemesis, and the promise of a utopian community in the Black Hills was hoisted on its own petard.

★

By the mid-1980s, cooler heads had recognized that the only way that the Sioux would ever get their land back was through an act of Congress. Toward this end, the Sioux tribes got together and chartered an organization called the Black Hills Steering Committee and empowered two members to penetrate the legislative wilderness.

Gerald Clifford was an Oglala from Pine Ridge who had earned an engineering degree from the South Dakota School of Mines at the age of nineteen. After working in the aerospace industry in California, he answered a more spiritual calling and spent several years in a Roman Catholic monastery in Italy before finally returning to his roots on the reservation. "The Lakota were placed around the Black Hills for a purpose by God," Clifford said, articulating his own brand of liberation theology. "[I]t is a moral imperative that we reject the idea of selling the land."

As its other coordinator, the steering committee chose Clifford's wife, Charlotte Black Elk, great-granddaughter of the Lakota holy man and granddaughter of Ben Black Elk, Rushmore's "Fifth Face." Today, Charlotte Black Elk requests that the specifics of her education—where and when she got her degrees in law and molecular biology—go unmentioned. ("I'd rather fool white people into thinking I'm a dumb Indian.") But suffice it to say, her bona fides, not to mention her bloodlines and steadfast commitment to Lakota causes, made her a worthy mate to Clifford. With added help from Mario Gonzalez, Black Elk and Clifford set about drafting legislation that would please a majority of their fellow Sioux and, if all went according to plan, win the favor of a majority of the U.S. Congress.

The bill they drafted was extraordinary, and the man they persuaded to sponsor it was no less remarkable. Before his election to the U.S. Senate, Bill Bradley had been a basketball star at Princeton and a Rhodes Scholar. During his post-grad years playing for the New York Knicks, he had participated in a summer basketball clinic on Pine Ridge, where the pride and poverty of the Lakota had made a lasting impression. When the Black Hills Steering Committee approached him about sponsoring their bill, Bradley consented—never mind that he represented New Jersey, a state with no discernible Indian constituency of its own.

The bill that Bradley introduced in the Senate in July 1985 was, from a Sioux perspective, a compromise. Rather than call for the return of the entire Black Hills—the "heart" of which covers roughly two million acres—it merely sought title to the 1.3 million acres of federal land overseen by the U.S. Forest Service, the Bureau of Land Management, and the National Park Service. The one exception was Mount Rushmore—although the bill did request that the Sioux be given first preference in bidding for the concessions there. As for the nearly 300,000 acres of private property checkerboarded throughout the Black Hills, that land would remain private for the time being, although again the Sioux asked for a right of first refusal to purchase any private ground when it came up for sale.

The Sioux Nation Black Hills Act, as Bradley's bill was called, envisioned an immense "Sioux Park," which would be managed "in accordance with the traditional principle of 'respect the earth.'" Whites would be allowed access to the park, with the exception of certain sacred areas. The Sioux also asked for return of three sacred sites outside the hills: Inyan Kara Mountain and Devil's Tower, both in Wyoming, and Bear Butte, east of Sturgis. And finally, the bill stipulated that the Sioux would accept the money awarded by the Court of Claims and Supreme Court—$106 million and growing—as the basis of a "Permanent Investment Fund."

Compromise or not, the Bradley bill was still the most potentially radical event in the history of the Black Hills since Custer's foray in 1874. Like Custer, Bradley had Indian scouts to guide him; unlike Custer, he had no army to back him up. Conspicuous in its unwillingness to align with Bradley was South Dakota's congressional delegation: Senators Tom Daschle and Larry Pressler and Representative Tim

Johnson. To have expressed even lukewarm encouragement would have endangered, if not ended, their political careers. Conversely, their disavowal of the bill ensured its death: The Sioux Nation Black Hills Act never got out of committee.

Undaunted, the steering committee persuaded Bradley to introduce the bill again in March 1987. "Today, we make another attempt to right the long-standing injustice," he told his Senate colleagues. "After all the discussions about politics ... each of you must decide what you owe another human being. By this, I don't mean what you owe ... your family, or even some of your friends, but rather what you owe a stranger simply because he or she is a human being. ... It is for [this reason] that I have introduced the Black Hills bill."

This time the bill was all but thrown back in Bradley's face. When Wyoming senator Malcolm Wallop learned that Devil's Tower and Inyan Kara were on the block, he threatened to introduce his own legislation giving away the Statue of Liberty, a landmark visible from the shores of New Jersey. While South Dakota business leaders argued that passage of the bill would cripple the economy and lovers of the outdoors feared that it would hamper their ability to camp, hike, ski, hunt, and fish—and while the region's contingent of rednecks contemplated being overrun by a pack of longhaired ex-cons—the state's politicians endeavored to tread a diplomatic path. Republican governor George Mickelson, respected for his record of reconciliation with Indians, suggested as politely as possible that "[c]reating more division between the Sioux people and their fellow South Dakotans is not only wrong but a giant step backwards." Congressman Johnson, a Democrat, put the blame squarely on Bradley for sticking his nose where it didn't belong: "This is the kind of thing that happens when you're well meaning but don't know what you're doing. This is a little bit as though I told Senator Bradley, 'You have some problems in downtown Atlantic City. Let me fix them.'" For the second time, the Black Hills Act died in committee.

Yet even then it suffered a bizarre and pathetic purgatory in the hands of Phil Stevens, the multimillionaire chairman of Ultra Systems, an engineering firm headquartered in Newport Beach, California. Stevens, who purported to be the great-grandson of Henry Standing Bear, had first taken an interest in the Black Hills claim on a trip to Pine Ridge in 1986. He returned the next year and gradually persuaded various Oglala elders, including the venerable Grey Eagle Society, that he, not Bradley, was the man who could conquer the U.S. Congress. The Grey Eagles made Stevens an honorary chief, and even before Bradley had a chance to test (or retest) the waters of the Senate, Stevens muddied them by proposing that the compensation portion of the bill be upped to $3.1 billion. "He had the grandiosity that no psychiatrist can cure," Charlotte Black Elk recalls bitterly. "We had no choice but to back off and let the shit settle."

Meanwhile, Stevens did what all self-respecting activists do sooner or later in South Dakota: He staged a rally at Mount Rushmore. On August 16, 1988, he led a hundred Sioux (he had notified the Park Service to expect two thousand) on a mile-long march to Rushmore, where he took great pains to itemize the various injustices done to the Sioux Nation over the years. "We are not stupid savages," he harangued. "We are informed, reasonable people." Then, choosing an unfortunate image that showed greater sensitivity to his Newport Beach lifestyle than to his Native American roots, he demanded, "It's now time to step up to the bar and pay the bill." Further inspiration was provided that day by folksinger Joni Mitchell, who performed "Lakota," a song that she had recorded with the help of seventy-three-year-old Iron Eyes Cody, the Cherokee-Cree actor famous for weeping so convincingly in anti-litter commercials. Unlike the AIM-led events of years past, there were no hints of unruliness, and the Indians disbanded calmly by late afternoon.

Eventually, Stevens did come up with his own Black Hills bill, which was introduced in Congress as a personal favor by his Newport Beach congressman Matthew Martinez. But by then, Stevens had worn out his welcome in all camps, both native and non-native. "We are just a little sick and tired of . . . Stevens in his war bonnet, Stevens in his fur cap, Stevens in his leather . . . and Stevens as a spokesman for the Lakota Nation," snipped Lakota journalist Tim Giago. The Stevens bill, needless to say, was stillborn.

Looking back, the most enduring difference between Bradley and Stevens is that nobody in Indian Country holds a grudge against Bradley for his solemn efforts. Phil Stevens, on the other hand, remains a sore subject. To invoke his name among Lakota is to remind them of their misplaced trust in a (mostly) white savior, and of their most recent failure to recover the Black Hills. If Phil Stevens was as close as they got, then they never got very close at all.

The stepchild of Phil Stevens has to be Kevin Costner. In 1990—which also happened to be the centennial of the massacre at Wounded Knee—Costner released his epic western, *Dances with Wolves*, filmed in South Dakota, directed by and starring himself. He played Lieutenant John Dunbar, a miraculous survivor of the Civil War who, in order to distance himself from the trauma and impurity of eastern civilization, chooses assignment to a remote outpost in Dakota Territory, where he sets up camp alone, Robinson Crusoe–like—to heal, to ruminate, and "to see the frontier . . . before it's gone." (Dunbar's Friday is an inquisitive wolf, with which, out of loneliness and with feral abandon, he inevitably dances.) Over time, Dunbar makes contact with the local Lakota, and in the course of absorbing and admiring their ways, he joins in their buffalo hunt and offers counsel on what they can expect from the far less sympathetic white men—his fellow soldiers—who number "like the stars" and are already beginning to rattle their sabers on the edge of Indian Country. For the sake of romantic tidiness (and presumably not to sidestep ancient Hollywood taboos against miscegenation), Dunbar is paired with the plucky and pretty Stands with Fist, a white captive raised by the Indians.

Dances with Wolves was the Next Big Thing for South Dakota, more defining than *North by Northwest* and nearly as attention-grabbing as Mount Rushmore itself. The prairie looks absolutely delicious through Costner's lens, a symphony of grass and rivers. "The country is everything I dreamed it could be. There can be no place like this on earth," Dunbar writes in his journal.

Westerns have been filmed in South Dakota almost since the studios were able to take cameras on location. "It is difficult to estimate the magnitude of the publicity which the Black Hills will receive ... as a result of this wonderful production," exclaimed the *Rapid City Journal* in 1925, the year Universal filmed the silent shoot-'em-up *Deadwood Dick* not far from the spot where Gutzon Borglum was then planning to carve his colossal monument. Unfortunately, most of the westerns filmed in the region since then, while flattering to the local scenery, have wound up insulting their subject matter and often their audiences. The ultimate atrocity, undoubtedly, was *Chief Crazy Horse* (1955), starring Victor Mature. "*Chief Crazy Horse* ... pays a Technicolor installment on Hollywood's mountain of debt to the American Indian," *Time* intoned. "After years of getting clobbered, the redskins this time win three battles in a row over the U.S. cavalry. What's more the embattled Sioux are given Victor Mature as their peerless leader, but sad to say, when silhouetted against the sky in war paint and feathers, Mature looks more like an aggrieved turtle than an eagle of the plains."

It was against this backdrop, and this still enormous mountain of Hollywood debt, that Kevin Costner shot *Dances with Wolves*. By all accounts, he tried his best to be authentic and politically correct. And in some ways he succeeded. He hired 175 Indians (and no whites) to play the native parts. Instead of having Indians speak pidgin English, he sent his actors to Lakota language school—and obliged audiences to read English subtitles in many scenes. Costumes were made of genuine buffalo, deerskin, and feathers, under the guidance of Lakota consultants. Set designers had trained at the Smithsonian. And so on.

The movie was a hit, winning seven Academy Awards, including Best Picture, and returning more than $500 million on an $18 million investment. And at first blush at least, it won high praise from Native Americans for portraying them as complex human beings. "They are not beggars and thieves. They are not the boogey men they have been made out to be," Lieutenant Dunbar observes. "They are eager to laugh, devoted to family, dedicated to each other." For his sensitivity, not to mention the money and attention the movie brought to the Lakota, Costner was made an honorary tribal member in a well-publicized ceremony in Washington on the eve of the *Dances with Wolves* premiere. "I think for our people it will be a classic," cast member Tantoo Cardinal told the *Los Angeles Times* after finally seeing the finished movie. Doris Leader Charge, one of the Lakota tutors and translators, pronounced: "They've gotten it right this time."

Not all the reviews were in, however. After the initial hype died down, the scholars began to respond, and with decidedly thinner applause. They questioned the chronology of Costner's narrative (the Sioux apparently were not at war with the Pawnees precisely when he said they were) and the nuance of language (male actors, it turned out, had been taught an inflection reserved for female speech).

Perhaps the most penetrating critic of the film was Louis Owens, a professor of literature at the University of Oklahoma who is of Choctaw, Cherokee, as well as Irish heritage. "*Dances with Wolves* is, from beginning to end, the perfect, exquisite reenactment of the whole colonial enterprise in America," Owens lectured with academic sanctimony, "and it is the most insidious vehicle yet for this familiar message because it comes beautifully disguised as its opposite." His point was that, beneath the movie's authenticity and apparent sympathy toward Indians, it is essentially the tale of a white intruder who insinuates himself into the Indians' pristine world to feed off its vitality before returning to his own trammeled corner of the map. Like a "psychic vampire," Owens averred, Dunbar becomes "more and more 'Indian' until, in the final absurdity, he is a better Indian than the Indian themselves. As the Indians grow more weak and vulnerable to the advancing edge of Euramerican civilization, Dunbar becomes stronger. When Dunbar has absorbed everything possible from the fragile Lakota band, the Indians become disposable. It is time then to erase and replace the Indian—the ultimate fantasy of the colonizer come true."

Other critics have called Costner's epic *Lawrence of South Dakota*. Like Phil Stevens, another Southern Californian, Costner and his alter ego, Lieutenant Dunbar, play Indian for a while and then drift off, righteous and replenished.

Except that in Costner's case, he did not drift off entirely. A month before *Dances with Wolves* was to open in Rapid City, he and his brother Dan purchased a building on Main Street in Deadwood, once the gambling haunt of Wild Bill Hickok and now the only place in South Dakota—besides Indian reservations—where anything other than video gambling is legal. Gossip immediately spread that the brothers were going into the gaming business, although no one realized the dimension of their dream. Two years later, the brothers bought 85 acres on a hill above Deadwood and announced plans to develop a five-star hotel and casino. With no irony intended, they named their resort-to-be "the Dunbar." The theme would be Old West, with numerous wood-sided buildings and even a railroad linking Deadwood to the Rapid City airport, forty miles away. Not surprisingly, the estimated cost swelled from $60 million to $100 million, and then to twice that. With the prospect of six hundred new jobs and an incalculable gush of cash from tourists and gamblers—just as mining in the Deadwood area was beginning to dry up—the business community received Costner as a savior.

No one really raised an eyebrow until 1995, when the Costners bought an additional 585 very scenic acres in Spearfish Canyon, twelve miles away, and proposed trading them for 630 acres of Forest Service land adjacent to the Dunbar on which they wanted to build a championship golf course. This sort of swap happens all the time, only this time the Costners didn't have designs on any garden-variety national forest; they were messing with *Paha Sapa*, property that the Sioux still claimed as their own, property whose loss Lieutenant Dunbar had lamented so evocatively, property on which Kevin and Dan Costner now hoped to make a bundle. Some Indians even contended that the proposed location for the tenth hole had once been a sun dance site. Despite widespread opposition, including a demonstration, the Costner brothers and the Forest Service turned a cold shoulder to the Sioux and consummated the land swap.

After so much negative publicity from Indians and environmentalists, the Costners have become extremely guarded about their plans and schedule. But when and if the Dunbar opens, its entrance will be decorated with a colossal, *Wars of America*–scale bronze of a Lakota buffalo hunt—not unlike the one Costner had reenacted in his movie and no Indian has participated in since. "Can you see that you will always be my friend?" the Lakota warrior Wind in His Hair tells the departing Dunbar at the end of *Dances with Wolves*. The answer is supposed to be obvious. But at that point, Wind in His Hair had yet to see the coming attractions.

No discussion of the Sioux's relationship to the Black Hills would be complete without revisiting Crazy Horse Memorial. Korczak Ziolkowski died in 1982, well short of completion of his colossal monument. Yet in the ensuing years, the resolve of his second wife, Ruth, and their children has been as keen as the drills they use to shape their mountain. Nor have the Ziolkowskis wavered from their mantra that the sculpture is being done at the behest of Indians. Which is not to say that it is absolutely necessary for Indians to visit Crazy Horse in great numbers—whites are the ones with money—yet for the sake of legitimacy, those same money-spending tourists must be assured that visiting Crazy Horse is a good thing, not just for the Ziolkowskis, but for Indians in general.

The task of pleasing all camps at once—Indians and whites, locals and visitors—is not an easy one. The prevailing fear among South Dakotans, the *Rapid City Journal* once editorialized, is that "any more mountains in imitation of Rushmore would cheapen that great sculpture and largely destroy its significance." And so Ziolkowski had to prove Crazy Horse's worthiness. In a 1954 speech to the Kiwanis Club of Hot Springs, he explained that the previous year nearly a quarter of a million visitors had come to Crazy Horse. The public could scoff at his artistic vision, but as a "tourist gimmick"—Ziolkowski's words—Crazy Horse was already a boon to the local economy. He also reminded the public that his goal had never been to feather his own nest. (Anybody could see that he wasn't getting rich off of blasting and bulldozing.) Rather, he underscored his objective to honor and aid Native Americans. Before his death, he drafted a 220-page master plan that mapped out an Indian university, museum, and health center at the foot of the mountain—all linked by a four-lane boulevard, the Avenue of the Chiefs, all paid for by tourist dollars. Who dared frown on that?

Because Crazy Horse Memorial is a privately controlled, nonprofit organization (the Ziolkowskis say that they have actually turned down offers of federal assistance), nobody knows exactly how many people pay the admission fee ($8 a person, $19 the carload) each day or how many Crazy Horse miniatures, mugs, and T-shirts they purchase. It's a safe guess, however, that visitors now exceed a million annually, and judging from the tireless trilling of the tills in the gift shop and the Laughing Water Restaurant, cash receipts likely approach $50,000 on busy days. Things are going so well, in fact, that the Ziolkowskis acknowledge that they are not in any hurry to complete the sculpture.

People seem to like the fact that it is a work in progress, a Sphinx in the rough. Dynamite blasts are part of the entertainment, and granite chunks from the mountain are absolutely free.

As for the rest of the master plan, only the avenue, the museum (although not the one envisioned in the master plan), and the first inklings of the university are evident. At the rear of the visitor center, behind Ziolkowski's original home and studio, is a stone-clad building dedicated to Indian crafts. In its basement, Donovin Sprague, a Lakota whose great-great-grandfather was one of Crazy Horse's uncles, offers a couple of classes each semester under the auspices of the American Indian Studies Department at Black Hills State University, where he also teaches. Sprague knows a great deal about flute making and treaty law, but he also plays electric guitar and manages Indian rock bands on the side. "Once we had smoke signals," he jokes. "Now I use e-mail." Since he set up the curriculum at Crazy Horse in 1996, most of his classes have been craft-related—quill work, feather work, bead work—and most of his students so far have been white. But despite the slow start and sparse native enrollment, he is happy with the setup. "I don't have a problem with Crazy Horse [as a monument]," he explains. "I'd love to teach what I teach anywhere, but I'm not sure that it would get the same attention if this monument weren't here. . . . This place attracts people from all over the world."

Sprague is especially pleased that Crazy Horse Memorial provides free admission to Indians and free space for them to show and sell their crafts. He is proud that the Ziolkowskis have given out more than $300,000 in scholarships to Indians. And he is hopeful that in another five years or so, Indian University of North America, as the emerging Crazy Horse program is now officially called, will have its own building. "I enjoy what I'm doing," he says, "and the way I look at it, the more people who know about Crazy Horse, by whatever means, the better."

Yet for every Donovin Sprague, there are many more Indians who regard Crazy Horse Memorial as a transgression on a scale at least as grand as Mount Rushmore, if not more so. During the 1970s and 1980s, when Rushmore was the focus of intermittent demonstrations, Crazy Horse was exempted, even though the scar it was leaving on the breast of *Paha Sapa* is deep. Various AIM leaders were said to be friends of the Ziolkowskis, and besides, Rushmore was a vastly more redolent backdrop for protests against white wickedness. In recent years, however, as Crazy Horse has become more and more of a cash cow, an increasing number of Indians have begun speaking out against it. "So many of us hate that thing," says Charmaine Whiteface, an Oglala who works with the Sierra Club. Lakota journalist Jodi Rave Lee is another member of the disgruntled majority. Despite the Ziolkowskis' sincere efforts to involve Indians in the memorial—through exhibits, conferences, classes, scholarships, and ceremonies on Native American Day (South Dakota's adaptation of Columbus Day)—Lee still cannot avoid the "gnawing feeling . . . that the Ziolkowski family appears to be one more entity exploiting tribal land and the name of Crazy Horse."

Still others see the fate of Crazy Horse Memorial as foretold. Lakota religion, like Christianity, holds that a great day of reckoning will eventually come to cleanse the Earth of its impurities and those who caused them. Crazy Horse, it is said, will be one of the horsemen of that apocalypse, returning as thunder. "Crazy Horse is not one to be trifled with," advises Ben Rhodd, a Potawatomi from Kansas who has lived and led sun dances among the Lakota for the past thirty years. "I've been in *yuwipi* [a séance-like healing ceremony] and felt his presence, and I can tell you he definitely doesn't like that thing [Crazy Horse Memorial]. In fact," Rhodd says with an ominous pause, "we've known since 1984 that he was going to take it out."

The Ziolkowskis answer the warning with their own thunder, another thousand tons of rock blown off of *Paha Sapa*. Their work is now concentrated on the horse's head and Crazy Horse's outstretched arm. Years ago, as Korczak Ziolkowski was first contemplating the design of his mountain sculpture, someone, perhaps Henry Standing

Bear, had told him about an encounter between Crazy Horse and a white man. "Where are your lands now?" the white man asked impertinently. "My lands are where my dead lie buried," Crazy Horse is supposed to have replied. Inspired by that anecdote, Ziolkowski conceived a colossal Indian mounted on horseback, his granite arm—the index finger alone will be thirty-seven feet long—pointing eastward toward the prairie, toward the reservation—and, incidentally, *away* from the Black Hills.

Ziolkowski, meanwhile, is buried not on the East Coast, where the bones of his immigrant parents presumably lie, but in a tomb of his own design at the foot of the rugged mountain he first staked as a mining claim. "I think it would be better for you to pursue your creative efforts where you are not hampered by any other ways of doing things," Gutzon Borglum had written in his 1939 letter firing Ziolkowski, a copy of which is mounted like a shield of honor on the wall at Crazy Horse Memorial. Since that fateful date, Ziolkowski and his family have been called many things, but nobody has ever accused them of failing to do whatever they pleased—the American dream writ large.

14

PRESIDENTS VIEW

T HIS TIME I came at the Black Hills from a different direction. On July 2, 2001, I bought a microwaved ham sandwich at Big Bat's Texaco in the heart of Pine Ridge and ate it in the car as I drove toward Wounded Knee. The primary objective of the trip was to see the fireworks display at Mount Rushmore the following night, but before I immersed myself in those gay festivities, I decided to detour to a more out-of-the-way, but no less crucial, American monument. Several years before, the South Dakota Department of Tourism had come up with a catchy slogan, "Great Faces, Great Places," mostly as a plug for Rushmore, a landmark that, according to surveys, the vast majority of people recognize, but too few of whom associate with South Dakota. Wounded Knee is renowned, too, but so far no one has built a splashy advertising campaign around it.

I had hoped to see Oliver Red Cloud, eighty-three-year-old great-grandson of the great Lakota chief, but on the afternoon I arrived on Pine Ridge, he was called into an impromptu meeting of Oglala tribal leaders to discuss how best to fight a recent U.S. Supreme Court decision that allowed state law enforcement officials to come on the reservation for the purpose of investigating and prosecuting crimes committed elsewhere. Instead of an interview with Red Cloud, I was obliged to listen to him on KILI, the Pine Ridge radio station, which broadcast the meeting live. "The Supreme Court has to understand that we are a treaty tribe," tribal adviser Johnson Holy Rock scolded as I turned off the pavement and parked by the Wounded Knee graveyard, where Big Foot and his fellow victims of the 1890 massacre are buried. Close by are the ruins of Sacred Heart Catholic Church, ground zero of the 1973 AIM takeover. "Pine Ridge Reservation was not a gift from the United States," Holy Rock lectured. "We fought for it with our blood. . . . The treaty recognizes that we have our own laws. We're not about to trade our freedom for something that has only the appearance of freedom."

"That's right. We're different. We're Oglala," Red Cloud chimed in. For the next hour, he and his fellow elders explained to their people via radio how and why they would stand up to this latest invasion of their homeland.

The names of the Wounded Knee victims are engraved on a single gravestone, a tapered, eight-foot column with an ornamental urn on top, not unlike the markers in a thousand non-native cemeteries. Big Foot's name tops the list, and the names that follow parse like haiku: Living Bear, Afraid of Bear, Shoots the Bear. Picked Horses, Ghost Horse, Chase in Winter. Big Skirt, Bird Shakes, Spotted Thunder. At the foot of the marker lay an assortment of offerings to the dead: cigarettes, artificial roses, turkey feathers, seashells, and a Ziploc bag containing a handful of Dorito chips and two Fifth Avenue candy bars.

As I jotted down this inventory, I was approached by three boys, none older than ten, on knobby mountain bikes. Their summer crewcuts were growing out, and they exhibited the universal ennui of kids who live too far from town with not enough to do. Wounded Knee is their playground. When I asked how they were spending their vacation, they mentioned Little League, then asked me for money to buy equipment. When I raised a skeptical eye, they spun their bikes and galloped off toward home. On the foundation walls of Sacred Heart Church were spray-painted words less dulcet: "Slow Killers," "Fuck the Hill Billys," and "WG Locoz"—this last probably a gang tag. The view from the battered front steps reminded me of Palestine: hills and gullies I know to be historic, but now too poor to inspire more than pity.

Leaving Wounded Knee, I drove seven miles north to the village of Manderson, still on the reservation. Across from the post office, a woman in a sleeveless red-white-and-blue blouse was selling fireworks out of her Bronco. Two of her customers rode pinto horses. Steering off the pavement again, I paralleled a palisade of burnt buttes until the road dead-ended at Charlotte Black Elk's driveway. Somewhere other than here, her well-built house would be called "ranch style." It sits in the throat of an otherwise undisturbed canyon, offering fine views of the jagged uplands from its comfortable deck. As I entered the front gate, I was struck by the stench of something dead. Other people have birdbaths and whirligigs in their yards. Charlotte Black Elk, for some reason, had a ripe buffalo carcass nearby.

Intentionally, I had not prepared a long list of questions. Really I just wanted to meet the notorious Charlotte Black Elk, whom so many people had told me about. (Gerald Clifford, her ex-husband, had died in 2000.) Besides, she had agreed to see me only if I paid her for her time. I had protested and put off the visit for a year, hoping she would change her terms. Never before had I paid for an interview, and I still could not quite believe that, of all people, this woman of such high character, who had been interviewed hundreds of times by reporters from all over the world, would be the one to deflower me. Initially I had hung up on her when she asked for money. Then I had called back and inquired what her rate was. She said flatly, "I'm a lawyer. I get three hundred and twenty-five dollars an hour." I asked her what I could expect to get for that exorbitant sum—access to her records on the Black Hills land claim, archives on her Black Elk forebears? "No," she said, "you just get to talk to me."

And so I bought an hour of Charlotte Black Elk's time, thinking that if she would stick it to the *wasicu*, I would have the final word on her. I half expected the leather and frown of a dominatrix. Instead I was greeted by a slim, cordial, very pretty woman in her mid to late fifties, with long hennaed hair, a floral skirt, and a white lace blouse. She had just come from a wake, at which an aunt's coffin had been laid out in a tepee. Her patent-leather sandals and painted toenails were covered in a soft layer of dust. Her smile was warm and streetwise, the twinkle in her dark eyes mischievous, and all the while, she chain-smoked Sun Dance cigarettes.

It was at this meeting that she filled me in on the sour demise of the Black Hills Act. Mostly, though, I just let the meter run, and the conversation drifted all over creation. I asked her how Nicholas Black Elk, her great-grandfather, had managed to justify Catholicism with his traditional beliefs. "What Black Elk saw," she answered, "was that Jesus was a very good Lakota." And how did she feel about her grandfather Ben Black Elk schmoozing for tips at Mount Rushmore? "To anyone who would listen, he told them to love the Black Hills and treat them with respect," she replied, this time a bit defensively. "And he was always telling his own people to hang on to their language." When I asked about Crazy Horse Memorial, she told me that Ben Black Elk had actually climbed Thunderhead Mountain in the early days and fasted and prayed that the Crazy Horse monument would never be built.

"Does Ruth Ziolkowski know that?" I asked.

"Oh, she'll just say, 'You must have been talking to Charlotte.'"

Talking to Charlotte, though, was enthralling. We came back around to the Black Hills claim. "I get asked all the time to rekindle [federal legislation]," she admitted, "and I always say no." But that does not mean she has lost hope of ever getting the hills back. "Indian kids today are more radical than we ever were, though in a very different way, and they're even more committed to the Black Hills. When I talk at schools on the reservations, I meet students all the time who are studying forestry or business so they will be ready when they have to manage those resources.... Look at the latest Census—South Dakota is a state of old white women and young Indians. Say what you want, but we're the new brain trust. We're the people who are staying." With that, her daughter came out on the porch. Charlotte introduced her and announced proudly that she would be entering medical school at Georgetown in the fall. "[Return of the Hills] may not happen in *my* lifetime," Charlotte declared, "but I know it will."

I asked if she too believes in a final reckoning. By way of answering, she reminded me that she was one of the authors of the study that used "stellar theology" to determine the date when the Lakota first emerged from Wind Cave and walked on the earth. (She says 3,500 years ago.) Next she brought up the infrared photos of the Black Hills taken from outer space. The Lakota have always believed that the Black Hills form the outline of a buffalo, with prominent peaks on the perimeter, such as Devil's Tower and Bear Butte, positioned as the hump, horns, hooves, etc. The hills themselves are the heart of the buffalo—the heart of everything that is. When NASA came along a few years back with a photo—red, no less—that showed the Black Hills more or less in the shape of a heart—not a valentine, but the actual organ—many Lakota took the news not so much as a revelation but as a confirmation. Charlotte Black Elk, holder of degrees in biology and law, descendant of *the* Black Elk, shot me a look and smiled. "Our sacred pipe is very new, only a couple of thousand years old," she said enigmatically. "Imagine what it still has to teach us."

I steered her back to the prophecy of a final reckoning. "I'm positive that forces of nature will take care of the desecrations," she offered finally. "The earth will cleanse itself. We've already had earthquakes in the Black Hills. Not big ones, but someday—who knows?—they could level Mount Rushmore and Crazy Horse. Right now nature is only smacking mosquitoes. One day she's going to pull out the Raid."

When I tried to tease her about her choice of such an environmentally harmful pesticide, she cut me off: "You know what I mean."

Too quickly, my watch said the hour was up, and there was an awkward pause while I waited to see if she would actually ask for money. She did. I suggested a check. She preferred cash. I asked for a receipt, and she drew up a document that read: "Be it known that I, Charlotte A. Black Elk, have received the amount of three hundred and twenty-five dollars ($325) for cultural consulting from John Taliaferro this 2 day of July, 2001." I never asked about the buffalo in the yard. She never brought it up.

Sunset was basting the Badlands as I drove north by northwest across Red Shirt Table toward the Black Hills. On KILI, the tribal elders had signed off, and the disc jockey was spinning nothing but blues, including, by request, "The Sky Is Crying" and two versions of "I've Got Dreams to Remember." Electric blues is the music of African-Americans who migrated from southern fields, looking for work and a better life in the big cities. To Native Americans, it is the music they brought from the cities back to the reservation, and in its passion and pain, angst and insight, it is an astoundingly good fit.

I stayed that night at the Presidents View Resort, a hotel perched on a narrow shelf carved into the mountainside, one hundred feet above the main drag of Keystone. From the parking lot and from some, but not all, of the rooms, Mount Rushmore can be seen, four miles distant, especially at night when the floodlights are on. The Presidents View is the flagship of Bill Durst, who owns or leases twenty-seven of the thirty-some businesses in the snug quarter mile that is "downtown" Keystone.

I had first met him a year earlier, and with very little prompting, he had told me the story of how he had managed to acquire more keys to Keystone than anyone else. At first I had been taken aback by his playboyish fringe-over-the-ears haircut and his rayon shirt with its surfboard and palm-tree motif. But I couldn't help but admire his easy intelligence and uninhibited ambition. Here was a man who knew how to keep his eye on the prize, and, what is more, truly loved doing so. "You see that stop light out there?" he asked, flicking his curly head in the direction of Keystone's one and only traffic signal, at the intersection of Highways 16A and 40. "That is the busiest intersection in South Dakota. Every year, three million people drive through it headed for Mount Rushmore. They get off the interstate, climb into the Black Hills, see a few trees, and for most of them, this is their first stop. . . . Their dollars are still fresh and clean, and they save them for me."

As we were talking, a tour bus pulled up outside the front door. "You call that an air brake," he said as the bus gasped to a halt. "I call that a five-thousand-dollar bill. And you know what? That bus will only be here twelve and a half hours, and this year we'll have a couple hundred of 'em. Now, that's slick money." In a 210-day tourist season, Durst claims that his occupancy rate is 109 percent—however he manages that—while the state average is only 89.

Durst has made his money a lot of different ways over the years, although he knows hotels as well as anything. His parents ran the old Harney Hotel in Rapid City, and when his father died in the early 1960s, he and his mother kept it going, catering to the crews constructing missile silos in western South Dakota, along with their female acquaintances. By nineteen, Durst was on his own, running a café in Keystone and living in the apartment above. "I started making money right off," he recalled, his voice graveled by endless Winstons. "At the end of every day, I would take what I earned upstairs, paper my floor in ones and tens and twenties, and walk all over it." Back then, he did his deals on "a handshake and two shots of whiskey." And when someone crossed him—well, he could be "as crazy as a pet coon," in the words of one former associate. At fifty-five, Durst has put aside some of his scrappiness, but he is no less wily, in a Bogart sort of way. He still has the smile of an impish night clerk, and he has a way of flashing it contagiously when he's talking about his beloved enterprises in Keystone, his own little Andorra.

Durst remembers the early days of the tourist boom the way prospectors remember the first gold strikes—which is to say, with fondness but also with poetic license. "The only thing between Rapid City and here, besides the Gaslight [restaurant] in Rockerville, was Sitting Bull Caverns," he recounted. "Bill Duhamel would sit up on the hill in his jeep and ride tourists down the back to his cave. The other guy was Earl Brockelsby. When cars would overheat coming [into the Black Hills], he'd hose down their radiators—the equivalent of free ice water at Wall Drug. He kept a bunch of rattlesnakes in a swimming pool behind his gas station, and while people waited for their cars to cool down, he'd charge them a nickel or dime to watch him handle them. That was the start of Reptile Gardens."

"Keystone these days," Durst told me, "is a Monopoly game, and you've got to play Monopoly." He has drilled for oil in Wyoming, built a high-rise in Dallas, developed a casino in Deadwood, and owned a Black Hills gold jewelry outlet, but now his full attention is on Keystone. The big flood of 1972 was horrendously traumatic to the hills, but it was not without a silver lining. For instance, it allowed Keystone to widen Main Street, and low-interest disaster loans gave people like Durst a chance to improve their holdings. Nowadays, three out of every four dollars he earns come from lodging. So far he has approximately two hundred rooms; he intends to up that number to three hundred in the next few years.

In 1986, he bought the first of two prefab motels: One was originally built to house oilfield workers in Williston, North Dakota; the other, added in 1993, he salvaged from a bankrupt truck stop outside Rapid City. He sawed them in pieces, hauled them to Keystone, spliced them back together, dressed his new edifice with a new façade, and named it the White House Resort Motel—a seventy-four-room oxymoron that suits his clientele perfectly. "The people who come here are families—farmers from essentially the nine nearest states," he explained. "They want a clean room and a bargain, a Sunday kind of town. We give 'em that, a lot of red, white, and blue, and we plant a bunch of flowers so their wives will feel safe. And because we offer a good rate on the room, they can afford a twelve-dollar T-shirt [at one of Durst's Main Street shops] and a seventeen-dollar meal instead of a seven-dollar meal [at one of his restaurants]. . . . They lick a little ice cream, lick some more, spend some money."

"You know," Durst continued, "when you're from Iowa you'll probably never get around to going to Washington, D.C. But you can see Mount Rushmore, and while you're doing that, you can stay at the White House."

Given the tightness of the canyon that cups Keystone, Durst figured that for his next move, the best way to go was up. And so he scraped off a ledge from the mountain that hovers directly over downtown Keystone and built (this time from scratch) the 120-room Presidents View, which opened in 1995. "People laughed when I said I was going to blast away this mountain," he related as we sat in his Jeep Cherokee in the parking lot, gazing westward, "but I looked across at Rushmore and said, 'If Borglum can do that, I can do this.'"

We turned our heads and studied the porte cochere and front elevation of his pride and joy—a sort of Caesar's Palace by way of the Corn Palace, the tourist Taj in eastern South Dakota bejeweled with corncobs. "With dynamite, a bulldozer, and a backhoe you can go several different ways," he continued. "You can dig for gold or you can build a motel. You can make more money from tourists than you can from a mine. So I built a motel." Night and day, the enormous flashing sign at the front entrance of Presidents View proclaims: "Fine Economy Lodging," "Newly Open," "Kids Free," "Indoor Pool," "Free HBO," "Meal Deal." Sometimes it blinks "Singles $49.95," although Durst informs me with a sneaky grin that there are only eight singles in the entire hotel. Just above the blinking sign, an eighty-foot flagpole waves a twenty-five-foot by thirty-five-foot American flag—by Durst's reckoning the largest in South Dakota.

Every time I am in Keystone I think of Gutzon Borglum and his abiding concern that trinket stands would eventually hem in Mount Rushmore and then creep up the mountain toward the monument itself, like vines strangling a tropical temple. Before turning in, I couldn't resist making one more list, this time of the storefronts in the heart of Keystone: Wild Star Gifts ("Black Hills Gold, Discounted Prices"), Where the Buffalo Roam, The Daisy Chain ("You Pick, You Choose—Almost Nothing Over $2.99"), Billy Bob's Best Buy, Smokey's Family Restaurant, Old West Photo Shop, Rushmore Trading Post, Roughriders Leather, Ruby House, Red Garter, Lil' Trader, The Taffy Shop, The Indians, and Mini Donuts.

With the money he's made playing Monopoly, Durst has built himself a million-dollar house on a hill overlooking Rapid City, where he expects to live for the rest of his life. And in the next year or two, he intends to break ground on yet another hotel—this one carved even farther up the mountain, eighty feet *above* the Presidents View. "Sitting on a mountaintop is my style," he told me, with the self-satisfaction of a man who has just passed Go and knows that the hotels on Boardwalk and Park Place are his.

Later, when I asked him what Mount Rushmore means to him, his answer was infused with reverence and gratitude: "You make your own luck, but I can tell you, Rushmore is the greatest thing that ever happened to me.... I've still got a lot of chiseling to do, but when and if I ever get done, I'll be able to go up on Mount Rushmore and see *my* dream come true." In that regard, I suppose, Bill Durst has a lot in common not only with Borglum, but with Black Elk as well: What one sees *from* Rushmore is as integral to life as what one sees when looking *at* it.

★

The following morning, the third of July, I left my car on the upper level of the Mount Rushmore parking complex and ate breakfast in the Buffalo Dining Room. The choices were "George Washington" (oatmeal, toast, and fruit); "Thomas Jefferson" (French toast); "Teddy Roosevelt" (biscuits and gravy), and "Abraham Lincoln" (waffles). The fireworks were not scheduled until 9:20 that night, but by nine in the morning, scores of early birds were already holding seats in the amphitheater and unfolding their lawn chairs and blankets in the choicest spots on the Grand View Terrace and the Avenue of Flags—twelve hours of waiting for twenty minutes of pyrotechnics.

The crowd was expected to be one of the biggest in Rushmore history. Some were tourists who by fortunate coincidence happened to be in the Black Hills for the occasion; others had arranged their vacations to be at Mount Rushmore on this day; but the largest portion by far were "locals," not only from Rapid City and western South Dakota, but also from four surrounding states: Nebraska, Wyoming, Montana, and North Dakota. Many had driven five or six hours one way and would turn around and drive all the way home later that night. And unlike most other Independence Day gatherings of this scale—rodeos, ball games, NASCAR races—this particular congregation would pass the day entirely, unimaginably, without benefit of beer. Alcohol, while never for sale at Rushmore, is not actually verboten, although nobody seems to partake of it on these hallowed grounds.

I met up with Rushmore superintendent Dan Wenk and Chief Ranger Mike Pflaum outside the administration building. They were headed up the mountain to inspect the fireworks emplacements. Wenk is forty-nine, with sandy hair and a dimpled chin that gives him a slightly Dudley Do-Right mien. A landscape architect by training, he had helped to design the grounds at the Gateway Arch in St. Louis (the most recent of America's colossal monuments) and then had spent five years in Yellowstone, where he had given the environs of Old Faithful their first makeover in decades. He became Rushmore's superintendent in 1985. Wenk is a new breed of Park Service executive. He runs a cordial but no-nonsense office, plays well with Washington, and if truth be told, he'd rather spend his weekends on the golf course than in the backcountry. He seldom wears his Park Service uniform, and even on this July 3, a special occasion demanding official dress, he had forgotten his ranger shirt and had to borrow one—a size too small—from Mike Pflaum, whose job, it seems, entailed having to remember the little things that never cross Wenk's mind, or desk.

By his own admission, Wenk was nearing the end of his tour of duty at Rushmore. During his tenure, he orchestrated a total makeover of the memorial that included the demolition and replacement of the old visitor center, gift shop, and restaurant; construction of a new amphitheater, museum, employee dormitory, and parking garage; installation of a state-of-the-art security system; completion of the Hall of Records (albeit a bare-bones version of Borglum's ideal); and implementation of a program to repair and monitor flaws in the presidential faces. Nearly all of the above—approximately $60 million worth—was paid for with private funds. For his formidable accomplishments, Wenk would soon be kicked upstairs to direct the Park Service's Denver Service Center, which oversees the region that includes Rushmore. Yet plenty of people in South Dakota will always remember him as the man who "spoiled" the Shrine of Democracy. Some say that's why he prefers not to wear a uniform; incognito, he avoids having strangers come up to him and bitch about the changes.

From the beginning, Wenk knew that he faced a pronounced dilemma. On one hand, running Rushmore can be a fairly straightforward job. "This place is about mom, apple pie, and the American flag. Everybody gets it," Wenk told me during one of several conversations we had over the course of a year. At the same time, however, Rushmore is the dynamo that drives the $300-million-a-year Black Hills tourist industry and also a beloved keepsake to those who live within its gravitational pull. "Quickly I realized that I was managing something besides a national shrine," Wenk said. "It was much more local than that. I discovered that everybody in Rapid City and the Black Hills had an opinion on what was best for Mount Rushmore." Some wanted it to stay just the way it was. Others wanted Rushmore to spiff up its act in order to make South Dakota and the Black Hills that much more seductive to visitors. Either way, Wenk laughed, "I was the guy with a big target painted on his back."

While Wenk was taking heat, his baby was being loved to death. The facilities he inherited were geared to handle one million visitors a year. By the early 1970s, however, the crush was double that. Compared to most western parks, Rushmore is small, only twelve hundred acres, and the area actually used by visitors is less than twenty acres. On the busiest days of summer, with crowds routinely exceeding twenty thousand, Rushmore felt like Grand Central Station at rush hour. The parking lots were full most of the time; the roads to and from the mountain were likewise jammed three months out of the year; and when visitors finally jostled their way onto the memorial grounds, they found little to engage them for very long. "It was a pit stop, a photo op," explained Carolyn Mollers, who worked at the Rushmore soda fountain as a college student and years later became president of the Mount Rushmore Memorial Society.

"The visitor center was just a desk for answering questions, or you could watch films on tiny TV sets," Wenk elaborated. As he began traveling around the state, trying out his ideas for innovations at Rushmore, he discovered that many of the people he met were apprehensive of anything new; they all clung to the memory of the first time they had piled out of the family station wagon, scampered along the pine-shaded path to the viewing terrace, and bought a rubber tomahawk at the gift shop. But when Wenk inquired when they had last visited Rushmore, he learned that hadn't been in a long time. Why not? Too crowded, they'd say.

In 1986, Wenk was approached by a publicist for actor Charlton

Heston, who explained that Heston was interested in doing for Mount Rushmore what Detroit auto executive Lee Iacocca had recently done for the Statue of Liberty: He would rally America to restore one of its most cherished icons. In the end, Heston did not follow through on his offer, but the notion of a white knight inspired Wenk to think big, and for the first time, he dared to believe that he could accomplish his immodest goals entirely through private philanthropy. With the blessing of his superiors at the Park Service and the help of the Rushmore Memorial Society's newly formed Preservation Fund, Wenk set out to raise $40 million. With luck, he figured he could complete his grand design in time for the memorial's fiftieth birthday in 1991.

The headwind he encountered was formidable. When the Park Service proposed widening the highway between Rushmore and Keystone, locals lambasted the plan as extravagant, environmentally intrusive, and downright sacrilegious. Back in the 1920s, Borglum and Peter Norbeck had laid out the original road to follow the contour of the land and to provide tantalizing glimpses of Mount Rushmore. "The new road is more like a ski run," fumed Gene Koevenig, retired head of maintenance at Rushmore and perhaps the most outspoken opponent of the Wenk regime. And when Wenk recommended replacing the old concession building, he made enemies of Kay Steuerwald, who had run the restaurant and gift shop for nearly forty years, not to mention movie buffs, who considered the *North by Northwest* location a precious landmark.

Meanwhile, owners of Keystone businesses worried that any expansion of services at Rushmore would rob them of revenues. Rushmore was in danger of becoming "too commercial," they warned self-righteously. From the other flank, the Sierra Club and an ad hoc group called the Mount Rushmore Environmental Coalition threatened a lawsuit demanding that Wenk prepare a full-blown environmental impact statement (instead of a mere environmental *assessment*) before unlimbering the wrecking ball. A group calling itself Citizens Protecting

Rushmore pledged to keep Rushmore "in the state it is right now." "They're playing Russian roulette with the focal point of South Dakota," growled Pauline Casey, a status-quo proponent and owner of Bear Country USA, the drive-through zoo that has fed on Rushmore tourists since 1972.

The most prickly issue of all was parking. As early as 1967, planners had suggested a monorail between Keystone and Rushmore, and perhaps connecting other attractions in the Black Hills as well. (Futurism was rampant in those days: At about the same time, developers proposed building a revolving restaurant atop Harney Peak, connected by tram to Sylvan Lake.) Even though the monorail idea went nowhere, it did make a certain amount of sense. On busy days, Rushmore is the third largest city in South Dakota, requiring all the services expected of a comparable urban center: water, sewage, safety, and of course traffic management. More parking that could be more easily accessed and take up less acreage was essential, especially when one factored in all the new diversions that Wenk had in mind: expanded trails, a museum, and interpretive programs. Visitors were likely to stay not just for an hour or so, as they had done in the past, but for two or three hours, slowing turnover in the parking lots even further.

The Park Service rejected the idea of remote parking and instead opted for a bigger, on-site facility, multi-tiered so that its "footprint" would not have to take over the *entire* mountain. The cost was predicted to be an additional $15 million. While the Preservation Fund figured that it could locate a certain number of Charlton Hestons or Lee Iacoccas to underwrite a new amphitheater or visitor center, it realized that the list of big-name, big-money people willing to have their name on a parking garage was considerably shorter. Casting about for a solution, Wenk finally came up with the idea of selling a "possessory interest," which, simply put, enabled a private concessionaire to build and run the parking garage. He was not yet out of the weeds, however. The 1929 act authorizing Rushmore stipulated, "No charge shall ever be made for admission to the memorial grounds or for viewing the memorial." Yet to pay for its investment, and to make a few bucks besides, the parking concessionaire would surely need to collect a fee. Wenk went before the public and clarified that it would not be an *admission* fee per se, but a *parking* fee. The hornets of dissent, already agitated, went through the roof.

"I took them on as straight as I could," Wenk recounted. Still, he was stung. "People would stage-whisper behind my back at restaurants so they could tell their friends they'd told me off," he recalled. On the golf course at Arrowhead Country Club in Rapid City, other players would spin by in their carts and lob snide remarks. But all it ever amounted to was talk. Wenk and the Park Service listened politely and then continued to execute its master plan.

All the while, the Preservation Fund pressed ahead with its fund-raising campaign. Sale of commemorative coins, not unlike the ones Borglum had conceived for Stone Mountain, helped some, and the Homestake Mining Company and the Gannett Foundation (later renamed the Freedom Forum), chaired by former South Dakotan Al Neuharth, each pledged a million dollars. "We were just as naïve as Borglum had been," Carolyn Mollers said, shaking her head in happy hindsight. "With stars in our eyes we just kept at it, pitching the American Dream."

One of the Preservation Fund's more effective TV ads presented images of toppled statues of Lenin in the Soviet Union, followed by close-ups of Mount Rushmore. The voice-over advised: "Build a monument to tyranny and oppression and one day people will tear it down. But build a monument to freedom and democracy, and people will give anything to keep it standing forever." And give they did. Unlike the 1930s, when the Depression had made it so difficult for Borglum, Boland, Robinson, Norbeck et al. to raise money from private sources, the 1990s were flush, and after eight years of toil, the Preservation Fund was near its $40 million goal. Most gratifying were the contributions of South Dakota residents themselves, their checks helping to drown out the static of dissent. Borglum's daughter Mary Ellis Vhay, and his grandchildren, Robin Borglum Carter and James Borglum, were also conspicuous in their support, both financial and moral. (Lincoln Borglum had died in 1986.) They made it known that they believed in Rushmore's future as well as its past.

Wenk never came close to meeting his 1991 deadline. The last phase of construction was not completed until 1998. While first-time visitors don't know what they missed, returnees and many locals are slow to warm to the new layout. As I walked from my car to the visitors center on July 3, I overtook a couple in their seventies, clutching cameras and frowning. "They've ruined it," I heard them say. The last time they had visited Rushmore had been forty years ago.

The most grievous eyesore, as ever, is parking. The multilevel parking structure is the first thing visitors encounter as they drive up the mountain, and although they can now find a parking space much more easily, the eight-dollar fee is significant, and holders of National Park passes must pay full price like everyone else because the garage is not run by the Park Service. Nor is there anything vaguely rustic about the approach to the memorial. Arriving at Mount Rushmore is like driving up to any shopping mall in America. All the goodies are on the inside; the exterior is generic and bland.

The architecture of the new orientation plaza, restaurant, gift shop, and visitor center is entirely without wood and color. Surfaces are glass or granite, smooth and honest, but their rigidity and unstinting grayness create an effect that is altogether institutional. The broad colonnade of the front entrance and the connecting columns of the Avenue of Flags are doubtless intended as a cathedralesque preamble to the altar of Mount Rushmore, but they also radiate the overbearing authoritarianism of the Vatican's Piazza San Pietro or Berlin's Brandenburg Gate. And while Borglum had managed to find sufficient granite on Mount Rushmore to carve four presidents, the Park Service imported granite from Minnesota to complete its latest additions—an epic outrage in the eyes of the loyal opposition.

The most common complaint of all, though, is that the new construction tends to dwarf the sculpture. Wenk was quick to stress that by tearing down the old concession building, which, to be frank, did monopolize one of the best spots for viewing the mountain, he not only opened up better sight lines, but, from a philosophical standpoint, he rousted the money changers, if not from the temple entirely, then at least from the front pew. In that respect, he made the right call. Yet there is no getting around the fact that the new 40,000-square-foot concession complex, while more politely positioned aft of the main viewing terrace, is broader than the four faces of Mount Rushmore. Borglum intended his mountain carving to be a shining example of the Colossal Age. Now the sculpture must compete with several other colossi, including the concession building, the visitor center, and a two-thousand-seat amphitheater. Mount Rushmore, as set against its $40 million foreground ($60 million with the parking garage included), remains a marvel, but the awe it is capable of inspiring is now more relative than unique.

On the other hand—and to the credit of the National Park Service and its architects—once you have negotiated the parking garage, strolled down the Avenue of Flags, distanced yourself from the gift shop and visitor center, and taken a stand on the Grand View Terrace, the elegance of the overall design becomes breathtakingly self-evident. The effect is like standing on the bow of a ship, looking forward. Without too much difficulty, you can ignore the presence of the dreadnought behind and beneath you, and you are free to embrace Rushmore the way the tired and poor once greeted the Statue of Liberty. Indeed, the experience is not unlike democracy itself. You can savor the moment as a member of a group, or you can shut out the madding crowd and commune with the presidents, just you and the four of them. This is what Borglum had wished for. And at the new

Rushmore, all nostalgia and second-guessing aside, this exquisite wish has yet to be rescinded.

At 10:30, Dan Wenk, Mike Pflaum, and I hiked briskly along the new Presidential Trail, which fits along the base of the talus just below the faces like an orchestra pit at the opera. Only recently have ordinary civilians been able to get so close to the presidents. You can look right up their noses, as Alfred Hitchcock had wanted. Halfway along the boardwalk, just before it begins its descent to Borglum's studio, we stopped at a padlocked gate. Pflaum unlocked it; we passed through and began hiking up the steep slope to the right of Abraham Lincoln. The gate is a sore subject among Park Service personnel, and it even has a nickname that Pflaum would not tell me, although I'd wager it's something very close to "Daschle's Door."

Every year, thousands of rock climbers come from all over the world to challenge the twisted granite of Rushmore National Memorial, although it is illegal to climb anywhere near the faces; the fine for trespassing can be as high as $500. Yet in 1997, a blatant exception was made. In this instance, an exclusive group of climbers was given a deluxe tour; the price of admission was $5,000 apiece. That, anyway, is how the press chose to characterize "A Black Hills Weekend With Tom & Linda Daschle," a fundraising junket hosted by South Dakota's senior U.S. senator and his wife.

On September 13, Daschle, accompanied by Dan Wenk, escorted a small group of political contributors—including lobbyists for the tobacco, aerospace, and telecommunications industries—up the same path we were now following, through another locked gate, past the Hall of Records, and up a metal stairway to the very summit of Mount Rushmore. Daschle had been an ardent and active friend of Rushmore (and Wenk) during the recent development campaign and had been to the top several times before. But that was before the public had learned that President Clinton had been renting out the Lincoln bedroom to Democratic contributors. Suddenly there was egg on Daschle's face and mud on the Shrine of Democracy. Editorials accused him of "Mining Mt. Slushmore."

"The founding fathers must be spinning in their graves," scolded Republican senator John McCain, the most prominent champion of campaign-finance reform. Since his 1997 contretemps, Daschle, needless to say, has been somewhat more discriminating in his itinerary, and Wenk has been more selective about whom he takes through Daschle's Door. I was grateful to have been invited. We wasted no time moving upward into the cover of juniper and ponderosa.

In the spirit of full disclosure, I will say that I had already been up Rushmore twice before in the company of Mike Pflaum, a bearded, affable, and dedicated ranger who, in his late forties, is chronically recovering from one sports injury after another (today a pulled hamstring—softball). Even so, he was able to chug along much faster than Wenk, who does much better in golf cleats on level ground. A year earlier, Pflaum had led me on a scramble to the Indian camp behind the faces and explained to me the security measures the Park Service has put in place in recent years. "Most of the threats we've gotten since the Indian days are from white males," he told me. In October 1987, several members of the environmental group Greenpeace sneaked onto the mountain unmolested and hung a banner that read "We the People Say No to Acid Rain" just below George Washington's chin. After President George Bush announced that he would attend the fiftieth-anniversary celebration in 1991, Rushmore was barraged with more serious threats, Pflaum said. "Even on the day of his visit we were given a report that a convoy of vehicles and a horse trailer full of explosives was headed for Mount Rushmore. Let's face it—we're a readymade stage for anyone who wants to get their message on CNN."

After the 1995 bombing of the Murrah Federal Building in Oklahoma City and the 1996 crash of TWA Flight 800, Rushmore was designated as one of several national landmarks (the list also included the Golden Gate Bridge, Gateway Arch, Independence Hall, the Statue of Liberty, Washington Monument, and Lincoln Memorial) in need of special protection. Almost without having to ask, Rushmore was given a generous $3.6 million to beef up security. From a command center in the administration building, rangers can now monitor critical areas of the memorial via a system of sophisticated cameras. Roving, remote-controlled eyes can inspect the frost on Roosevelt's moustache, read license plates in the parking garage, locate lost kids, or bust bikers trying to sneak joints. Ever since Borglum first carved eyes on the four faces, many visitors to Mount Rushmore have had the uncanny sensation that they're being watched. Now, however, they're being scrutinized by an entirely different presence—Big Brother, one of democracy's necessary safeguards. (After learning of the attacks on the World Trade Center on September 11, 2001, the Park Service closed Rushmore for the rest of the day, and Pflaum says he wasted no time in drafting a request for "even more training, more cameras, more money.")

Yet on this particular day, the bombers had been given the run of the mountain. In the canyon by the Hall of Records, we entered a thicket of mortar tubes, bristling sheaves of ordnance aimed skyward, each tube holding a firework shell. Borglum had shot off fireworks at the 1939 dedication of Theodore Roosevelt, but no one had dared repeat the stunt until Wenk took a chance in 1998 at the grand celebration of the completion of the new facilities. In order not to upstage smaller but more established Independence Day celebrations around the region, he chose July 3 as Rushmore's day. The first year, dense clouds postponed the event until the fifth. Fewer than ten thousand people showed up, but the fireworks—twelve hundred shells in fourteen minutes—did not disappoint. The following year, the show came off without a hitch, and the crowd was twice as large.

In 2000, Wenk had reason to second-guess the tradition he had started. The Black Hills were especially dry, and fire danger was commensurately high. (Later that summer, a woman pulled off the road south of Custer, dropped a match onto pine needles, notified no one, and within days, 80,000 acres of Black Hills National Forest were toast.) Wenk decided to go ahead with the July 3 fireworks anyway, but five minutes after the first rocket was fired, flames were visible in the surrounding timber. Pflaum had three dozen men with water packs stationed throughout the memorial, but still, he admitted, "We had fifteen to eighteen fires, five of them big enough to have names. All told, though, we burned less than two acres." The crowd that day was the largest in Rushmore's history—nearly forty thousand. It was also the best day for Amfac, the park concessionaire, which grossed $113,000 in hot dogs, ice cream, and T-shirts. Several million more people watched the spectacle on television, although not one station (or newspaper) mentioned the fires that took till dawn to extinguish.

In light of this sooty record, Wenk was especially anxious about the 2001 show. Conditions were every bit as dry as the previous year. Zambelli, famous for its fireworks displays above New York Harbor and the Washington Mall, stood ready to fire off thirty-three hundred shells in twenty minutes, twice the spectacle—and three times the sparks—of the year before. This time, though, Wenk had promised his superiors in the Park Service that if the "probability of ignition"—a fire index based on humidity and temperature—was too high at show time, he would call off the evening. As we filed past the bundles of rockets, which had taken sixty helicopter trips to place among the presidents, Wenk figured the chances of timely consummation at fifty-fifty. "It takes a lot of people to put something like this together," he said with a tight grin, "but I'm the only one whose ass is on the line if it doesn't go right." Instead of "ass," he might as well have said his entire career. Meanwhile, the Zambelli crew stood about, relaxed but at the ready, like stevedores who had just unloaded a cargo of exotic fruit and now had a vested interest in not letting it rot.

Leaving the canyon, we climbed the metal stairs that lead to the back of George Washington's head. In a way, standing on top of Mount Rushmore is no different from standing on any other summit: The view is what first commands your attention, not the stone beneath your feet. From my perch atop Washington, I could look west to Harney Peak, south to Mount Coolidge, and east to the Badlands, where cumulus clouds merged with the prairie horizon. To the north, the boomtown architecture of Keystone was evident.

Yet to stand on Rushmore is about much more than elevation. It makes you feel like Jonah approaching the whale: You sense the mass, but soon enough you are absorbed by the sum of its parts. My first impulse, after taking my bearings, was to run my hand across the surface of Washington's granite wig. It is astoundingly smooth, not due to weather, not yet anyway, but rather from the devoted "bumping" of handheld jackhammers. I have sat on curbs much coarser than this. With a little imagination, I could have been touching petrified bone.

Crossing from Washington to Jefferson was easy enough, but to get to Roosevelt and then Lincoln, we had to grab a rope and shinny down a steep, eight-foot crevasse behind Jefferson, and then carefully traverse a five-foot-wide pegmatite dike, bejeweled with rose quartz, between Roosevelt and Lincoln—the only cartilage that connects the latter to his three neighbors. Sheer drops on either side remind one of just how little rock Borglum had left when he finally got Roosevelt squared away. The reward, though, is well worth the scramble, for the crown of Lincoln's head is the best spot from which to admire the other presidents. The spikes of "light" in their eyes are delicate and clever. To examine the frames of Roosevelt's glasses from so close is to be let in on a delicious parlor prank. The joke is not spoiled; it's enhanced.

Not that Rushmore is without blemishes. As good as Borglum was at reading the rock and making adjustments—for instance, when he tilted Jefferson to avoid a fault line—he ultimately had to accept the vagaries of Black Hills geology. Yet streaks of slightly darker or lighter granite are better than benign; if anything, they add character to the "living rock" (and invite the tabloids to speculate on presidential "tears"). What concerns the Park Service are actual cracks. In recent years, engineers have used a technology called photogrammetry to map more than 140 fractures in the twenty or so blocks of granite that make up Mount Rushmore. Most are virtually invisible and of little concern. However, three fractures bear watching: one across Lincoln's nose, one along the shock of hair on Roosevelt's left forehead, and, biggest of all, one that demarcates the right frontal lobe of Washington's skull.

To keep track of these seams, engineers have installed electronic monitors, called "linear variable displacement transfusers," to record the movement of the cracks. Not surprisingly, the cracks widen in winter as cold contracts the rock and shrink according to the heat of summer. The good news is that the annual cycle of the most active fracture (Washington's head) is no more than one-fourth of one-hundredth of an inch—hardly a tectonic shimmy. But even while scientists assure that Rushmore isn't going anywhere soon, they do warn that moisture could seep into cracks, freeze, and widen them further. Over tens of thousands of years, such a trend could cause more serious headaches.

Borglum had forestalled this monumental drift by sealing cracks with a mixture of granite dust, white lead, and linseed oil. Park Service maintenance workers now apply silicon not unlike the stuff used in caulking skylights. Also they have been careful to camouflage the monitors, although from a few feet away the small gray discs fastened to the heads of Washington, Roosevelt, and Lincoln resemble the gadgets that sense brain waves.

Before leaving the summit, I looked down one last time, hoping to discern the patch on Jefferson's lip. But Borglum's men had done their job well; no scar is discernible today. From far away or up close, this will always be my favorite aspect of Mount Rushmore: Jefferson's mouth is sublime, as if shaped by a thumb pressed into fresh clay instead of a beastly jackhammer banged against billion-year-old granite. The slight curve of the lips is every bit as subtle as the dimple Michelangelo gave to *David's* knee.

Back down at the Hall of Records, Wenk and Pflaum posed for photos with the fireworks crew, and for good luck we all signed our names to the biggest shell, a cannonball of powder and psychedelia about the size of a coconut. The men had stashed their tarps and extra gear in the hall, which after sixty years is still a gaping aperture, a mineshaft gone bust. In 1998, to fulfill the dream of the Borglum family, a Park Service crew drilled a rectangular vault in the solid granite floor of the eighty-foot tunnel, which was then lined with titanium. In a ceremony on August 9, more than a hundred people—including four generations of Borglums—gathered to witness the interment of a teakwood box. Inside the box were placed sixteen porcelain panels on which had been etched the Constitution, the Declaration of Independence, the Bill of Rights, and the Gettysburg Address; short profiles of the four Rushmore presidents and Borglum himself; an account of how Rushmore came to be; and, finally, a thumbnail history of the United States, entitled "The Meaning of Mount Rushmore." A twelve-hundred pound capstone was lowered over the box, sealing the tablets away for safekeeping.

By noon, we were off the mountain, and I left Wenk and Pflaum to deal with the remainder of their hectic day. The temperature had climbed above eighty, and the sun beat on the glass and granite of Rushmore's new buildings, turning the pavement of the Grand View Terrace and the Avenue of Flags into vast cookie sheets. It was a good day to bake, as evidenced by the throngs that continued to pour like so much batter from the parking garage. By early afternoon, the amphitheater and the prime spots along the walls and walkways were fully occupied by patient patriots. Some had brought ice chests, paperbacks, crosswords, and headphones, although most seemed content just to sit and wait and burn.

On a trip to the restroom just inside the front entrance, I took particular notice of an overweight man in a lawn chair, wearing a tank top on

which was rubricated "Walk for Jesus 2000." He and his wife were playing cards with another couple, using their ice chest for tricks and dis-
cards. The first time I spied my erstwhile walker, he was inhaling a hot
dog, and every time I passed by his little camp after that, he was clutching cards in one paw and a different gustatory delight in the other: a leaning tower of ice cream, a jug of Coca-Cola, a slab of processed cheese. In
the course of waiting for the fireworks, his skin turned—rather fittingly, I
thought—from bologna pink to a sort of ketchupy red.

The rest of the day passed easily enough. At one o'clock, the Lakota
band Brulé—the same group that had been invited to play for *Regis and
Kathie Lee*—performed a set of New Agey native tunes. At five sharp,
four F-16 fighter jets from the South Dakota Air National Guard thun-
dered by, followed by more music, this time from the Circle B Cowboys, who played authentic songs from the Old West and Civil War.

I spent part of the afternoon sitting on the balustrade outside the gift
shop. Seeking shade just below me were a couple and their young son,
perhaps five years old. Dad had bought the boy two small flags—one of
their home state of Indiana, the other the Stars and Stripes—and the
child stood twiddling them as his father read aloud from *The U.S. Presidents Sticker Book*, a slim volume of presidential profiles with a centerfold
of stickers bearing their portraits. In this heat, with the fireworks still
hours off, none of us was in a hurry to move, not even the kid, who
stood mercifully still, except for the occasional wave of his flags, while
his dad finished the entire book. Feeling a bit droopy myself, I let the
parade of chief executives meander across my brain like sheep.

"George Washington had two adopted daughters—but that's not
why he's one of the most famous fathers in history," the litany began.
We learned that Andrew Jackson "liked to throw big parties"; at one of
them, "a wheel of cheese weighing 1,400 pounds was eaten in two
hours." Each president was awarded a "Fun Fact." Jefferson's was that
he kept a pet mockingbird in the White House. Lincoln, whom the
book celebrates as "the greatest president the United States has ever

had," is further singled out as the first president to wear a beard in the White House. For his part, Teddy Roosevelt is credited with building up his wimpy body, capturing a Spanish fort, and encouraging the Panama Canal. Other presidents don't come off nearly as well, however. Ulysses S. Grant "stole government money." Nixon got "caught in a scandal." The book had apparently gone to press before Bill Clinton could test the author's talents as a euphemist.

The book is especially astute about at least one thing: Abraham Lincoln is the greatest president America has ever had. In Rushmore's Buffalo Dining Room, where I went next, there is a voting booth in which visitors can cast ballots for their favorite president. Every year, Lincoln wins the contest hands down, earning nearly twice as many votes as the nearest challenger, George Washington. More newsworthy, though, is the Fun Fact that Ronald Reagan is hot on Washington's heels, only three thousand votes behind. No wonder the crusade to have Reagan added to Rushmore seems never to die.

The idea first caught fire in 1988, when the editor of the conservative *American Spectator* presented President Reagan with a picture of Rushmore, which he had doctored to include Reagan's face. After Reagan left office, a group of his devotees formed the Reagan Legacy Project with the aim of getting Reagan's name and/or image added to as many things as possible. As a result of their lobbying, Washington's National Airport is now Reagan National, and a $4 billion aircraft carrier and the second-biggest government building in the country (after the Pentagon) bear his moniker. So far, the National Park Service and those who like Rushmore just the way it is have succeeded in repelling the "Ron on the Rock" forces, as they are now called, thanks to assistance from South Dakota's two (Democratic) senators and timely memos from engineers, whose recent evaluation of the mountain has determined that the granite to Washington's right or Lincoln's left is too unstable to accommodate a fifth face.

Nevertheless, every year or so Reagan's name crops up again. Occasionally someone even suggests making over one of the existing faces—Roosevelt is the name mentioned most frequently—to look like the Gipper. "Would you repaint the *Mona Lisa*?" responds Jim Popovich, Rushmore's chief of interpretation, trying his best to be diplomatic. Yet returns at the Rushmore voting booth would suggest some amount of sympathy for such a surgery. After all, Reagan is already more popular than two of the presidents on the mountain.

Toward the end of the afternoon, I strolled out to the upper deck of the parking garage in order to survey the line of traffic coming up the hill from Keystone. Highway 16A was bumper to bumper, with a steady stream of pedestrians making better time along the shoulder. Several yards away from me, an Indian man in shorts and a Chevy cap stood against the railing, doing the same thing I was. I sidled over and struck up a conversation. He, his family, and a group of friends had convoyed five hours from Bismarck, North Dakota, but when he pulled the lead car into the Rushmore entrance, his wife, who was following behind, kept going and disappeared down the hill in the direction of Keystone. To get back up would take hours. My companion had already waited forty-five minutes. "She's starting to piss me off," he said without enthusiasm.

He told me he was half Dakota Sioux, half Assiniboine. I asked him why, as an Indian, he had brought his family to Mount Rushmore. He allowed that the four presidents were "ignorant white people," but said that the kids had begged to see the fireworks. On the subject of ignorant white men, he had a lot more to impart: "There are a lot of them out there. Some of them won't even serve you on Christmas day."

"Oh?" I prodded.

"That's right, my family and I were refused food at a truck stop in Bismarck on Christmas day. No service. I got even, though. I sued the bastards . . . got $236,000, and opened my own restaurant. One of those guys [who refused to serve us] came in once, and I recognized him. He ordered a couple of tacos and fries. I threw them in his face and said get out of *my* place, you bastard."

I waited around a few more minutes as he continued to study the creeping traffic, then I bid him goodbye and turned back toward Rushmore. By nine o'clock, as darkness fell, I was dehydrated and seated with my back to a rock outcropping, off to the side of the visitor center. I wondered how Wenk's "probability of ignition" index was shaping up. The air still seemed hot and dry to me. But then at 9:20, right on schedule, the first rocket glared and the public-address system in the amphitheater broke into the *Star Wars* theme.

The wait had been worth it. For the next twenty minutes, thirty thousand spectators and another ten million television viewers were dazzled and transfixed by the greatest display of fireworks any (or at least the vast majority) of us had ever seen. Colors burst, splashed, sparkled, and streamed ecstatically, haloing the presidents, who seemed to beam with nationalistic pleasure. When the sound system moved on to the theme from *The Bridge on the River Kwai*, the rockets whistled along. When it was time for Louis Armstrong's "What a Wonderful World," the heavens fairly bloomed. Not until the granite against which I was leaning seemed actually to shudder did I allow myself a fleeting thought of Charlotte Black Elk's cosmic can of Raid.

Having been briefed on last year's sideshow, I kept an eye peeled for sparks falling on timber. I watched as one or two licks of light settled on the wooded slope north of the faces, but they seemed to die out. More conspicuous was the shooting star that landed smack in the middle of the junipers clinging to the talus slope just below the sculpture. Right as the fireworks came to a crescendo, one of these trees appeared to burst into flames, and smoke began to funnel up Teddy Roosevelt's nose. Just then, and I'm sure quite by coincidence, the canned soundtrack ended and a live rock-and-roll band from Ellsworth Air Force Base broke into a rousing version of "Great Balls of Fire."

★

That night I left my window open at the Presidents View. At dawn on the Fourth of July, I awoke to the metronome of helicopters—Zambelli's launchers being lifted from Mount Rushmore. From the parking lot I could see a lone chopper hovering over the heads of the presidents. In a few seconds, it ascended, a bundle in tow, and disappeared beyond my line of sight. The sky, thankfully, was free of smoke. I learned later that the fire beneath the faces had burned mostly pine needles and that six similar fires on the mountain had consumed less than an acre all told. Wenk's daring call had not jeopardized his career after all; not long after, he was promoted to Denver and awarded the prestigious Ben Black Elk Award, given each year to the individual who has made the greatest contribution to South Dakota tourism.

I chose not to return to Rushmore. Instead I spent the Fourth of July wandering half-randomly through the Black Hills, eventually winding up at Crazy Horse. I paid my eight dollars, drove up the Avenue of the Chiefs, and mingled with the other Independence Day tourists. In a crowd of a thousand or so, I was able to spot only three or four Indians. I had been to Crazy Horse at least a half-dozen times before, and I had even been up on the mountain to stare the chief full in the face. As art, I have concluded, Crazy Horse is a far cry from Mount Rushmore. If anything, its closest cousin is the Statue of Liberty—big and symbolic but lacking any grace of form, and both have those lifeless eyes that Borglum would not abide in his own work.

Progress—that's what I decided that Crazy Horse was ultimately all about. For all the back story about Indian culture and heritage—Henry Standing Bear's letter, Donovin Sprague's university—what really seemed to catch the imagination of my fellow visitors is the inexorable grunt of progress. There is something deeply satisfying about watching another man dig a hole. And that is what the Ziolkowski family is essentially doing: They are not so much *erecting* a monument as they are digging a hole in the sky in which to bury Crazy Horse. When and if the Ziolkowskis ever finish their gargantuan excavation, that's when we'll know that Crazy Horse is actually dead. And remembering what General Sheridan had said about the only good Indians being the dead ones, then the deader Crazy Horse gets, the more non–Native America will love him. Meanwhile, Ruth Ziolkowski and her children are already mining a mother lode of tourists, the precious metal of the new Black Hills. And that thump we hear whenever dynamite gouges another layer of flesh from the mountainside is not the groan of Crazy Horse, who, after all, was stoical when stabbed, but rather the sound of Doane Robinson's next shoe dropping.

Wrung out at last, I withdrew from the Black Hills. After Crazy Horse, I backtracked toward Rapid City, passing more of my favorite tourist attractions. First came Cosmos Mystery Area ("See It. Feel It. It's Wacky."), a fun house where for six dollars you can watch a Dr. Pepper can roll uphill. Several miles farther on is Reptile Gardens, which is now a world-class zoo, although beneath its Animal Planet sophistication, it still features Death Row—an exhibit of "the 10 Most Deadly Snakes in the World"—and, for a quarter, lets you ask questions of a chicken. ("Do I need to go on a diet?" "Will Hillary dump the turkey?")

Reptile Gardens and so many other Black Hills tourist businesses—Crazy Horse, Rushmore Cave, Bear Country USA, Sitting Bull Crystal Caverns, and Wall Drug—are now in the hands of the next (and, in some cases, third) generation, whose DNA tells them that tourism is a family affair. Because the clans all grew up together, they stick up for one another, boost one another's businesses. Over the last half-century, they have achieved critical mass—the Black Hills as "destination"—which allows them to live quite comfortably, and respectably, for that matter. New England has its Mayflower descendants, New York its Knickerbockers. In the Black Hills, the Brockelsby, Ziolkowski, Pullen,

Casey, Duhamel, and Husted clans are aristocracy. And so is James Borglum, Gutzon's grandson, who dwells almost reclusively on the family ranch in Hermosa.

Sprouting up around these venerable fixtures is a weed bed of arrivistes, whose crass charms I have absorbed on numerous drives between Rushmore and Rapid City. For irony, I am especially partial to the Fort Hays Dances with Wolves Film Set, featuring a Chuckwagon Supper, 99¢ Cowboy Pancakes, and a cluster of souvenir shops ringing a faux-faded building that is recognizable for about two seconds in the Costner movie. Then, too, I cannot help but be drawn to two groups of presidential statues that have recently joined the catalogue of Black Hills curiosities. One group has taken a stand on prominent street corners in Rapid City; the other group I found encamped in the parking lot of a ski area outside of Lead. From a certain perspective, they are the ultimate compliment to Gutzon Borglum. From another, they are the ultimate insult.

In the early 1990s, not long after the collapse of the Soviet Union, Rapid City furniture manufacturer Don Perdue took a trip to Russia, where he says he saw statues of Lenin lying in alleyways. How delicious it would be, Perdue thought, if these obsolete Soviet monuments could be melted down and made into bronzes of American presidents. The Soviet scheme soon proved impractical, but Perdue was stuck on his idea of presidential bronzes. He formed a nonprofit foundation called the City of Presidents and commissioned four South Dakota sculptors to start at either end of the presidential parade and work toward the middle. First out of the foundry were George Washington, John Adams, Ronald Reagan (Perdue's hero), and George Bush. (Perdue detests Bill Clinton, so he ruled against sitting presidents.)

In 2000, life-size bronze likenesses of these four were installed in downtown Rapid City, all within a block of one another. Washington stands, sword at his side, like a captured chess piece; Adams is a pudgy panhandler in a frock coat; Reagan poses bucolically in his *Death Valley*

Days duds; and Bush guards a globe, an ungainly retirement gift he's lugging home from the office. Next up: Jefferson, John Quincy Adams, Gerald Ford, and Jimmy Carter, and in ten more years, if all goes according to Perdue's plan, every one of the chief executives, even Bill Clinton, will grace the City of Presidents—"From the Mountain to Main Street." Inevitably, Perdue predicts that a new wave of visitors will flock to his Parthenon on the prairie, much the way Doane Robinson had originally envisioned they would be drawn to Mount Rushmore.

Borglum had his share of opponents when he started in on Mount Rushmore, but nothing like the critics who sprang to the ramparts to repel the affront of the City of Presidents. Their brief went something like this: 1) The project is undemocratic, rammed down the public's throat by Perdue without undergoing proper review; 2) postponing Clinton was a deliberate partisan insult; 3) the art does not reflect the diversity (landscape, Indians, local heroes) of the region; and 4) it's just plain lousy art that will turn Rapid City into the laughing stock of the universe. As the debate heated up, the complainers began referring to Perdue and his allies as "fascists"; those in favor of Perdue's presidents called the naysayers "Nazis"—each side rejecting the other's definition of what is art, what is good art, and what is good for the community. Ultimately, opponents filed a lawsuit to block the project, only to have a local judge rule against them.

On the day I paid my final visit to Perdue's presidents, I noticed that someone had spat in George Bush's face. And as I studied the sculptures, I could not help recalling the statement Borglum had made in the Mount Rushmore annual report of 1932: "To fall into the class of real art, the completed figure must stir the beholder, not because it may be a striking likeness. . . . It should characterize him in his spiritual aspect and so dramatize it that no intelligent beholder can escape its power. Unless it does this and more, it is a failure as a work of inspirational portraiture." For George Bush and the other City of Presidents pieces, I don't think Borglum could have worked up a gob of spit if he tried.

By contrast, and much to my surprise, the set of colossal presidential busts that I found mustered in the parking lot of the Deer Mountain ski area disarmed me with their brashness. They, too, are the product of private enterprise, the creation of Texas sculptor David Adickes. In the early 1990s, Adickes had visited Mount Rushmore and was frustrated at not being able to see the faces up close. His response was to sculpt 20-foot-tall busts of all forty-three presidents. But when he initially endeavored to display them near Williamsburg, Virginia, he was shunned out of town. Critics called his oversized oeuvre "the tackiest project to exploit and pollute America's heritage" since the Disney movie *Pocahontas*.

One town's kitsch is another town's culture, and the town of Lead, wincing after the announced closing of the Homestake gold mine, has allowed Adickes to develop a twenty-acre Presidents Park, where the busts will be arranged in shady grottoes and accompanied by short biographies. On my visit, though, the presidents loitered in the afternoon sun like Buddhas on a back lot. In the off-season, Deer Mountain is the home of Andy's Trail Rides, and as I drove up, a string of Andy's horses loafed in the shade of LBJ, Ike, and FDR, switching flies off themselves and the presidents. Perhaps it was the unpretentious setting, or perhaps it was because the monuments seemed so beatifically off duty, but I had a great deal of fun walking among them.

They wore little stick-on nametags, like conventioneers; only "Teddy" was identified by his first name. Some of the faces are better rendered than others. For instance, Calvin Coolidge, whom I thought I knew so well, was a stranger to me here. Bill Clinton is a J. C. Penney mannequin. But despite the unevenness of execution, every one of the busts offers at least a flicker of vitality. Even the presidents we don't remember (Franklin Pierce, Chester Arthur) seem outwardly tickled to be included, and of course to be so big. Again, the key is the eyes. David Adickes had borrowed Borglum's (and Daniel Chester French's) trick, and so forty-two heads (George W. Bush not yet present) looked out at me as fixedly as I might look at myself in the mirror. Was I mistaken, or was Martin Van Buren actually attempting a smile, his concrete muttonchops streaming like the boughs of ponderosa in the forest behind him? Borglum might never forgive me, but I had made a few friends at Deer Mountain.

I left the Black Hills the way I had entered a year earlier, passing quickly through Sturgis, downright laconic absent its horde of Harleys, and turned north in the direction of Slim Buttes. By nine o'clock, I was once again bedded down among the Castles. To the south, in the direction of the Black Hills, I could make out thunder and twinges of lightning. In the night it rained at first, but by 3:00 A.M. the moon was out, a day past full.

After spending so much time knocking about the monuments of the West and the world, I regretted that I had never measured the Slim Buttes monument, so at dawn I again parked beside it, took out my tape measure, and noted its dimensions. In truth, though, I had come to pay my respects one more time to the Siege Ravine, in which American Horse and his followers had been cornered and killed. Trespassing once more, I climbed through the fence and strode across the rolling uplands toward the spot I now knew by heart. Wet grass darkened my jeans. Redwing blackbirds made light of me, darting from one ripening soapberry to the next. A whitetail buck in new velvet bounded ahead, disappearing into the very ravine I was seeking. Still in the mood for measurements, I counted the number of strides it took to circle the entire ravine—350. How horribly impossible it must have been for the twenty or so Lakota attempting to hide in its limited recesses. How much like fish in a barrel they must have seemed to several hundred famished soldiers.

At the head of the ravine stands a box elder. It is too young to have been here in American Horse's day, but even so it marks the spot from which his Lakota might have escaped if they'd been only a few minutes farther ahead of the Army. I dug in my pockets for some sort of offering, finally took out my wallet, and came upon my most recent admission ticket to Crazy Horse Memorial. It was bright orange, like Halloween candy, and bore the words "Crazy Horse $8.00." I felt a bit silly, but just the same, I pushed the stub into a knot in the box elder.

The Slim Buttes monument is a white concrete obelisk, six feet, six inches tall, twelve inches at its widest, and it rests on an eighteen-inch base. Its manifest purpose is to commemorate a battle in which three white men perished, with only minor mention of Indian victims. The actual design of the obelisk, I have come to understand, originated with the Egyptians a very long time ago.

ACKNOWLEDGMENTS
AND BIBLIOGRAPHIC NOTES

First and above all, I would like to express my respect and gratitude to the staff of Mount Rushmore National Memorial, whose dedication, generosity, wisdom, and warmth are the lifeblood of the Rushmore I came to know during numerous visits over nearly three years of research. Some of them have since moved on, but all have left their mark on this manuscript. Best wishes to Dan Wenk, Mike Pflaum, Jim Popovich, Bruce Van Vort, and Judy Olson. And an extra-special thanks to Mount Rushmore curator Bruce Weisman for guiding me through the memorial's extraordinary museum and archives, which he manages so meticulously.

An even richer trove of information on Mount Rushmore and Gutzon Borglum is the Gutzon Borglum Papers in the Manuscript Division, Library of Congress, Washington, D.C. Unless otherwise noted below, the correspondence, journals, memoranda, clippings, and records that inform my narrative are drawn from the Borglum Papers, an archive of more than 70,000 items. This includes the incomplete draft of Borglum's never-published memoir, *The One Man War*.

Additionally, I am indebted to the following institutions: the Rapid City Public Library; the Special Collections Department of the Woodruff Library, Emory University; the Schlesinger Library, Radcliffe Institute, Harvard University; and the South Dakota State Historical Society Archives.

I would also like to acknowledge the many authors who have scaled Mount Rushmore before me. They have provided me with a point of departure, even though the path I chose for *Great White Fathers* is mine alone. My distinguished predecessors include Lincoln Borglum, *My Father's Mountain: Mt. Rushmore National Memorial and How It Was Carved* (1965); Robin Borglum Carter, *Gutzon Borglum: His Life and Work* (1998); Robert J. Casey and Mary Borglum, *Give the Man Room: The Story of Gutzon Borglum* (1952); Robert J. Dean, *Living Granite: The Story of Borglum and the Mount Rushmore Memorial* (1949); Gilbert C. Fite, *Mount Rushmore* (1952); Rosa Portell, ed., *Out of Rushmore's Shadow: The Artistic Development of Gutzon Borglum (1867–1941)* (1999); Willadene Price, *Gutzon Borglum: Artist and Patriot* (1961); Judith St. George, *The Mount Rushmore Story* (1985); San Francisco Art Institute, *Rushmore—Another Look: Surveying the American Icon* (1976); Howard Shaff and Audrey Karl Shaff, *Six Wars at a Time: The Life and Times of Gutzon Borglum, Sculptor of Mount Rushmore* (1985); Rex Alan Smith, *The Carving of Mount Rushmore* (1985); and June Culp Zeitner and Lincoln Borglum, *Unfinished Dream: Mount Rushmore* (1976). Another worthy book, Jesse Larner, *Mount Rushmore: An Icon Reconsidered* (2002), appeared after I had already completed my own manuscript.

Pertinent articles about Borglum and Rushmore include Edward F. Bigelow, "Beauty in the Life of a Portrayer of Beauty," *The Guide to Nature* 4:5 (September 1911), 164–175; Albert Boime, "Patriarchy Fixed in Stone: Gutzon Borglum's Mount Rushmore," *American Art* 5:1–2 (Winter/Spring 1991), 142–167; William Bulow, "My Days with Gutzon Borglum," *Saturday Evening Post* 219 (11 January 1947), 24–25, 106; Charles D'Emery, "Carving the Largest Monument in the World," *The Mentor* 16:1 (February 1928), 42–48; James C. Derieux, "A Sculptor Who Rode to Fame on Horseback," *American Magazine* 92:1 (January 1924), 12–14, 66–72; E. M. Halliday, "Carving the American Colossus," *American Heritage* 28:4 (June 1977), 180–187; Rupert Hughes, "The Sculpture of Gutzon Borglum," *Appleton's Magazine* 8:6 (December 1906), 709–717; Donald Dale Jackson, "Gutzon Borglum's odd and awesome portraits in granite," *Smithsonian* 23:5 (August 1992), 64–75; George Marvin, "Gutzon Borglum: A Mechanic, Horseman, Politician, and Apostle of American Art," *World's Work* 33:2 (June 1914), 198–200; Leila Mechlin, "Gutzon Borglum, Painter and Sculptor," *International Studio* 28:110 (April 1906), 35–43; "The 'Moment of Intensity' in Gutzon Borglum's Sculpture," *Current Opinion* 56:5 (May 1914), 379–380; David Perlman, "Four for the Ages," *New York Times Magazine* (25 August 1940), 8–9, 18; and Jim Pomeroy, "The Versatile Talent of Gutzon Borglum," *Current Literature* 40:5 (May 1906), 499–502. Also see the Rushmore chapter in William Williamson, *William Williamson: Student, Homesteader, Teacher, Lawyer, Judge, Congressman and Trusted Friend* (1964), and *The Black Hills Engineer* 18:4 (November 1930), an entire issue devoted to Mount Rushmore.

Borglum wrote dozens of articles in his day. Some of the most provocative are "Aesthetic Activities in America: An Answer to His Critics," *The Craftsman* 15:3 (December 1908), 301–307; "Art That Is Real and American," *World's Work* 33:2 (June 1914), 200–217; "The Betrayal of the People by a False Democracy," *The Craftsman* 22:1 (April 1912), 3–9; "Individuality, Sincerity and Reverence in American Art," *The Craftsman* 15:1 (October 1908), 3–6; "The New Deal," *North American Review* 235:4 (April 1933), 350–353; and "The World as I Want It," *Forum and Century* 93:2 (February 1935), 112–113.

Researching and writing *Great White Fathers* would not have been possible—nor would I have had much fun—without the patience, professionalism, and friendship of Bill Harlan, Dale Lamphere, Jane Murphy, Tom Griffith, Mark Zwonitzer, Laura McKellar, Rosa Portell, and Patrick Walsh. My editors at PublicAffairs, Peter Osnos, Geoff Shandler, and especially Kate Darnton, offered sterling guidance and encouragement, and in giving me their best, they brought out the best in me.

And finally, I would like to thank Robin Borglum Carter, daughter of Lincoln Borglum, granddaughter of Gutzon Borglum. She kindly shared her own voluminous archive of family correspondence, clippings, mementos, and photographs. She served as a thoughtful guide as I slogged through the thicket of research and rumors, always aiming me toward reasoned truth and away from shallow assumptions. She read my manuscript with a stern but respectful eye. Admittedly, it is hard to have one's family history told by a stranger, but Robin, perhaps more than anyone, appreciates that Mount Rushmore and Gutzon Borglum now belong to history, and to the future. In this respect, she is a chip off the old block.

Chapter 1: American Horse

The best single source on the fighting at Slim Buttes is Jerome A. Greene, *Slim Buttes, 1876: An Episode of the Great Sioux War* (1982). Three eyewitnesses recorded vivid details of the Big Horn and Yellowstone Expedition, the Siege of the Ravine, and the Starvation March: John G. Bourke, *On the Border with Crook* (1891, reprint 1971); Captain Charles King, *Campaigning with Crook* (1880, reprint 1964); and John F. Finerty, *War-Path and Bivouac, or The Conquest of the Sioux* (1890, reprint 1994). My trips to Slim Buttes were aided by Paul L. Hedren, *Traveler's Guide to the Great Sioux War: The Battlefields, Forts, and Related Sites of America's Greatest Indian War* (1996). Photographs of the Starvation March are reproduced in Wesley R. Hurt and William E. Lass, *Frontier Photographer: Stanley J. Morrow's Dakota Years* (1956). Also of interest is Julia B. McGillycuddy, *McGillycuddy, Agent* (1941, reprinted as *Blood on the Moon: Valentine McGillycuddy and the Sioux*, 1990).

The most concise history of the Sturgis Rally and Races is Bill Harlan, "Unplanned party," *Rapid City Journal* (6 August 2000). For the demographics of the rally, see Jeffery B. Zeiger, "1995 Sturgis Rally & Races Attendee Survey Results," Center for Business and Tourism, Black Hills State University, 15 September 1995. Thanks to Bill Honerkamp, president of Black Hills, Badlands, and Lakes Association, for helping me to frame the economic and cultural impact of Sturgis.

I got the lay of the land from Sven G. Froiland, *Natural History of the Black Hills and Badlands* (1990); Edward Raventon, *Island in the Plains: A Black Hills Natural History* (1994); and Joseph P. Connolly, "The Geology of Mount Rushmore and Vicinity," *Black Hills Engineer* 18:4 (November 1930), 355–366. Far and away the best guidebook to the state is T. D. Griffith, *South Dakota* (2d ed., 1998). Also relevant is the Federal Writers' Project, *A South Dakota Guide* (1938).

Chapter 2: The Thieves Road

Every inch, seemingly every twitch, of George Armstrong Custer's controversial life has been examined, and the 1874 Black Hills expedition is no exception. The most succinct source is Donald Jackson's *Custer's Gold: The United States Cavalry Expedition of 1874* (1966). Newspaper accounts of the trip, as well as the reports of Custer and several of his officers and companions, appear in George Armstrong Custer, "Opening the Black Hills: Custer's Report," *South Dakota Historical Collections* 7 (1914), 583–594; and Herbert Krause and Gary D. Olson, *Prelude to Glory: A Newspaper Accounting of Custer's 1874 Expedition to the Black Hills* (1974). Also indispensable is the scholarship of Watson Parker, particularly *Gold in the Black Hills* (1966) and "The Majors and the Miners: The Role of the U.S. Army in the Black Hills Gold Rush," *Journal of the West* 11:1 (January 1972), 99–113. Other useful sources include: Donald Progulske, *Yellow Ore, Yellow Hair, Yellow Pine* (1974); Progulske with Frank J. Shideler, *Following Custer* (1982); Lawrence A. Frost, ed., *With Custer in '74: James Calhoun's Diary of the Black Hills Expedition* (1979); Cleophas C. O'Harra, "Custer's Black Hills Expedition of 1874," *Black Hills Engineer* 17:4 (November 1929), 220–286; O'Harra, "The Discovery of Gold in the Black Hills," *Black Hills Engineer* 17:4 (November 1929), 286–299; George Bird Grinnell, *Two Great Scouts and Their Pawnee Battalion: The Experiences of Frank J. North and Luther H. North, Pioneers in the Great West, 1856–1882* (1928); John F. Reiger, ed., *The Passing of the Great West: Selected Papers of George Bird Grinnell* (1972); and Richard Slotkin, "'... & Then the Mare Will Go!': An 1875 Black Hills Scheme by Custer, Holladay, and Buford," *Journal of the West* 15:3 (July 1976), 60–77. Of the numerous biographical assessments of Custer, I most cherish Evan S. Connell, *Son of the Morning Star* (1984) and Frederic F. Van de Water, *Glory-Hunter: A Life of General Custer* (1934). And for those who crave sweets, I call attention to Captain Ralph Bonehill's novel for young readers, *With Custer in the Black Hills; or A Young Scout among the Indians* (1902).

Richard Irving Dodge's trip to the Black Hills the year after Custer's is chronicled in Dodge, *The Black Hills: A Minute Description of the Routes, Scenery, Soil, Climate, Timber, Gold, Geology, Zoology, etc.* (1876), and Wayne R. Kime, ed., *The Black Hills Journals of Colonel Richard Irving Dodge* (1996). The arrival of the Sioux in the Dakotas is estimated by any number of white authorities, including Waldo R. Wedel, *Prehistoric Man on the Great Plains* (1961); Larry J. Zimmerman, *Peoples of Prehistoric South Dakota* (1985); and George E. Hyde, *Red Cloud's Folk: A History of the Oglala Sioux Indians* (1937, reprint 1975). Lakota star theology charts a different chronology in Ronald Goodman, ed., *Lakota Star Knowledge: Studies in Lakota Star Theology* (1992). The wisdom of Black Elk is passed along via John Neihardt, *Black Elk Speaks: Being the Life Story of a Holy Man of the Oglala Sioux* (1932, reprint 1998). Also valuable is James R. Walker, *Lakota Belief and Ritual* (1980).

Lewis and Clark report rumors of strange doings in the "Black Mountains" via Gary E. Moulton, ed., *The Journals of the Lewis and Clark Expedition*, vol. 3 (1987). Edwin Deming hears the moans of a "Great White Giant" in *Five Indian Tribes of the Upper Missouri: Sioux, Arickaras, Assiniboines, Crees, Crows* (1961).

There are several noteworthy histories of the Black Hills and the Dakotas. I value Roderick Peattie, ed., *The Black Hills* (1952); Robert J. Casey, *The Black Hills and Their Incredible Characters* (1949); Herbert S. Schell, *History of South Dakota* (3d ed., revised 1975); Bruce Nelson, *Land of the Dacotahs* (1946); Howard Roberts Lamar, *Dakota Territory, 1861–1889* (1956); Harold E. Briggs, *Frontiers of the Northwest: A History of the Upper Missouri Valley* (1940); and Weston Arthur Goodspeed, ed., *The Province and the States: A History of the Province of Louisiana under France and Spain, and of the Territories and States of the United States Formed Therefrom*, vol. 6 (1904).

The library of books and articles on the Black Hills gold rush and the early development of that region is vast and rich. I am again beholden to the writings of Parker: *Gold in the Black Hills* (1966) and *Deadwood: The Golden Years* (1981). The canon of Black Hills literature begins with Annie Tallent, *The Black Hills, or the Last Hunting Grounds of the Dakotahs* (1899, reprint 1974); John S. McClintock, *Pioneer Days in the Black Hills: Accurate History and Facts Related by One of the Early Day Pioneers* (1939, reprint 2000); Richard B. Hughes, *Pioneer Years in the Black Hills* (1957, reprint 1999); Estelline Bennett, *Old Deadwood Days* (1928, reprint 1982); and Agnes Wright Spring, *The Cheyenne and Black Hills Stage and Express Routes* (1948). Other sources I found compelling include: Briggs, "The Black Hills Gold Rush," *North Dakota Historical Quarterly* 5:2 (January 1931), 71–99; Briggs, "The Great Dakota Boom, 1879 to 1886," *North Dakota Historical Quarterly* 4:2 (January 1930), 78–108; John D. McDermott, ed., *Gold Rush: The Black Hills Story* (2001); Joe E. Milner, *Cali-*

fornia Joe, Noted Scout and Indian Fighter (1935); Jerry Bryan, *An Illinois Gold Hunter in the Black Hills* (1960); H. N. Maguire, *The Black Hills and American Wonderland* (1877); Herman Palais, "A Study of the Trails to the Black Hills Gold Fields," *South Dakota Historical Collections* 25 (1951), 215–262; O. W. Coursey, *Beautiful Black Hills: A Comprehensive Treatise on the Black Hills of South Dakota, non-technical, for Popular Reading* (1926); and Paul Fatout, *Ambrose Bierce and the Black Hills* (1956).

My survey of early guide books, promotional literature, and firsthand accounts of early visits by whites to the Black Hills led me to "The Black Hills—Their Value, Regardless of Gold," *Potter's American Magazine* 5 (August 1875), 616–620; Seth Bullock, "An Account of Deadwood and the Northern Black Hills in 1876," *South Dakota Historical Collection* 31 (1962), 287–364; Leander P. Richardson, "A Trip to the Black Hills," *Scribner's Monthly* 13:6 (April 1877), 748–756; Coleman E. Bishop, "The Black Hills of Dakota," *The Chautauquan* 7:9 (June 1887), 538–541; Edwin A. Curley, *Guide to the Black Hills, Comprising the Travels of the Author and his Special Artist* (1877); Parker, "Booming the Black Hills," *South Dakota History* 11:1 (Winter 1980), 35–52; Chicago and North Western Railway, *The Black Hills, South Dakota: The Richest Hundred Miles Square in the World* (1912); and William H. Russell, "Promoters and Promotion Literature of Dakota Territory," *South Dakota Historical Collections* 26 (1952), 434–455.

On western mining in general and Black Hills mining specifically, I have consulted Joseph H. Cash, "A History of Lead, South Dakota, 1876–1900," *South Dakota Historical Collections* 34 (1968), 33–141; Cash, *Working the Homestake* (1973); C. B. Glasscock, *The Big Bonanza* (1961); William S. Greever, *The Bonanza West: The Story of Western Mining Rushes, 1848–1900* (1963); *The Black Hills Engineer* 14:3 (May 1926), an entire issue devoted to Homestake; and Linn Carr, *History of the Homestake Gold Mine* (1994).

The history of the Sioux Nation and white America's impact on it could fill its own library. Among the many texts I studied are Ralph K. Andrist, *The Long Death: The Last Days of the Plains Indians* (1964); James C. Olson, *Red Cloud and the Sioux Problem* (1965); George E. Hyde, *Red Cloud's Folks: A History of the Oglala Sioux Indians* (1937); Hyde, *A Sioux Chronicle* (1956); Robert M. Utley, *The Last Days of the Sioux Nation* (1963); Doane Robinson, *A History of the Dakota or Sioux Indians* (1904, reprint 1956); William K. Powers, *Oglala Religion* (1975); Francis Paul Prucha, *The Great Father: The United States Government and the American Indians*, vols. 1 and 2 (1984, combined edition 1995); and Edward Lazarus, *Black Hills White Justice: The Sioux Nation versus the United States, 1775 to the Present* (1991).

The life of Crazy Horse is pieced together from Stephen M. Ambrose, *Crazy Horse and Custer: The Parallel Lives of Two American Warriors* (1975); Mari Sandoz, *Crazy Horse: The Strange Man of the Oglalas* (1942); Larry McMurtry, *Crazy Horse*

(1999); Richard G. Hardorff, ed., *The Death of Crazy Horse: A Tragic Episode in Lakota History* (1998); and Tom Buecker, "Crazy Horse: The Search for the Elusive (and Improbable) Photo of [the] Famous Oglala Chief," *Greasy Grass Magazine* 14 (May 1998), 26–35. The best account of Sitting Bull's life is Utley, *The Lance and the Shield: The Life and Times of Sitting Bull* (1993).

Leland D. Case's observation that the Black Hills lacked a medieval period can be found in his historical essay, "Where B.C. Means Before Custer," in Peattie, *The Black Hills*, 33.

For a detailed appreciation of the boom and bust of Dakota agriculture in the early decades of the twentieth century, see Pamela M. Nelson, *After the West Was Won: Homesteaders and Town-Builders in Western South Dakota, 1900–1917* (1986); Nelson, *The Prairie Winnows Out Its Own: The West River Country of South Dakota in the Years of Depression and Dust* (1996); James H. Shideler, *Farm Crisis, 1919–1923* (1957); and Mary Wilma M. Hargreaves, *Dry Farming in the Northern Great Plains, 1900–1925* (1957). For a more personal vantage point on the Dakota prairie in the early twentieth century, see George S. Reeves, *A Man from South Dakota* (1950).

Doane Robinson's character and deeds are revealed through his collected papers at the South Dakota State Historical Archives, Pierre. Peter Norbeck's papers are housed in the Richardson Archives, University of South Dakota, Vermillion, although most of his correspondence pertinent to Mount Rushmore is also contained within the Borglum Papers. Additionally, Gilbert C. Fite has written a serviceable biography of Norbeck, *Peter Norbeck: Prairie Statesman* (1948).

Chapter 3: Garden of the Gods

I was steered through the panoramic history of American highways by Curt McConnell, *Coast to Coast by Automobile: The Pioneering Trips, 1899–1908* (2000); Drake Hokanson, *The Lincoln Highway: Main Street across America* (1999); John B. Rae, *The Road and the Car in American Life* (1971); Jean Labatut and Wheaton J. Lane, eds., *Highways in Our National Life: A Symposium* (1950); Phil Patton, *Open Road: A Celebration of the American Highway* (1986); Val Hart, *The Story of American Roads* (1950); Frederic L. Paxson, "The Highway Movement, 1916–1935," *The American Historical Review* 51:2 (January 1946), 236–253; Albert C. Rose, "Historic American Highways," *Annual Report of the Board of Regents of the Smithsonian Institution,* 1939; Warren James Belasco, *Americans on the Road: From Autocamp to Motel, 1910–1945* (1979); John A. Jakle, *The Tourist: Travel in Twentieth-Century North America* (1985); John F. Sears, *Sacred Places: American Tourist Attractions in the Nineteenth Century* (1989); Carey S. Bliss, *Autos across America: A Bibliography of Transcontinental Automobile Travel: 1903–1940* (1972); Michael L. Berger, *The Devil Wagon in God's*

Country: The Automobile and Social Change in Rural America, 1893–1929 (1979); Alice A. Ridge and John William Ridge, *Introducing the Yellowstone Trail: A Good Road from Plymouth Rock to Puget Sound, 1912–1930* (2000); Elizabeth Eiselen, "The Tourist Industry of a Modern Highway: U.S. 16 in South Dakota," *Economic Geography* 21:39 (July 1945), 221–230; John E. Miller, *Looking for History on Highway 14* (1993); Art Buntin, "20th Century Pioneering: The Road and Auto Frontier in Northern S.D.," *The Karl E. Mundt Historical & Educational Foundation Series No. 15, 18th Dakota History Conference, April 10–12, 1986 Papers* (1987); and James Cracco, "History of the South Dakota Highway Department, 1919–1941," master's thesis, University of South Dakota, 1969. Emily Post's account of her cross-country car trip is entitled *By Motor to the Golden Gate* (1916).

I first learned about Lorado Taft's "Big Injun" from Karal Ann Marling, *The Colossus of Roads: Myth and Symbol along the American Highway* (1984). For more on Taft, see Josephine Craven Chandler, "Eagle's Nest Camp, Barbizon of Chicago Artists," *Art and Archaeology* 12:5 (November 1921), 194–204; Hamlin Garland, "The Art of Lorado Taft," *The Mentor* 11:9 (October 1923), 19–34; Timothy J. Garvey, *Public Sculptor: Lorado Taft and the Beautification of Chicago* (1988); James L. Riedy, *Chicago Sculpture* (1981); Ira J. Bach and Mary Lackritz Gray, *A Guide to Chicago's Public Sculpture* (1983); Lorado Taft, *The History of American Sculpture* (1903, revised 1924); Taft, "The Joyous Adventure of Bringing Art to the People," *American Magazine of Art* 19:8 (August 1928), 422–425; and Taft, "The Monuments of Chicago," *Art and Archaeology* 12:3–4 (September–October 1921), 120–127.

Thanks to Marcy West for pointing out the parallel between Mount Rushmore and New Hampshire's Old Man of the Mountain and for directing me to two germane books: Frances Ann Johnson Hancock, *Saving the Great Stone Face: The Chronicle of the Old Man of the Mountain* (1984), and John Mudge, *The Old Man's Reader: History and Legends of Franconia Notch* (1995).

Chapter 4: Great Man

My education on Great Men led me to G. W. F. Hegel, *Lectures on the Philosophy of History* (translated from the 3d German ed. by J. Sibree, 1857); Robert S. Hartman, "The Significance of Hegel for History," introduction to Hegel, *Reason in History: A General Introduction to the Philosophy of History* (1953); M. Victor Cousin, *Course of the History of Modern Philosophy* (1882); Sidney Hook, *The Hero in History: A Study in Limitation of Possibility* (1943); Thomas Carlyle, *On Heroes, Hero-Worship, & the Heroic in History* (notes and introduction by Michael K. Goldberg, 1993); B. H. Lehman, *Carlyle's Theory of the Hero: Its Sources, Development, History, and Influence on Carlyle's Work* (1966); Simon Heffer, *Moral Desperado: A Life of Thomas Carlyle* (1995); Kenneth Marc Harris, *Carlyle and Emerson: Their Long Debate* (1978); Ralph

Waldo Emerson, *Essays and Lectures* (1983); Robert D. Richardson Jr., *Emerson: The Mind on Fire* (1995); and Gay Wilson Allen, *Waldo Emerson: A Biography* (1981).

Borglum's early years are pieced together from *The One Man War*, his unfinished autobiography, scraps of which survive in his papers at the Library of Congress. I am also indebted to the genealogical legwork undertaken by Shaff and Shaff in *Six Wars at a Time*; Robin Borglum Carter's family archives and input were likewise essential. Borglum's "I was born in the Golden West..." first appeared in Borglum, "Art That Is Real and American," and later in J. Walker McSpadden, *Famous Sculptors of America* (1924).

Borglum's moon-chasing memory is repeated in Mary Borglum, *Give the Man Room*, 33. His speculation on why he ran away from home as a boy appears in Derieux, "A Sculptor Who Rode to Fame on Horseback," 14.

Borglum's emergence from "a wilderness of dabblers" is noted in the *Los Angeles Times* (17 September 1887).

There are two useful biographies of Jessie Benton Fremont: Catherine Coffin Phillips, *Jessie Benton Frémont: A Woman Who Made History* (1935); and Pamela Herr, *Jessie Benton Fremont: A Biography* (1987).

The notice in the Omaha newspaper regarding Borglum's upcoming trip to Europe was reprinted in the *Los Angeles Times* (30 June 1890).

My appreciation of Auguste Rodin was enriched by Ruth Butler, *Rodin: The Shape of Genius* (1993); and Jacques Vilain et al., *Rodin at the Musée Rodin* (1996). Borglum wrote his own tribute to Rodin: "Auguste Rodin," *The Artist* 32:264 (January 1902), 190–196.

The only book-length biography of Solon Borglum, A. Mervyn Davies's *Solon H. Borglum: "A Man Who Stands Alone"* (1974), is thorough, but it must be taken with a grain of salt, as Davies, who is Solon Borglum's son-in-law, bears an obvious grudge against Uncle Gutzon. For a more objective assessment of Solon Borglum's talents, see Arthur Goodrich, "The Frontier in Sculpture," *The World's Work* 3:5 (March 1902), 1857–1874; Frank Sewall, "A Sculptor of the Prairie," *The Century Magazine* 58:2 (June 1904), 247–251; Louise Eberle, "In Recognition of an American Artist," *Scribner's Magazine* 72:3 (September 1922), 379–384; Charles H. Caffin, *American Masters of Sculpture* (1903, reprint 1913); Taft, *The History of American Sculpture*; Michael Forrest, *Art Bronzes* (1988); and Patricia Janis Broder, *Bronzes of the American West* (1974).

Chapter 5: Art for America

Nowadays, statues in the park are not the hottest subject within art history circles, yet the genre is marked by a number of surprisingly well-turned texts, the most trenchant of which is Michele H. Bogart, *Public Sculpture and the Civic Ideal in New*

York City, 1890–1930 (1997). For a discussion of the City Beautiful movement, see William H. Wilson, *The City Beautiful Movement* (1989). Books devoted to specific sculptors include: John H. Dryfhout, *The Work of Augustus Saint-Gaudens* (1982); Michael Richman, *Daniel Chester French: An American Sculptor* (1976); and James M. Dennis, *Karl Bitter: Architectural Sculptor, 1867–1915* (1967). For sculpture by city (in addition to the books on Chicago sculpture cited earlier), I toured James M. Goode, *The Outdoor Sculpture of Washington, D.C.: A Comprehensive Historical Guide* (1974); Philip H. Viles Jr., *National Statuary Hall: Guidebook for a Walking Tour* (1996); George Gurney, *Sculpture and the Federal Triangle* (1985); John W. Reps, *Monumental Washington: The Planning and Development of the Capital Center* (1967); Constance McLaughlin Green, *Washington: Capital City, 1879–1950* (1963); Lewis I. Sharp, *New York City Public Sculpture by 19th-Century American Artists* (1974); Joseph Lederer, *All Around the Town: A Walking Guide to Outdoor Sculpture in New York City* (1975); Meredith Arms Bzdak, *Public Sculpture in New Jersey: Monuments to Collective Identity* (1999); and Francis F. Beirne, *The Amiable Baltimoreans* (1951). I have mentioned some of the general texts on American sculpture already (e.g., Taft, *The History of American Sculpture*; McSpadden, *Famous Sculptors of America*), to which I now add H. W. Janson, *Nineteenth-Century Sculpture* (1985); Albert TenEyck Gardner, *Yankee Stonecutters: The First American School of Sculpture, 1800–1850* (1945); Charles H. Caffin, *American Masters of Sculpture* (1913); Adeline Adams, *The Spirit of American Sculpture* (1929); Chandler Rafton Post, *A History of European and American Sculpture from the Early Christian Period to the Present Day*, vol. 2 (1921); William H. Gerdts, *American Neo-Classic Sculpture* (1973); Marion E. Gridley, *America's Indian Statues* (1966); Wayne Craven, *Sculpture in America* (1968, revised 1984); Tom Armstrong et al., *200 Years of American Sculpture* (1976); Thayer Tolles, ed., *American Sculpture in the Metropolitan Museum of Art, Volume I: A Catalogue of Works by Artists Born before 1865* (1999) and *Volume II: A Catalogue of Works by Artists Born between 1865 and 1885* (2001). Also see Janson, *The Rise and Fall of the Public Monument* (1976); and Ruth Mirolli, "Monuments for the Middle Class," in Mirolli, ed., *Nineteenth Century French Sculpture: Monuments for the Middle Class* (1971).

For a peek inside the world's fairs, I relied upon Carolyn Kinder Carr et al., *Reviewing the White City: American Art at the 1893 World's Fair* (1993); Robert W. Rydell, *All the World's Fair* (1984); and *Brush and Pencil* 13:3 (December 1903), an entire issue devoted to the sculpture at the 1904 Louisiana Purchase Exposition in St. Louis.

The "Jewish-looking beards" on the angels of St. John the Divine are examined in "Salon of the Dilettanti–I: Those Abolished Girl Angels," *Brush and Pencil* 16:6 (December 1905), 221–226. Also see "The Shattered Angels—An Art Tragedy," *New York Times* (15 October 1905).

For the controversy over the Grant memorial, additional sources beyond Borglum's own records include Charles Hall Garrett, "The New American Sculptor," *Munsey's Magazine* 29:4 (July 1903), 545–552; Mrs. Benjamin S. Church, "A Great American Sculptor: Henry Merwin Shrady," *Journal of American History* 7:2 (April–May–June 1913), 1004–1014; and Dennis R. Montagna, *Henry Merwin Shrady's Ulysses S. Grant Memorial in Washington, D.C.: A Study in Iconography, Content and Patronage*, Ph.D. dissertation, University of Delaware, 1987. The fate of the original Custer monument at West Point is recounted in Minnie Dubbs Millbrook, "A Monument to Custer," in *The Great Sioux War, 1876–77: The Best from "Montana the Magazine of Western History"* (1991).

Imagery of Lincoln has been as carefully documented as his life. Borglum's essay, "The Beauty of Lincoln," appeared in *Everybody's Magazine* 22:2 (February 1910), 216–220. The reception and perception of Lincoln down through history are discussed brilliantly in Merrill D. Peterson, *Lincoln in American Memory* (1994). Also illuminating are: Lauriston Bullard, *Lincoln in Marble and Bronze* (1952); Harold Holzer et al., *The Lincoln Image: Abraham Lincoln and the Popular Print* (1984); Holzer, *Washington and Lincoln Portrayed: National Icons in Popular Prints* (1993); Noble E. Cunningham Jr., *Popular Images of the Presidency: From Washington to Lincoln* (1991); Franklin B. Mead, *Heroic Statues in Bronze of Abraham Lincoln, Introducing the Hoosier Youth of Paul Manship* (1932); Charles Hamilton and Lloyd Ostendorf, *Lincoln in Photographs: An Album of Every Known Pose* (1985); and Mark S. Reinhart, *Abraham Lincoln on Screen: A Filmography of Dramas and Documentaries Including Television, 1903–1998* (1999).

Eugene Meyer's career is chronicled in Merlo J. Pusey, *Eugene Meyer* (1974).

A handy anthology of Ruskin is *The Lamp of Beauty: Writings on Art* (1959, 3d ed. 1995). Also see Roger B. Stein, *John Ruskin and Aesthetic Thought in America, 1840–1900* (1967).

Borglum followed up his October 1908 *Craftsman* essay on "Individuality, Sincerity and Reverence" with "Aesthetic Activities in America: An Answer to His Critics," *The Craftsman* 15:3 (December 1908), 301–307.

William Ordway Partridge's views on art are published in *Art for America* (1894). Also see Marjorie Pingel Balge, *William Ordway Partridge (1861–1930): American Art Critic and Sculptor*, Ph.D. dissertation, University of Delaware, 1982.

My appreciation of Phidias and his similarities to Borglum derive from Andrew Stewart, *Greek Sculpture: An Exploration*, vol. 1 (1990); Gisela M. A. Richter, *The Sculpture and Sculptors of the Greeks* (4th ed., 1970); John Boardman, *Greek Sculpture: The Classical Period* (1985); and Plutarch, *The Rise and Fall of Athens: Nine Greek Lives* (1960).

Chapter 6: Insurgent Among Insurgents

The standard text on the Armory show remains Milton W. Brown, *The Story of the Armory Show* (1963).

One of the distinguishing characteristics of Theodore Roosevelt scholarship is that so much of it is so good. Of the numerous biographies, I am partial to Henry F. Pringle, *Theodore Roosevelt* (1931); David McCullough, *Mornings on Horseback* (1981); H. W. Brands, *T. R.: The Last Romantic* (1997); and two volumes by Edmund Morris, *The Rise of Theodore Roosevelt* (1979) and *Theodore Rex* (2001). One of the best book-length evaluations of Roosevelt was never published as an actual book: Richard H. Collin, *The Image of Theodore Roosevelt in American History and Thought, 1885–1965*, Ph.D. dissertation, New York University, 1966.

Other sources relating to Roosevelt's Progressivism, near-assassination, and public image include George E. Mowry, *Theodore Roosevelt and the Progressive Movement* (1946); Mowry, *Theodore Roosevelt and the Birth of Modern America* (1958); Vincent P. DeSantis, *The Shaping of Modern America: 1877–1916* (1973); John Allen Gable, *The Bull Moose Years: Theodore Roosevelt and the Progressive Party* (1978); Stuart R. Sherman, *Americans* (1922); William Allen White, *Masks in the Pageant* (1928); Joseph Bucklin Bishop, ed., *Theodore Roosevelt and His Time: Shown in His Letters*, vol. 1 (1920); and Oliver E. Remey et al., *The Attempted Assassination of Ex-President Theodore Roosevelt* (1912, reprint 1978). The rush to memorialize Roosevelt is discussed in "The Proposed Roosevelt Memorial in Washington," *The Outlook* 141:17 (23 December 1925), 632–633; "Are You Ready for the Question," *The Outlook* 141:17 (23 December 1925), 624; Oswald Garrison Villard, "Creating Reputations, Ltd.," *The American Mercury* 4:16 (April 1925), 385–389; and Alan Havig, "Presidential Images, History, and Homage: Memorializing Theodore Roosevelt, 1919–1967," *American Quarterly* 30:4 (Fall 1978), 514–532.

To place Borglum's Progressivism in a more local context, see Herbert Janick, "The Mind of the Connecticut Progressive," *Mid-America* 52:2 (April 1970), 83–101.

Chapter 7: Size Matters

My perspective of the Statue of Liberty was changed forever by Marvin Trachtenberg, "The Statue of Liberty: Transparent Banality or Avant-Garde Conundrum?" *Art in America* 62:3 (May–June 1974), 36–43, and by his subsequent book, *The Statue of Liberty* (1976). In the former, Trachtenberg wrote, "Her [Liberty's] image is somehow familiar and enters effortlessly into the consciousness, being already part of the common visual language, like words of a native tongue." Trachtenberg is also the source of Gustav Eiffel's remark, "There is in the colossal an attraction, a particular charm. . . ." Liberty is masterfully placed in the context of colossalism in Pierre Provoyeur, "Bartholdi and the Colossal Tradition," in New York Public Library et al., *Liberty: The French-American Statue in Art and History* (1986).

The first I heard of the 1916 explosion on Black Tom Island was in Christian Blanchet and Bertrand Dard, *Statue of Liberty: The First Hundred Years* (1985). My descriptions of that event derive from accounts in the *New York Times*.

The best single source on the origins and tradition of colossal sculpture is Virginia Bush, *The Colossal Sculpture of the Cinquecento* (1976). Bush is the one who quotes Vasari's observation on *gran maniera*.

In addition to the abundant material relevant to Stone Mountain contained within the Borglum Papers, I was enlightened by correspondence, minutes, legal documents, and other records within the Stone Mountain Collection, Special Collections Department, Robert W. Woodruff Library, Emory University, Atlanta, Georgia (used by permission). The best one-volume overview of Stone Mountain is David B. Freeman, *Carved in Stone: The History of Stone Mountain* (1997). A less objective, but nonetheless valuable, chronicle of the monument was written shortly after Borglum's blowup there: Gerald W. Johnson, *The Undefeated* (1927). More succinct but also useful are Harkness Kenimer, *History of Stone Mountain (The 8th Wonder of the World)* (1993); and Willard Neal, *Georgia's Stone Mountain* (n.d.).

The genesis of the Daughters of the Confederacy and its campaign to erect Confederate monuments is told floridly in Mary B. Poppenheim et al., *The History of the United Daughters of the Confederacy*, vol. 1 (1925).

The article in *The Nation* so critical of Stone Mountain appeared without a byline as "Sculpturing a Mountain," *The Nation* 105:2719 (9 August 1917), 140. Other journals, while relishing controversy, were far less harsh: "Mountain a Monument: Gutzon Borglum Proposes to Carve the Solid Granite of Stone Mountain into a Wonderful Confederate Memorial," *New York Times*, Magazine Section (2 January 1916), 1–2; Derieux, "A Sculptor Who Rode to Fame on Horseback"; "Making a Monument Out of a Mountain: Stone Mountain Memorial—Greatest Work of Sculpture in History," *Scientific American* 131:2 (August 1924), 90; "Uncivil War Over the Confederate Memorial," *The Literary Digest* 84:11 (14 March 1925), 28–30; "Borglum, As Seen by His Fellow Artists," *The Literary Digest* 84:12 (12 March 1925), 26–28; Gerald W. Johnson, "Sophocles in Georgia," *The Century Magazine* 112:5 (September 1926), 565–571; Craig F. Thompson, "The Stone Mountain Fiasco," *Plain Talk* 2:4 (April 1928), 393–398; and "Turning a Mountain into a Memorial," *DuPont Magazine* 19:1 (January 1925), 7, 12. Borglum himself published several articles on the subject, including "The Confederate Memorial," *The World's Work* 34:4 (August 1917), 437–446; and "Moulding a Mountain," *The Forum* 70:4 (October 1923), 2019–2026. Additional reporting on Stone Mountain is provided by the *Atlanta Constitution* and the *Atlanta Journal*.

I likewise relied on the *Constitution* and the *Journal* for descriptions of how *Birth of a Nation* was received in Atlanta. The birth of *Birth* and its impact on America in general are discussed thoroughly in Richard Schickel, *D. W. Griffith: An American Life* (1984); and Robert Lang, ed.; *The Birth of a Nation: D.W. Griffith, Director (1994)*.

Borglum's files on the aircraft investigation within the Library of Congress are massive, daunting, and in some respects as engrossing as a spy thriller. For a vivid glimpse of the Wright brothers, the historic flight at Fort Myer, and their inadvertent link to the war scandal, see Fred Howard, *Wilbur and Orville: A Biography of the Wright Brothers* (1987); and Tom D. Crouch, *The Bishop's Boys: A Life of Wilbur and Orville Wright* (1989). Edward A. Deeds is defended and venerated in Isaac F. Marcosson, *Colonel Deeds: Industrial Builder* (1948).

Borglum's effort to win the Gómez commission in Cuba is described maliciously in the autobiography of his rival, Pompeo Coppini, *From Dawn to Sunset* (1949).

H. L. Mencken's dismissal of Theodore Roosevelt appears in Mencken, *Prejudices: Second Series* (1920). John Dewey's tribute comes from Dewey, "Theodore Roosevelt," *The Dial* 66:783 (8 February 1919), 115–117.

My summary of the Nonpartisan League is gleaned from Robert L. Morlan, *Political Prairie Fire: The Nonpartisan League, 1915–1922* (1955), by far the best book on the topic. Also helpful were Charles N. Glabb et al., *The North Dakota Political Tradition* (1981); Theodore Saloutos, *Agricultural Discontent in the Midwest, 1900–1939* (1951); Edward C. Blackorby, *Prairie Rebel: The Public Life of William Lemke* (1963); Nelson, *Land of the Dacotahs* (1946); Gilbert C. Fite, "Peter Norbeck and the Defeat of the Nonpartisan League in South Dakota," *Mississippi Valley Historical Review* 33:2 (September 1946), 217–236; William C. Pratt, "Socialism on the Northern Plains, 1900–1924," *South Dakota History* 18:1/2 (Spring/Summer 1988), 1–35; and Pratt, "Rural Radicalism on the Northern Plains, 1912–1950," *Montana the Magazine of Western History* 42:1 (Winter 1992), 42–55.

Borglum's insistence that he would rather carve Stone Mountain than be president appears in Derieux, "A Sculptor Who Rode to Fame on Horseback."

Chapter 8: A Rock and a Hard Place

All of the following helped me appreciate the full magnitude of the Ku Klux Klan's second coming in the twentieth century: David M. Chalmers, *Hooded Americanism: The History of the Ku Klux Klan* (1987); Nancy MacLean, *Behind the Mask of Chivalry: The Making of the Second Ku Klux Klan* (1994); Wyn Craig Wade, *The Fiery Cross: The Ku Klux Klan in America* (1987); Kenneth T. Jackson, *The Ku Klux Klan in* the City, 1915–1930 (1967); Charles C. Alexander, *The Ku Klux Klan in the Southwest* (1965); John Higham, *Strangers in the Land: Patterns of American Nativism, 1860–1925* (1955); David H. Bennett, *Party of Fear: The American Far Right from Nativism to the Militia Movement* (rev. ed., 1995); Leonard J. Moore, "Historical Interpretations of the 1920's Klan: The Traditional View and the Populist Revision," *Journal of Social History* 24:2 (Winter 1990), 341–357; Lee N. Allen, "The McAdoo Campaign for the Presidential Nomination in 1924," *Journal of Southern History* 19:2 (May 1963), 211–228; Charles O. Jackson, "William J. Simmons: A Career in Ku Kluxism," *Georgia Historical Quarterly* 50:4 (December 1966), 351–365; Robert L. Duffus, "Salesmen of Hate: The Ku Klux Klan," *World's Work* 46:1 (May 1923), 31–38; Duffus, "How the Ku Klux Klan Sells Hate," *World's Work* 46:2 (June 1923), 174–183; Duffus, "The Ku Klux Klan in the Middle West," *World's Work* 46:4 (August 1923), 363–372; and Clement Charlton Moseley, *Invisible Empire: A History of the Ku Klux Klan in Twentieth Century Georgia, 1915–1965*, Ph.D. dissertation, University of Georgia, 1968. In *The Fiery Cross*, 165, Wade alleges that President Harding took the Klan oath in the White House.

Regarding David C. Stephenson and the Indiana Klan specifically, see William Lutholtz, *Grand Dragon: D. C. Stephenson and the Ku Klux Klan in Indiana* (1991); Francis X. Busch, *Guilty or Not Guilty? An Account of the Trials of The Leo Frank Case, The D. C. Stephenson Case, the Samuel Insull Case, The Alger Hiss Case* (1952); Robert Coughlan, "Konklave in Kokomo," in Isabel Leighton, ed., *The Aspirin Age, 1919–1941* (1949); and Emma Lou Thornbrough, "Segregation in Indiana during the Klan Era of the 1920's," *Mississippi Valley Historical Review* 47:4 (March 1961), 594–618.

My knowledge of U.S. coins comes from Walter Breen, *Walter Breen's Complete Encyclopedia of U.S. and Colonial Coins* (1988); Mort Reed, *Encyclopedia of U.S. Coins* (1969); and Ted Schwarz, *A History of United States Coinage* (1980).

Borglum's search for suitable rock on which to carve his Black Hills memorial is described colorfully in Smith, *The Carving of Mount Rushmore*, 90–97.

The flap over whether to erect a Roosevelt memorial or a Jefferson memorial in Washington's Tidal Basin is sorted out in Peterson, *The Jefferson Image in the American Mind* (1960), 420–423; "Jefferson Monument to Have Precedence," *New York Times* (4 July 1926), 16; "The Proposed Roosevelt Memorial in Washington," *The Outlook* 141:17 (23 December 1925), 632–634; "Roosevelt vs. Wilson: Fourth Round," *The Nation* 122:3159 (20 January 1926), 52; and Alan Havig, "Presidential Images, History, and Homage: Memorializing Theodore Roosevelt, 1919–1967," *American Quarterly* 30:4 (Fall 1978), 514–532.

Chapter 9: Cliff Notes

Calvin Coolidge stands out among his contemporaries the way a man in a beige cardigan might stand out in a kaleidoscope of carnival costumes. Here are some of the sources that informed my portrayal of him: John L. Blair, "'I do not choose to run for President in Nineteen Twenty Eight,'" *Vermont History* 30:3 (July 1962), 177–195; Gamaliel Bradford, *The Quick and the Dead* (1929); William J. Bulow, "When Cal Coolidge Came to Visit Us," *The Saturday Evening Post* 219:27 (4 January 1947), 22–23, 65–66; Calvin Coolidge, *The Autobiography of Calvin Coolidge* (1931); Grace Coolidge, ed., "The Real Calvin Coolidge: A First-Hand Story of His Life Told by 50 People Who Knew Him Best," *Good Housekeeping* 100: 2, 3, 4, 5, 6 (February–June 1935); Robert H. Ferrell, *The Presidency of Calvin Coolidge* (1998); Claude M. Fuess, *Calvin Coolidge: The Man from Vermont* (1940); Robert E. Gilbert, *The Mortal Presidency: Illness and Anguish in the White House* (1992); John Earl Haynes, ed., *Calvin Coolidge and the Coolidge Era* (1998); Peter R. Levin, *Seven by Chance: The Accidental Presidents* (1948); C. C. O'Harra, ed., *The Black Hills Engineer* 15:4 (November 1927), an entire issue dedicated to Coolidge's 1927 visit to South Dakota; Donald R. McCoy, *Calvin Coolidge: The Quiet President* (1967); Ishbel Ross, *Grace Coolidge and Her Era: The Story of a President's Wife* (1962); Robert Sobel, *Coolidge: An American Enigma* (1998); Edmund W. Starling, as told to Thomas Sugrue, *Starling of the White House: The Story of the Man Whose Secret Service Detail Guarded Five Presidents from Woodrow Wilson to Franklin D. Roosevelt* (1946); and William Allan White, *A Puritan in Babylon: The Story of Calvin Coolidge* (1938).

For the passages explaining how Mount Rushmore was designed and carved, I relied on records at Mount Rushmore National Memorial and within the Borglum Papers. I also would like to reemphasize my indebtedness to Fite, *Mount Rushmore*; Shaff and Shaff, *Six Wars at a Time*; and Smith, *The Carving of Mount Rushmore*. In many instances, these authors availed themselves of the same primary sources as I, but at the time they were researching their books, they also were able to interview a number of the actual workers on the mountain, nearly all of whom had died by the time I came along.

I read Nathaniel Hawthorne's "The Great Stone Face" in *Hawthorne's Short Stories* (1946). Hawthorne was a serious student of sculpture, basing an entire novel, *The Marble Faun* (1860), on a Roman statue and the American expatriates who come under its spell.

Of the many books and articles on George Washington, I relied most readily on Borglum's essay "Carving the Real Washington," *New York Herald Tribune* (30 June 1929); Karal Ann Marling, *George Washington Slept Here: Colonial Revivals and American Culture, 1876–1986* (1988); Barry Schwartz, *George Washington: The Making of an American Symbol* (1987); Garry Wills, *Cincinnatus: George Washington and the Enlightenment; Images of Power in Early America* (1984); and W. E. Woodward, *George*

Washington: The Image and the Man (1926). Rupert Hughes's biography of Washington was published in three volumes: *George Washington: The Human Being and the Hero, 1732–1762* (1926); *George Washington: The Rebel and the Patriot, 1762–1777* (1927); and *George Washington: The Savior of the States, 1777–1781* (1930). I read Mason L. Weems's *The Life of Washington* in a 1974 Limited Editions Club reprint that includes a nifty introduction by Henry Steele Commager. Likewise trenchant are Thomas A. Bailey, *Presidential Greatness: The Image and the Man from George Washington to the Present* (1966); William Alfred Bryan, *George Washington in American Literature, 1775–1865* (1952); John C. Fitzpatrick, "The George Washington Scandals," *Scribner's Magazine* 81:4 (April 1927), 389–395; Jay Fliegelman, *Prodigals and Pilgrims: The American Revolution against Patriarchal Authority, 1750–1800* (1982); Lawrence J. Friedman, *Inventors of the Promised Land* (1975); "'Humanizing' George Washington," *The Literary Digest* 91:6 (6 November 1926), 24–25; Paul K. Longmore, *The Invention of George Washington* (1988); Bernard Mayo, *Myths and Men: Patrick Henry, George Washington, Thomas Jefferson* (1959); George W. Nordham, *George Washington: Vignettes and Memorabilia* (1977); "Washington Dismounted from His High Horse," *The Literary Digest* 87:11 (12 December 1925), 50, 52; "Washington—Man or Waxwork?" *The Nation* 122:3160 (27 January 1926), 75; Dixon Wecter, *The Hero in America: A Chronicle of Hero-Worship* (1941); and Woodward, "On the Trail of Greatness," *Bookman* 64:5 (January 1927), 551–555. Woodward's "debunking" of Washington is discussed in Wesley Frank Craven, *The Legend of the Founding Fathers* (1956), 160–164. Woodward first coined the term in his novel *Bunk* (1923). Hawthorne's remark about seeing Washington naked is quoted in Marshall W. Fishwick, *American Heroes: Myth and Reality* (1954), 38. Regarding Washington's false teeth: They are sometimes referred to as "sea-horse teeth," although they were actually made of hippopotamus ivory, according to Woodward, *George Washington: The Image and the Man*, 390.

On Washington expressly as a work of art, see Noble E. Cunningham Jr., *Popular Images of the Presidency: From Washington to Lincoln* (1991); Gustavus A. Eisen, *Portraits of Washington*, vols. 1–3 (1932); Charles Henry Hart, "Life Portraits of George Washington," *McClure's Magazine* 8:4 (February 1897), 290–308; Ellen G. Miles, *George and Martha Washington: Portraits from the Presidential Years* (1999); Mark Edward Thistlewaite, *The Image of George Washington: Studies in Mid-Nineteenth Century History Painting* (1979); Frances Davis Whittemore, *George Washington in Sculpture* (1933); Wendy C. Wick, *George Washington, An American Icon: The Eighteenth-Century Graphic Portraits* (1982); John S. Hallam, "Houdon's *Washington* in Richmond: Some New Observations," *The American Art Journal* 10:2 (November 1978), 72–80; and Christine DeFazio et al., *Houdon: An Exhibition of Sculpture from the Collection of Michael Hall, Esq.* (1998).

Chapter 10: Worthy of Immortality

On the mercurial nature of Thomas Jefferson, by far the most original, comprehensive, and illuminating source is Peterson, *The Jefferson Image in the American Mind*. It was Peterson who clued me in to Theodore Roosevelt's dislike of Jefferson (335–336), Franklin Roosevelt's admiration of him (351–352), and the contextual importance of Claude G. Bowers, *Jefferson and Hamilton: The Struggle for Democracy in America* (1925). Teddy Roosevelt's unfiltered disparagement of Jefferson can be found in Bishop, ed., *Theodore Roosevelt and His Time: Shown in His Letters*, vol. 1, 23–24, 71. Perhaps the best single-volume biographies of Jefferson are Peterson, *Thomas Jefferson and the New Nation* (1970); and Joseph J. Ellis, *American Sphinx: The Character of Thomas Jefferson* (1996). Other revelatory writings on Jefferson include Peter S. Onuf, ed., *Jeffersonian Legacies* (1993); Onuf, "The Scholar's Jefferson," *The William and Mary Quarterly*, Third Series 50:4 (October 1993), 673–699; Paul Leicester Ford, "Thomas Jefferson in Undress," *Scribner's Magazine* 12:4 (October 1892), 509–516; Douglas L. Wilson, "Thomas Jefferson and the Character Issue," *The Atlantic Monthly* 270:5 (November 1992), 57–74; Eric L. McKitrick, "The View from Jefferson's Camp," *The New York Review of Books* 15:11 (17 December 1970), 35–38; Garry Wills, "The Aesthete," *The New York Review of Books* 40:14 (12 August 1993), 6–10; Wills, "Storm over Jefferson," *The New York Review of Books* 47:5 (23 March 2000), 16–18; Eric S. Lander and Joseph J. Ellis, "Founding Father," *Nature* 396:6706 (5 November 1998), 13–14, 27–28; Jan Ellen Lewis and Onuf, *Sally Hemings and Thomas Jefferson: History, Memory, and Civic Culture* (1999); Mayo, *Myths and Men*; and Wecter, *The Hero in America*. Artistic renderings of Jefferson are catalogued in Alfred L. Bush, *The Life Portraits of Thomas Jefferson* (1987); Susan R. Stein, *The Worlds of Thomas Jefferson at Monticello* (1993); Noble E. Cunningham, *The Image of Thomas Jefferson in the Public Eye: Portraits for the People, 1800–1809* (1981); and Cunningham, *Popular Images of the Presidency*.

I am grateful to Rex Alan Smith for allowing me to borrow the anecdote in which Borglum demands credit at the Keystone gas station and the one in which he instructs Red Anderson to turn his back on the carving and "feel it."

Lorena Hickok's grim observations of the Dust Bowl are collected in Richard Lowitt and Maurine Beasley, eds., *One Third of a Nation: Lorena Hickok Reports on the Great Depression* (1981). The stoic optimism of "Next Year Country" is expressed in Reeves, *A Man from South Dakota*. Also see Lowitt, *The New Deal and the West* (1984).

Details of Franklin Roosevelt's visit to South Dakota come from the Borglum Papers and the *Rapid City Journal*.

For sources relating to the treatment of Lincoln by artists and authors during the Rushmore years, see my notes regarding Lincoln in chapter 5. For public response to Sandburg's biography of Lincoln, see Penelope Nevin, *Carl Sandburg: A Biography* (1991).

Chapter 11: Sorry Old Warrior

H. Rider Haggard first published *She* in 1887; I read a paperback reprint (1991). It has been adapted several times for the movies; the 1935 version of *She* is available from King Video. I became aware of the architectural link between *King Kong* and *She* through Marla Harper's review of the latter in the *Washington Post* (27 August 1989). The similarity between the film's doors and stairs and those in Borglum's design of the Hall of Records is indeed remarkable. I absorbed more details about *She*, the movie, from the Internet Movie Database (imdb.com). I also wish to call attention to two valuable documents on the Hall of Records. The first is Paul Higbee, *Mount Rushmore's Hall of Records* (1999); this is an illustrated booklet published by the Mount Rushmore History Association. The second is Enid T. Thompson, "Gutzon Borglum's Concept of the Hall of Records at Mount Rushmore" (1974); it is an internal report prepared for the National Park Service and available only in the Mount Rushmore National Memorial Archives.

Regarding the "Million-Dollar Chisel," see Samuel Lubell and Walter Everett, "Mountain Man," *Scribner's Commentator* 7:5 (March 1940), 29–44. The article was then reprinted as "The Man Who Carves Mountains," *Reader's Digest* 36:217 (May 1940), 113–115.

For perspective on the sculpture of the Texas Centennial, see Commission of Control for Texas Centennial Celebrations, *Monuments Erected by the State of Texas to Commemorate the Centenary of Texas Independence* (1938); and Kenneth B. Ragsdale, *Centennial '36: The Year America Discovered Texas* (1987).

Borglum's essay, "The World As I Want It," appears in *The Forum and Century* 93:2 (February 1935), 112–113.

Correspondence to and from Rose Arnold Powell comes from two sources: the Rose Arnold Powell Papers, Schlesinger Library, Radcliffe Institute, Harvard University, Cambridge, Massachusetts (used by permission); and the Borglum Papers. Also see Simon Schama, *Landscape and Memory* (1995), 385–411.

Chapter 12: Expedient Exaggeration

The Duhamel Trading Post and the relationship between the Duhamel family and the Lakota is memorialized in Dale Lewis, *Duhamel: From Ox Cart . . . to Television* (1993).

I am indebted to Richard N. Ellis for his introduction to the reprint editions of

Luther Standing Bear's books, *My People the Sioux* (1928, reprint 1975) and *Land of the Spotted Eagle* (1933, reprint 1978). Two other pertinent documents are Ellis, "Luther Standing Bear: 'I would raise him to be an Indian,'" in L. G. Moses and Raymond Wilson, eds., *Indian Lives: Essays on Nineteenth- and Twentieth-Century Native American Leaders* (1985); and Chief Standing Bear, "The Tragedy of the Sioux," *The American Mercury* 24:95 (November 1931), 273–278.

The history of the Black Hills land claim is chronicled in Lazarus, *Black Hills, White Justice*.

Black Elk's life and vision are immortalized in Neihardt, *Black Elk Speaks*. His 1936 visit to Mount Rushmore is recorded in the *Rapid City Journal* (28 August 1936).

Borglum's plan to erect memorials to Lakota chiefs in Nebraska is discussed in the "Sioux Memorial Issue" (sometimes referred to as the "Pine Ridge Number") of *Nebraska History* 21:4 (October–December 1940), specifically two articles by Borglum, "Memorials to the Sioux Indians," 253–255, and "People's Memorials— and Their Monuments," 287–290; and a third un-bylined piece, "Indian Tribe in Granite Is Next Plan of Gutzon Borglum, Sculptor of Mount Rushmore," 291–292. I am also grateful to Robin Borglum Carter for sharing her file of correspondence between Everett P. Wilson and her father, Lincoln Borglum.

My education on Korczak Ziolkowski and Crazy Horse Memorial comes from numerous visits to the memorial; interviews with Ziolkowski's widow, Ruth, and memorial publicist Robb DeWall; correspondence and clippings in the Borglum Papers and the Rapid City Public Library; and two books by DeWall: *Korczak: Storyteller in Stone* (1984) and *Carving a Dream* (1992). Lame Deer's critique of Crazy Horse Memorial appears in John (Fire) Lame Deer and Richard Erdoes, *Lame Deer: Seeker of Visions* (1972). The *Rapid City Journal*'s account of the memorial's dedication appeared on June 4, 1948.

The story of *North by Northwest*, both on screen and behind the scenes, is told through a rich variety of sources. The movie itself is available on video through MGM/UA Vintage Classics. Ernest Lehman's screenplay was published in book form: Lehman, *North by Northwest* (1972). Various reviews and essays on the movie are compiled in James Naremore, ed., *North by Northwest: Alfred Hitchcock, Director* (1993), including the *Cahiers du Cinéma* interview in which Hitchcock remarked that "art comes before democracy" (178). Other books on Hitchcock and his craft include Dan Auiler, *Hitchcock's Notebooks: An Authorized and Illustrated Look Inside the Creative Mind of Alfred Hitchcock* (1999); John W. Finler, *Hitchcock in Hollywood* (1992); Donald Spoto, *The Art of Alfred Hitchcock: Fifty Years of His Motion Pictures* (1979); Spoto, *The Dark Side of Genius: The Life of Alfred Hitchcock* (1983); and John Russell Taylor, *Hitch: The Life and Times of Alfred Hitchcock* (1978). MGM's activities in South Dakota are covered in the *Rapid City Journal* (16–17 September 1958).

Hitchcock's rhetorical query, "How can you tell who a spy is these days?" appeared in the *Journal* (15 May 1958). The conflict between the studio and the National Park Service is smartly summarized in Todd David Epp, "Alfred Hitchcock's 'Expedient Exaggerations' and the Filming of *North by Northwest* at Mount Rushmore," *South Dakota History* 23:3 (Fall 1993), 181–196. News clippings and Park Service correspondence and memos are preserved in the Mount Rushmore Archives. For background on Karl Mundt, see Scott N. Heidepriem, *A Fair Chance for a Free People: Biography of Karl E. Mundt, United States Senator* (1988); Larry Pressler, *U.S. Senators from the Prairie* (1982); and John E. Miller, "Two Visions of the Great Plains: *The Plow That Broke the Plains* and South Dakotans' Reaction to It," *Upper Midwest History* 2 (1982), 1–12. Also see Robert L. Snyder, *Pare Lorentz and the Documentary Film* (1968).

The Rushmore archives and Robin Borglum Carter both maintain wonderful files of various cartoons, comics, advertisements, homages, spoofs, and spin-offs relating to Mount Rushmore. The archives have also collected clippings, correspondence, memoranda, programs, photographs, and ephemera related to special events at Rushmore, from the Telstar telecast to presidential visits. Thanks to Bruce Van Vort, Rushmore's concessionaire, for sending me my own copy of the *Live with Regis and Kathie Lee* tapes.

Chapter 13: Doksa Black Hills

Most of the details relating to Indian protests and security issues at Mount Rushmore were gleaned from correspondence, memoranda, internal reports, news clippings, handbills, and ephemera in the Mount Rushmore archives. Another rich, albeit subjective, source was Russell Means with Marvin J. Wolf, *Where White Men Fear to Tread: The Autobiography of Russell Means* (1995). Further reading includes Lazarus, *Black Hills, White Justice*; Paul Chaat Smith and Robert Allen Warrior, *Like a Hurricane: The Indian Movement from Alcatraz to Wounded Knee* (1996); Mario Gonzalez and Elizabeth Cook-Lynn, *The Politics of Hallowed Ground: Wounded Knee and the Struggle for Indian Sovereignty* (1999); Peter Matthiessen, *In the Spirit of Crazy Horse* (1983); Rolland Dewing, *Wounded Knee II* (1995); Tim Giago, *Notes from Indian Country*, vols. 1 and 2 (1984 and 1999); Vine DeLoria Jr., *Custer Died for Your Sins* (1969); Deloria and Clifford M. Lytle, *American Indians, American Justice* (1983); Rex Weyler, *Blood on the Land: The Government and Corporate War Against First Americans* (1982); Robert Burnette and John Koster, *The Road to Wounded Knee* (1974); Stanley David Lyman, *Wounded Knee 1973: A Personal Account* (1993); Alvin M. Josephy Jr., "Wounded Knee and all that—What the Indians want," *New York Times Magazine* (18 March 1973), 18–19, 66–67, 70, 74, 76, 82; Clyde

D. Dollar, "The Second Tragedy at Wounded Knee: A 1970s Confrontation and Its Historical Roots," *The American West* 10:5 (September 1973), 4–11, 58–61; Terri Schultz, "Bamboozle Me Not at Wounded Knee," *Harper's* 246:1477 (June 1973), 46–48, 53–56; Bella Stumbo, "A World Apart: Indian Activists Dennis Banks and Russell Means Are Back Together—but Hardly United—in a Forgotten Slice of America Called Wounded Knee," *Los Angeles Times Magazine* (15 June 1986), 10–19, 21; and William Greider, "The Heart of Everything That Is," *Rolling Stone* 499 (7 May 1987), 37–38, 40, 60, 62, 64. I am also grateful for interviews with former park employees Leo Zwetzig and Gene Koevenig and former FBI agent Tom Greene, Cheyenne River Sioux Tribe chairman Gregg Bourland, and attorney Mario Gonzalez. Aubrie James, staff assistant to U.S. senator Tim Johnson, and Tim Giago of the *Lakota Journal* were generous to share their offices' files on the Black Hills land claim and the Bradley bill.

The Indian rap sheet against the Rushmore presidents comes from several sources. Charlotte Black Elk reminded me of the "skin scalping" charge against George Washington in our interview of July 2, 2001. Russell Means compares Washington's anti-Indian activities to My Lai in *Where White Men Fear to Tread.* Jefferson's posture is examined in Anthony F. C. Wallace, *Jefferson and the Indians: The Tragic Fate of the First Americans* (1999); and Bernard W. Sheehan, *Seeds of Extinction: Jeffersonian Philanthropy and the American Indian* (1974). Abraham Lincoln's role in the Black Hawk War, including his battle with "mosquetoes," is revealed in David Herbert Donald, *Lincoln* (1995). "The Great Sioux Uprising," including the postmortem by Dr. Mayo, is revisited in Andrist, *The Long Death.* Mario Gonzalez lodges his complaint against Theodore Roosevelt in *The Politics of Hallowed Ground.*

The film *Dances with Wolves* is available on video from Metro-Goldwyn-Mayer Contemporary Classics. The following newspaper articles examine the making and impact of *Dances with Wolves* and the Dunbar development in Deadwood: Pat Dobbs, "Costner purchases Deadwood building," *Rapid City Journal* (20 October 1990); "Indians feel good about 'Dances with Wolves,'" *Rapid City Journal* (21 October 1990); Geraldine Baum, "Kevin Costner's Dance with the Sioux," *Los Angeles Times* (28 October 1990); Elaine Dutka, "Costner Takes a Stand," *Los Angeles Times Magazine* (4 November 1990); Sheila Benson, "Costner's Magic with 'Wolves,'" *Los Angeles Times* (9 November 1990); Vincent Canby, "A Soldier at One With the Sioux," *New York Times* (9 November 1990); Edward Guthmann, "Indians Call Costner a Friend," *San Francisco Chronicle* (10 November 1990); Christine Jackson, "'Dances' debuts in S.D.," *Rapid City Journal* (19 November 1990); Daniel Golden, "The Sioux Offscreen," *Boston Globe* (5 December 1990); Pauline Kael, "New Age Daydreams," *The New Yorker* 66:44 (17 December 1990), 115–116; Eric Harrison, "For

Lakota, 'Dances' Can't Keep Wolf from the Door," *Los Angeles Times* (29 July 1991); Pat Doyle, "Is Costner now John Dunbad?" (Minneapolis) *Star Tribune* (19 February 1995); Alix Sharkey, "Indian Giver," *The Guardian* (London) (8 April 1995); Bill Harlan, "Bad Days at Black Hills for Developer Costner," *Los Angeles Times* (25 May 1995); Tim Velder, "All aboard Dunrail train in '02?" *Rapid City Journal* (21 October 2000); Velder, "Homestake demands judgment," *Rapid City Journal* (14 March 2001); Velder, "Dunbar: financing foiled again," *Rapid City Journal* (6 November 2001); Denise Ross, "Sculpture may go up in Deadwood," *Rapid City Journal* (9 November 2001); and Velder, "Judge: Costners owe Homestake $1.2 million," *Rapid City Journal* (10 January 2002). Louis Owens's essay, "Apocalypse at the Two-Socks Hop: Dancing with the Vanishing American," is included in his collection, *Mixedblood Messages: Literature, Film, Family, Place* (1998).

Early optimism of the benefits of movies to the Black Hills is expressed in "Movie Producers See Big Future in Black Hills," *Rapid City Journal* (28 August 1925). Victor Mature is glimpsed as an "aggrieved turtle" in "Three Up, Three Down," *Time* 65:22 (30 May 1955), 86.

For sources on Crazy Horse Memorial, see my notes for chapter 12. I conducted interviews with Robb DeWall, Ruth Ziolkowski, Charmaine Whiteface, Ben Rhodd, Donovin Sprague, and many others throughout 2001. Syndicated columnist Jodi Rave Lee shared her "gnawing feeling" about Crazy Horse Memorial in "Setting for newspaper conference troubling," *Rapid City Journal* (19 May 2001).

Chapter 14: Presidents View

For my account of the campaign to improve the facilities at Mount Rushmore and the opposition it faced, I relied on clippings, reports, minutes, transcripts, and ephemera in the Mount Rushmore National Memorial Archives and on interviews with Dan Wenk, Carolyn Mollers, Tom Griffith, and Gene Koevenig.

Regarding the brouhaha over "Daschle's Door," see Ann Reilly Dowd, "Look Who's Cashing in on Congress," *Money* 26:12 (December 1997), 128–138; Ruth Marcus, "Daschle Event Gives Supporters Trip to Top of Mount Rushmore," *Washington Post* (10 October 1997); "How to Climb Mt. Rushmore," *Washington Post* (12 October 1997); "Mining Mt. Slushmore," *Orange County Register* (16 October 1997); "Daschle denies selling access to Rushmore," *Rapid City Journal* (11 October 1997); "Ethics complaint targets Daschle's Rushmore visit," *Rapid City Journal* (28 October 1997); Bill Harlan, "Justice reviews Daschle's Rushmore trip," *Rapid City Journal* (6 November 1998).

The cracks, monitoring, and maintenance of the presidential faces are described in Denise J. Smith, "Mapping the Faces: The Survey of Mount Rushmore," *P.O.B.*

[Point of Beginning] 15:4 (April–May 1990); "Mount Rushmore: Saving Face," *Compressed Air* (July/August 1992), 8–13; and "Mount Rushmore Protected with Silicone Sealant," *Material News* (Dow Corning) (November/December 1991), 6–8. Even more informative were interviews with consulting engineer Douglas Blankenship of Respec, Inc., and Chief Ranger Mike Pflaum.

The U.S. Presidents Sticker Book is by Karen Stillman (1999). The campaign to add Ronald Reagan to Rushmore is chronicled in David Kamp, "Ronnie on the Rocks," *GQ* 68:10 (October 1998), 242–247, 282–284; Paulette Tobin, "Conservative groups want to add Reagan to Rushmore," *Rapid City Journal* (15 May 1989); Khiota Therrien, "Will Reagan Be Chiseled Out?" *Washington Post* (15 February 1999); Anthony Ramirez, "Will the Gipper Ever Get a Piece of the Rock?" *New York Times* (11 February 2001); and sundry memoranda and correspondence in the Mount Rushmore National Memorial Archives.

To appreciate the City of Presidents statuary, I interviewed Don Perdue, the project's originator and leading proponent, and Denise DuBroy, a Rapid City artist and the project's most outspoken critic. Both of them shared letters and documents relating to publicity, public meetings, and legal proceedings. I also followed the controversy through articles in the *Rapid City Journal*. David Adickes's quest to create a Presidents Park near Lead is chronicled in various articles in the *Journal*.

INDEX

Borglum's health and, 94
Borglum's politics and, 138, 139
health of, 293
marriage of, 118
Stone Mountain and, 182, 203
Borglum, Mary Ellis (daughter)
birth of, 162
education of, 270
Rushmore and, 280
Borglum, Solon (brother), 100
Armory Show and, 128
art career of, 96, 101
background of, 69
Grant commission and, 91
Lincoln commission and, 118
as sculptor, 81–83
Stone Mountain and, 155
Bourland, Gregg, 353
Bowers, Claude G., 252–53
Boylan, John, 216, 251
Bradley, Bill, 368–70
Bradley, John Edward, 277, 296
Brancusi, Constantin, 129
Brenner, Victor, 196
Brokaw, Tom, 342–43
Browere, John Henri, 249
Brush and Pencil, 99
Bryan, William Jennings, 133
Buffalo Chips. *See* White, Jonathan
Bull Moose Party. *See* National Progressive
Party
Bulow, William, 224
Bunyan, Paul, 150, 239
Bureau of Indian Affairs, 32, 354
Bureau of Land Management, 369
The Burghers of Calais (Rodin), 79
Burnham, Daniel, 90
Burroughs, John, 216
Bush, George H., 343, 400
Bush, George W., 414
Bushfield, Harlan, 297, 311
Butler, William Mill, 290
Butterfield, Daniel, 131

Calhoun, James, 23
Cammerer, Arno, 271
Camp Robinson, 38
Canada, 7, 11
Canary, "Calamity Jane," 36, 39
Cardinal, Tantoo, 374

Carhenge, 327
Carlyle, Thomas, 66, 67, 103
Carter, Jimmy, 340
Carter, Robin Borglum, 186, 397
Case, Francis, 288, 289
Case, Leland, 43
Case, Ralph, 365
Casey, Pauline, 395
Cathedral of St. John the Divine, 99, 204
Causici, Henrico, 246
CCC. *See* Civilian Conservation Corps
Central Trust, 215
Century Club, 118
Champion, James, 270
Charge, Doris Leader, 374
Cher, 2
Cheyenne, 7, 25, 34
Chicago and North Western Railway, 15, 264
Chicago Public Library, 132
Children's Founder's Role, 183
Christo, 17, 158
Citizens Protecting Rushmore, 394–95
City Beautiful movement, 89–90
City of Presidents, 412–15
Civilian Conservation Corps (CCC), 277
Clark, William, 27, 54, 95, 212, 352
Clarke, Edward Young, 187–88
Clinton, William Jefferson, 2, 340, 400
Cody, Buffalo Bill, 42, 54
Cody, Iron Eyes, 371
Coleman, Charles, 332
Collier, John, 68, 322
colossal sculpture, 149–53, 239–40
Colossus of Rhodes, 53, 59, 126, 150
Colt, Samuel, 173
Columbian Fountain (Macmonnies), 89
Columbus, Christopher, 152, 239
Columbus Fountain (Taft), 53
Commercial Club, 213, 235
Commission for the Celebration for the
Two Hundredth Anniversary of the
Birth of George Washington, 245
Conception (Borglum), 130
Confederate national memorial. *See* Stone
Mountain Memorial
Congress
Fort Laramie Treaty and, 24
Great Sioux Reservation and, 40
Lincoln Memorial and, 49
national highways and, 50
Stone Mountain and, 183

PublicAffairs is a publishing house founded in 1997. It is a tribute to the standards, values, and flair of three persons who have served as mentors to countless reporters, writers, editors, and book people of all kinds, including me.

I.F. STONE, proprietor of *I. F. Stone's Weekly*, combined a commitment to the First Amendment with entrepreneurial zeal and reporting skill and became one of the great independent journalists in American history. At the age of eighty, Izzy published *The Trial of Socrates*, which was a national bestseller. He wrote the book after he taught himself ancient Greek.

BENJAMIN C. BRADLEE was for nearly thirty years the charismatic editorial leader of *The Washington Post*. It was Ben who gave the *Post* the range and courage to pursue such historic issues as Watergate. He supported his reporters with a tenacity that made them fearless and it is no accident that so many became authors of influential, best-selling books.

ROBERT L. BERNSTEIN, the chief executive of Random House for more than a quarter century, guided one of the nation's premier publishing houses. Bob was personally responsible for many books of political dissent and argument that challenged tyranny around the globe. He is also the founder and longtime chair of Human Rights Watch, one of the most respected human rights organizations in the world.

For fifty years, the banner of Public Affairs Press was carried by its owner Morris B. Schnapper, who published Gandhi, Nasser, Toynbee, Truman, and about 1,500 other authors. In 1983, Schnapper was described by *The Washington Post* as "a redoubtable gadfly." His legacy will endure in the books to come.

Peter Osnos, *Publisher*